1993

SOLUTIONS MANUAL 1-14

Accounting Principles

SEVENTEENTH EDITION

D0608176

PHILIP E. FESS
Professor Emeritus of Accountancy
University of Illinois, Champaign-Urbana

CARL S. WARREN
Professor of Accounting
University of Georgia, Athens

COLLEGE DIVISION South-Western Publishing Co.

Cincinnati Ohio

AB70RY1

Copyright © 1993
by South-Western Publishing Co.
Cincinnati, Ohio

Sponsoring Editor: Mark Hubble
Senior Developmental Editor: Ken Martin
Developmental Editor: Mary H. Draper
Production Editor: Leslie Kauffman
Associate Editor: Nancy Watson
Cover Designer: Craig LaGesse Ramsdell
Cover and Title Illustrator: David Lesh
Marketing Manager: Randy G. Haubner

ISBN: 0-538-81861-1

1 2 3 4 DH 5 4 3 2

Printed in the United States of America

TABLE OF CONTENTS

Page

CHAPTER 1

DISCUSSION QUESTIONS

1. Investors (owners) and prospective investors; bankers and suppliers (creditors); government agencies; employees and their union representatives; management.

2. Accountants serving a particular business firm, governmental agency, not-for-profit organization, etc., as an employee are said to be engaged in private accounting. Accountants who render accounting services to clients on a fee basis, or who are employed by such accountants, are said to be engaged in public accounting.

3. a. The requirements for the CMA, mentioned in the text, are:

   (1) College degree or equivalent.
   (2) Two years of experience in management accounting.
   (3) Successful completion of written examination.

   b. The requirements for the CPA, mentioned in the text, are:

   (1) Education (college degree is required).
   (2) Experience (usually some experience in public accounting).
   (3) Written examination (the uniform examination prepared by the American Institute of Certified Public Accountants).

   Other requirements, not mentioned in the textbook but listed here for the sake of completeness, are:
   (4) Age (minimum of 21 is common).
   (5) Residence (most states require residence or place of business within the state for minimum of one year).
   (6) Citizenship (most states require that applicant be a U.S. citizen or has declared intention of becoming one).

4. Ethics are moral principles of rightness that guide the conduct of individuals whether operating alone or as members of groups such as professions and businesses.

5. Financial accounting, auditing, cost accounting, management accounting, tax accounting, accounting systems, budgetary accounting, international accounting, not-for-profit accounting, social accounting, accounting instruction.

6. Generally accepted accounting principles (GAAP) are established by research, accepted accounting practices, and pronouncements of authoritative bodies.

7. a. American Institute of Certified Public Accountants
   b. Certified Internal Auditor
   c. Certified Management Accountant
   d. Certified Public Accountant
   e. Financial Accounting Standards Board
   f. Generally Accepted Accounting Principles

8. a. The three principal forms are (1) sole proprietorship, (2) partnership, and (3) corporation.
   b. Sole proprietorship
   c. Corporation

9. According to the cost principle, the monetary record for properties and services purchased by a business is recorded in terms of cost.

10. $95,000

11. a. The land should be recorded at $75,000 at the time of acquisition.
    b. No. (The offer of $150,000 and the increase in the assessed value should not be recognized in the accounting records.)
    c. (1) $100,000 ($175,000 − $75,000)
       (2) $175,000

12. a. $250,000
    b. Liabilities (the rights of creditors) and owner's equity (the rights of the owner)

13. Assets, liabilities, and owner's equity

14. a. $65,000
    b. $250,000
    c. $550,000

15. a. Increase assets and increase owner's equity.
    b. Increase assets and increase owner's equity.
    c. Increase assets and decrease assets.
    d. Decrease assets and decrease owner's equity.
    e. Increase assets and increase liabilities.

16. a. (1) Total assets increased $15,000.
       (2) No change in liabilities.
       (3) Owner's equity increased $15,000.

    b. (1) Total assets decreased $35,000.
       (2) Total liabilites decreased $35,000.
       (3) No change in owner's equity.

17. a. Revenue, $95,000
    b. Expenses, $81,000
    c. Net income, $14,000

18. An account receivable is a claim against a customer for goods or services sold. An account payable is an amount owed to a creditor for goods or services purchased. Therefore, an account receivable in the records of the seller is an account payable in the records of the purchaser.

19. a. Net loss

20. b. Net income

21. Increase in owner's investment and revenue

22. a. 1, 2
b. 3, 4

23. Income statement, statement of owner's equity, balance sheet, and statement of cash flows. The income statement presents a summary of the revenues and expenses of a business entity for a specific period of time. The statement of owner's equity indicates the changes in owner's equity that have occurred over a specified period of time. The balance sheet presents a list of the assets, liabilities, and owner's equity of a business entity as of a specific date. The statement of cash flows presents a summary of cash receipts and cash payments of a business entity for a specific period of time.

24. a. 2, 3, 4
b. 1

25. a. Net income or net loss
b. Owner's equity at the end of the period

26. a. $345,000 − $ 95,000 = $250,000
$250,000 − $260,000 = $ 10,000 net loss
b. $345,000 − $ 95,000 = $250,000
$250,000 − $260,000 + $ 30,000 = $20,000 net income

27. Operating activities, investing activities, financing activities

28. a. 3, 4
b. 2
c. 1

29. $15,188.2 million ($106,434.8 − $91,246.6)

ETHICS DISCUSSION CASE Acceptable professional conduct requires that Joan Kelley supply the Pioneer National Bank with all the relevant financial statements necessary for the bank to make an informed decision. Therefore, Joan should provide the complete set of financial statements. These can be supplemented with a discussion of the net loss in the past year or other supplementary data explaining why granting the loan is a good investment by the bank.

EXERCISES

Ex. 1-1 As in many ethics issues, there is no one right answer. The *Naples Daily News* reported on this issue in these terms: "...the company covered up the first report and the local newspaper uncovered the company's secret. The company was forced to not locate here (Collier County)...It became patently clear that doing the least that is legally allowed is not enough...."

Ex. 1-2 a. $37,000 ($15,500 + $21,500)
  b. $32,750 ($62,750 − $30,000)
  c. $38,000 ($57,000 − $19,000)

Ex. 1-3 a. liability
  b. asset
  c. owner's equity
  d. asset
  e. asset
  f. owner's equity

Ex. 1-4 1. c   6. a
  2. e   7. a
  3. c   8. d
  4. c   9. e
  5. e   10. e

Ex. 1-5 a. (1) Sale of services for cash, $9,000.
      (2) Payment of expenses, $3,250.
      (3) Payment of cash to suppliers, $2,300.
      (4) Purchase of supplies on account, $600.
      (5) Withdrawal of cash by owner, $1,950.
      (6) Purchase of land for cash, $4,000.
      (7) Recognition of cost of supplies used, $680.
  b. $2,500 ($4,500 − $2,000)
  c. $3,120 ($19,620 − $16,500)
  d. $5,070 ($9,000 − $3,250 − $680)
  e. $3,120 ($5,070 − $1,950)

Ex. 1-6 It would be incorrect to say that the owner had incurred a net loss of $1,000. The excess of the withdrawals over the net income for the period is a decrease in the amount of owner's equity in the enterprise.

Ex. 1-7 Company A:

Owner's equity at end of year ($620,000 − $265,000) ...	$355,000
Owner's equity at beginning of year ($525,000 − $190,000)	335,000
Increase in owner's equity − net income	$ 20,000

Ex. 1-7, Concluded

Company B:

Increase in owner's equity (as determined for A)	$ 20,000
Add withdrawals.	40,000
Net income	$ 60,000

Company C:

Increase in owner's equity (as determined for A)	$ 20,000
Deduct additional investment.	50,000
Net loss.	$ (30,000)

Company D:

Increase in owner's equity (as determined for A)	$ 20,000
Deduct additional investment.	50,000
	$ (30,000)
Add withdrawals.	40,000
Net income	$ 10,000

Ex. 1-8   Balance sheet items: (1), (2), (4), (5), (6), (10)

Ex. 1-9   Income statement items: (3), (7), (8), (9)

Ex. 1-10

JOAN BENNY COMPANY
Statement of Owner's Equity
For Month Ended September 30, 1993

Joan Benny, capital, September 1, 1993.		$39,950
Net income for month	$4,750	
Less withdrawals	3,000	
Increase in owner's equity		1,750
Joan Benny, capital, September 30, 1993		$41,700

Ex. 1-11

CHAVEZ SERVICES
Income Statement
For Month Ended June 30, 19—

Fees earned.		$5,400
Operating expenses:		
Wages expense.	$1,700	
Rent expense.	900	
Supplies expense.	250	
Miscellaneous expense.	50	
Total operating expenses		2,900
Net income		$2,500

Ex. 1-12

I. Owner's equity at end of year
($315,000 − $185,000)............................... **$130,000**
Owner's equity at beginning of year
($270,000 − $160,000)............................. 110,000
Increase in owner's equity......................... $ 20,000
Deduct increase due to net income
($87,750 − $72,750)............................... 15,000
$ 5,000
Add withdrawals 20,000
    Additional investment in business .... $ 25,000

II. Owner's equity at end of year ($95,000 − $25,000).. $ 70,000
Owner's equity at beginning of year
($70,000 − $35,000)............................. 35,000
Increase in owner's equity......................... $ 35,000
Add withdrawals 18,000
$ 53,000
Deduct additional investment 12,000
Increase due to net income .... $ 41,000
Add expenses 32,000
    Revenue.. $ 73,000

III. Owner's equity at end of year ($94,000 − $87,000).. $ 7,000
Owner's equity at beginning of year
($90,000 − $76,000)............................. 14,000
Decrease in owner's equity......................... $ (7,000)
Deduct decrease due to net loss
($88,100 − $89,600)............................... −(1,500)
$ (5,500)
Deduct additional investment 5,000
    Withdrawals................................... $ (10,500)

IV. Owner's equity at end of year ($79,000 − $52,000).. $ 27,000
Deduct increase due to net income
($99,000 − $78,000)............................... 21,000
$ 6,000
Add withdrawals 23,000
$ 29,000
Deduct additional investment 20,000
$ 9,000
Add liabilities at beginning of year................. 22,750
    Assets at beginning of year..................... $ 31,750

Ex. 1-13

a.

L. KEATON INTERIORS
Balance Sheet
May 31, 19—

Assets

Cash	$10,150
Accounts receivable	10,300
Supplies	975
Total assets	$21,425

Liabilities

Accounts payable	$ 7,720

Owner's Equity

Leon Keaton, capital	13,705
Total liabilities and owner's equity	$21,425

L. KEATON INTERIORS
Balance Sheet
June 30, 19—

Assets

Cash	$12,050
Accounts receivable	13,400
Supplies	750
Total assets	$26,200

Liabilities

Accounts payable	$ 9,900

Owner's Equity

Leon Keaton, capital	16,300
Total liabilities and owner's equity	$26,200

b.

Owner's equity, June 30	$16,300
Owner's equity, May 31	13,705
Net income	$ 2,595

c.

Owner's equity, June 30	$16,300
Owner's equity, May 31	13,705
Increase in owner's equity	$ 2,595
Add withdrawal	4,000
Net income	$ 6,595

WHAT'S WRONG WITH THIS?

1. All financial statements should contain the name of the business in their heading.
2. The statement of owner's equity should be labeled to cover the month ended June 30, 19—.
3. The net income on the statement of owner's equity does not agree with the net income on the income statement.
4. In the statement of owner's equity, "withdrawals" should be deducted from "net income for the month." This results in a decrease in owner's equity of $125.
5. Accounts payable should be listed as a liability on the balance sheet.
6. Supplies should be listed as an asset on the balance sheet.
7. The balance sheet assets should equal the sum of liabilities and owner's equity.

Corrected financial statements would be as follows:

COX REALTY
Income Statement
For Month Ended June 30, 19—

Sales commissions		$6,100
Operating expenses:		
Office salaries expense	$2,150	
Rent expense	1,800	
Automobile expense	400	
Supplies expense	125	
Miscellaneous expense	250	
Total operating expenses		4,725
Net income		$1,375

COX REALTY
Statement of Owner's Equity
For Month Ended June 30, 19—

Investment during the month		$7,500
Net income for the month	$1,375	
Less withdrawals	1,500	
Decrease in owner's equity		125
Carol Cox, capital, June 30, 19—		$7,375

What's Wrong?, Concluded

COX REALTY
Balance Sheet
June 30, 19—

Assets

Cash...	$7,250
Supplies	325
Total assets..................................	$7,575

Liabilities

Accounts payable	$ 200

Owner's Equity

Carol Cox, capital	7,375
Total liabilities and owner's equity	$7,575

PROBLEMS

Prob. 1-1A

1.

	Assets			= Liabilities +	Owner's Equity	
	Cash	+ Accounts Receivable	+ Supplies	= Accounts Payable	+ Ruth Ruhl, Capital	
a.	+8,000				+8,000	Investment
b.	−4,000				−4,000	Rent Expense
Bal.	4,000				4,000	
c.			+1,950	+1,950		
Bal.	4,000		1,950	1,950	4,000	
d.	+2,500				+2,500	Fees earned
Bal.	6,500		1,950	1,950	6,500	
e.	− 975			− 975		
Bal.	5,525		1,950	975	6,500	
f.		+2,250			+2,250	Fees earned
Bal.	5,525	2,250	1,950	975	8,750	
g.	−1,755				− 980	Auto expense
					− 775	Misc. expense
Bal.	3,770	2,250	1,950	975	6,995	
h.	−1,500				−1,500	Salaries expense
Bal.	2,270	2,250	1,950	975	5,495	
i.			−1,025		−1,025	Supplies expense
Bal.	2,270	2,250	925	975	4,470	
j.	−1,200				−1,200	Withdrawal
Bal.	1,070	2,250	925	975	3,270	

Prob. 1-1A, Concluded

2. Owner's equity is the right of owners to the assets of the business. These rights are increased by owner's investments and revenues. These rights are decreased by owner's withdrawals and expenses.

Prob. 1-2A

1.
PELICAN TRAVEL
Income Statement
For Year Ended October 31, 1994

Fees earned		$84,530
Operating expenses:		
Wages expense	$25,500	
Rent expense	24,000	
Utilities expense	4,500	
Supplies expense	1,125	
Miscellaneous expense	1,750	
Total operating expenses		56,875
Net income		$27,655

2.
PELICAN TRAVEL
Statement of Owner's Equity
For Year Ended October 31, 1994

Jim Rudd, capital, November 1, 1993		$4,500
Net income for the year	$27,655	
Less withdrawals	25,000	
Increase in owner's equity		2,655
Jim Rudd, capital, October 31, 1994		$7,155

3.
PELICAN TRAVEL
Balance Sheet
October 31, 1994

Assets

Cash	$6,500
Supplies	865
Total assets	$7,365

Liabilities

Accounts payable	$ 210

Owner's Equity

Jim Rudd, capital	7,155
Total liabilities and owner's equity	$7,365

Prob. 1-3A

1.

MARY HALL SERVICES
Income Statement
For Month Ended April 30, 19—

Fees earned		$8,100
Operating expenses:		
Salaries expense	$1,900	
Rent expense	1,800	
Auto expense	1,250	
Supplies expense	450	
Miscellaneous expense	350	
Total operating expenses		5,750
Net income		$2,350

2.

MARY HALL SERVICES
Statement of Owner's Equity
For Month Ended April 30, 19—

Investment during month		$5,000
Net income for month	$2,350	
Less withdrawals	2,000	
Increase in owner's equity		350
Mary Hall, capital, April 30, 19—		$5,350

3.

MARY HALL SERVICES
Balance Sheet
April 30, 19—

Assets

Cash	$1,225
Accounts receivable	4,350
Supplies	275
Total assets	$5,850

Liabilities

Accounts payable	$ 500

Owner's Equity

Mary Hall, capital	5,350
Total liabilities and owner's equity	$5,850

Prob. 1-4A

1.

	Assets		= Liabilities +	Owner's Equity	
	Cash	+ Supplies =	Accounts Payable +	Doris Lusk, Capital	
a.	+ 7,500			+7,500	Investment
b.	− 4,100			− 4,100	Rent Expense
Bal.	3,400			3,400	
c.		+750	+750		
Bal.	3,400	750	750	3,400	
d.	− 500		−500		
Bal.	2,900	750	250	3,400	
e.	+14,100			+14,100	Sales commissions
Bal.	17,000	750	250	17,500	
f.	− 3,000			− 3,000	Withdrawal
Bal.	14,000	750	250	14,500	
g.	−2,250			− 1,900	Auto expense
				− 350	Misc. expense
Bal.	11,750	750	250	12,250	
h.	− 4,150			− 4,150	Salaries expense
Bal.	7,600	750	250	8,100	
i.		−550		− 550	Supplies expense
Bal.	7,600	200	250	7,550	

2.

LUSK REALTY
Income Statement
For Month Ended August 31, 19—

Sales commissions		$14,100
Operating expenses:		
Office salaries expense...........................	$4,150	
Rent expense...	4,100	
Automobile expense	1,900	
Supplies expense	550	
Miscellaneous expense............................	350	
Total operating expenses............................		11,050
Net income		$ 3,050

Prob. 1-4A, Concluded

LUSK REALTY
Statement of Owner's Equity
For Month Ended August 31, 19—

Investment during the month		$7,500
Net income for the month	$3,050	
Less withdrawals	3,000	
Increase in owner's equity		50
Doris Lusk, capital, August 31, 19—		$7,550

LUSK REALTY
Balance Sheet
August 31, 19—

Assets

Cash	$7,600
Supplies	200
Total assets	$7,800

Liabilities

Accounts payable	$ 250

Owner's Equity

Doris Lusk, capital	7,550
Total liabilities and owner's equity	$7,800

Prob. 1-5A

1.

Assets				=	Liabilities +	Owner's Equity
Cash +	Accounts Receivable	+ Supplies +	Land =		Accounts Payable +	Karen Guy, Capital
6,250 +	12,100	+ 900	+ 25,000 =		7,800 +	Karen Guy, Capital
	44,250			=	7,800 +	Karen Guy, Capital
	36,450			=		Karen Guy, Capital

Prob. 1-5A, Continued

2.

	Assets				=	Liabilities +	Owner's Equity	
	Cash	+ Accounts Receivable	+ Supplies	+ Land	=	Accounts Payable	+ Karen Guy, Capital	
Bal.	6,250	12,100	900	25,000		7,800	36,450	
(a)	+10,750						+10,750	Dry cleaning sales
Bal.	17,000	12,100	900	25,000		7,800	47,200	
(b)	−2,000						−2,000	Rent expense
Bal.	15,000	12,100	900	25,000		7,800	45,200	
(c)			+820			+820		
Bal.	15,000	12,100	1,720	25,000		8,620	45,200	
(d)	−7,800					−7,800		
Bal.	7,200	12,100	1,720	25,000		820	45,200	
(e)		+6,920					+6,920	Dry cleaning sales
Bal.	7,200	19,020	1,720	25,000		820	52,120	
(f)						+7,700	−7,700	Dry cleaning expense
Bal.	7,200	19,020	1,720	25,000		8,520	44,420	
(g)	−5,570						−2,400	Wages expense
							−1,580	Truck expense
							−960	Utilities expense
							−630	Miscellaneous expense
Bal.	1,630	19,020	1,720	25,000		8,520	38,850	
(h)	+8,100	−8,100						
Bal.	9,730	10,920	1,720	25,000		8,520	38,850	
(i)			−970				−970	Supplies expense
Bal.	9,730	10,920	750	25,000		8,520	37,880	

Prob. 1-5A, Concluded

3a.
GUY DRY CLEANERS
Income Statement
For Month Ended May 31, 19—

Dry cleaning sales		$17,670
Operating expenses:		
Dry cleaning expense	$7,700	
Wages expense	2,400	
Rent expense	2,000	
Truck expense	1,580	
Supplies expense	970	
Utilities expense	960	
Miscellaneous expense	630	
Total operating expenses		16,240
Net income		$ 1,430

3b.
GUY DRY CLEANERS
Statement of Owner's Equity
For Month Ended May 31, 19—

Karen Guy, capital, May 1, 19—	$36,450
Net income for the month	1,430
Karen Guy, capital, May 31, 19—	$37,880

3c.
GUY DRY CLEANERS
Balance Sheet
May 31, 19—

Assets

Cash	$ 9,730
Accounts receivable	10,920
Supplies	750
Land	25,000
Total assets	$46,400

Liabilities

Accounts payable	$ 8,520

Owner's Equity

Karen Guy, capital	37,880
Total liabilities and owner's equity	$46,400

Prob. 1-6A

1.

GRAF SERVICES
Income Statement
For Year Ended December 31, 19—

Fees Earned...		$99,250
Operating expenses:		
Wages expense..	$29,700	
Rent expense...	12,000	
Utilities expense.....................................	8,100	
Supplies expense.....................................	4,800	
Taxes expense..	4,500	
Advertising expense..................................	3,000	
Miscellaneous expense...............................	1,250	
Total operating expenses...........................		63,350
Net income...		$35,900

2.

GRAF SERVICES
Statement of Owner's Equity
For Year Ended December 31, 19—

Tom Graf, capital, January 1, 19—......................		$20,450
Net income for the year...............................	$35,900	
Less withdrawals......................................	30,000	
Increase in owner's equity		5,900
Tom Graf, capital, December 31, 19—...................		$26,350

3.

GRAF SERVICES
Balance Sheet
December 31, 19—

Assets

Cash..		$ 7,200
Accounts receivable		21,000
Supplies		2,750
Total assets		$30,950

Liabilities

Accounts payable......................................	$3,100	
Wages payable	1,500	
Total liabilities..		$ 4,600

Owner's Equity

Tom Graf, capital......................................		26,350
Total liabilities and owner's equity......................		$30,950

Prob. 1-1B

1.

	Assets			= Liabilities +	Owner's Equity	
	Cash	+ Accounts Receivable +	Supplies =	Accounts Payable +	David Key, Capital	
a.	+5,000				+5,000	Investment
b.	−2,500				−2,500	Rent Expense
Bal.	2,500				2,500	
c.			+850	+850		
Bal.	2,500		850	850	2,500	
d.	− 625			−625		
Bal.	1,875		850	225	2,500	
e.	+3,250				+3,250	Fees earned
Bal.	5,125		850	225	5,750	
f.	−1,030				− 780	Auto expense
					− 250	Misc. expense
Bal.	4,095		850	225	4,720	
g.	−1,500				−1,500	Salaries expense
Bal.	2,595		850	225	3,220	
h.			−575		− 575	Supplies expense
Bal.	2,595		275	225	2,645	
i.		+2,350			+2,350	Fees earned
Bal.	2,595	2,350	275	225	4,995	
j.	−1,000				−1,000	Withdrawal
Bal.	1,595	2,350	275	225	3,995	

2. Owner's equity is the right of owners to the assets of the business. These rights are increased by owner's investments and revenues. These rights are decreased by owner's withdrawals and expenses.

Prob. 1-2B

1.   **COLE TRAVEL SERVICE**
                                    Income Statement
                              For Year Ended June 30, 1994

Fees earned		$68,775
Operating expenses:		
Wages expense	$24,900	
Rent expense	9,900	
Utilities expense	8,500	
Supplies expense	4,550	
Taxes expense	1,800	
Miscellaneous expense	825	
Total operating expenses		50,475
Net income		$18,300

2.   **COLE TRAVEL SERVICE**
                              Statement of Owner's Equity
                              For Year Ended June 30, 1994

E. F. Cole, capital, July 1, 1993		$5,400
Net income for the year	$18,300	
Less withdrawals	18,000	
Increase in owner's equity		300
E. F. Cole, capital, June 30, 1994		$5,700

3.   **COLE TRAVEL SERVICE**
                                    Balance Sheet
                                    June 30, 1994

Assets

Cash	$6,125
Supplies	675
Total assets	$6,800

Liabilities

Accounts payable	$1,100

Owner's Equity

E. F. Cole, capital	5,700
Total liabilities and owner's equity	$6,800

Prob. 1-3B

1.

JACK HYDE SERVICES
Income Statement
For Month Ended July 31, 19—

Fees earned		$6,750
Operating expenses:		
Rent expense	$2,000	
Salaries expense	1,000	
Auto expense	780	
Supplies expense	125	
Miscellaneous expense	375	
Total operating expenses		4,280
Net income		$2,470

2.

JACK HYDE SERVICES
Statement of Owner's Equity
For Month Ended July 31, 19—

Investment during month		$2,500
Net income for month	$2,470	
Less withdrawals	1,200	
Increase in owner's equity		1,270
Jack Hyde, capital, July 31, 19—		$3,770

3.

JACK HYDE SERVICES
Balance Sheet
July 31, 19—

Assets

Cash	$1,895
Accounts receivable	1,750
Supplies	425
Total assets	$4,070

Liabilities

Accounts payable	$ 300

Owner's Equity

Jack Hyde, capital	3,770
Total liabilities and owner's equity	$4,070

Prob. 1-4B

1.

	Assets		= Liabilities +	Owner's Equity	
	Cash	+ Supplies =	Accounts Payable +	Leo Egan, Capital	
a.	+ 5,000			+ 5,000	Investment
b.	− 3,600			− 3,600	Rent Expense
Bal.	1,400			1,400	
c.		+825	+825		
Bal.	1,400	825	825	1,400	
d.	− 500		−500		
Bal.	900	825	325	1,400	
e.	+11,100			+11,100	Sales commissions
Bal.	12,000	825	325	12,500	
f.	− 2,000			− 2,000	Withdrawal
Bal.	10,000	825	325	10,500	
g.	− 1,450			− 900	Auto expense
				− 550	Misc. expense
Bal.	8,550	825	325	9,050	
h.	− 2,950			− 2,950	Salaries expense
Bal.	5,600	825	325	6,100	
i.		−425		− 425	Supplies expense
Bal.	5,600	400	325	5,675	

2.

EGAN REALTY
Income Statement
For Month Ended July 31, 19—

Sales commissions		$11,100
Operating expenses:		
Rent expense.	$3,600	
Office salaries expense.	2,950	
Automobile expense	900	
Supplies expense	425	
Miscellaneous expense.	550	
Total operating expenses.		8,425
Net income		$ 2,675

Prob. 1-4B, Concluded

EGAN REALTY
Statement of Owner's Equity
For Month Ended July 31, 19—

Investment during the month		$5,000
Net income for the month	$2,675	
Less withdrawals	2,000	
Increase in owner's equity		675
Leo Egan, capital, July 31, 19—		$5,675

EGAN REALTY
Balance Sheet
July 31, 19—

Assets

Cash	$5,600
Supplies	400
Total assets	$6,000

Liabilities

Accounts payable	$ 325

Owner's Equity

Leo Egan, capital	5,675
Total liabilities and owner's equity	$6,000

Prob. 1-5B

1.

	Assets			=	Liabilities +	Owner's Equity
	Accounts				Accounts	
Cash +	Receivable +	Supplies +	Land =		Payable +	Karen Guy, Capital
5,400 +	6,750 +	560 +	10,000 =		3,880 +	Karen Guy, Capital
		22,710		=	3,880 +	Karen Guy, Capital
		18,830		=		Karen Guy, Capital

Prob. 1-5B, Continued

2.

	Assets				= Liabilities +	Owner's Equity	
	Cash +	Accounts Receivable +	Supplies +	Land =	Accounts Payable +	Karen Guy, Capital	
Bal.	5,400	6,750	560	10,000	3,880	18,830	
(a)	−1,450					−1,450	Rent expense
Bal.	3,950	6,750	560	10,000	3,880	17,380	
(b)		+7,150				+7,150	Dry cleaning sales
Bal.	3,950	13,900	560	10,000	3,880	24,530	
(c)	−1,680				−1,680		
Bal.	2,270	13,900	560	10,000	2,200	24,530	
(d)			+310		+310		
Bal.	2,270	13,900	870	10,000	2,510	24,530	
(e)	+3,600					+3,600	Dry cleaning sales
Bal.	5,870	13,900	870	10,000	2,510	28,130	
(f)	+3,750	−3,750					
Bal.	9,620	10,150	870	10,000	2,510	28,130	
(g)					+3,400	−3,400	Dry cleaning expense
Bal.	9,620	10,150	870	10,000	5,910	24,730	
(h)	−3,225					−1,800	Wages expense
						− 725	Truck expense
						− 510	Utilities expense
						− 190	Miscellaneous expense
Bal.	6,395	10,150	870	10,000	5,910	21,505	
(i)			−570			− 570	Supplies expense
Bal.	6,395	10,150	300	10,000	5,910	20,935	

Prob. 1-5B, Concluded

3a.

GUY DRY CLEANERS
Income Statement
For Month Ended June 30, 19—

Dry cleaning sales		$10,750
Operating expenses:		
Dry cleaning expense	$3,400	
Wages expense	1,800	
Rent expense	1,450	
Truck expense	725	
Supplies expense	570	
Utilities expense	510	
Miscellaneous expense	190	
Total operating expenses		8,645
Net income		$ 2,105

3b.

GUY DRY CLEANERS
Statement of Owner's Equity
For Month Ended June 30, 19—

Karen Guy, capital, June 1, 19—	$18,830
Net income for the month	2,105
Karen Guy, capital, June 30, 19—	$20,935

3c.

GUY DRY CLEANERS
Balance Sheet
June 30, 19—

Assets

Cash	$ 6,395
Accounts receivable	10,150
Supplies	300
Land	10,000
Total assets	$26,845

Liabilities

Accounts payable	$ 5,910

Owner's Equity

Karen Guy, capital	20,935
Total liabilities and owner's equity	$26,845

Prob. 1-6B

1.

BENNETT CONSULTANTS
Income Statement
For Year Ended July 31, 1994

Fees Earned...		$827,500
Operating expenses:		
Wages expense......................................	$412,000	
Rent expense.......................................	165,000	
Utilities expense....................................	65,750	
Taxes expense......................................	33,500	
Advertising expense................................	30,000	
Supplies expense...................................	19,750	
Miscellaneous expense..............................	8,125	
Total operating expenses.........................		734,125
Net income		$ 93,375

2.

BENNETT CONSULTANTS
Statement of Owner's Equity
For Year Ended July 31, 1994

Bob Bennett, capital, August 1, 1993		$157,890
Net income for the year...............................	$93,375	
Less withdrawals.....................................	50,000	
Increase in owner's equity		43,375
Bob Bennett, capital, July 31, 1994		$201,265

3.

BENNETT CONSULTANTS
Balance Sheet
July 31, 1994

Assets

Cash..		$ 64,515
Accounts receivable		69,750
Supplies		6,250
Land..		150,000
Total assets		$290,515

Liabilities

Accounts payable.....................................	$78,000	
Wages payable	11,250	
Total liabilities......................................		$ 89,250

Owner's Equity

Bob Bennett, capital..................................		201,265
Total liabilities and owner's equity......................		$290,515

Mini-Case 1

1.

	Assets		= Liabilities +	Owner's Equity	
	Cash	+ Supplies =	Accounts Payable +	A. Gage, Capital	
a.	+ 300			+ 300	Investment
b.	− 150	+150			
Bal.	150	150		300	
c.	− 75			− 75	Rent expense
Bal.	75	150		225	
d.	− 50		+50	− 100	Rent expense
Bal.	25	150	50	125	
e.	+ 950			+ 950	Service revenue
Bal.	975	150	50	1,075	
f.	+ 150			+ 150	Service revenue
Bal.	1,125	150	50	1,225	
g.	− 300			− 300	Salary expense
Bal.	825	150	50	925	
h.	− 75			− 75	Miscellaneous expense
Bal.	750	150	50	850	
i.	+ 240			+ 240	Service revenue
Bal.	990	150	50	1,090	
j.		− 70		− 70	Supplies expense
Bal.	990	80	50	1,020	
k.	− 600			− 600	Withdrawal
Bal.	390	80	50	420	

2.

VINES TENNIS SERVICES
Income Statement
For Month Ended September 30, 19—

Service revenue		$1,340
Operating expenses:		
Salary expense	$300	
Rent expense...	175	
Supplies expense	70	
Miscellaneous expense...............................	75	
Total operating expenses...............................		620
Net income		$ 720

Mini-Case 1, Continued

3.
VINES TENNIS SERVICES
Statement of Owner's Equity
For Month Ended September 30, 19—

Investment during the month		$300
Net income for the month	$720	
Less withdrawal	600	
Increase in owner's equity		120
Ana Gage, capital, September 30, 19—		$420

4.
VINES TENNIS SERVICES
Balance Sheet
September 30, 19—

Assets
Cash	$390
Supplies	80
Total assets	$470

Liabilities
Accounts payable	$ 50

Owner's Equity
Ana Gage, capital	420
Total liabilities and owner's equity	$470

5.

a.

Vines Tennis Services would provide Ana with $80 more income per month than work as a waitress. This amount is computed as follows:

Net income of Vines Tennis Services, per month	$720
Earnings as waitress, per month:	
20 hours per week × $8 per hour × 4 weeks	640
Difference	$ 80

b.

Other factors that Ana should consider before discussing a long-term arrangement with Vines Tennis Club include the following:

Ana should consider whether the results of operations for September are indicative of what to expect each month. For example, Ana should consider whether club members will continue to request lessons or use the ball machine during the winter months when interest in tennis may slacken. Ana should evaluate whether the additional income of $80 per month from Vines Tennis Services is worth the risk being taken and the effort being expended.

Mini-Case 1, Concluded

Ana should also consider how much her investment in Vines Tennis Services could have earned if invested elsewhere. For example, if the initial investment of $300 had been deposited in a money market or savings account at 5% interest, it would have earned $1.25 interest in September, or $15 for the year.

Note to Instructors: Numerous other considerations could be mentioned by students, such as the ability of Ana to withdraw cash from Vines Tennis Services for personal use. Unlike a money market account or savings account, some of her investment in Vines Tennis Services will be in the form of supplies (tennis balls, etc.) which may not be readily convertible to cash. The objective of this mini-case is not to mention all possible considerations, but rather to encourage students to begin thinking about the use of accounting information in making business decisions.

CHAPTER 2

DISCUSSION QUESTIONS

1. An account is a form designed to record changes in a particular asset, liability, owner's equity, revenue, or expense.

2. An account is a form designed to record changes in a particular asset, liability, owner's equity, revenue, or expense. A ledger is a group of related accounts that form a complete unit.

3. Chart of accounts

4. The sequence of accounts in the ledger corresponds generally to the sequence of accounts as they appear in the balance sheet, followed by the accounts as they appear in the income statement.

5. The terms debit and credit may signify either an increase or decrease, depending upon the nature of the account. For example, debits signify an increase in asset and expense accounts; they signify a decrease in liability, owner's capital, and revenue accounts.

6. Journal

7. Posting is the process by which data in journal entries are transferred to the appropriate accounts.

8. (a) debit, (b) debit, (c) credit

9. Liabilities and owner's equity are both equities which have claims or rights to assets as indicated by the accounting equation of Assets = Liabilities + Owner's Equity. Therefore, the same rules of debits and credits apply to both liabilities and owner's equity.

10. a. Decrease in owner's equity
    b. Increase in expense

11. a. Increase in owner's equity
    b. Increase in revenue

12. a. Liability-credit   f. Asset-debit
    b. Asset-debit   g. Revenue-credit
    c. Expense-debit   h. Owner's equity
    d. Owner's equity   (capital)-credit
       (drawing)-debit   i. Asset-debit
    e. Asset-debit   j. Expense-debit

13. a. $12,225 ($11,725 + $14,000 − $13,500)
    b. Credit

14. (a) Assuming that there have been no errors, the credit balance in the cash account resulted from drawing checks for $575 in excess of the amount of cash on deposit. (b) The $575 credit balance in the cash account as of June 30 is a liability owed to the bank; it is usually referred to as an "overdraft" and should be classified on the balance sheet as a liability.

15. 1. credit only (b)
    2. debit and credit (c)
    3. debit only (a)
    4. debit and credit (c)
    5. debit only (a)
    6. debit and credit (c)
    7. debit only (a)

16. b. Business transaction occurs
    d. Business document prepared
    c. Entry recorded in journal
    a. Entry posted to ledger

17. a. Record the date, June 11, and the amount, $875, in the credit section of the fees earned account.
    b. Record the journal page number, 32, in the posting reference column of the fees earned account.
    c. Record the account number, 41, in the posting reference column of the journal.

18. When an entry has been posted to the accounts, the account number is inserted in the journal in the posting reference column.

19. (a) The revenue was earned in June. (b) (1) Debit Accounts Receivable and credit Fees Earned or other appropriately titled revenue account. (2) Debit Cash and credit Accounts Receivable.

20. a. A trial balance is a listing of the debit and the credit balances of every account in the ledger (arranged in parallel columns) with the columnar totals inserted below.
    b. The trial balance is a proof of the equality of the debits and the credits in the ledger.

21. No. Errors may have been made that had the same erroneous effect on both debits and credits, such as failure to record and/or post a transaction, recording the same transaction more than once, and posting a transaction correctly to the wrong account.

22. The listing of $3,675 is a slide; the listing of $5,400 is a transposition.

23. a. The error would not cause the trial balance to be out of balance because the same error occurred on both the debit side and the credit side of the trial balance.

   b. The answer would not be the same. The error would cause the debit total of the trial balance to exceed the credit total by $270.

24. Inequality of trial balance totals would be caused by errors described in (a) and (c).

25. The correction is made by drawing a line through the error and inserting the correct title or amount immediately above.

26. The preferred procedure is to journalize and post a correcting entry debiting Accounts Receivable and crediting Accounts Payable.

27. a. $7,853,100 ($8,271,100 − $418,000)
   b. 5.1% ($418,000 ÷ $8,271,100)

ETHICS DISCUSSION CASE Acceptable ethical conduct requires that Ted look for the difference. If Ted cannot find the difference within a reasonable amount of time, he should confer with his supervisor as to what action should be taken so that the financial statements can be prepared by the 5 o'clock deadline. Ted's responsibility to his employer is to act with integrity, objectivity, and due care, so that users of the financial statements will not be misled.

EXERCISES

Ex. 2-1

Balance Sheet Accounts	Income Statement Accounts
1. Assets	**4. Revenue**
11 Cash	41 Fees Earned
12 Accounts Receivable	**5. Expenses**
13 Supplies	51 Wages Expense
14 Prepaid Insurance	52 Rent Expense
15 Equipment	53 Supplies Expense
2. Liabilities	59 Miscellaneous Expense
21 Accounts Payable	
22 Unearned Rent	
3. Owner's Equity	
31 R. Bailey, Capital	
32 R. Bailey, Drawing	

Note: The order of some of the accounts within the major classifications is somewhat arbitrary, as in accounts 13–14 and accounts 51–53. In a new enterprise, the order of magnitude of balances in such accounts is not determinable in advance. The magnitude may also vary from period to period.

Ex. 2-2 a. and b.

	Account Debited		Account Credited	
Transaction	Type	Effect	Type	Effect
1	asset	+	capital	+
2	asset	+	asset	−
3	asset	+	asset	−
			liability	+
4	expense	+	asset	−
5	asset	+	revenue	+
6	liability	−	asset	−
7	asset	+	asset	−
8	drawing	+	asset	−
9	expense	+	asset	−

Ex. 2-3
GROSS SERVICES
Trial Balance
June 30, 19—

Cash...	6,825	
Accounts Receivable	4,000	
Supplies	1,050	
Equipment	13,950	
Accounts Payable		5,000
Debra Gross, Capital.............................		15,000
Debra Gross, Drawing	2,500	
Service Revenue		12,500
Operating Expenses	4,175	
	32,500	32,500

Ex. 2-4 a. Debit (negative) balance of $4,000. ($20,000 − $18,000 − $6,000)

           b. Yes. The balance sheet prepared at December 31 will balance, with Donna Drabeck, Capital being reported in the owner's equity section as a negative $4,000.

Ex. 2-5 a. The increase of $7,500 in the cash account does not indicate earnings of that amount. Other assets may have increased or decreased, and liabilities and owner's equity may have increased or decreased.

           b. $40,000 ($32,500 + $897,500 − $890,000)

Ex. 2-6 a. $24,750 ($12,750 + $26,000 − $14,000)

           b. $23,600 ($21,000 + $22,500 − $19,900)

           c. $27,800 ($30,500 − $27,700 + $25,000)

Ex. 2-7 19—

May	1	Rent Expense	1,500	
		Cash		1,500
	3	Supplies	270	
		Cash		270
	5	Advertising Expense	350	
		Cash		350
	5	Office Equipment	4,200	
		Accounts Payable		4,200
	8	Cash	5,600	
		Accounts Receivable		5,600
	12	Accounts Payable	2,150	
		Cash		2,150
	15	Joseph Rago, Drawing	1,800	
		Cash		1,800
	25	Miscellaneous Expense	90	
		Cash		90
	27	Utilities Expense	195	
		Cash		195
	29	Accounts Receivable	9,150	
		Fees Earned		9,150
	31	Utilities Expense	430	
		Cash		430

Ex. 2-8 a.

(1)	Supplies	720	
	Accounts Payable		720
(2)	Accounts Receivable	2,210	
	Fees Earned		2,210
(3)	Cash	1,100	
	Accounts Receivable		1,100
(4)	Accounts Payable	500	
	Cash		500

b.

	Cash				Accounts Payable	
(3)	1,100	(4)	500	(4)	500	(1)	720

	Supplies				Fees Earned	
(1)	720					(2)	2,210

	Accounts Receivable		
(2)	2,210	(3)	1,100

Ex. 2-9

POGUE COMPANY
Trial Balance
August 31, 19—

Cash	18,950	
Accounts Receivable	20,500	
Supplies	4,100	
Prepaid Insurance	3,150	
Land	125,000	
Accounts Payable		19,710
Unearned Rent		10,000
Notes Payable		25,000
R. Pogue, Capital		120,290
R. Pogue, Drawing	28,000	
Fees Earned		325,000
Wages Expense	190,000	
Rent Expense	48,000	
Utilities Expense	41,500	
Supplies Expense	5,900	
Insurance Expense	5,000	
Miscellaneous Expense	9,900	
	500,000	500,000

Ex. 2-10

BRETT CARPET SERVICES
Trial Balance
December 31, 19—

Cash	5,700	
Accounts Receivable	17,000	
Prepaid Insurance	3,300	
Equipment	45,000	
Accounts Payable		7,950
Unearned Rent		840
Fran Brett, Capital		61,250
Fran Brett, Drawing	24,000	
Service Revenue		64,940
Wages Expense	33,400	
Advertising Expense	5,200	
Miscellaneous Expense	1,380	
	134,980	134,980

Ex. 2-11

Error	(a) Out of Balance	(b) Difference	(c) Larger Total
1	yes	$360	credit
2	no	—	—
3	yes	750	debit
4	yes	1,000	debit
5	no	—	—
6	yes	180	credit
7	yes	1,730	debit

Ex. 2-12 a.

Supplies	500	
Cash		500

b.

A.C. Boyle, Drawing	2,500	
Miscellaneous Expense		2,500

c.

Rent Expense	800	
Supplies Expense		800

WHAT'S WRONG WITH THIS?

1. The trial balance should be dated October 31, 19—.
2. The Accounts Receivable balance should be in the debit column.
3. The Accounts Payable balance should be in the credit column.
4. The Ann Mason, Drawing balance should be in the debit column.
5. The Service Revenue balance should be in the credit column.
6. The two column totals are added incorrectly.

A corrected trial balance would be as follows:

MASON COMPANY
Trial Balance
October 31, 19—

Cash	4,010	
Accounts Receivable	14,400	
Prepaid Insurance	2,400	
Equipment	41,200	
Accounts Payable		5,850
Salaries Payable		750
Ann Mason, Capital		49,600
Ann Mason, Drawing	9,000	
Service Revenue		37,900
Salary Expense	18,400	
Advertising Expense	4,200	
Miscellaneous Expense	490	
	94,100	94,100

PROBLEMS

Prob. 2-1A

1. and 2.

Cash			
(a)	10,000	(b)	1,500
(g)	2,100	(c)	2,500
1,510	*12,100*	(e)	900
		(f)	850
		(h)	75
		(i)	3,000
		(j)	400
		(m)	1,250
		(n)	115
			10,590

Accounts Receivable	
(l)	3,150

Supplies	
(e)	900

Prepaid Insurance	
(f)	850

Automobiles	
(c)	9,500

Equipment	
(d)	6,000

Notes Payable			
(j)	400	(c)	7,000
		6,600	

Accounts Payable			
(i)	3,000	(d)	6,000
		(k)	110
	3,110		*6,110*

Lisa Kent, Capital			
		(a)	10,000

Professional Fees			
		(g)	2,100
		(l)	3,150
			5,250

Rent Expense	
(b)	1,500

Salary Expense	
(m)	1,250

Automobile Expense	
(n)	115

Blueprint Expense	
(k)	110

Miscellaneous Expense	
(h)	75

Prob. 2-1A, Concluded

3.   **LISA KENT, ARCHITECT**
Trial Balance
February 28, 19—

Cash	1,510	
Accounts Receivable	3,150	
Supplies	900	
Prepaid Insurance	850	
Automobiles	9,500	
Equipment	6,000	
Notes Payable		6,600
Accounts Payable		3,110
Lisa Kent, Capital		10,000
Professional Fees		5,250
Rent Expense	1,500	
Salary Expense	1,250	
Automobile Expense	115	
Blueprint Expense	110	
Miscellaneous Expense	75	
	24,960	24,960

Prob. 2-2A

1.

(a)	Cash	5,000	
	Janet Lopes, Capital		5,000
(b)	Rent Expense	3,000	
	Cash		3,000
(c)	Supplies	4,500	
	Accounts Payable		4,500
(d)	Accounts Payable	2,900	
	Cash		2,900
(e)	Cash	29,750	
	Sales Commissions		29,750
(f)	Automobile Expense	2,900	
	Miscellaneous Expense	1,950	
	Cash		4,850
(g)	Office Salaries Expense	8,000	
	Cash		8,000
(h)	Supplies Expense	1,325	
	Supplies		1,325
(i)	Janet Lopes, Drawing	5,000	
	Cash		5,000

Prob. 2-2A, Concluded

2.

Cash			
(a)	5,000	(b)	3,000
(e)	29,750	(d)	2,900
11,000	*34,750*	(f)	4,850
		(g)	8,000
		(i)	5,000
			23,750

Supplies			
(c)	4,500	(h)	1,325
3,175			

Accounts Payable			
(d)	2,900	(c)	4,500
		1,600	

Janet Lopes, Capital			
		(a)	5,000

Janet Lopes, Drawing		
(i)	5,000	

Sales Commissions		
	(e)	29,750

Office Salaries Expense		
(g)	8,000	

Rent Expense		
(b)	3,000	

Automobile Expense		
(f)	2,900	

Supplies Expense		
(h)	1,325	

Miscellaneous Expense		
(f)	1,950	

3.

LOPES REALTY
Trial Balance
July 31, 19—

Cash...	11,000	
Supplies	3,175	
Accounts Payable.................................		1,600
Janet Lopes, Capital.............................		5,000
Janet Lopes, Drawing............................	5,000	
Sales Commissions		29,750
Office Salaries Expense..........................	8,000	
Rent Expense	3,000	
Automobile Expense..............................	2,900	
Supplies Expense.................................	1,325	
Miscellaneous Expense	1,950	
	36,350	36,350

4. a. $29,750
   b. $17,175
   c. $12,575

Prob. 2-3A

1.   **JOURNAL**   **Pages 1 and 2**

Date	Description	Post. Ref.	Debit	Credit
19—				
June 5	Cash...........................	11	15,000	
	Tom Morgan, Capital	31		15,000
5	Rent Expense	53	950	
	Cash...........................	11		950
7	Equipment........................	16	6,250	
	Accounts Payable	22		6,250
8	Truck.........................	18	15,000	
	Cash...........................	11		7,500
	Notes Payable........................	21		7,500
10	Supplies......................	13	525	
	Cash...........................	11		525
12	Cash...........................	11	600	
	Fees Earned............................	41		600
15	Wages Expense	51	800	
	Cash...........................	11		800
20	Prepaid Insurance	14	725	
	Cash...........................	11		725
22	Accounts Receivable	12	1,950	
	Fees Earned...........................	41		1,950
24	Truck Expense	55	310	
	Accounts Payable	22		310
26	Cash...........................	11	650	
	Fees Earned............................	41		650
28	Supplies......................	13	190	
	Accounts Payable	22		190
29	Utilities Expense........................	54	390	
	Cash...........................	11		390
29	Miscellaneous Expense	59	95	
	Cash...........................	11		95
30	Cash...........................	11	1,300	
	Accounts Receivable....................	12		1,300
30	Wages Expense	51	1,200	
	Cash...........................	11		1,200
30	Accounts Payable	22	2,500	
	Cash...........................	11		2,500
30	Tom Morgan, Drawing...................	32	2,000	
	Cash...........................	11		2,000

Prob. 2-3A, Continued

2.

GENERAL LEDGER

Cash 11

Date	Item	Post. Ref.	Dr.	Cr.	Balance Dr.	Balance Cr.
19—						
June 5	....	1	15,000	......	15,000	......
5	....	1	......	950	14,050	......
8	....	1	......	7,500	6,550	......
10	....	1	......	525	6,025	......
12	....	1	600	......	6,625	......
15	....	1	......	800	5,825	......
20	....	1	......	725	5,100	......
26	....	2	650	......	5,750	......
29	....	2	......	390	5,360	......
29	....	2	......	95	5,265	......
30	....	2	1,300	......	6,565	......
30	....	2	......	1,200	5,365	......
30	....	2	......	2,500	2,865	......
30	....	2	......	2,000	865	......

Accounts Receivable 12

Date	Item	Post. Ref.	Dr.	Cr.	Balance Dr.	Balance Cr.
19—						
June 22	....	1	1,950	......	1,950	......
30	....	2	......	1,300	650	......

Supplies 13

Date	Item	Post. Ref.	Dr.	Cr.	Balance Dr.	Balance Cr.
19—						
June 10	....	1	525	......	525	......
28	....	2	190	......	715	......

Prepaid Insurance 14

Date	Item	Post. Ref.	Dr.	Cr.	Balance Dr.	Balance Cr.
19—						
June 20	....	1	725	......	725	......

Equipment 16

Date	Item	Post. Ref.	Dr.	Cr.	Balance Dr.	Balance Cr.
19—						
June 7	....	1	6,250	......	6,250	......

Prob. 2-3A, Continued

Truck   18

Date	Item	Post. Ref.	Dr.	Cr.	Balance Dr.	Balance Cr.
19—						
June 8	....	1	15,000	......	15,000	......

Notes Payable   21

Date	Item	Post. Ref.	Dr.	Cr.	Balance Dr.	Balance Cr.
19—						
June 8	....	1	......	7,500	.....	7,500

Accounts Payable   22

Date	Item	Post. Ref.	Dr.	Cr.	Balance Dr.	Balance Cr.
19—						
June 7	....	1	......	6,250	.....	6,250
24	....	1	......	310	.....	6,560
28	....	2	......	190	.....	6,750
30	....	2	2,500	......	.....	4,250

Tom Morgan, Capital   31

Date	Item	Post. Ref.	Dr.	Cr.	Balance Dr.	Balance Cr.
19—						
June 5	....	1	......	15,000	.....	15,000

Tom Morgan, Drawing   32

Date	Item	Post. Ref.	Dr.	Cr.	Balance Dr.	Balance Cr.
19—						
June 30	....	2	2,000	......	2,000	......

Fees Earned   41

Date	Item	Post. Ref.	Dr.	Cr.	Balance Dr.	Balance Cr.
19—						
June 12	....	1	......	600	.....	600
22	....	1	......	1,950	.....	2,550
26	....	2	......	650	.....	3,200

Wages Expense   51

Date	Item	Post. Ref.	Dr.	Cr.	Balance Dr.	Balance Cr.
19—						
June 15	....	1	800	......	800	......
30	....	2	1,200	......	2,000	......

Prob. 2-3A, Concluded

Rent Expense   **53**

Date	Item	Post. Ref.	Dr.	Cr.	Balance Dr.	Balance Cr.
19— June 5	....	1	950	......	950	......

Utilities Expense   **54**

Date	Item	Post. Ref.	Dr.	Cr.	Balance Dr.	Balance Cr.
19— June 29	....	2	390	......	390	......

Truck Expense   **55**

Date	Item	Post. Ref.	Dr.	Cr.	Balance Dr.	Balance Cr.
19— June 24	....	1	310	......	310	......

Miscellaneous Expense   **59**

Date	Item	Post. Ref.	Dr.	Cr.	Balance Dr.	Balance Cr.
19— June 29	....	2	95	......	95	......

3.

MORGAN DECORATORS
Trial Balance
June 30, 19—

	Dr.	Cr.
Cash..	865	
Accounts Receivable.......................................	650	
Supplies	715	
Prepaid Insurance...	725	
Equipment	6,250	
Truck	15,000	
Notes Payable...		7,500
Accounts Payable..		4,250
Tom Morgan, Capital		15,000
Tom Morgan, Drawing	2,000	
Fees Earned		3,200
Wages Expense..	2,000	
Rent Expense	950	
Utilities Expense	390	
Truck Expense...	310	
Miscellaneous Expense	95	
	29,950	29,950

Prob. 2-4A

2. and 3.   **JOURNAL**   **Pages 97 and 98**

Date		Description	Post. Ref.	Debit	Credit
19—					
June	1	Rent Expense............................	53	2,000	
		Cash..................................	11		2,000
	2	Equipment.............................	18	10,500	
		Accounts Payable	22		10,500
	3	Supplies...............................	13	725	
		Accounts Payable	22		725
	6	Cash...................................	11	10,025	
		Accounts Receivable.................	12		10,025
	6	Accounts Payable	22	5,240	
		Cash..................................	11		5,240
	8	Cash...................................	11	75	
		Supplies	13		75
	10	Prepaid Insurance	14	495	
		Cash..................................	11		495
	15	Laboratory Expense.....................	56	395	
		Cash..................................	11		395
	20	Cash...................................	11	100	
		Accounts Receivable.................	12		100
	24	Accounts Payable	22	550	
		Equipment............................	18		550
	26	Frank Saul, Drawing....................	32	2,750	
		Cash..................................	11		2,750
	30	Accounts Receivable	12	7,770	
		Professional Fees.....................	41		7,770
	30	Cash...................................	11	9,610	
		Professional Fees.....................	41		9,610
	30	Salary Expense.........................	51	4,050	
		Cash..................................	11		4,050
	30	Miscellaneous Expense	59	420	
		Cash..................................	11		420
	30	Utilities Expense.......................	55	610	
		Cash..................................	11		610
	30	Utilities Expense.......................	55	130	
		Cash..................................	11		130
	30	Utilities Expense.......................	55	280	
		Cash..................................	11		280

Prob. 2-4A, Continued

1. and 3.

Cash 11

Date		Item	Post. Ref.	Dr.	Cr.	Balance Dr.	Balance Cr.
19—							
June	1	Balance.....................	√	.....	.....	5,075	.....
	1	....	97	.....	2,000	3,075	.....
	6	....	97	10,025	.....	13,100	.....
	6	....	97	.....	5,240	7,860	.....
	8	....	97	75	.....	7,935	.....
	10	....	97	.....	495	7,440	.....
	15	....	97	.....	395	7,045	.....
	20	....	97	100	.....	7,145	.....
	26	....	97	.....	2,750	4,395	.....
	30	....	98	9,610	.....	14,005	.....
	30	....	98	.....	4,050	9,955	.....
	30	....	98	.....	420	9,535	.....
	30	....	98	.....	610	8,925	.....
	30	....	98	.....	130	8,795	.....
	30	....	98	.....	280	8,515	.....

Accounts Receivable 12

Date		Item	Post. Ref.	Dr.	Cr.	Balance Dr.	Balance Cr.
19—							
June	1	Balance.....................	√	.....	.....	15,110	.....
	6	....	97	.....	10,025	5,085	.....
	20	....	97	.....	100	4,985	.....
	30	....	98	7,770	.....	12,755	.....

Supplies 13

Date		Item	Post. Ref.	Dr.	Cr.	Balance Dr.	Balance Cr.
19—							
June	1	Balance.....................	√	.....	.....	1,140	.....
	3	....	97	725	.....	1,865	.....
	8	....	97	.....	75	1,790	.....

Prepaid Insurance 14

Date		Item	Post. Ref.	Dr.	Cr.	Balance Dr.	Balance Cr.
19—							
June	1	Balance.....................	√	.....	.....	3,700	.....
	10	....	97	495	.....	4,195	.....

Prob. 2-4A, Continued

Equipment   18

Date	Item	Post. Ref.	Dr.	Cr.	Balance Dr.	Balance Cr.
19—						
June 1	Balance....................	√	......	......	52,200	......
2	....	97	10,500	......	62,700	......
24	....	97	......	550	62,150	......

Accounts Payable   22

Date	Item	Post. Ref.	Dr.	Cr.	Balance Dr.	Balance Cr.
19—						
June 1	Balance....................	√	....	......	.....	9,850
2	....	97	....	10,500	.....	20,350
3	....	97	....	725	.....	21,075
6	....	97	5,240	......	......	15,835
24	....	97	550	......	.....	15,285

Frank Saul, Capital   31

Date	Item	Post. Ref.	Dr.	Cr.	Balance Dr.	Balance Cr.
19—						
June 1	Balance....................	√	....	....	.....	67,375

Frank Saul, Drawing   32

Date	Item	Post. Ref.	Dr.	Cr.	Balance Dr.	Balance Cr.
19—						
June 26	....	97	2,750	......	2,750	......

Professional Fees   41

Date	Item	Post. Ref.	Dr.	Cr.	Balance Dr.	Balance Cr.
19—						
June 30	....	98	....	7,770	.....	7,770
30	....	98	....	9,610	.....	17,380

Salary Expense   51

Date	Item	Post. Ref.	Dr.	Cr.	Balance Dr.	Balance Cr.
19—						
June 30	....	98	4,050	......	4,050	......

Rent Expense   53

Date	Item	Post. Ref.	Dr.	Cr.	Balance Dr.	Balance Cr.
19—						
June 1	....	97	2,000	......	2,000	......

Prob. 2-4A, Concluded

Utilities Expense   55

Date	Item	Post. Ref.	Dr.	Cr.	Balance Dr.	Balance Cr.
19—						
June 30	....	98	610	......	610	......
30	....	98	130	......	740	......
30	....	98	280	......	1,020	......

Laboratory Expense   56

Date	Item	Post. Ref.	Dr.	Cr.	Balance Dr.	Balance Cr.
19—						
June 15	....	97	395	......	395	......

Miscellaneous Expense   59

Date	Item	Post. Ref.	Dr.	Cr.	Balance Dr.	Balance Cr.
19—						
June 30	....	98	420	......	420	......

4.   FRANK SAUL, M.D.
                                 Trial Balance
                                 June 30, 19—

	Dr.	Cr.
Cash..	8,515	
Accounts Receivable.................................	12,755	
Supplies	1,790	
Prepaid Insurance...................................	4,195	
Equipment	62,150	
Accounts Payable....................................		15,285
Frank Saul, Capital..................................		67,375
Frank Saul, Drawing	2,750	
Professional Fees		17,380
Salary Expense......................................	4,050	
Rent Expense	2,000	
Utilities Expense	1,020	
Laboratory Expense	395	
Miscellaneous Expense	420	
	100,040	100,040

5. a. $6,545. ($17,380 − $4,050 − $2,000 − $1,020 − $395 − $420 − $2,950)
   b. $3,795. ($6,545 − $2,750)
   c. $71,170. ($67,375 + $3,795)

Prob. 2-5A

2. and 3.   **JOURNAL**   **Pages 18 and 19**

Date	Description	Post. Ref.	Debit	Credit
19—				
Apr. 1	Rent Expense...............................	52	1,500	
	Cash	11		1,500
3	Office Supplies	14	375	
	Accounts Payable	21		375
5	Prepaid Insurance........................	13	1,650	
	Cash	11		1,650
7	Cash	11	18,200	
	Accounts Receivable	12		18,200
15	Salary and Commission Expense..........	51	16,650	
	Cash	11		16,650
15	Land	16	55,000	
	Cash	11		11,000
	Notes Payable	22		44,000
15	Accounts Receivable	12	19,100	
	Fees Earned	41		19,100
18	Accounts Payable........................	21	4,150	
	Cash	11		4,150
20	Accounts Payable........................	21	75	
	Office Supplies	14		75
23	Cash	11	16,700	
	Accounts Receivable	12		16,700
24	Advertising Expense......................	53	1,550	
	Cash	11		1,550
27	Cash	11	350	
	Salary and Commission Expense........	51		350
28	Automobile Expense......................	54	715	
	Cash	11		715
29	Miscellaneous Expense....................	59	215	
	Cash	11		215
30	Accounts Receivable	12	16,300	
	Fees Earned	41		16,300
30	Salary and Commission Expense..........	51	19,850	
	Cash	11		19,850
30	J. J. Barr, Drawing	32	2,000	
	Cash	11		2,000

Prob. 2-5A, Continued

1. and 3.

Cash   11

Date	Item	Post. Ref.	Dr.	Cr.	Balance Dr.	Balance Cr.
19—						
Apr. 1	Balance	√	......	......	36,150	......
1	....	18	......	1,500	34,650	......
5	....	18	......	1,650	33,000	......
7	....	18	18,200	......	51,200	......
15	....	18	......	16,650	34,550	......
15	....	18	......	11,000	23,550	......
18	....	18	......	4,150	19,400	......
23	....	18	16,700	......	36,100	......
24	....	18	......	1,550	34,550	......
27	....	19	350	......	34,900	......
28	....	19	......	715	34,185	......
29	....	19	......	215	33,970	......
30	....	19	......	19,850	14,120	......
30	....	19	......	2,000	12,120	......

Accounts Receivable   12

Date	Item	Post. Ref.	Dr.	Cr.	Balance Dr.	Balance Cr.
19—						
Apr. 1	Balance................	√	......	......	28,750	......
7	....	18	......	18,200	10,550	......
15	....	18	19,100	......	29,650	......
23	....	18	......	16,700	12,950	......
30	....	19	16,300	......	29,250	......

Prepaid Insurance   13

Date	Item	Post. Ref.	Dr.	Cr.	Balance Dr.	Balance Cr.
19—						
Apr. 1	Balance	√	......	......	1,100	......
5	....	18	1,650	......	2,750	......

Office Supplies   14

Date	Item	Post. Ref.	Dr.	Cr.	Balance Dr.	Balance Cr.
19—						
Apr. 1	Balance................	√			715	......
3	....	18	375	......	1,090	......
20	....	18	......	75	1,015	......

Prob. 2-5A, Continued

Land 16

Date	Item	Post. Ref.	Dr.	Cr.	Balance Dr.	Balance Cr.
19—						
Apr. 15	....	18	55,000	......	55,000	....

Accounts Payable 21

Date	Item	Post. Ref.	Dr.	Cr.	Balance Dr.	Balance Cr.
19—						
Apr. 1	Balance................	✓	......	......	....	6,175
3	....	18	......	375	....	6,550
18	....	18	4,150	......	....	2,400
20	....	18	75	......	....	2,325

Notes Payable 22

Date	Item	Post. Ref.	Dr.	Cr.	Balance Dr.	Balance Cr.
19—						
Apr. 15	....	18	......	44,000	....	44,000

J. J. Barr, Capital 31

Date	Item	Post. Ref.	Dr.	Cr.	Balance Dr.	Balance Cr.
19—						
Apr. 1	Balance................	✓	......	......	....	40,840

J. J. Barr, Drawing 32

Date	Item	Post. Ref.	Dr.	Cr.	Balance Dr.	Balance Cr.
19—						
Apr. 1	Balance................	✓	......	......	2,000	....
30	....	19	2,000	......	4,000	....

Fees Earned 41

Date	Item	Post. Ref.	Dr.	Cr.	Balance Dr.	Balance Cr.
19—						
Apr. 1	Balance................	✓	......	......	....	125,500
15	....	18	......	19,100	....	144,600
30	....	19	......	16,300	....	160,900

Salary and Commission Expense 51

Date	Item	Post. Ref.	Dr.	Cr.	Balance Dr.	Balance Cr.
19—						
Apr. 1	Balance................	✓	......	......	92,100	......
15	....	18	16,650	......	108,750	......
27	....	19	......	350	108,400	......
30	....	19	19,850	......	128,250	......

Prob. 2-5A, Concluded

Rent Expense   52

Date	Item	Post. Ref.	Dr.	Cr.	Balance Dr.	Balance Cr.
19—						
Apr. 1	Balance.............	√	......	......	4,500	......
1	....	18	1,500	......	6,000	......

Advertising Expense   53

Date	Item	Post. Ref.	Dr.	Cr.	Balance Dr.	Balance Cr.
19—						
Apr. 1	Balance.............	√	......	......	3,900	......
24	....	18	1,550	......	5,450	......

Automobile Expense   54

Date	Item	Post. Ref.	Dr.	Cr.	Balance Dr.	Balance Cr.
19—						
Apr. 1	Balance.............	√	......	......	2,750	......
28	....	19	715	......	3,465	......

Miscellaneous Expense   59

Date	Item	Post. Ref.	Dr.	Cr.	Balance Dr.	Balance Cr.
19—						
Apr. 1	Balance.............	√	......	......	550	......
29	....	19	215	......	765	......

4.
LAKESIDE REALTY
Trial Balance
April 30, 19—

	Dr.	Cr.
Cash	12,120	
Accounts Receivable	29,250	
Prepaid Insurance	2,750	
Office Supplies	1,015	
Land	55,000	
Accounts Payable		2,325
Notes Payable		44,000
J. J. Barr, Capital		40,840
J. J. Barr, Drawing	4,000	
Fees Earned		160,900
Salary and Commission Expense	128,250	
Rent Expense	6,000	
Advertising Expense	5,450	
Automobile Expense	3,465	
Miscellaneous Expense	765	
	248,065	248,065

Prob. 2-6A

1. Totals of preliminary trial balance: Debit $30,403.84
   Credit $34,878.10

2. Difference between preliminary trial balance totals: $ 4,474.26

3. Errors in trial balance:
   (a) Rent Expense debit balance of $1,540 listed as credit balance.
   (b) Advertising Expense of $275 omitted.

4. Errors in account balances:
   (a) Prepaid Insurance balance of $395.50 totaled as $295.50.

5. Errors in posting:
   (a) Cash entry of March 1 for $1,540 posted as $1,450 (transposition).
   (b) Miscellaneous Expense entry of March 25 for $121.40 posted as $12.14 (slide).
   (c) Wages Expense entry of March 31 for $1,890 posted as $890.

6. Mar. 31 Advertising Expense 53 125.00
   Cash 11   125.00

7.

DONAHUE TV REPAIR
Trial Balance
March 31, 19—

Cash..	8,291.00	
Supplies	997.90	
Prepaid Insurance.............................	395.50	
Land..	16,625.00	
Notes Payable.................................		6,500.00
Accounts Payable.............................		1,077.50
Ann Donahue, Capital........................		17,760.20
Ann Donahue, Drawing	1,350.00	
Service Revenue...............................		8,000.40
Wages Expense.................................	3,018.60	
Utilities Expense	436.60	
Advertising Expense...........................	400.00	
Rent Expense	1,540.00	
Miscellaneous Expense	283.50	
	33,338.10	33,338.10

Prob. 2-7A

1.   **BELL CARPET INSTALLATION**
                                      Trial Balance
                                    August 31, 19—

Cash..	3,720	
Accounts Receivable.......................................	7,125	
Supplies	1,100	
Prepaid Insurance..	550	
Equipment	15,500	
Notes Payable..		10,000
Accounts Payable......................................		3,910
John Bell, Capital.......................................		14,300
John Bell, Drawing	8,000	
Fees Earned...		49,980
Wages Expense..	28,500	
Rent Expense	6,400	
Advertising Expense......................................	3,200	
Gas, Electricity, and Water Expense.......................	3,150	
Miscellaneous Expense	945	
	78,190	78,190

2. No. The trial balance indicates only that the debits and credits are equal. Any errors that have the same effect on debits and credits will not affect the balancing of the trial balance.

Prob. 2-1B

1. and 2.

<table>
<tr><td colspan="4" align="center">Cash</td></tr>
<tr><td>(a)</td><td>10,000</td><td>(b)</td><td>3,300</td></tr>
<tr><td>(g)</td><td>1,725</td><td>(c)</td><td>1,200</td></tr>
<tr><td>2,887</td><td>11,725</td><td>(d)</td><td>225</td></tr>
<tr><td></td><td></td><td>(f)</td><td>510</td></tr>
<tr><td></td><td></td><td>(h)</td><td>2,100</td></tr>
<tr><td></td><td></td><td>(i)</td><td>65</td></tr>
<tr><td></td><td></td><td>(l)</td><td>1,000</td></tr>
<tr><td></td><td></td><td>(m)</td><td>68</td></tr>
<tr><td></td><td></td><td>(n)</td><td>300</td></tr>
<tr><td></td><td></td><td>(o)</td><td>70</td></tr>
<tr><td></td><td></td><td></td><td>8,838</td></tr>
</table>

<table>
<tr><td colspan="2" align="center">Accounts Receivable</td></tr>
<tr><td>(k)</td><td>2,500</td></tr>
</table>

<table>
<tr><td colspan="2" align="center">Supplies</td></tr>
<tr><td>(d)</td><td>225</td></tr>
</table>

<table>
<tr><td colspan="2" align="center">Prepaid Insurance</td></tr>
<tr><td>(f)</td><td>510</td></tr>
</table>

<table>
<tr><td colspan="2" align="center">Automobiles</td></tr>
<tr><td>(b)</td><td>14,300</td></tr>
</table>

<table>
<tr><td colspan="2" align="center">Equipment</td></tr>
<tr><td>(e)</td><td>4,200</td></tr>
</table>

<table>
<tr><td colspan="4" align="center">Notes Payable</td></tr>
<tr><td>(n)</td><td>300</td><td>(b)</td><td>11,000</td></tr>
<tr><td></td><td></td><td></td><td>10,700</td></tr>
</table>

<table>
<tr><td colspan="4" align="center">Accounts Payable</td></tr>
<tr><td>(h)</td><td>2,100</td><td>(e)</td><td>4,200</td></tr>
<tr><td></td><td></td><td>(j)</td><td>75</td></tr>
<tr><td></td><td>2,175</td><td></td><td>4,275</td></tr>
</table>

<table>
<tr><td colspan="4" align="center">Hector Cruz, Capital</td></tr>
<tr><td></td><td></td><td>(a)</td><td>10,000</td></tr>
</table>

<table>
<tr><td colspan="4" align="center">Professional Fees</td></tr>
<tr><td></td><td></td><td>(g)</td><td>1,725</td></tr>
<tr><td></td><td></td><td>(k)</td><td>2,500</td></tr>
<tr><td></td><td></td><td></td><td>4,225</td></tr>
</table>

<table>
<tr><td colspan="2" align="center">Rent Expense</td></tr>
<tr><td>(c)</td><td>1,200</td></tr>
</table>

<table>
<tr><td colspan="2" align="center">Salary Expense</td></tr>
<tr><td>(l)</td><td>1,000</td></tr>
</table>

<table>
<tr><td colspan="2" align="center">Automobile Expense</td></tr>
<tr><td>(o)</td><td>70</td></tr>
</table>

<table>
<tr><td colspan="2" align="center">Blueprint Expense</td></tr>
<tr><td>(j)</td><td>75</td></tr>
</table>

<table>
<tr><td colspan="2" align="center">Miscellaneous Expense</td></tr>
<tr><td>(i)</td><td>65</td></tr>
<tr><td>(m)</td><td>68</td></tr>
<tr><td></td><td>133</td></tr>
</table>

Prob. 2-1B, Concluded

3.   **HECTOR CRUZ, ARCHITECT**
Trial Balance
November 30, 19—

Cash...	2,887	
Accounts Receivable..............................	2,500	
Supplies	225	
Prepaid Insurance.................................	510	
Automobiles	14,300	
Equipment	4,200	
Notes Payable		10,700
Accounts Payable.................................		2,175
Hector Cruz, Capital		10,000
Professional Fees		4,225
Rent Expense	1,200	
Salary Expense...................................	1,000	
Automobile Expense..............................	70	
Blueprint Expense	75	
Miscellaneous Expense	133	
	27,100	27,100

Prob. 2-2B

1.	(a)	Cash..	15,000	
		Rob Petrie, Capital		15,000
	(b)	Rent Expense................................	12,000	
		Cash...		12,000
	(c)	Supplies.....................................	5,900	
		Accounts Payable		5,900
	(d)	Accounts Payable	4,000	
		Cash...		4,000
	(e)	Cash	41,500	
		Sales Commissions............................		41,500
	(f)	Rob Petrie, Drawing............................	10,000	
		Cash...		10,000
	(g)	Automobile Expense	3,900	
		Miscellaneous Expense	1,950	
		Cash...		5,850
	(h)	Office Salaries Expense........................	10,000	
		Cash...		10,000
	(i)	Supplies Expense	2,250	
		Supplies......................................		2,250

Prob. 2-2B, Concluded

2.

Cash			
(a)	15,000	(b)	12,000
(e)	41,500	(d)	4,000
14,650	56,500	(f)	10,000
		(g)	5,850
		(h)	10,000
			41,850

Supplies			
(c)	5,900	(i)	2,250
3,650			

Accounts Payable			
(d)	4,000	(c)	5,900
			1,900

Rob Petrie, Capital			
		(a)	15,000

Rob Petrie, Drawing			
(f)	10,000		

Sales Commissions			
		(e)	41,500

Rent Expense			
(b)	12,000		

Office Salaries Expense			
(h)	10,000		

Automobile Expense			
(g)	3,900		

Supplies Expense			
(i)	2,250		

Miscellaneous Expense			
(g)	1,950		

3.

MIDSTATE REALTY
Trial Balance
July 31, 19—

Cash	14,650	
Supplies	3,650	
Accounts Payable		1,900
Rob Petrie, Capital		15,000
Rob Petrie, Drawing	10,000	
Sales Commissions		41,500
Rent Expense	12,000	
Office Salaries Expense	10,000	
Automobile Expense	3,900	
Supplies Expense	2,250	
Miscellaneous Expense	1,950	
	58,400	58,400

4. a. $41,500
   b. $30,100
   c. $11,400

Prob. 2-3B

1.   JOURNAL   Pages 1 and 2

Date	Description	Post. Ref.	Debit	Credit
19—				
July 10	Cash	11	10,000	
	Jane Morse, Capital	31		10,000
10	Rent Expense...........................	53	600	
	Cash	11		600
11	Truck..................................	18	9,000	
	Cash	11		3,000
	Notes Payable	21		6,000
12	Equipment	16	1,700	
	Accounts Payable	22		1,700
14	Supplies................................	13	885	
	Cash	11		885
14	Prepaid Insurance.......................	14	420	
	Cash	11		420
15	Cash	11	510	
	Fees Earned	41		510
16	Supplies................................	13	240	
	Accounts Payable	22		240
17	Wages Expense..........................	51	600	
	Cash	11		600
21	Accounts Payable........................	22	1,700	
	Cash	11		1,700
24	Accounts Receivable	12	2,100	
	Fees Earned	41		2,100
26	Truck Expense	55	225	
	Accounts Payable	22		225
26	Cash	11	1,050	
	Fees Earned	41		1,050
27	Utilities Expense	54	205	
	Cash	11		205
27	Miscellaneous Expense....................	59	73	
	Cash	11		73
28	Cash	11	1,420	
	Accounts Receivable	12		1,420
31	Wages Expense..........................	51	1,350	
	Cash	11		1,350
31	Jane Morse, Drawing	32	1,500	
	Cash	11		1,500

Prob. 2-3B, Continued

2.

Cash   11

Date	Item	Post. Ref.	Dr.	Cr.	Balance Dr.	Cr.
19—						
July 10	....	1	10,000	......	10,000	......
10	....	1	......	600	9,400	......
11	....	1	......	3,000	6,400	......
14	....	1	......	885	5,515	......
14	....	1	......	420	5,095	......
15	....	1	510	......	5,605	......
17	....	1	......	600	5,005	......
21	....	2	......	1,700	3,305	......
26	....	2	1,050	......	4,355	......
27	....	2	......	205	4,150	......
27	....	2	......	73	4,077	......
28	....	2	1,420	......	5,497	......
31	....	2	......	1,350	4,147	......
31	....	2	......	1,500	2,647	......

Accounts Receivable   12

Date	Item	Post. Ref.	Dr.	Cr.	Balance Dr.	Cr.
19—						
July 24	....	2	2,100	......	2,100	......
28	....	2	......	1,420	680	......

Supplies   13

Date	Item	Post. Ref.	Dr.	Cr.	Balance Dr.	Cr.
19—						
July 14	....	1	885	......	885	......
16	....	1	240	......	1,125	......

Prepaid Insurance   14

Date	Item	Post. Ref.	Dr.	Cr.	Balance Dr.	Cr.
19—						
July 14	....	1	420	......	420	......

Equipment   16

Date	Item	Post. Ref.	Dr.	Cr.	Balance Dr.	Cr.
19—						
July 12	....	1	1,700	......	1,700	......

Prob. 2-3B, Continued

Truck   18

| | | | | | Balance | |
Date	Item	Post. Ref.	Dr.	Cr.	Dr.	Cr.
19—						
July 11	....	1	9,000	......	9,000	......

Notes Payable   21

19—						
July 11	....	1	......	6,000	......	6,000

Accounts Payable   22

19—						
July 12	....	1	......	1,700	......	1,700
16	....	1	......	240	......	1,940
21	....	2	1,700	......	......	240
26	....	2	......	225	......	465

Jane Morse, Capital   31

19—						
July 10	....	1	......	10,000	......	10,000

Jane Morse, Drawing   32

19—						
July 31	....	2	1,500	......	1,500	......

Fees Earned   41

19—						
July 15	....	1	......	510	......	510
24	....	2	......	2,100	......	2,610
26	....	2	......	1,050	......	3,660

Wages Expense   51

19—						
July 17	....	1	600	......	600	......
31	....	2	1,350	......	1,950	......

Rent Expense   53

19—						
July 10	....	1	600	......	600	......

Prob. 2-3B, Concluded

Utilities Expense 54

Date	Item	Post. Ref.	Dr.	Cr.	Balance Dr.	Balance Cr.
19—						
July 27	....	2	205	......	205	......

Truck Expense 55

Date	Item	Post. Ref.	Dr.	Cr.	Balance Dr.	Balance Cr.
19—						
July 26	....	2	225	......	225	......

Miscellaneous Expense 59

Date	Item	Post. Ref.	Dr.	Cr.	Balance Dr.	Balance Cr.
19—						
July 27	....	2	73	......	73	......

3.

MORSE DECORATORS
Trial Balance
July 31, 19—

	Dr.	Cr.
Cash	2,647	
Accounts Receivable	680	
Supplies	1,125	
Prepaid Insurance	420	
Equipment	1,700	
Truck	9,000	
Notes Payable		6,000
Accounts Payable		465
Jane Morse, Capital		10,000
Jane Morse, Drawing	1,500	
Fees Earned		3,660
Wages Expense	1,950	
Rent Expense	600	
Utilities Expense	205	
Truck Expense	225	
Miscellaneous Expense	73	
	20,125	20,125

Prob. 2-4B

2. and 3.   **JOURNAL**   **Pages 97 and 98**

Date	Description	Post. Ref.	Debit	Credit
19—				
May 1	Rent Expense........................	53	2,100	
	Cash	11		2,100
2	Equipment	18	8,500	
	Accounts Payable	22		8,500
5	Supplies...........................	13	850	
	Accounts Payable	22		850
6	Cash	11	8,925	
	Accounts Receivable	12		8,925
7	Accounts Payable..................	22	5,620	
	Cash	11		5,620
10	Cash	11	75	
	Supplies..........................	13		75
10	Prepaid Insurance.................	14	545	
	Cash	11		545
15	Laboratory Expense	56	345	
	Cash	11		345
20	Cash	11	100	
	Accounts Receivable	12		100
24	Accounts Payable..................	22	250	
	Equipment........................	18		250
26	Chris Dunn, Drawing...............	32	2,200	
	Cash	11		2,200
28	Miscellaneous Expense.............	59	420	
	Cash	11		420
30	Utilities Expense	55	510	
	Cash	11		510
30	Utilities Expense	55	130	
	Cash	11		130
30	Utilities Expense	55	225	
	Cash	11		225
31	Accounts Receivable	12	8,200	
	Professional Fees	41		8,200
31	Cash	11	9,910	
	Professional Fees	41		9,910
31	Salary Expense	51	4,650	
	Cash	11		4,650

Prob. 2-4B, Continued

1. and 3.

Cash   11

Date	Item	Post. Ref.	Dr.	Cr.	Balance Dr.	Balance Cr.
19—						
May 1	Balance	✓	....	.....	5,925	.....
1		97	....	2,100	3,825	.....
6		97	8,925	.....	12,750	.....
7		97	....	5,620	7,130	.....
10		97	75	....	7,205	
10		97	....	545	6,660	.....
15		97	....	345	6,315	.....
20		97	100	....	6,415	
26		97	....	2,200	4,215	.....
28		98	....	420	3,795	.....
30		98	....	510	3,285	.....
30		98	....	130	3,155	.....
30		98	....	225	2,930	.....
31		98	9,910	.....	12,840	.....
31		98	....	4,650	8,190	.....

Accounts Receivable   12

Date	Item	Post. Ref.	Dr.	Cr.	Balance Dr.	Balance Cr.
19—						
May 1	Balance	✓	....	.....	15,160	.....
6		97	....	8,925	6,235	.....
20		97	....	100	6,135	.....
31		98	8,200	.....	14,335	.....

Supplies   13

Date	Item	Post. Ref.	Dr.	Cr.	Balance Dr.	Balance Cr.
19—						
May 1	Balance	✓	....	.....	1,240	.....
5		97	850	.....	2,090	.....
10		97	....	75	2,015	.....

Prepaid Insurance   14

Date	Item	Post. Ref.	Dr.	Cr.	Balance Dr.	Balance Cr.
19—						
May 1	Balance	✓	....	.....	3,500	.....
10		97	545	.....	4,045	.....

Prob. 2-4B, Continued

Equipment   18

Date	Item	Post. Ref.	Dr.	Cr.	Balance Dr.	Balance Cr.
19—						
May 1	Balance	√	....	.....	55,600	......
2	....	97	8,500	.....	64,100	......
24	....	97	....	250	63,850	......

Accounts Payable   22

Date	Item	Post. Ref.	Dr.	Cr.	Balance Dr.	Balance Cr.
19—						
May 1	Balance	√	....	.....	......	9,850
2	....	97	....	8,500	.....	18,350
5	....	97	....	850	.....	19,200
7	....	97	5,620	.....	.....	13,580
24	....	97	250	.....	.....	13,330

Chris Dunn, Capital   31

Date	Item	Post. Ref.	Dr.	Cr.	Balance Dr.	Balance Cr.
19—						
May 1	Balance	√	....	.....	......	71,575

Chris Dunn, Drawing   32

Date	Item	Post. Ref.	Dr.	Cr.	Balance Dr.	Balance Cr.
19—						
May 26	....	97	2,200	.....	2,200	......

Professional Fees   41

Date	Item	Post. Ref.	Dr.	Cr.	Balance Dr.	Balance Cr.
19—						
May 31	....	98	....	8,200	......	8,200
31	....	98	....	9,910	......	18,110

Salary Expense   51

Date	Item	Post. Ref.	Dr.	Cr.	Balance Dr.	Balance Cr.
19—						
May 31	....	98	4,650	.....	4,650	......

Rent Expense   53

Date	Item	Post. Ref.	Dr.	Cr.	Balance Dr.	Balance Cr.
19—						
May 1	....	97	2,100	.....	2,100	......

Prob. 2-4B, Concluded

Utilities Expense 55

Date	Item	Post. Ref.	Dr.	Cr.	Balance Dr.	Balance Cr.
19—						
May 30	....	98	510	.....	510	......
30	....	98	130	.....	640	......
30	....	98	225	.....	865	......

Laboratory Expense 56

Date	Item	Post. Ref.	Dr.	Cr.	Balance Dr.	Balance Cr.
19—						
May 15	....	97	345	.....	345	......

Miscellaneous Expense 59

Date	Item	Post. Ref.	Dr.	Cr.	Balance Dr.	Balance Cr.
19—						
May 28	....	97	420	.....	420	......

4.

CHRIS DUNN, M.D.
Trial Balance
May 31, 19—

	Dr.	Cr.
Cash..	8,190	
Accounts Receivable................................	14,335	
Supplies..	2,015	
Prepaid Insurance.................................	4,045	
Equipment......................................	63,850	
Accounts Payable.................................		13,330
Chris Dunn, Capital...............................		71,575
Chris Dunn, Drawing...............................	2,200	
Professional Fees.................................		18,110
Salary Expense...................................	4,650	
Rent Expense....................................	2,100	
Utilities Expense.................................	865	
Laboratory Expense...............................	345	
Miscellaneous Expense............................	420	
	103,015	103,015

5. a. $7,880. ($18,110 − $4,650 − $2,100 − $865 − $345 − $420 − $1,850)
   b. $5,680. ($7,880 − $2,200)
   c. $77,255. ($71,575 + $5,680)

Prob. 2-5B

2. and 3.

| | | JOURNAL | | Pages 18 and 19 |
| | | | | |

Date	Description	Post. Ref.	Debit	Credit
19—				
May 1	Rent Expense..............................	52	2,500	
	Cash	11		2,500
2	Office Supplies	14	425	
	Accounts Payable.......................	21		425
3	Prepaid Insurance........................	13	1,925	
	Cash	11		1,925
9	Cash	11	21,000	
	Accounts Receivable	12		21,000
15	Salary and Commission Expense	51	19,650	
	Cash	11		19,650
15	Land	16	50,000	
	Cash	11		10,000
	Notes Payable	22		40,000
15	Accounts Receivable	12	20,900	
	Fees Earned	41		20,900
18	Accounts Payable........................	21	5,650	
	Cash	11		5,650
20	Accounts Payable........................	21	50	
	Office Supplies	14		50
29	Cash	11	19,200	
	Accounts Receivable	12		19,200
29	Advertising Expense	53	2,150	
	Cash	11		2,150
29	Cash	11	500	
	Salary and Commission Expense.........	51		500
30	Automobile Expense......................	54	850	
	Cash	11		850
30	Miscellaneous Expense....................	59	215	
	Cash	11		215
31	Accounts Receivable	12	19,300	
	Fees Earned	41		19,300
31	Salary and Commission Expense	51	19,850	
	Cash	11		19,850
31	P. E. Combs, Drawing......................	32	10,000	
	Cash	11		10,000

Prob. 2-5B, Continued

1. and 3.

Cash 11

Date	Item	Post. Ref.	Dr.	Cr.	Balance Dr.	Balance Cr.
19—						
May 1	Balance	√	......	......	39,500	......
1		18	......	2,500	37,000	......
3		18	......	1,925	35,075	......
9		18	21,000		56,075	......
15		18	......	19,650	36,425	......
15		18	......	10,000	26,425	......
18		18	......	5,650	20,775	......
29		18	19,200	......	39,975	......
29		18	......	2,150	37,825	......
29		19	500	......	38,325	......
30		19	......	850	37,475	......
30		19	......	215	37,260	......
31		19	......	19,850	17,410	......
31		19	......	10,000	7,410	......

Accounts Receivable 12

Date	Item	Post. Ref.	Dr.	Cr.	Balance Dr.	Balance Cr.
19—						
May 1	Balance	√	......	......	28,600	......
9		18	......	21,000	7,600	......
15		18	20,900	......	28,500	......
29		18	......	19,200	9,300	......
31		19	19,300	......	28,600	......

Prepaid Insurance 13

Date	Item	Post. Ref.	Dr.	Cr.	Balance Dr.	Balance Cr.
19—						
May 1	Balance	√	......	......	750	......
3		18	1,925	......	2,675	......

Office Supplies 14

Date	Item	Post. Ref.	Dr.	Cr.	Balance Dr.	Balance Cr.
19—						
May 1	Balance	√	......	......	625	......
2		18	425	......	1,050	......
20		18	......	50	1,000	......

Prob. 2-5B, Continued

Land   16

| | | Post. | | | Balance | |
| | | | | | Dr. | Cr. |
Date	Item	Ref.	Dr.	Cr.	Dr.	Cr.
19—						
May 15	....	18	50,000	......	50,000	....

Accounts Payable   21

		Post.			Balance	
19—						
May 1	Balance	√	......	......	......	9,250
2	....	18	......	425	......	9,675
18	....	18	5,650	......	......	4,025
20	....	18	50	......	......	3,975

Notes Payable   22

		Post.			Balance	
19—						
May 15	....	18	......	40,000	....	40,000

P. E. Combs, Capital   31

		Post.			Balance	
19—						
May 1	Balance	√	......	......	......	63,025

P. E. Combs, Drawing   32

		Post.			Balance	
19—						
May 1	Balance	√	......	......	20,000	......
31	....	19	10,000	......	30,000	....

Fees Earned   41

		Post.			Balance	
19—						
May 1	Balance	√	......	......	....	157,750
15	....	18	......	20,900	....	178,650
31	....	19	......	19,300	....	197,950

Salary and Commission Expense   51

		Post.			Balance	
19—						
May 1	Balance	√	......	......	122,100	......
15	....	18	19,650	......	141,750	......
29	....	19	......	500	141,250	......
31	....	19	19,850	......	161,100	......

Prob. 2-5B, Concluded

Rent Expense 52

			Post.			Balance	
Date	Item		Ref.	Dr.	Cr.	Dr.	Cr.
19—							
May 1	Balance	....	√	......	......	9,000	....
1	....		18	2,500	......	11,500	....

Advertising Expense 53

19—							
May 1	Balance	....	√	......	......	4,900	....
29	....		18	2,150	......	7,050	....

Automobile Expense 54

19—							
May 1	Balance	....	√	......	......	3,950	....
30	....		19	850	......	4,800	....

Miscellaneous Expense 59

19—							
May 1	Balance	....	√	......	......	600	....
30	....		19	215	......	815	....

4.
COMBS REALTY
Trial Balance
May 31, 19—

	Dr.	Cr.
Cash	7,410	
Accounts Receivable	28,600	
Prepaid Insurance	2,675	
Office Supplies	1,000	
Land	50,000	
Accounts Payable		3,975
Notes Payable		40,000
P. E. Combs, Capital		63,025
P. E. Combs, Drawing	30,000	
Fees Earned		197,950
Salary and Commission Expense	161,100	
Rent Expense	11,500	
Advertising Expense	7,050	
Automobile Expense	4,800	
Miscellaneous Expense	815	
	304,950	304,950

Prob. 2-6B

1. Totals of preliminary trial balance: Debit $30,403.84

                                                       Credit $34,878.10

2. Difference between preliminary trial balance totals: $ 4,474.26

3. Errors in trial balance:
   (a) Rent Expense debit balance of $1,540 listed as credit balance.
   (b) Advertising Expense of $275 omitted.

4. Errors in account balances:
   (a) Prepaid Insurance balance of $395.50 totaled as $295.50.

5. Errors in posting:
   (a) Cash entry of March 1 for $1,540 posted as $1,450 (transposition).
   (b) Miscellaneous Expense entry of March 25 for $121.40 posted as $12.14 (slide).
   (c) Wages Expense entry of March 31 for $1,890 posted as $890.

6. Mar. 31   Utilities Expense........................   52   160.00

                 Cash   11   160.00

7.

DONAHUE TV REPAIR
Trial Balance
March 31, 19—

Cash...	8,256.00	
Supplies	997.90	
Prepaid Insurance.............................	395.50	
Land..	16,625.00	
Notes Payable.................................		6,500.00
Accounts Payable..............................		1,077.50
Ann Donahue, Capital..........................		17,760.20
Ann Donahue, Drawing	1,350.00	
Service Sales..................................		8,000.40
Wages Expense................................	3,018.60	
Utilities Expense	596.60	
Advertising Expense...........................	275.00	
Rent Expense	1,540.00	
Miscellaneous Expense	283.50	
	33,338.10	33,338.10

Prob. 2-7B

1.

WELLS PHOTOGRAPHY
Trial Balance
October 31, 19—

Cash	5,825	
Accounts Receivable	10,100	
Supplies	1,250	
Prepaid Insurance	950	
Equipment	12,500	
Notes Payable		7,500
Accounts Payable		3,100
Elaine Wells, Capital		11,740
Elaine Wells, Drawing	7,500	
Fees Earned		80,750
Wages Expense	48,150	
Rent Expense	7,500	
Advertising Expense	5,250	
Gas, Electricity, and Water Expense	3,150	
Miscellaneous Expense	915	
	103,090	103,090

2. No. The trial balance indicates only that the debits and credits are equal. Any errors that have the same effect on debits and credits will not affect the balancing of the trial balance.

Mini-Case 2

1. Although the titles and numbers of accounts may differ, depending on how expenses are classified, the following accounts would be adequate for recording transaction data for Peck Caddy Service:

Account #	Account Title
1. Assets	
11	Cash
12	Accounts Receivable
13	Supplies
2. Liabilities	
21	Accounts Payable
3. Owner's Equity	
31	Fran Peck, Capital
32	Fran Peck, Drawing
4. Revenues	
41	Service Revenue
5. Expenses	
51	Rent Expense
52	Supplies Expense
53	Salary Expense
54	Utilities Expense
55	Miscellaneous Expense

2.

PECK CADDY SERVICE
Income Statement
For Month Ended June 30, 19—

Service revenue		$2,825
Operating expenses:		
Rent expense	$1,100	
Supplies expense	625	
Salary expense	220	
Utilities expense	85	
Miscellaneous expense	110	
Total operating expenses		2,140
Net income		$ 685

Note to Instructors: Students may have prepared slightly different income statements, depending upon the titles of the major expense classifications chosen. Regardless of the classification of expenses, however, the total sales, total operating expenses, and net income should be as presented above.

T accounts are not required for the preparation of the income statement of Peck Caddy Service. The following presentation illustrates one solution using T accounts. Alternative solutions are possible if students used different accounts. In presenting the following T account solution, instructors may wish

Mini-Case 2, Continued

to emphasize the advantages of using T accounts (or a journal and four-column accounts) when a large number of transactions must be recorded.

	Cash						11
19—			19—				
June 1	1,000		June 1	100			
15	990		2	190			
25	150		2	50			
30	1,475		3	500			
1,730	3,615		15	110			
			17	180			
			20	500			
			28	60			
			30	55			
			30	30			
			30	110			
				1,885			

	Accounts Receivable				12
19—			19—		
June 15	210		June 25	150	
30	150				
210	360				

	Supplies				13
19—			19—		
June 2	190		June 30	625	
7	325				
22	280				
170	795				

	Accounts Payable				21
19—			19—		
June 17	180		June 3	500	
20	500		7	325	
	680		22	280	
			425	1,105	

	Fran Peck, Capital				31
			19—		
			June 1	1,000	

	Service Revenue				41
			19—		
			June 15	990	
			15	210	
			30	1,475	
			30	150	
				2,825	

	Rent Expense				51
19—					
June 1	100				
3	1,000				
1,100					

	Supplies Expense				52
19—					
June 30	625				

	Salary Expense				53
19—					
June 15	110				
30	110				
220					

	Utilities Expense				54
19—					
June 30	55				
30	30				
85					

	Miscellaneous Expense				55
19—					
June 2	50				
28	60				
110					

Mini-Case 2, Concluded

3. **$1,730, computed in the following manner:**

Cash receipts:

Initial investment	$1,000
Cash sales	2,465
Collections on accounts	150
Total cash receipts during June	$3,615

Cash disbursements:

Rent expense	$1,100	
Supplies purchased for cash	190	
Salary expense.....................................	220	
Payment for supplies on account.....................	180	
Utilities expense	85	
Miscellaneous expense	110	
Total cash disbursements during June..............		1,885
Cash on hand according to records....................		$1,730*

*If the student used T accounts in completing part (2), or this part, this amount ($1,730) should agree with the balance of the cash account.

4. The difference of $1,310 between the cash on hand according to records ($1,730) and the cash on hand according to the count ($420) could be due to many factors, including errors in the record keeping and withdrawals made by Fran.

CHAPTER 3

DISCUSSION QUESTIONS

1. a. Under cash basis accounting, revenues are reported in the period in which cash is received and expenses are reported in the period in which cash is paid.
   b. Under accrual basis accounting, revenues are reported in the period in which they are earned and expenses are reported in the period in which they are incurred in producing revenues.

2. a. 1994
   b. 1993

3. a. 1994
   b. 1993

4. Accrual basis

5. Yes. The cash amount listed on the trial balance is normally the amount of cash on hand and needs no adjustment at the end of the period.

6. No. The amount listed on the trial balance, before adjustments, normally represents the cost of the inventory of supplies at the beginning of the period plus the cost of the supplies purchased during the period. Some of the supplies have been used; therefore, an adjustment is necessary for the supplies used before the amount for the balance sheet is determined.

7. Adjusting entries are necessary at the end of an accounting period to bring the ledger up to date.

8. Adjusting entries bring the ledger up to date as a normal part of the accounting cycle. Correcting entries correct errors in the ledger.

9. Deferred expenses (prepaid expenses), deferred revenues (unearned revenues), accrued expenses (accrued liabilities), accrued revenues (accrued assets), and plant assets (depreciation).

10. Statement (b): Increases the balance of an expense account.

11. Yes, because every adjusting entry affects expenses or revenues.

12. a. The balance is the sum of the beginning balance and the amount of the insurance premiums paid during the period.
    b. The balance is the unexpired premiums at the end of the period.

13. a. The rights acquired represent an asset.
    b. The justification for debiting Rent Expense is that when the ledger is summarized in a trial balance at the end of the month, statements prepared, etc., the rent will have become an expense. Hence, no adjusting entry will be necessary.

14. a. Supplies expense (or expenses) will be understated. Net income will be overstated.
    b. Supplies (or assets) will be overstated. Owner's equity will be overstated.

15. a. Rent income (or revenues) will be understated. Net income will be understated.
    b. Net income will be understated. Owner's equity at the end of the period will be understated.
    c. Unearned rent (or liabilities) will be overstated. Owner's equity will be understated.

16. a. Salary expense (or expenses) will be understated. Net income will be overstated.
    b. Salaries payable (or liabilities) will be understated. Owner's equity will be overstated.

17. a. Salary expense (or expenses) will be overstated. Net income will be understated.
    b. Balance sheet will be correct.

18. a. Fees earned (or revenues) will be understated. Net income will be understated.
    b. Accounts (fees) receivable (or assets) will be understated. Owner's equity will be understated.

19. Plant assets are tangible assets that are permanent or have a long life and are used in the business.

20. Depreciation is the expense related to the decrease in usefulness of plant assets. In accounting, it represents the systematic allocation of a plant asset's cost to expense.

21. Accumulated Depreciation—Equipment

22. a. The portion of the cost of a plant asset deducted from revenue of the period is debited to Depreciation Expense. It is a cost expiration for the period. The reduction in the plant asset account is recorded by a credit to Accumulated Depreciation rather than to the plant asset account. The use of the contra asset account facilitates the presentation of original cost and accumulated depreciation on the balance sheet.

b. Depreciation Expense—debit balance; Accumulated Depreciation—credit balance.
c. It is not customary for the balances of the two accounts to be equal in amount.
d. Depreciation Expense appears in the income statement; Accumulated Depreciation appears in the balance sheet.

23. Book value of the plant asset.

24. a. Depreciation expense (or expenses) will be understated. Net income will be overstated.
b. Accumulated depreciation will be understated and plant assets overstated (or assets overstated). Owner's equity will be overstated.

25. a. Deferred expense (prepaid expense): 4, 7
b. Deferred revenue (unearned revenue): 2, 8
c. Accrued expense (accrued liability): 1, 3, 6
d. Accrued revenue (accrued asset): 5

26. a. Revenue: 1, 7
b. Expense: 3, 8
c. Asset: 4, 5
d. Liability: 2, 6

27. A work sheet is a working paper used to assist in preparing adjusting entries (and financial statements).

28. $1,790,400,000 ($2,921,900,000 − $1,131,500,000)

29. a. $121,863,000
($54,962,000 + $16,949,000 + $37,804,000 + $12,148,000)
b. 62.4% ($121,863,000 ÷ $195,444,000)

ETHICS DISCUSSION CASE Paul Martinez behaved in an ethical manner. Although the accrual basis is most widely used, the cash basis is acceptable for small service enterprises (such as Martinez Real Estate) which have few receivables and payables.

EXERCISES

Ex. 3-1 a. $50,000 ($75,000 − $25,000)

b. No. Depreciation is an allocation of the cost of the equipment to the periods benefiting from its use. It does not necessarily relate to value or loss of value.

Ex. 3-2 Supplies Expense 2,150
      Supplies 2,150

Ex. 3-3 a. Insurance Expense............................. 4,900
      Prepaid Insurance....................... 4,900

b. Insurance Expense............................. 4,900
      Prepaid Insurance....................... 4,900

Ex. 3-4 a. Insurance Expense............................. 5,600
      Prepaid Insurance....................... 5,600

b. Insurance Expense............................. 5,100
      Prepaid Insurance....................... 5,100

Ex. 3-5 Unearned Fees 2,500
      Fees Earned 2,500

Ex. 3-6 a. Salary Expense 6,000
      Salaries Payable 6,000

b. Salary Expense 9,000
      Salaries Payable 9,000

Ex. 3-7 a. Taxes Expense............................. 8,000
      Prepaid Taxes............................ 8,000
      Taxes Expense............................. 12,600
      Taxes Payable 12,600

b. $20,600

Ex. 3-8 a. $1,800 ($750 + $1,050)
b. $11,600 ($11,900 − $300)

Ex. 3-9 a. Accounts Receivable........................... 4,950
      Fees Earned 4,950

b. No. If the cash basis of accounting is used, revenues are recognized only when the cash is received. Therefore, earned but unbilled revenues would not be recognized in the accounts and no adjusting entry would be necessary.

Ex. 3-10 a.   Unearned Fees 6,500
           Fees Earned   6,500

     b.   Accounts Receivable.......................... 3,750
           Fees Earned   3,750

Ex. 3-11 Depreciation Expense............................ 420
      Accumulated Depreciation   420

Ex. 3-12 a.   Depreciation Expense.......................... 2,500
           Accumulated Depreciation   2,500

     b.   (1) Depreciation expense would be understated.
           Net income would be overstated.
        (2) Accumulated depreciation would be under-
           stated and total assets would be overstated.
           Owner's equity would be overstated.

Ex. 3-13 a.   Supplies Expense............................. 1,350
           Supplies...................................   1,350

     b.   Depreciation Expense.......................... 690
           Accumulated Depreciation   690

WHAT'S WRONG WITH THIS?

1. The debit in the Adjustments column for Laundry Supplies [adjustment (a)] should be a credit. The adjusted balance for Laundry Supplies would therefore be $1,840.
2. Laundry Equipment should appear as a debit in both the Trial Balance and Adjusted Trial Balance columns.
3. Accumulated Depreciation should be a credit in both the Trial Balance and Adjusted Trial Balance columns.
4. The adjustment for depreciation [adjustment (c)] should have a debit to Depreciation Expense and a credit to Accumulated Depreciation.
5. If prepared correctly, the totals of the Dr. and Cr. columns would be equal in the Trial Balance, Adjustments, and Adjusted Trial Balance columns.
6. The Wages Payable should be a credit in the Adjustments column.

WHAT'S WRONG?, Concluded

A corrected partial work sheet would be as follows:

LAKESIDE LAUNDROMAT
Work Sheet
For Year Ended July 31, 1994

Account Title	Trial Balance Dr.	Trial Balance Cr.	Adjustments Dr.		Adjustments Cr.		Adjusted Trial Balance Dr.	Adjusted Trial Balance Cr.
Cash	7,790	......	....		....		7,790	......
Laundry Supplies	4,750	......	....		(a)	2,910	1,840	......
Prepaid Insurance	2,825	......	....		(b)	1,500	1,325	......
Laundry Equipment	85,600	......	....		....		85,600	......
Accumulated Depreciation	......	55,700	....		(c)	5,720	......	61,420
Accounts Payable	......	4,950	....		....		......	4,950
Alex Black, Capital	......	30,900	....		....		......	30,900
Alex Black, Drawing	18,000	......	....		....		18,000	......
Laundry Revenue	......	76,900	....		....		......	76,900
Wages Expense	24,500	......	(d)	850	....		25,350	......
Rent Expense	15,575	......	....		....		15,575	......
Utilities Expense	8,500	......	....		....		8,500	......
Miscellaneous Expense	910	......	....		....		910	......
	168,450	168,450						
Laundry Supplies Expense	......	......	(a)	2,910	....		2,910	......
Insurance Expense	......	......	(b)	1,500	....		1,500	......
Depreciation Expense	......	......	(c)	5,720	....		5,720	......
Wages Payable	......	......	....		(d)	850	......	850
				10,980		10,980	175,020	175,020

PROBLEMS

Prob. 3-1A

1. a. Supplies Expense 755
        Supplies 755

    b. Unearned Rent...................................... 900
        Rent Income 900

    c. Wages Expense 3,100
        Wages Payable 3,100

    d. Accounts Receivable 7,500
        Fees Earned....................................... 7,500

    e. Depreciation Expense 550
        Accumulated Depreciation 550

Prob. 3-1A, Concluded

2. Adjusting entries are a planned part of the accounting process to update the accounts. Correcting entries are not planned, but arise only when necessary to correct errors.

Prob. 3-2A

a.	Accounts Receivable	8,650	
	Fees Earned		8,650
b.	Supplies Expense	2,325	
	Supplies		2,325
c.	Rent Expense	24,000	
	Prepaid Rent		24,000
d.	Depreciation Expense	4,750	
	Accumulated Depreciation		4,750
e.	Unearned Fees	3,650	
	Fees Earned		3,650
f.	Wages Expense	750	
	Wages Payable		750

Prob. 3-3A

1.

J.L. RHODES SERVICES
Work Sheet
For Year Ended December 31, 19—

Account Title	Trial Balance Dr.	Trial Balance Cr.	Adjustments Dr.		Adjustments Cr.		Adjusted Trial Balance Dr.	Adjusted Trial Balance Cr.
Cash	3,950	.....		....		....	3,950	......
Accounts Receivable	2,125	.....	(a)	875		....	3,000	......
Supplies	1,990	.....		....	(b)	1,100	890	......
Prepaid Insurance	1,800	.....		....	(c)	1,250	550	......
Equipment	20,000	.....		....		....	20,000	......
Accumulated Depreciation	......	5,200		....	(d)	2,000	......	7,200
Accounts Payable	......	3,700		....		....	......	3,700
Unearned Rent	......	600	(e)	200		....	......	400
J.L. Rhodes, Capital	......	14,555		....		....	......	14,555
J.L. Rhodes, Drawing	18,000	.....		....		....	18,000	......
Service Revenue	......	39,900		....	(a)	875	......	40,775
Wages Expense	7,300	.....	(f)	150		....	7,450	......
Rent Expense	7,200	.....		....		....	7,200	......
Utilities Expense	880	.....		....		....	880	......
Miscellaneous Expense	710	.....		....		....	710	......
	63,955	63,955						
Supplies Expense	......	.....	(b)	1,100		....	1,100	......
Insurance Expense	......	.....	(c)	1,250		....	1,250	......
Depreciation Expense	......	.....	(d)	2,000		....	2,000	......
Rent Income				....	(e)	200	......	200
Wages Payable				....	(f)	150	......	150
				5,575		5,575	66,980	66,980

2.

	Error (a) Over-stated	Error (a) Under-stated	Error (b) Over-stated	Error (b) Under-stated
1. Net income for the year would be...	$1,100	....	$150	....
2. Assets at December 31 would be....	$1,100	....	$–0–	$–0–
3. Liabilities at December 31 would be .	$ –0–	$–0–	....	$150
4. Owner's equity at December 31 would be	$1,100	....	$150	....

Prob. 3-4A

19—

June 30	Supplies Expense	5,315	
	Supplies		5,315
30	Insurance Expense	2,500	
	Prepaid Insurance		2,500
30	Depreciation Expense—Equipment...............	12,790	
	Accumulated Depreciation—Equipment.........		12,790
30	Depreciation Expense—Automobiles	8,650	
	Accumulated Depreciation—Automobiles.......		8,650
30	Utilities Expense................................	420	
	Accounts Payable		420
30	Salary Expense.................................	3,400	
	Salaries Payable..............................		3,400
30	Unearned Service Fees	3,775	
	Service Fees Earned...........................		3,775

Prob. 3-5A

a.	Accounts Receivable	2,550	
	Fees Earned		2,550
b.	Supplies Expense......................................	490	
	Supplies...		490
c.	Depreciation Expense	1,100	
	Accumulated Depreciation...........................		1,100
d.	Unearned Fees	900	
	Fees Earned		900
e.	Wages Expense..	175	
	Wages Payable......................................		175

Prob. 3-6A

1, 2, 3

ELSTER BOWL
Work Sheet
For Year Ended December 31, 19—

Account Title	Trial Balance Dr.	Trial Balance Cr.	Adjustments Dr.		Adjustments Cr.		Adjusted Trial Balance Dr.	Adjusted Trial Balance Cr.
Cash........................	9,700	....	....		....		9,700	......
Prepaid Insurance..............	3,400	....	....	(a)	2,700		700	......
Supplies......................	1,950	....	....	(b)	1,500		450	......
Land.........................	50,000	....	....		....		50,000	......
Building......................	141,500	....	....		....		141,500	......
Accumulated Depr.— Building ..	......	91,700	....	(c)	1,620		......	93,320
Equipment....................	90,100	....	....		....		90,100	......
Accumulated Depr.— Equipment	......	65,300	....	(d)	5,500		......	70,800
Accounts Payable..............	......	7,500	....		....		......	7,500
Unearned Rent.................	......	6,000	(e) 4,000		....		......	2,000
Cathy Elster, Capital	......	70,700	....		....		......	70,700
Cathy Elster, Drawing..........	20,000	....	....		....		20,000	......
Bowling Revenue	......	218,400	....		....		......	218,400
Salaries and Wages Expense ...	80,200	....	(f) 2,000		....		82,200	......
Utilities Expense...............	28,200	....	....		....		28,200	......
Advertising Expense...........	19,000	....	....		....		19,000	......
Repairs Expense	11,500	....	....		....		11,500	......
Miscellaneous Expense.........	4,050	....	....		....		4,050	......
	459,600	459,600						
Insurance Expense..............	....	......	(a) 2,700		....		2,700	......
Supplies Expense	....	......	(b) 1,500		....		1,500	......
Depr. Expense—Building	....	......	(c) 1,620		....		1,620	......
Depr. Expense—Equipment	....	......	(d) 5,500		....		5,500	......
Rent Income	....	......	....	(e)	4,000		......	4,000
Salaries and Wages Payable	....	......	....	(f)	2,000		......	2,000
			17,320		17,320		468,720	468,720

4.

19—

		Dr.	Cr.
Dec. 31	Insurance Expense.................................	2,700	
	Prepaid Insurance.................................		2,700
31	Supplies Expense.................................	1,500	
	Supplies...		1,500
31	Depreciation Expense—Building	1,620	
	Accumulated Depreciation—Building..............		1,620
31	Depreciation Expense—Equipment	5,500	
	Accumulated Depreciation—Equipment		5,500
31	Unearned Rent	4,000	
	Rent Income.....................................		4,000
31	Salaries and Wages Expense	2,000	
	Salaries and Wages Payable		2,000

Prob. 3-7A

1.

a.	Supplies Expense	1,750	
	Supplies		1,750
b.	Accounts Receivable	3,900	
	Fees Earned		3,900
c.	Depreciation Expense	300	
	Accumulated Depreciation		300
d.	Wages Expense	2,500	
	Wages Payable		2,500

2.

	Net Income	Total Assets	Total Liabilities	Total Owner's Equity
Reported amounts	$39,750	$89,700	$30,200	$59,500
Corrections:				
Adjustment (a)	− 1,750	− 1,750	0	− 1,750
Adjustment (b)	+ 3,900	+ 3,900	0	+ 3,900
Adjustment (c)	− 300	− 300	0	− 300
Adjustment (d)	− 2,500	0	+ 2,500	− 2,500
Corrected amounts	$39,100	$91,550	$32,700	$58,850

Prob. 3-1B

1.

a.	Accounts Receivable	8,250	
	Fees Earned		8,250
b.	Supplies Expense	1,565	
	Supplies		1,565
c.	Wages Expense	4,350	
	Wages Payable		4,350
d.	Unearned Rent	1,000	
	Rent Income		1,000
e.	Depreciation Expense	600	
	Accumulated Depreciation		600

2. Adjusting entries are a planned part of the accounting process to update the accounts. Correcting entries are not planned, but arise only when necessary to correct errors.

Prob. 3-2B

a. Supplies Expense 1,950
    Supplies...   1,950

b. Depreciation Expense 4,950
    Accumulated Depreciation   4,950

c. Rent Expense 18,000
    Prepaid Rent.....................................   18,000

d. Wages Expense 525
    Wages Payable...................................   525

e. Unearned Fees.................................... 4,350
    Fees Earned......................................   4,350

f. Accounts Receivable 4,750
    Fees Earned......................................   4,750

Prob. 3-3B

1.

J. L. RHODES SERVICES
Work Sheet
For Year Ended December 31, 19—

Account Title	Trial Balance Dr.	Trial Balance Cr.	Adjustments Dr.	Adjustments Cr.	Adjusted Trial Balance Dr.	Adjusted Trial Balance Cr.
Cash......................................	3,950	.....			3,950	......
Accounts Receivable	2,125	.....	(a) 875	....	3,000	......
Supplies	1,990	.....	....	(b) 1,100	890	......
Prepaid Insurance	1,800	.....	....	(c) 1,250	550	......
Equipment..............................	20,000	.....	....	....	20,000	......
Accumulated Depreciation	......	5,200	....	(d) 2,000	......	7,200
Accounts Payable	......	3,700	....	....	......	3,700
Unearned Rent.........................	......	600	(e) 200	....	......	400
J. L. Rhodes, Capital	......	14,555	....	....	......	14,555
J. L. Rhodes, Drawing	18,000	.....	....	....	18,000	......
Service Revenue	......	39,900	....	(a) 875	......	40,775
Wages Expense	7,300	.....	(f) 150	....	7,450	......
Rent Expense	7,200	.....	....	....	7,200	......
Utilities Expense.......................	880	.....	....	....	880	......
Miscellaneous Expense.................	710	.....	....	....	710	......
	63,955	63,955				
Supplies Expense	......	.....	(b) 1,100	....	1,100	......
Insurance Expense	......	.....	(c) 1,250	....	1,250	......
Depreciation Expense..................	......	.....	(d) 2,000	....	2,000	......
Rent Income	......	.....	....	(e) 200	......	200
Wages Payable.........................	......	.....	....	(f) 150	......	150
			5,575	5,575	66,980	66,980

Prob. 3-3B, Concluded

2.

	Error (a)		Error (b)	
	Over-stated	Under-stated	Over-stated	Under-stated
1. Net income for the year would be . . .	$1,250	. . . .	. . . .	$875
2. Assets at December 31 would be. . . .	$1,250	. . . .	. . . .	$875
3. Liabilities at December 31 would be .	$ –0–	$–0–	$–0–	$–0–
4. Owner's equity at December 31 would be.	$1,250	. . . .	. . . .	$875

Prob. 3-4B

19—

Dec. 31	Supplies Expense.	6,420	
	Supplies.		6,420
31	Insurance Expense.	2,000	
	Prepaid Insurance.		2,000
31	Depreciation Expense—Buildings	4,800	
	Accumulated Depreciation—Buildings.		4,800
31	Depreciation Expense—Trucks.	18,100	
	Accumulated Depreciation—Trucks		18,100
31	Utilities Expense	600	
	Accounts Payable.		600
31	Salary Expense	1,450	
	Salaries Payable		1,450
31	Unearned Service Fees.	6,580	
	Service Fees Earned		6,580

Prob. 3-5B

a.	Supplies Expense	990	
	Supplies.		990
b.	Accounts Receivable	3,025	
	Fees Earned		3,025
c.	Depreciation Expense	950	
	Accumulated Depreciation.		950
d.	Wages Expense.	210	
	Wages Payable.		210
e.	Unearned Fees	800	
	Fees Earned		800

Prob. 3-6B

1, 2, 3

MIDTOWN BOWL
Work Sheet
For Year Ended December 31, 19—

Account Title	Trial Balance Dr.	Trial Balance Cr.	Adjustments Dr.		Adjustments Cr.		Adjusted Trial Balance Dr.	Adjusted Trial Balance Cr.
Cash	10,200	....	....		....		10,200	......
Prepaid Insurance	3,900	....	....		(a)	3,075	825	......
Supplies	2,450	....	....		(b)	2,000	450	......
Land	50,000	....	....		....		50,000	......
Building	141,500	....	....		....		141,500	......
Accumulated Depr.— Building	....	95,700	....		(c)	1,500	......	97,200
Equipment	90,100	....	....		....		90,100	......
Accumulated Depr.— Equipment	....	65,300	....		(d)	5,500	......	70,800
Accounts Payable	....	7,500	....		....			7,500
Unearned Rent	....	4,000	(e)	2,000	....			2,000
John Fox, Capital	....	70,700	....		....			70,700
John Fox, Drawing	20,000	....	....		....		20,000	
Bowling Revenue	....	218,400	....		....		......	218,400
Salaries and Wages Expense	78,700	....	(f)	1,900	....		80,600	......
Utilities Expense	28,200	....	....		....		28,200	......
Advertising Expense	19,000	....	....		....		19,000	......
Repairs Expense	13,500	....	....		....		13,500	......
Miscellaneous Expense	4,050	....	....		....		4,050	......
	461,600	461,600						
Insurance Expense	....	....	(a)	3,075	....		3,075	......
Supplies Expense	....	....	(b)	2,000	....		2,000	......
Depr. Expense—Building	....	....	(c)	1,500	....		1,500	......
Depr. Expense—Equipment	....	....	(d)	5,500	....		5,500	......
Rent Income	....	....	....		(e)	2,000	......	2,000
Salaries and Wages Payable	....	....	....		(f)	1,900	......	1,900
			15,975		15,975		470,500	470,500

Prob. 3-6B, Concluded

4.

19—

Dec. 31	Insurance Expense....................................	3,075	
	Prepaid Insurance.................................		3,075
31	Supplies Expense....................................	2,000	
	Supplies..		2,000
31	Depreciation Expense—Building....................	1,500	
	Accumulated Depreciation—Building.............		1,500
31	Depreciation Expense—Equipment	5,500	
	Accumulated Depreciation—Equipment		5,500
31	Unearned Rent	2,000	
	Rent Income......................................		2,000
31	Salaries and Wages Expense	1,900	
	Salaries and Wages Payable		1,900

Prob. 3-7B

1.

a.	Accounts Receivable	5,900	
	Fees Earned..		5,900
b.	Supplies Expense	3,100	
	Supplies		3,100
c.	Depreciation Expense	1,300	
	Accumulated Depreciation		1,300
d.	Wages Expense	3,250	
	Wages Payable		3,250

2.

	Net Income	Total Assets	Total Liabilities	Total Owner's Equity
Reported amounts	$60,500	$127,250	$46,500	$80,750
Corrections:				
Adjustment (a)	+ 5,900	+ 5,900	0	+ 5,900
Adjustment (b)	− 3,100	− 3,100	0	− 3,100
Adjustment (c)	− 1,300	− 1,300	0	− 1,300
Adjustment (d)	− 3,250	0	+ 3,250	− 3,250
Corrected amounts	$58,750	$128,750	$49,750	$79,000

Mini-Case

1. There are several indications that adjusting entries were not recorded before the financial statements were prepared including:
   a. All expenses on the income statement are identified as "paid" items and not as "expenses."
   b. No expense is reported on the income statement for depreciation and no accumulated depreciation is reported on the balance sheet.
   c. No supplies, accounts payable, or wages payable are reported on the balance sheet.
2. Likely accounts requiring adjustment include:
   a. Truck for depreciation.
   b. Supplies (paid) expense for supplies on hand.
   c. Insurance (paid) expense for unexpired insurance.
   d. Wages accrued.
   e. Utilities accrued.

CHAPTER 4

DISCUSSION QUESTIONS

1. No. The work sheet is a device used by the accountant to facilitate the preparation of statements and the recording of adjusting and closing entries.

2. a. Income statement: 2, 4, 7
   b. Balance sheet: 1, 3, 5, 6, 8, 9, 10

3. a. Asset: 2, 5, 7, 8, 12
   b. Liability: 1, 11
   c. Revenue: 4, 9
   d. Expense: 3, 6, 10

4. Net loss. The expenses exceed the revenues.

5. Net income. The revenues exceed the expenses by $91,500.

6. (a) Current assets are composed of cash and other assets that may reasonably be expected to be realized in cash, or sold or consumed in the near future through the normal operations of the business. (b) Plant assets are composed of tangible assets used in the business that are of a permanent or relatively fixed nature.

7. a. Current asset: 1, 2, 4
   b. Plant asset: 3, 5, 6

8. Current liabilities are liabilities that will be due within a short time (usually one year or less) and that are to be paid out of current assets. Liabilities that will not be due for a comparatively long time (usually more than one year) are called long-term liabilities.

9. Revenue, expense, and drawing accounts are generally referred to as temporary accounts.

10. Adjusting and closing entries apply to the last day of the fiscal period and hence are recorded as of that date. The entries are actually journalized and posted some time later, since it is generally not feasible to record them on the last day of the period.

11. Closing entries are necessary at the end of an accounting period to (1) transfer the balances in temporary accounts to permanent accounts and (2) prepare the temporary accounts for use in accumulating data for the following accounting period.

12. Adjusting entries bring the accounts up to date while closing entries reduce the revenue, expense, and drawing accounts to zero balances for use in accumulating data for the following accounting period.

13. 1. The first entry closes all income statement accounts with credit balances by transferring the total to the credit side of Income Summary.
    2. The second entry closes all income statement accounts with debit balances by transferring the total to the debit side of Income Summary.
    3. The third entry closes Income Summary by transferring its balance, the net income or net loss for the year, to the owner's capital account.
    4. The fourth entry closes Drawing by transferring its balance to the owner's capital account.

14. a. Expense accounts
    b. Revenue accounts

15. Owner's capital account

16. Owner's capital account

17. c. Fees Earned
    d. Salaries Expense
    e. Depreciation Expense—Buildings
    h. Supplies Expense

18. a. Accounts Receivable
    b. Accumulated Depreciation
    c. Cash
    d. Supplies
    f. Wages Payable
    g. Equipment
    i. S. D. Sands, Capital

19. The purpose of the post-closing trial balance is to make sure that the ledger is in balance at the beginning of the next period.

20. Fiscal year

21. The natural business year is the fiscal year that ends when business activities have reached the lowest point in the annual operating cycle.

22. January is more likely to have a lower level of business activity than is December for a department store. Therefore the additional work to adjust and close the accounts and prepare the financial statements can more easily be performed at the end of January than at the end of December.

23. d, g, f, e, a, c, b

24. All the companies listed are general merchandisers whose busiest time of the year is during the Christmas buying season, which extends through most

of December. Traditionally, the lowest point of business activity for general merchandisers will be near the end of January and the beginning of February. Thus, these companies have chosen their natural business year for their fiscal years.

ETHICS DISCUSSION CASE It is generally accepted practice to date the adjusting and closing entries as of the last day of the accounting period, even though they were actually prepared and posted at a later date. It is often not possible to gather the necessary adjusting entry data until after the end of the accounting period. Hence, as a practical matter, the adjusting and closing entries are prepared at a later date and entered as if they had been prepared on the last day of the accounting period. In this way, the underlying accounting records will agree with the resulting financial statements. Thus, the accountant behaved in an ethical manner in entering the adjusting and closing entries.

EXERCISES

Ex. 4-1

A. D. FINNEY COMPANY
Income Statement
For Year Ended June 30, 19—

Fees Earned....................................		$92,500
Operating expenses:		
Salaries expense	$37,100	
Rent expense................................	18,000	
Utilities expense	8,500	
Depreciation expense.......................	2,100	
Supplies expense...........................	2,050	
Insurance expense..........................	1,500	
Miscellaneous expense......................	1,750	
Total operating expenses		71,000
Net income		$21,500

Ex. 4-2

J. J. HENDERSON CO.
Income Statement
For Year Ended October 31, 19—

Service revenue		$71,200
Operating expenses:		
Wages expense..............................	$26,750	
Rent expense................................	24,000	
Utilities expense	8,500	
Depreciation expense.......................	4,000	
Insurance expense..........................	3,900	
Supplies expense...........................	3,100	
Miscellaneous expense......................	2,250	
Total operating expenses		72,500
Net loss		$ 1,300

Ex. 4-3

SAMPRAS SERVICES
Statement of Owner's Equity
For Year Ended December 31, 19—

P.C. Sampras, capital, January 1, 19—		$62,500
Net income for year	$40,250	
Less withdrawals	30,000	
Increase in owner's equity		10,250
P.C. Sampras, capital, December 31, 19—		$72,750

Ex. 4-4

JOHN CHANG COMPANY
Statement of Owner's Equity
For Year Ended March 31, 19—

John Chang, capital, April 1, 19—		$60,500
Net loss for year	$10,500	
Withdrawals	24,000	
Decrease in owner's equity		34,500
John Chang, capital, March 31, 19—		$26,000

Ex. 4-5 Since current liabilities are usually due within one year, $60,000 would be reported as a current liability on the balance sheet. The remainder of $190,000 ($250,000 − $60,000) would be reported as a long-term liability on the balance sheet.

Ex. 4-6

LEEDS COMPANY
Balance Sheet
June 30, 19—

Assets

Current assets:		
Cash..	$ 6,150	
Accounts receivable	9,920	
Supplies	4,750	
Prepaid insurance	3,100	
Prepaid rent.................................	2,400	
Total current assets.........................		$26,320
Plant assets:		
Equipment	$60,600	
Less accumulated depreciation	21,100	39,500
Total assets.................................		$65,820

Liabilities

Current liabilities:		
Accounts payable............................	$12,750	
Salaries payable	3,750	
Unearned fees...............................	1,000	
Total liabilities		$17,500

Owner's Equity

Robert Leeds, capital.........................		48,320
Total liabilities and owner's equity		$65,820

Ex. 4-7 The income summary account is used to close the revenue and expense accounts. The $357,500 represents expense account balances and the $378,000 represents revenue account balances that have been closed.

Ex. 4-8 a. Income Summary............................ 72,000
         Wayne Ferrara, Capital   72,000

      Wayne Ferrara, Capital 36,000
         Wayne Ferrara, Drawing.....................   36,000

    b. $135,500 ($99,500 + $72,000 − $36,000)

Ex. 4-9 Feb. 28 Fees Earned........................... 55,000
         Income Summary.......................   55,000

      28 Income Summary....................... 38,000
         Wages Expense...........................   21,500
         Rent Expense............................   9,000
         Supplies Expense   5,500
         Miscellaneous Expense.................   2,000

      28 Income Summary....................... 17,000
         L. M. Dunn, Capital....................   17,000

      28 L. M. Dunn, Capital 20,000
         L. M. Dunn, Drawing   20,000

Ex. 4-10

PARRISH MACHINE REPAIRS
Post-Closing Trial Balance
July 31, 19—

Cash...	8,500	
Accounts Receivable	11,250	
Supplies	900	
Equipment	31,500	
Accumulated Depreciation—Equipment...........		15,130
Accounts Payable		6,250
Salaries Payable................................		3,500
Unearned Rent		4,000
Jane Parrish, Capital............................		23,270
	52,150	52,150

Ex. 4-11 a. (1) Sales Salaries Expense 3,600
           Salaries Payable.......................   3,600

      (2) Accounts Receivable 2,750
           Fees Earned   2,750

    b. (1) Salaries Payable 3,600
           Sales Salaries Expense   3,600

      (2) Fees Earned 2,750
           Accounts Receivable   2,750

Ex. 4-12 a. (1) Payment (last payday in year)
　　　　　　(2) Adjusting (accrual of wages at end of year)
　　　　　　(3) Closing
　　　　　　(4) Reversing
　　　　　　(5) Payment (first payday in following year)

　　　　b. (1) Wages Expense . . . . 　7,500
　　　　　　　　　Cash . . . . 　　　　　7,500

　　　　　　(2) Wages Expense . . . . 　3,000
　　　　　　　　　Wages Payable . . . . 　　　　　3,000

　　　　　　(3) Income Summary 248,500
　　　　　　　　　Wages Expense . . . . 　　　　248,500

　　　　　　(4) Wages Payable . . . . 　3,000
　　　　　　　　　Wages Expense . . . . 　　　　　3,000

　　　　　　(5) Wages Expense . . . . 　7,500
　　　　　　　　　Cash . . . . 　　　　　7,500

WHAT'S WRONG WITH THIS?

1. Date of statement should be "July 31, 1994" and not "For Year Ended July 31, 1994."
2. Accounts payable should be current liability.
3. Land should be plant asset.
4. "Accumulated depreciation" should be deducted from related plant asset.
5. An adding error was made in determining the amount of total plant assets.
6. Accounts receivable should be current asset.
7. Net loss would be reported on income statement.
8. Wages payable should be current liability.
9. Total assets does not equal total liabilities and owner's equity.

WHAT'S WRONG?, Concluded

A corrected balance sheet would be as follows:

EASTLAND SERVICES
Balance Sheet
July 31, 1994

Assets

Current assets:

Cash	$ 6,170	
Accounts receivable	5,390	
Supplies	590	
Prepaid insurance	845	
Total current assets		$12,995

Plant assets:

Land		$20,000	
Building	$55,500		
Less accumulated depreciation	23,525	31,975	
Equipment	$28,250		
Less accumulated depreciation	17,340	10,910	
Total plant assets			62,885
Total assets			$75,880

Liabilities

Current liabilities:

Accounts payable	$ 5,390	
Wages payable	975	
Total liabilities		$ 6,365

Owner's Equity

Paul Beck, capital	69,515
Total liabilities and owner's equity	$75,880

PROBLEMS

Prob. 4-1A

1.

SUDS LAUNDROMAT
Work Sheet
For Year Ended July 31, 1994

Account Title	Trial Balance Dr.	Trial Balance Cr.	Adjustments Dr.	Adjustments Cr.	Adjusted Trial Balance Dr.	Adjusted Trial Balance Cr.	Income Statement Dr.	Income Statement Cr.	Balance Sheet Dr.	Balance Sheet Cr.
Cash	6,290				6,290				6,290	
Laundry Supplies	3,850			(a) 2,910	940				940	
Prepaid Insurance	2,400			(b) 1,500	900				900	
Laundry Equipment	81,600				81,600				81,600	
Accumulated Depreciation		52,700		(c) 5,220		57,920				57,920
Accounts Payable		3,950				3,950				3,950
J.R. Barr, Capital		33,900				33,900				33,900
J.R. Barr, Drawing	16,600				16,600				16,600	
Laundry Revenue		66,900				66,900		66,900		
Wages Expense	22,900		(d) 850		23,750		23,750			
Rent Expense	14,400				14,400		14,400			
Utilities Expense	8,500				8,500		8,500			
Miscellaneous Expense	910				910		910			
	157,450	157,450								
Laundry Supplies Expense			(a) 2,910		2,910		2,910			
Insurance Expense			(b) 1,500		1,500		1,500			
Depreciation Expense			(c) 5,220		5,220		5,220			
Wages Payable				(d) 850		850				850
			10,480	10,480	163,520	163,520	57,190	66,900	106,330	96,620
Net Income							9,710			9,710
							66,900	66,900	106,330	106,330

Prob. 4-1A, Continued

2.

SUDS LAUNDROMAT
Income Statement
For Year Ended July 31, 1994

Laundry revenue		$66,900
Operating expenses:		
Wages expense	$23,750	
Rent expense	14,400	
Utilities expense	8,500	
Depreciation expense	5,220	
Laundry supplies expense	2,910	
Insurance expense	1,500	
Miscellaneous expense	910	
Total operating expenses		57,190
Net income		$ 9,710

SUDS LAUNDROMAT
Statement of Owner's Equity
For Year Ended July 31, 1994

J.R. Barr, capital, August 1, 1993		$33,900
Net income for the year	$ 9,710	
Less withdrawals	16,600	
Decrease in owner's equity		6,890
J.R. Barr, capital, July 31, 1994		$27,010

Prob. 4-1A, Continued

SUDS LAUNDROMAT
Balance Sheet
July 31, 1994

Assets

Current assets:

Cash	$ 6,290	
Laundry supplies	940	
Prepaid insurance.....................................	900	
Total current assets.................................		$ 8,130

Plant assets:

Laundry equipment.....................................	$81,600	
Less accumulated depreciation	57,920	23,680
Total assets		$31,810

Liabilities

Current liabilities:

Accounts payable......................................	$ 3,950	
Wages payable	850	
Total liabilities......................................		$ 4,800

Owner's Equity

J. R. Barr, capital	27,010
Total liabilities and owner's equity......................	$31,810

3.   **Adjusting Entries**

1994

July 31	Laundry Supplies Expense	2,910	
	Laundry Supplies		2,910
31	Insurance Expense.................................	1,500	
	Prepaid Insurance................................		1,500
31	Depreciation Expense..............................	5,220	
	Accumulated Depreciation........................		5,220
31	Wages Expense....................................	850	
	Wages Payable...................................		850

Prob. 4-1A, Concluded

4.   <u>Closing Entries</u>

1994

July 31	Laundry Revenue	66,900	
	Income Summary		66,900
31	Income Summary	57,190	
	Wages Expense		23,750
	Rent Expense....................................		14,400
	Utilities Expense.................................		8,500
	Miscellaneous Expense		910
	Laundry Supplies Expense.......................		2,910
	Insurance Expense		1,500
	Depreciation Expense		5,220
31	Income Summary	9,710	
	J.R. Barr, Capital................................		9,710
31	J.R. Barr, Capital	16,600	
	J.R. Barr, Drawing		16,600

Prob. 4-2A

1.
<u>Adjusting Entries</u>

1994

April 30	Accounts Receivable	4,000	
	Service Fees Earned		4,000
30	Supplies Expense	5,310	
	Supplies		5,310
30	Insurance Expense	925	
	Prepaid Insurance		925
30	Depreciation Expense—Equipment	2,790	
	Accumulated Depreciation—Equipment		2,790
30	Utilities Expense	220	
	Accounts Payable		220
30	Salary Expense	3,480	
	Salaries Payable		3,480
30	Taxes Expense	1,200	
	Taxes Payable		1,200
30	Unearned Rent	250	
	Rent Income		250

2.
<u>Closing Entries</u>

April 30	Service Fees Earned	185,200	
	Rent Income	250	
	Income Summary		185,450
30	Income Summary	147,170	
	Salary Expense		115,780
	Rent Expense		15,600
	Supplies Expense		5,310
	Depreciation Expense—Equipment		2,790
	Utilities Expense		2,940
	Taxes Expense		2,115
	Insurance Expense		925
	Miscellaneous Expense		1,710
30	Income Summary	38,280	
	J.R. Riley, Capital		38,280
30	J.R. Riley, Capital	18,300	
	J.R. Riley, Drawing		18,300

Prob. 4-2A, Concluded

3.   **RILEY COMPANY**
Statement of Owner's Equity
For Year Ended April 30, 1994

J. R. Riley, capital, May 1, 1993		$33,975
Net income for the year...............................	$38,280	
Less withdrawals.......................................	18,300	
Increase in owner's equity		19,980
J. R. Riley, capital, April 30, 1994........................		$53,955

4. The balance of J. R. Riley capital on April 30, 1994, would have been $2,745 debit ($33,975 + $38,280 − $75,000). This negative balance would be reported in the owner's equity section of the balance sheet.

Prob. 4-3A

1.

SALAZAR COMPANY
Work Sheet
For Month Ended January 31, 1994

Account Title	Trial Balance Dr.	Trial Balance Cr.	Adjustments Dr.	Adjustments Cr.	Adjusted Trial Balance Dr.	Adjusted Trial Balance Cr.	Income Statement Dr.	Income Statement Cr.	Balance Sheet Dr.	Balance Sheet Cr.
Cash	4,507.01				4,507.01				4,507.01	
Accounts Receivable	550.00		(a) 700.00		1,250.00				1,250.00	
Supplies	1,648.56			(b) 1,198.56	450.00				450.00	
Prepaid Insurance	790.70			(c) 80.00	710.70				710.70	
Land	20,000.00				20,000.00				20,000.00	
Building	55,500.00				55,500.00				55,500.00	
Accum. Depr.—Building		23,400.00		(d) 110.00		23,510.00				23,510.00
Equipment	28,000.00				28,000.00				28,000.00	
Accum. Depr.—Equipment		17,200.00		(e) 115.00		17,315.00				17,315.00
Accounts Payable		5,141.50				5,141.50				5,141.50
Unearned Rent		200.00	(f) 100.00			100.00				100.00
C. E. Salazar, Capital		61,815.10				61,815.10				61,815.10
C. E. Salazar, Drawing	2,000.00				2,000.00				2,000.00	
Service Revenue		11,985.67		(a) 700.00		12,685.67		12,685.67		
Wages Expense	4,799.80		(g) 975.00		5,774.80		5,774.80			
Rent Expense	910.00				910.00		910.00			
Utilities Expense	728.50				728.50		728.50			
Misc. Expense	307.70				307.70		307.70			
	119,742.27	119,742.27								
Supplies Expense			(b) 1,198.56		1,198.56		1,198.56			
Insurance Expense			(c) 80.00		80.00		80.00			
Depr. Expense—Building			(d) 110.00		110.00		110.00			
Depr. Expense—Equipment			(e) 115.00		115.00		115.00			
Rent Income				(f) 100.00		100.00		100.00		
Wages Payable				(g) 975.00		975.00				975.00
			3,278.56	3,278.56	121,642.27	121,642.27	9,224.56	12,785.67	112,417.71	108,856.60
Net Income							3,561.11			3,561.11
							12,785.67	12,785.67	112,417.71	112,417.71

Prob. 4-3A, Continued

2.

SALAZAR COMPANY
Income Statement
For Month Ended January 31, 1994

Revenues:		
Service revenue	$12,685.67	
Rent income.....................................	100.00	
Total revenues..................................		$12,785.67
Operating expenses:		
Wages expense.................................	$ 5,774.80	
Supplies expense	1,198.56	
Rent expense...................................	910.00	
Utilities expense................................	728.50	
Depreciation expense—equipment...............	115.00	
Depreciation expense—building	110.00	
Insurance expense	80.00	
Miscellaneous expense..........................	307.70	
Total operating expenses......................		9,224.56
Net income		$ 3,561.11

SALAZAR COMPANY
Statement of Owner's Equity
For Month Ended January 31, 1994

C. E. Salazar, capital, January 1, 1994		$56,815.10
Additional investment during the month...........		5,000.00
Total..		$61,815.10
Net income for the month	$ 3,561.11	
Less withdrawals..................................	2,000.00	
Increase in owner's equity		1,561.11
C. E. Salazar, capital, January 31, 1994		$63,376.21

Prob. 4-3A, Continued

SALAZAR COMPANY
Balance Sheet
January 31, 1994

Assets

Current assets:

Cash		$ 4,507.01
Accounts Receivable		1,250.00
Supplies		450.00
Prepaid insurance		710.70
Total current assets		$ 6,917.71

Plant assets:

Land			$20,000.00
Building	$55,500.00		
Less accumulated depreciation	23,510.00	31,990.00	
Equipment	$28,000.00		
Less accumulated depreciation	17,315.00	10,685.00	
Total plant assets			62,675.00
Total assets			$69,592.71

Liabilities

Current liabilities:

Accounts payable		$ 5,141.50
Wages payable		975.00
Unearned rent		100.00
Total liabilities		$ 6,216.50

Owner's Equity

C. E. Salazar, capital	63,376.21
Total liabilities and owner's equity	$69,592.71

Prob. 4-3A, Continued

3.

Adjusting Entries	Post. Ref.	Debit	Credit
19—			
Jan. 31 Accounts Receivable	12	700.00	
Service Revenue	41		700.00
31 Supplies Expense	52	1,198.56	
Supplies.............................	13		1,198.56
31 Insurance Expense	57	80.00	
Prepaid Insurance	14		80.00
31 Depreciation Expense—Building	54	110.00	
Accumulated Depreciation—Building	17		110.00
31 Depreciation Expense—Equipment....	56	115.00	
Accumulated Depreciation—			
Equipment..........................	19		115.00
31 Unearned Rent......................	23	100.00	
Rent Income	42		100.00
31 Wages Expense	51	975.00	
Wages Payable.....................	22		975.00

4.

Closing Entries	Post. Ref.	Debit	Credit
1994			
Jan. 31 Service Revenue	41	12,685.67	
Rent Income	42	100.00	
Income Summary	33		12,785.67
31 Income Summary	33	9,224.56	
Wages Expense	51		5,774.80
Rent Expense	53		910.00
Utilities Expense...................	55		728.50
Miscellaneous Expense	59		307.70
Supplies Expense	52		1,198.56
Insurance Expense	57		80.00
Depreciation Expense—Building	54		110.00
Depreciation Expense—Equipment..	56		115.00
31 Income Summary	33	3,561.11	
C. E. Salazar, Capital................	31		3,561.11
31 C. E. Salazar, Capital.................	31	2,000.00	
C. E. Salazar, Drawing	32		2,000.00

Prob. 4-3A, Continued

3. and 4.

Cash   11

Date	Item	Post. Ref.	Dr.	Cr.	Balance Dr.	Balance Cr.
1994						
Jan. 1	Balance	✓	....	....	1,259.50	......
3	....	23	....	910.00	349.50	......
4	....	23	5,000.00	....	5,349.50	......
5	....	23	....	86.40	5,263.10	......
7	....	23	800.00	....	6,063.10	......
8	....	23	400.00	....	6,463.10	......
8	....	23	....	2,584.10	3,879.00	......
8	....	23	1,695.30	....	5,574.30	......
10	....	24	....	510.20	5,064.10	......
12	....	24	....	2,319.60	2,744.50	......
15	....	24	2,718.32	....	5,462.82	......
16	....	24	....	1,000.00	4,462.82	......
19	....	24	....	2,135.50	2,327.32	......
22	....	24	....	370.20	1,957.12	......
22	....	24	3,992.21	....	5,949.33	......
24	....	25	....	527.76	5,421.57	......
26	....	25	....	2,480.20	2,941.37	......
30	....	25	....	156.50	2,784.87	......
30	....	25	....	26.48	2,758.39	......
31	....	25	....	1,000.00	1,758.39	......
31	....	25	3,029.84	....	4,788.23	......
31	....	25	....	281.22	4,507.01	......

Accounts Receivable   12

Date	Item	Post. Ref.	Dr.	Cr.	Balance Dr.	Balance Cr.
1994						
Jan. 1	Balance	✓	1,200.00	....	1,200.00	......
7	....	23	....	800.00	400.00	......
8	....	23	....	400.00	—	—
22	....	24	550.00	....	550.00	......
31	Adjusting	26	700.00	....	1,250.00	......

Prob. 4-3A, Continued

Supplies 13

Date	Item	Post. Ref.	Dr.	Cr.	Balance Dr.	Cr.
1994						
Jan. 1	Balance	√	....	....	610.60	....
10	....	24	510.20	....	1,120.80	....
27	....	25	527.76	....	1,648.56	....
31	Adjusting..........	26	....	1,198.56	450.00	....

Prepaid Insurance 14

Date	Item	Post. Ref.	Dr.	Cr.	Balance Dr.	Cr.
1994						
Jan. 1	Balance	√	....	....	420.50	....
22	....	24	370.20	....	790.70	....
31	Adjusting..........	26	....	80.00	710.70	....

Land 15

Date	Item	Post. Ref.	Dr.	Cr.	Balance Dr.	Cr.
1994						
Jan. 1	Balance	√	....	....	20,000.00	....

Building 16

Date	Item	Post. Ref.	Dr.	Cr.	Balance Dr.	Cr.
1994						
Jan. 1	Balance	√	....	....	55,500.00	....

Accumulated Depreciation—Building 17

Date	Item	Post. Ref.	Dr.	Cr.	Balance Dr.	Cr.
1994						
Jan. 1	Balance	√	....	....	....	23,400.00
31	Adjusting..........	26	....	110.00	....	23,510.00

Equipment 18

Date	Item	Post. Ref.	Dr.	Cr.	Balance Dr.	Cr.
1994						
Jan. 1	Balance	√	....	....	27,250.00	....
3	....	23	750.00	....	28,000.00	....

Accumulated Depreciation—Equipment 19

Date	Item	Post. Ref.	Dr.	Cr.	Balance Dr.	Cr.
1994						
Jan. 1	Balance	√	....	....	....	17,200.00
31	Adjusting..........	26	....	115.00	....	17,315.00

Prob. 4-3A, Continued

Accounts Payable 21

Date	Item	Post. Ref.	Dr.	Cr.	Balance Dr.	Cr.
1994						
Jan. 1	Balance	√	. . . .	. . . .	. . . .	8,625.50
3	. . . .	23	. . . .	750.00	. . . .	9,375.50
8	. . . .	23	2,584.10	. . . .	. . . .	6,791.40
19	. . . .	24	2,135.50	. . . .	. . . .	4,655.90
31	. . . .	25	. . . .	485.60	. . . .	5,141.50

Wages Payable 22

Date	Item	Post. Ref.	Dr.	Cr.	Balance Dr.	Cr.
1994						
Jan. 31	Adjusting.	26	. . . .	975.00	. . . .	975.00

Unearned Rent 23

Date	Item	Post. Ref.	Dr.	Cr.	Balance Dr.	Cr.
1994						
Jan. 1	Balance	√	. . . .	200.00	. . . .	200.00
31	Adjusting.	26	100.00	. . . .	. . . .	100.00

C. E. Salazar, Capital 31

Date	Item	Post. Ref.	Dr.	Cr.	Balance Dr.	Cr.
1994						
Jan. 1	Balance	√	. . . .	. . . .	. . . .	56,815.10
4	. . . .	23	. . . .	5,000.00	. . . .	61,815.10
31	Closing.	27	. . . .	3,561.11	. . . .	65,376.21
31	Closing.	27	2,000.00	. . . .	. . . .	63,376.21

C. E. Salazar, Drawing 32

Date	Item	Post. Ref.	Dr.	Cr.	Balance Dr.	Cr.
1994						
Jan. 16	. . . .	24	1,000.00	. . . .	1,000.00	. . . .
31	. . . .	25	1,000.00	. . . .	2,000.00	. . . .
31	Closing.	27	. . . .	2,000.00		

Income Summary 33

Date	Item	Post. Ref.	Dr.	Cr.	Balance Dr.	Cr.
1994						
Jan. 31	Closing.	27	. . . .	12,785.67	. . . .	12,785.67
31	Closing.	27	9,224.56	. . . .	3,561.11	. . . .
31	Closing.	27	3,561.11	. . . .		

Prob. 4-3A, Continued

Service Revenue   41

Date	Item	Post. Ref.	Dr.	Cr.	Balance Dr.	Balance Cr.
1994						
Jan. 8	....	23	....	1,695.30	....	1,695.30
15	....	24	....	2,718.32	....	4,413.62
22	....	24	....	3,992.21	....	8,405.83
22	....	24	....	550.00	....	8,955.83
31	....	25	....	3,029.84	....	11,985.67
31	Adjusting..........	26	....	700.00	....	12,685.67
31	Closing...........	27	12,685.67	....		

Rent Income   42

Date	Item	Post. Ref.	Dr.	Cr.	Balance Dr.	Balance Cr.
1994						
Jan. 31	Adjusting..........	26	....	100.00	....	100.00
31	Closing...........	27	100.00	....		

Wages Expense   51

Date	Item	Post. Ref.	Dr.	Cr.	Balance Dr.	Balance Cr.
1994						
Jan. 12	....	24	2,319.60	....	2,319.60	....
26	....	25	2,480.20	....	4,799.80	....
31	Adjusting..........	26	975.00	....	5,774.80	....
31	Closing...........	27	....	5,774.80		

Supplies Expense   52

Date	Item	Post. Ref.	Dr.	Cr.	Balance Dr.	Balance Cr.
1994						
Jan. 31	Adjusting..........	26	1,198.56	....	1,198.56	....
31	Closing...........	27	....	1,198.56		

Rent Expense   53

Date	Item	Post. Ref.	Dr.	Cr.	Balance Dr.	Balance Cr.
1994						
Jan. 3	....	23	910.00	....	910.00	....
31	Closing...........	27	....	910.00		

Depreciation Expense—Building   54

Date	Item	Post. Ref.	Dr.	Cr.	Balance Dr.	Balance Cr.
1994						
Jan. 31	Adjusting..........	26	110.00	....	110.00	....
31	Closing...........	27	....	110.00		

Prob. 4-3A, Concluded

Utilities Expense   55

Date	Item	Post. Ref.	Dr.	Cr.	Balance Dr.	Cr.
1994						
Jan. 5	....	24	86.40	....	86.40	......
30	....	25	156.50	....	242.90	......
31	....	25	485.60	....	728.50	......
31	Closing...........	26	....	728.50		

Depreciation Expense—Equipment   56

Date	Item	Post. Ref.	Dr.	Cr.	Balance Dr.	Cr.
1994						
Jan. 31	Adjusting.........	26	115.00	....	115.00	......
31	Closing...........	26	....	115.00		

Insurance Expense   57

Date	Item	Post. Ref.	Dr.	Cr.	Balance Dr.	Cr.
1994						
Jan. 31	Adjusting.........	26	80.00	....	80.00	......
31	Closing...........	26	....	80.00		

Miscellaneous Expense   59

Date	Item	Post. Ref.	Dr.	Cr.	Balance Dr.	Cr.
1994						
Jan. 30	....	25	26.48	....	26.48	......
31	....	25	281.22	....	307.70	......
31	Closing...........	26	....	307.70		

5.

SALAZAR COMPANY
Post-Closing Trial Balance
January 31, 1994

Cash....................................	4,507.01	
Accounts Receivable.............................	1,250.00	
Supplies	450.00	
Prepaid Insurance...............................	710.70	
Land..	20,000.00	
Building.......................................	55,500.00	
Accumulated Depreciation—Building		23,510.00
Equipment	28,000.00	
Accumulated Depreciation—Equipment............		17,315.00
Accounts Payable...............................		5,141.50
Wages Payable		975.00
Unearned Rent		100.00
C. E. Salazar, Capital		63,376.21
	110,417.71	110,417.71

Prob. 4-4A

1.

BEACON COMPANY
Work Sheet
For Year Ended June 30, 1994

Account Title	Trial Balance Dr.	Cr.	Adjustments Dr.	Cr.	Adjusted Trial Balance Dr.	Cr.	Income Statement Dr.	Cr.	Balance Sheet Dr.	Cr.
Cash	11,500				11,500				11,500	
Accounts Receivable	12,500		(a) 1,500		14,000				14,000	
Prepaid Insurance	2,400			(b) 1,050	1,350				1,350	
Supplies	1,950			(c) 1,500	450				450	
Land	40,000				40,000				40,000	
Building	100,500				100,500				100,500	
Accumulated Depr.—Building		81,700		(d) 1,620		83,320				83,320
Equipment	72,400				72,400				72,400	
Accumulated Depr.—Equipment		63,800		(e) 5,160		68,960				68,960
Accounts Payable		6,100				6,100				6,100
Unearned Rent		1,500	(g) 1,000			500				500
Joan Marone, Capital		60,500				60,500				60,500
Joan Marone, Drawing	24,000				24,000				24,000	
Fees Revenue		161,200		(a) 1,500		162,700		162,700		
Salaries and Wages Expense	60,200		(f) 1,950		62,150		62,150			
Advertising Expense	19,000				19,000		19,000			
Utilities Expense	18,200				18,200		18,200			
Repairs Expense	8,100				8,100		8,100			
Miscellaneous Expense	4,050				4,050		4,050			
	374,800	374,800								
Insurance Expense			(b) 1,050		1,050		1,050			
Supplies Expense			(c) 1,500		1,500		1,500			
Depr. Expense—Building			(d) 1,620		1,620		1,620			
Depr. Expense—Equipment			(e) 5,160		5,160		5,160			
Salaries and Wages Payable				(f) 1,950		1,950				1,950
Rent Income				(g) 1,000		1,000		1,000		
			13,780	13,780	385,030	385,030	120,830	163,700	264,200	221,330
Net Income							42,870			42,870
							163,700	163,700	264,200	264,200

Prob. 4-4A, Continued

2.

BEACON COMPANY
Income Statement
For Year Ended June 30, 1994

Revenues:		
Fees revenue	$162,700	
Rent income.......................................	1,000	
Total revenues..................................		$163,700
Operating expenses:		
Salaries and wages expense.......................	$ 62,150	
Advertising expense	19,000	
Utilities expense...................................	18,200	
Repairs expense	8,100	
Depreciation expense—equipment..................	5,160	
Depreciation expense—building	1,620	
Supplies expense	1,500	
Insurance expense	1,050	
Miscellaneous expense............................	4,050	
Total operating expenses.........................		120,830
Net income		$ 42,870

3.

BEACON COMPANY
Statement of Owner's Equity
For Year Ended June 30, 1994

Joan Marone, capital, July 1, 1993.....................		$60,500
Net income for year	$42,870	
Less withdrawals......................................	24,000	
Increase in owner's equity		18,870
Joan Marone, capital, June 30, 1994		$79,370

Prob. 4-4A, Concluded

4.

BEACON COMPANY
Balance Sheet
June 30, 1994

Assets

Current assets:

Cash	$11,500	
Accounts receivable	14,000	
Prepaid insurance........................	1,350	
Supplies	450	
Total current assets		$27,300

Plant assets:

Land...............................		$40,000	
Building............................	$100,500		
Less accumulated depreciation	83,320	17,180	
Equipment	$ 72,400		
Less accumulated depreciation	68,960	3,440	
Total plant assets			60,620
Total assets			$87,920

Liabilities

Current liabilities:

Accounts payable........................	$ 6,100	
Salaries and wages payable	1,950	
Unearned rent	500	
Total liabilities..........................		$ 8,550

Owner's Equity

Joan Marone, capital	79,370
Total liabilities and owner's equity......................	$87,920

5. $42,870 \div \$163,700 = 26.2\%$

Prob. 4-5A

JORDAN MACHINE REPAIRS
Work Sheet
For Year Ended July 31, 1994

2.

Account Title	Trial Balance Dr.	Trial Balance Cr.	Adjustments Dr.	Adjustments Cr.	Adjusted Trial Balance Dr.	Adjusted Trial Balance Cr.	Income Statement Dr.	Income Statement Cr.	Balance Sheet Dr.	Balance Sheet Cr.
Cash	6,491				6,491				6,491	
Supplies	4,295			(a) 3,993	302				302	
Prepaid Insurance	1,735			(b) 990	745				745	
Equipment	30,650				30,650				30,650	
Accum. Depr.—Equipment		9,750		(c) 3,380		13,130				13,130
Trucks	23,300				23,300				23,300	
Accum. Depr.—Trucks		6,400		(d) 4,400		10,800				10,800
Accounts Payable		2,015				2,015				2,015
J. J. Jordan, Capital		30,426				30,426				30,426
J. J. Jordan, Drawing	18,000				18,000				18,000	
Service Revenue		89,950				89,950		89,950		
Wages Expense	33,925		(e) 693		34,618		34,618			
Rent Expense	9,600				9,600		9,600			
Truck Expense	8,350				8,350		8,350			
Miscellaneous Expense	2,195				2,195		2,195			
	138,541	138,541								
Supplies Expense			(a) 3,993		3,993		3,993			
Insurance Expense			(b) 990		990		990			
Depr. Expense—Equipment			(c) 3,380		3,380		3,380			
Depr. Expense—Trucks			(d) 4,400		4,400		4,400			
Wages Payable				(e) 693		693				693
			13,456	13,456	147,014	147,014	67,526	89,950	79,488	57,064
Net Income							22,424			22,424
							89,950	89,950	79,488	79,488

Prob. 4-5A, Continued

3.

JORDAN MACHINE REPAIRS
Income Statement
For Year Ended July 31, 1994

Service revenue		$89,950
Operating expenses:		
Wages expense	$34,618	
Rent expense	9,600	
Truck expense	8,350	
Depreciation expense—trucks	4,400	
Supplies expense	3,993	
Depreciation expense—equipment	3,380	
Insurance expense	990	
Miscellaneous expense	2,195	
Total operating expenses		67,526
Net income		$22,424

JORDAN MACHINE REPAIRS
Statement of Owner's Equity
For Year Ended July 31, 1994

J. J. Jordan, capital, August 1, 1993		$30,426
Net income for the year	$22,424	
Less withdrawals	18,000	
Increase in owner's equity		4,424
J. J. Jordan, capital, July 31, 1994		$34,850

Prob. 4-5A, Continued

JORDAN MACHINE REPAIRS
Balance Sheet
July 31, 1994

Assets

Current assets:
Cash	$ 6,491	
Supplies	302	
Prepaid insurance.	745	
Total current assets		$ 7,538

Plant assets:
Equipment	$30,650		
Less accumulated depreciation	13,130	$17,520	
Trucks	$23,300		
Less accumulated depreciation	10,800	12,500	
Total plant assets			30,020
Total assets			$37,558

Liabilities

Current liabilities:
Accounts payable.	$ 2,015	
Wages payable	693	
Total liabilities.		$ 2,708

Owner's Equity

J. J. Jordan, capital	34,850
Total liabilities and owner's equity.	$37,558

1, 4, and 5

Cash   11

		Post.			Balance	
Date	Item	Ref.	Dr.	Cr.	Dr.	Cr.
1994						
July 31	Balance	√	. . . .	. . . .	6,491.00	. . . .

Supplies   13

1994						
July 31	Balance	√	. . . .	. . . .	4,295.00	. . . .
31	Adjusting.	26	. . . .	3,993.00	302.00	. . . .

Prob. 4-5A, Continued

Prepaid Insurance   14

Date	Item	Post. Ref.	Dr.	Cr.	Balance Dr.	Balance Cr.
1994						
July 31	Balance	√	....	....	1,735.00	....
31	Adjusting......	26	....	990.00	745.00	....

Equipment   16

Date	Item	Post. Ref.	Dr.	Cr.	Balance Dr.	Balance Cr.
1994						
July 31	Balance	√	....	....	30,650.00	....

Accumulated Depreciation—Equipment   17

Date	Item	Post. Ref.	Dr.	Cr.	Balance Dr.	Balance Cr.
1994						
July 31	Balance	√	....	....	....	9,750.00
31	Adjusting......	26	....	3,380.00	....	13,130.00

Trucks   18

Date	Item	Post. Ref.	Dr.	Cr.	Balance Dr.	Balance Cr.
1994						
July 31	Balance	√	....	....	23,300.00	....

Accumulated Depreciation—Trucks   19

Date	Item	Post. Ref.	Dr.	Cr.	Balance Dr.	Balance Cr.
1994						
July 31	Balance	√	....	....	....	6,400.00
31	Adjusting......	26	....	4,400.00	....	10,800.00

Accounts Payable   21

Date	Item	Post. Ref.	Dr.	Cr.	Balance Dr.	Balance Cr.
1994						
July 31	Balance	√	....	....	....	2,015.00

Wages Payable   22

Date	Item	Post. Ref.	Dr.	Cr.	Balance Dr.	Balance Cr.
1994						
July 31	Adjusting......	26	....	693.00	....	693.00

J. J. Jordan, Capital   31

Date	Item	Post. Ref.	Dr.	Cr.	Balance Dr.	Balance Cr.
1994						
July 31	Balance	√	....	....	....	30,426.00
31	Closing........	27	....	22,424.00	....	52,850.00
31	Closing........	27	18,000.00	....	....	34,850.00

Prob. 4-5A, Continued

J. J. Jordan, Drawing

32

Date	Item	Post. Ref.	Dr.	Cr.	Balance Dr.	Balance Cr.
1994						
July 31	Balance	√	....	....	18,000.00	....
31	Closing........	27	....	18,000.00		

Income Summary

33

Date	Item	Post. Ref.	Dr.	Cr.	Balance Dr.	Balance Cr.
1994						
July 31	Closing........	26	....	89,950.00	....	89,950.00
31	Closing........	26	67,526.00	....	....	22,424.00
31	Closing........	27	22,424.00	....		

Service Revenue

41

Date	Item	Post. Ref.	Dr.	Cr.	Balance Dr.	Balance Cr.
1994						
July 31	Balance	√	....	....	....	89,950.00
31	Closing........	26	89,950.00	....		

Wages Expense

51

Date	Item	Post. Ref.	Dr.	Cr.	Balance Dr.	Balance Cr.
1994						
July 31	Balance	√	....	....	33,925.00	....
31	Adjusting......	26	693.00	....	34,618.00	....
31	Closing........	26	....	34,618.00		

Supplies Expense

52

Date	Item	Post. Ref.	Dr.	Cr.	Balance Dr.	Balance Cr.
1994						
July 31	Adjusting......	26	3,993.00	....	3,993.00	....
31	Closing........	26	....	3,993.00		

Rent Expense

53

Date	Item	Post. Ref.	Dr.	Cr.	Balance Dr.	Balance Cr.
1994						
July 31	Balance	√	....	....	9,600.00	....
31	Closing........	26	....	9,600.00		

Depreciation Expense—Equipment

54

Date	Item	Post. Ref.	Dr.	Cr.	Balance Dr.	Balance Cr.
1994						
July 31	Adjusting......	26	3,380.00	....	3,380.00	....
31	Closing........	26	....	3,380.00		

Prob. 4-5A, Continued

Truck Expense 55

Date	Item	Post. Ref.	Dr.	Cr.	Balance Dr.	Balance Cr.
1994						
July 31	Balance	√	....	....	8,350.00	....
31	Closing........	26	....	8,350.00		

Depreciation Expense—Trucks 56

Date	Item	Post. Ref.	Dr.	Cr.	Balance Dr.	Balance Cr.
1994						
July 31	Adjusting......	26	4,400.00	....	4,400.00	....
31	Closing........	26	....	4,400.00		

Insurance Expense 57

Date	Item	Post. Ref.	Dr.	Cr.	Balance Dr.	Balance Cr.
1994						
July 31	Adjusting......	26	990.00	....	990.00	....
31	Closing........	26	....	990.00		

Miscellaneous Expense 59

Date	Item	Post. Ref.	Dr.	Cr.	Balance Dr.	Balance Cr.
1994						
July 31	Balance	√	....	....	2,195.00	....
31	Closing........	26	....	2,195.00		

4.

	Adjusting Entries	Post. Ref.	Debit	Credit
1994				
July 31	Supplies Expense.....................	52	3,993.00	
	Supplies.............................	13		3,993.00
31	Insurance Expense....................	57	990.00	
	Prepaid Insurance....................	14		990.00
31	Depreciation Expense—Equipment....	54	3,380.00	
	Accumulated Depreciation—Equipment	17		3,380.00
31	Depreciation Expense—Trucks........	56	4,400.00	
	Accumulated Depreciation—Trucks .	19		4,400.00
31	Wages Expense......................	51	693.00	
	Wages Payable......................	22		693.00

Prob. 4-5A, Concluded

5.

		Post. Ref.	Debit	Credit
	Closing Entries			
1994				
July 31	Service Revenue....................	41	89,950.00	
	Income Summary.................	33		89,950.00
31	Income Summary....................	33	67,526.00	
	Wages Expense	51		34,618.00
	Rent Expense.....................	53		9,600.00
	Truck Expense	55		8,350.00
	Miscellaneous Expense.............	59		2,195.00
	Supplies Expense	52		3,993.00
	Insurance Expense	57		990.00
	Depreciation Expense—Equipment..	54		3,380.00
	Depreciation Expense—Trucks......	56		4,400.00
31	Income Summary....................	33	22,424.00	
	J. J. Jordan, Capital	31		22,424.00
31	J. J. Jordan, Capital.................	31	18,000.00	
	J. J. Jordan, Drawing...............	32		18,000.00

6.

JORDAN MACHINE REPAIRS
Post-Closing Trial Balance
July 31, 1994

	Debit	Credit
Cash..	6,491.00	
Supplies	302.00	
Prepaid Insurance.........................	745.00	
Equipment	30,650.00	
Accumulated Depreciation—Equipment...............		13,130.00
Trucks......................................	23,300.00	
Accumulated Depreciation—Trucks		10,800.00
Accounts Payable...........................		2,015.00
Wages Payable		693.00
J. J. Jordan, Capital.......................		34,850.00
	61,488.00	61,488.00

Prob. 4-1B

E-Z COIN LAUNDRY
Work Sheet
For Year Ended October 31, 1994

Account Title	Trial Balance Dr.	Trial Balance Cr.	Adjustments Dr.	Adjustments Cr.	Adjusted Trial Balance Dr.	Adjusted Trial Balance Cr.	Income Statement Dr.	Income Statement Cr.	Balance Sheet Dr.	Balance Sheet Cr.
Cash	13,100				13,100				13,100	
Laundry Supplies	6,560			(a) 3,510	3,050				3,050	
Prepaid Insurance	2,750			(b) 1,800	950				950	
Laundry Equipment	84,100				84,100				84,100	
Accumulated Depreciation		45,200		(c) 4,600		49,800				49,800
Accounts Payable		6,100				6,100				6,100
Jan Marker, Capital		36,060				36,060				36,060
Jan Marker, Drawing	18,000				18,000				18,000	
Laundry Revenue		140,900				140,900		140,900		
Wages Expense	51,400		(d) 1,750		53,150		53,150			
Rent Expense	36,000				36,000		36,000			
Utilities Expense	13,650				13,650		13,650			
Miscellaneous Expense	2,700				2,700		2,700			
	228,260	228,260								
Laundry Supplies Expense			(a) 3,510		3,510		3,510			
Insurance Expense			(b) 1,800		1,800		1,800			
Depreciation Expense			(c) 4,600		4,600		4,600			
Wages Payable				(d) 1,750		1,750				1,750
			11,660	11,660	234,610	234,610	115,410	140,900	119,200	93,710
Net Income							25,490			25,490
							140,900	140,900	119,200	119,200

1.

Prob. 4-1B, Continued

2.

E-Z COIN LAUNDRY
Income Statement
For Year Ended October 31, 1994

Laundry revenue		$140,900
Operating expenses:		
Wages expense..	$53,150	
Rent expense..	36,000	
Utilities expense......................................	13,650	
Depreciation expense	4,600	
Laundry supplies expense...........................	3,510	
Insurance expense	1,800	
Miscellaneous expense..............................	2,700	
Total operating expenses..........................		115,410
Net income		$ 25,490

E-Z COIN LAUNDRY
Statement of Owner's Equity
For Year Ended October 31, 1994

Jan Marker, capital, November 1, 1993...................		$36,060
Net income for the year.................................	$25,490	
Less withdrawals.......................................	18,000	
Increase in owner's equity		7,490
Jan Marker, capital, October 31, 1994..................		$43,550

Prob. 4-1B, Continued

E-Z COIN LAUNDRY
Balance Sheet
October 31, 1994

Assets

Current assets:

Cash	$13,100	
Laundry supplies	3,050	
Prepaid insurance	950	
Total current assets		$17,100

Plant assets:

Laundry equipment	$84,100	
Less accumulated depreciation	49,800	34,300
Total assets		$51,400

Liabilities

Current liabilities:

Accounts payable	$ 6,100	
Wages payable	1,750	
Total liabilities		$ 7,850

Owner's Equity

Jan Marker, capital	43,550
Total liabilities and owner's equity	$51,400

3.   Adjusting Entries

1994

Oct. 31	Laundry Supplies Expense	3,510	
	Laundry Supplies		3,510
31	Insurance Expense	1,800	
	Prepaid Insurance		1,800
31	Depreciation Expense	4,600	
	Accumulated Depreciation		4,600
31	Wages Expense	1,750	
	Wages Payable		1,750

Prob. 4-1B, Concluded

4. <u>Closing Entries</u>

1994

Oct. 31	Laundry Revenue		140,900	
	Income Summary			140,900
	31	Income Summary	115,410	
		Wages Expense		53,150
		Rent Expense		36,000
		Utilities Expense		13,650
		Miscellaneous Expense		2,700
		Laundry Supplies Expense		3,510
		Insurance Expense		1,800
		Depreciation Expense		4,600
	31	Income Summary	25,490	
		Jan Marker, Capital		25,490
	31	Jan Marker, Capital	18,000	
		Jan Marker, Drawing		18,000

Prob. 4-2B

1.

<u>Adjusting Entries</u>

19—
Dec. 31 | Accounts Receivable............................. | 3,580 |
| Service Fees Earned .... | | 3,580

31 | Supplies Expense................................ | 6,420 |
| Supplies....................................... | | 6,420

31 | Insurance Expense.............................. | 1,600 |
| Prepaid Insurance............................ | | 1,600

31 | Depreciation Expense—Buildings............... | 4,800 |
| Accumulated Depreciation—Buildings......... | | 4,800

31 | Depreciation Expense—Equipment .... | 18,100 |
| Accumulated Depreciation—Equipment .... | | 18,100

31 | Utilities Expense .... | 400 |
| Accounts Payable............................. | | 400

31 | Salary Expense .... | 1,450 |
| Salaries Payable .... | | 1,450

31 | Taxes Expense.................................. | 920 |
| Taxes Payable .... | | 920

31 | Unearned Rent .... | 300 |
| Rent Income.................................. | | 300

2.

<u>Closing Entries</u>

19—
Dec. 31 | Service Fees Earned .... | 144,260 |
| Rent Income.................................. | 300 |
| Income Summary............................. | | 144,560

31 | Income Summary............................... | 120,000 |
| Salary Expense .... | | 72,650
| Depreciation Expense—Equipment............ | | 18,100
| Rent Expense................................ | | 9,000
| Supplies Expense .... | | 6,420
| Utilities Expense............................. | | 4,950
| Depreciation Expense—Buildings .... | | 4,800
| Taxes Expense............................... | | 1,520
| Insurance Expense .... | | 1,600
| Miscellaneous Expense....................... | | 960

31 | Income Summary.............................. | 24,560 |
| C.C. Furstner, Capital .... | | 24,560

31 | C.C. Furstner, Capital .... | 21,000 |
| C.C. Furstner, Drawing .... | | 21,000

Prob. 4-2B, Concluded

3.   **FURSTNER COMPANY**
                                    Statement of Owner's Equity
                              For Year Ended December 31, 19—

C.C. Furstner, capital, January 1, 1993		$124,890
Net income for the year.	$24,560	
Less withdrawals.	21,000	
Increase in owner's equity		3,560
C.C. Furstner, capital, December 31, 1994		$128,450

4. The balance of C.C. Furstner capital on December 31 would have been $50,550 debit ($124,890 + $24,560 − $200,000). This negative balance would be reported in the owner's equity section.

Prob. 4-3B

1.

SALAZAR COMPANY
Work Sheet
For Month Ended January 31, 1994

Account Title	Trial Balance Dr.	Trial Balance Cr.	Adjustments Dr.	Adjustments Cr.	Adjusted Trial Balance Dr.	Adjusted Trial Balance Cr.	Income Statement Dr.	Income Statement Cr.	Balance Sheet Dr.	Balance Sheet Cr.
Cash	4,507.01				4,507.01				4,507.01	
Accounts Receivable	550.00		(a) 750.00		1,300.00				1,300.00	
Supplies	1,648.56			(b) 1,097.96	550.60				550.60	
Prepaid Insurance	790.70			(c) 72.50	718.20				718.20	
Land	20,000.00				20,000.00				20,000.00	
Building	55,500.00				55,500.00				55,500.00	
Accum. Depr.—Building		23,400.00		(d) 125.00		23,525.00				23,525.00
Equipment	28,000.00				28,000.00				28,000.00	
Accum. Depr.—Equipment		17,200.00		(e) 95.00		17,295.00				17,295.00
Accounts Payable		5,141.50				5,141.50				5,141.50
Unearned Rent		200.00	(f) 100.00			100.00				100.00
C.E. Salazar, Capital		61,815.10				61,815.10				61,815.10
C.E. Salazar, Drawing	2,000.00				2,000.00				2,000.00	
Service Revenue		11,985.67		(a) 750.00		12,735.67		12,735.67		
Wages Expense	4,799.80		(g) 1,006.50		5,806.30		5,806.30			
Rent Expenes	910.00				910.00		910.00			
Utilities Expense	728.50				728.50		728.50			
Misc. Expense	307.70				307.70		307.70			
	119,742.27	119,742.27								
Supplies Expense			(b) 1,097.96		1,097.96		1,097.96			
Insurance Expense			(c) 72.50		72.50		72.50			
Depr. Expense—Building			(d) 125.00		125.00		125.00			
Depr. Expense—Equipment			(e) 95.00		95.00		95.00			
Rent Income				(f) 100.00		100.00		100.00		
Wages Payable				(g) 1,006.50		1,006.50				1,006.50
			3,246.96	3,246.96	121,718.77	121,718.77	9,142.96	12,835.67	112,575.81	108,883.10
Net Income							3,692.71			3,692.71
							12,835.67	12,835.67	112,575.81	112,575.81

Prob. 4-3B, Continued

2.

SALAZAR COMPANY
Income Statement
For Month Ended January 31, 1994

Revenues:		
Service revenue	$12,735.67	
Rent income	100.00	
Total revenues		$12,835.67
Operating expenses:		
Wages expense	$ 5,806.30	
Supplies expense	1,097.96	
Rent expense	910.00	
Utilities expense	728.50	
Depreciation expense—building	125.00	
Depreciation expense—equipment	95.00	
Insurance expense	72.50	
Miscellaneous expense	307.70	
Total operating expenses		9,142.96
Net income		$ 3,692.71

SALAZAR COMPANY
Statement of Owner's Equity
For Month Ended January 31, 1994

C. E. Salazar, capital, January 1, 1994		$56,815.10
Additional investment during the month		5,000.00
Total		$61,815.10
Net income for the month	$3,692.71	
Less withdrawals	2,000.00	
Increase in owner's equity		1,692.71
C. E. Salazar, capital, January 31, 1994		$63,507.81

Prob. 4-3B, Continued

SALAZAR COMPANY
Balance Sheet
January 31, 1994

Assets

Current assets:

Cash		$ 4,507.01
Accounts receivable		1,300.00
Supplies		550.60
Prepaid insurance..................		718.20
Total current assets		$ 7,075.81

Plant assets:

Land		$20,000.00
Building	$55,500.00	
Less accumulated depreciation	23,525.00	31,975.00
Equipment	$28,000.00	
Less accumulated depreciation	17,295.00	10,705.00
Total plant assets		62,680.00

Total assets	$69,755.81

Liabilities

Current liabilities:

Accounts payable..................	$ 5,141.50
Wages payable	1,006.50
Unearned rent.....................	100.00
Total liabilities.....................	$ 6,248.00

Owner's Equity

C. E. Salazar, capital.................	63,507.81
Total liabilities and owner's equity.....	$69,755.81

Prob. 4-3B, Continued

3.

Adjusting Entries	Post. Ref.	Debit	Credit
1994			
Jan. 31 Accounts Receivable	12	750.00	
Service Revenue	41		750.00
31 Supplies Expense	52	1,097.96	
Supplies............................	13		1,097.96
31 Insurance Expense	57	72.50	
Prepaid Insurance	14		72.50
31 Depreciation Expense—Building	54	125.00	
Accumulated Depreciation—Building	17		125.00
31 Depreciation Expense—Equipment....	56	95.00	
Accumulated Depreciation—Equipment.........................	19		95.00
31 Unearned Rent	23	100.00	
Rent Income	42		100.00
31 Wages Expense......................	51	1,006.50	
Wages Payable.....................	22		1,006.50

4.

Closing Entries			
1994			
Jan. 31 Service Revenue	41	12,735.67	
Rent Income........................	42	100.00	
Income Summary	33		12,835.67
31 Income Summary....................	33	9,142.96	
Wages Expense	51		5,806.30
Rent Expense......................	53		910.00
Utilities Expense...................	55		728.50
Miscellaneous Expense	59		307.70
Supplies Expense	52		1,097.96
Insurance Expense	57		72.50
Depreciation Expense—Building	54		125.00
Depreciation Expense—Equipment..	56		95.00
31 Income Summary....................	33	3,692.71	
C. E. Salazar, Capital...............	31		3,692.71
31 C. E. Salazar, Capital	31	2,000.00	
C. E. Salazar, Drawing	32		2,000.00

Prob. 4-3B, Continued

3. and 4.

Cash   11

Date		Item	Post. Ref.	Dr.	Cr.	Balance Dr.	Balance Cr.
1994							
Jan.	1	Balance	√	. . . .	. . . .	1,259.50	. . . .
	3	. . . .	23	. . . .	910.00	349.50	. . . .
	4	. . . .	23	5,000.00	. . . .	5,349.50	. . . .
	5	. . . .	23	. . . .	86.40	5,263.10	. . . .
	7	. . . .	23	800.00	. . . .	6,063.10	. . . .
	8	. . . .	23	400.00	. . . .	6,463.10	. . . .
	8	. . . .	23	. . . .	2,584.10	3,879.00	. . . .
	8	. . . .	23	1,695.30	. . . .	5,574.30	. . . .
	10	. . . .	24	. . . .	510.20	5,064.10	. . . .
	12	. . . .	24	. . . .	2,319.60	2,744.50	. . . .
	15	. . . .	24	2,718.32	. . . .	5,462.82	. . . .
	16	. . . .	24	. . . .	1,000.00	4,462.82	. . . .
	19	. . . .	24	. . . .	2,135.50	2,327.32	. . . .
	22	. . . .	24	. . . .	370.20	1,957.12	. . . .
	22	. . . .	24	3,992.21	. . . .	5,949.33	. . . .
	24	. . . .	25	. . . .	527.76	5,421.57	. . . .
	26	. . . .	25	. . . .	2,480.20	2,941.37	. . . .
	30	. . . .	25	. . . .	156.50	2,784.87	. . . .
	30	. . . .	25	. . . .	26.48	2,758.39	. . . .
	31	. . . .	25	. . . .	1,000.00	1,758.39	. . . .
	31	. . . .	25	3,029.84	. . . .	4,788.23	. . . .
	31	. . . .	25	. . . .	281.22	4,507.01	. . . .

Accounts Receivable   12

Date		Item	Post. Ref.	Dr.	Cr.	Balance Dr.	Balance Cr.
1994							
Jan.	1	Balance.	√	1,200.00	. . . .	1,200.00	. . . .
	7	. . . .	23	. . . .	800.00	400.00	. . . .
	8	. . . .	23	. . . .	400.00	—	—
	22	. . . .	24	550.00	. . . .	550.00	. . . .
	31	Adjusting.	26	750.00	. . . .	1,300.00	. . . .

Prob. 4-3B, Continued

Supplies   13

Date	Item	Post. Ref.	Dr.	Cr.	Balance Dr.	Balance Cr.
1994						
Jan. 1	Balance.......	√	....	....	610.60	....
10	....	24	510.20	....	1,120.80	....
27	....	25	527.76	....	1,648.56	....
31	Adjusting......	26	....	1,097.96	550.60	....

Prepaid Insurance   14

Date	Item	Post. Ref.	Dr.	Cr.	Balance Dr.	Balance Cr.
1994						
Jan. 1	Balance.......	√	....	....	420.50	....
22	....	24	370.20	....	790.70	....
31	Adjusting......	26	....	72.50	718.20	....

Land   15

Date	Item	Post. Ref.	Dr.	Cr.	Balance Dr.	Balance Cr.
1994						
Jan. 1	Balance.......	√	....	....	20,000.00	....

Building   16

Date	Item	Post. Ref.	Dr.	Cr.	Balance Dr.	Balance Cr.
1994						
Jan. 1	Balance.......	√	....	....	55,500.00	....

Accumulated Depreciation—Building   17

Date	Item	Post. Ref.	Dr.	Cr.	Balance Dr.	Balance Cr.
1994						
Jan. 1	Balance	√	....	....	....	23,400.00
31	Adjusting......	26	....	125.00	....	23,525.00

Equipment   18

Date	Item	Post. Ref.	Dr.	Cr.	Balance Dr.	Balance Cr.
1994						
Jan. 1	Balance	√	....	....	27,250.00	....
3	....	23	750.00	....	28,000.00	....

Accumulated Depreciation—Equipment   19

Date	Item	Post. Ref.	Dr.	Cr.	Balance Dr.	Balance Cr.
1994						
Jan. 1	Balance	√	....	....	....	17,200.00
31	Adjusting......	26	....	95.00	....	17,295.00

Prob. 4-3B, Continued

Accounts Payable

21

Date	Item	Post. Ref.	Dr.	Cr.	Balance	
					Dr.	Cr.
1994						
Jan. 1	Balance	√	....	....	....	8,625.50
3	....	23	....	750.00	....	9,375.50
8	....	23	2,584.10	....	....	6,791.40
19	....	24	2,135.50	....	....	4,655.90
31	....	25	....	485.60	....	5,141.50

Wages Payable

22

Date	Item	Post. Ref.	Dr.	Cr.	Balance	
1994						
Jan. 31	Adjusting......	26	....	1,006.50	....	1,006.50

Unearned Rent

23

Date	Item	Post. Ref.	Dr.	Cr.	Balance	
1994						
Jan. 1	Balance	√	....	200.00	....	200.00
31	Adjusting......	26	100.00	....	....	100.00

C. E. Salazar, Capital

31

Date	Item	Post. Ref.	Dr.	Cr.	Balance	
1994						
Jan. 1	Balance	√	....	....	....	56,815.10
4	....	23	....	5,000.00	....	61,815.10
31	Closing........	27	....	3,692.71	....	65,507.81
31	Closing........	27	2,000.00	....	....	63,507.81

C. E. Salazar, Drawing

32

Date	Item	Post. Ref.	Dr.	Cr.	Balance	
1994						
Jan. 16	....	24	1,000.00	....	1,000.00	....
31	....	25	1,000.00	....	2,000.00	....
31	Closing........	27	....	2,000.00		

Income Summary

33

Date	Item	Post. Ref.	Dr.	Cr.	Balance	
1994						
Jan. 31	Closing........	26	....	12,835.67	....	12,835.67
31	Closing........	26	9,142.96	....	....	3,692.71
31	Closing........	27	3,692.71	....		

Prob. 4-3B, Continued

Service Revenue 41

Date	Item	Post. Ref.	Dr.	Cr.	Balance Dr.	Balance Cr.
1994						
Jan. 8	....	23	....	1,695.30	....	1,695.30
15	....	24	....	2,718.32	....	4,413.62
22	....	24	....	3,992.21	....	8,405.83
22	....	24	....	550.00	....	8,955.83
31	....	25	....	3,029.84	....	11,985.67
31	Adjusting......	26	....	750.00	....	12,735.67
31	Closing........	26	12,735.67	....		

Rent Income 42

Date	Item	Post. Ref.	Dr.	Cr.	Balance Dr.	Balance Cr.
1994						
Jan. 31	Adjusting......	26	....	100.00	....	100.00
31	Closing........	26	100.00	....		

Wages Expense 51

Date	Item	Post. Ref.	Dr.	Cr.	Balance Dr.	Balance Cr.
1994						
Jan. 12	....	24	2,319.60	....	2,319.60	....
26	....	25	2,480.20	....	4,799.80	....
31	Adjusting......	26	1,006.50	....	5,806.30	....
31	Closing........	26	....	5,806.30		

Supplies Expense 52

Date	Item	Post. Ref.	Dr.	Cr.	Balance Dr.	Balance Cr.
1994						
Jan. 31	Adjusting......	26	1,097.96	....	1,097.96	....
31	Closing........	26	....	1,097.96		

Rent Expense 53

Date	Item	Post. Ref.	Dr.	Cr.	Balance Dr.	Balance Cr.
1994						
Jan. 3	....	23	910.00	....	910.00	....
31	Closing........	26	....	910.00		

Depreciation Expense—Building 54

Date	Item	Post. Ref.	Dr.	Cr.	Balance Dr.	Balance Cr.
1994						
Jan. 31	Adjusting......	26	125.00	....	125.00	....
31	Closing........	26	....	125.00		

Prob. 4-3B, Concluded

Utilities Expense 55

Date	Item	Post. Ref.	Dr.	Cr.	Balance Dr.	Balance Cr.
1994						
Jan. 5	....	24	86.40	....	86.40	....
30	....	25	156.50	....	242.90	....
31	....	25	485.60	....	728.50	....
31	Closing........	26	....	728.50		

Depreciation Expense—Equipment 56

Date	Item	Post. Ref.	Dr.	Cr.	Balance Dr.	Balance Cr.
1994						
Jan. 31	Adjusting......	26	95.00	....	95.00	....
31	Closing........	26	....	95.00		

Insurance Expense 57

Date	Item	Post. Ref.	Dr.	Cr.	Balance Dr.	Balance Cr.
1994						
Jan. 31	Adjusting......	26	72.50	....	72.50	....
31	Closing........	26	....	72.50		

Miscellaneous Expense 59

Date	Item	Post. Ref.	Dr.	Cr.	Balance Dr.	Balance Cr.
1994						
Jan. 30	....	25	26.48	....	26.48	....
31	....	25	281.22	....	307.70	....
31	Closing........	26	....	307.70		

5.

SALAZAR COMPANY
Post-Closing Trial Balance
January 31, 1994

Cash..	4,507.01	
Accounts Receivable..............................	1,300.00	
Supplies	550.60	
Prepaid Insurance..............................	718.20	
Land...	20,000.00	
Building......................................	55,500.00	
Accumulated Depreciation—Building		23,525.00
Equipment	28,000.00	
Accumulated Depreciation—Equipment.............		17,295.00
Accounts Payable..............................		5,141.50
Wages Payable		1,006.50
Unearned Rent		100.00
C. E. Salazar, Capital		63,507.81
	110,575.81	110,575.81

1.

WILLIS COMPANY
Work Sheet
For Year Ended June 30, 1994

Account Title	Trial Balance Dr.	Trial Balance Cr.	Adjustments Dr.	Adjustments Cr.	Adjusted Trial Balance Dr.	Adjusted Trial Balance Cr.	Income Statement Dr.	Income Statement Cr.	Balance Sheet Dr.	Balance Sheet Cr.
Cash	7,200				7,200				7,200	
Accounts Receivable	6,500		(a) 1,200		7,700				7,700	
Prepaid Insurance	3,400			(b) 2,700	700				700	
Supplies	1,950			(c) 1,500	450				450	
Land	50,000				50,000				50,000	
Building	137,500				137,500				137,500	
Accumulated Depr.—Building		51,700		(d) 1,620		53,320				53,320
Equipment	90,100				90,100				90,100	
Accumulated Depr.—Equipment		35,300		(e) 5,500		40,800				40,800
Accounts Payable		7,500				7,500				7,500
Unearned Rent		3,000	(g) 1,500			1,500				1,500
G. E. Willis, Capital		163,700				163,700				163,700
G. E. Willis, Drawing	20,000				20,000				20,000	
Fees Revenue		198,400		(a) 1,200		199,600		199,600		
Salaries and Wages Expense	80,200		(f) 2,000		82,200		82,200			
Advertising Expense	28,200				28,200		28,200			
Utilities Expense	19,000				19,000		19,000			
Repairs Expense	11,500				11,500		11,500			
Miscellaneous Expense	4,050				4,050		4,050			
	459,600	459,600								
Insurance Expense			(b) 2,700		2,700		2,700			
Supplies Expense			(c) 1,500		1,500		1,500			
Depr. Expense—Building			(d) 1,620		1,620		1,620			
Depr. Expense—Equipment			(e) 5,500		5,500		5,500			
Salaries and Wages Payable				(f) 2,000		2,000				2,000
Rent Income				(g) 1,500		1,500		1,500		
			16,020	16,020	469,920	469,920	156,270	201,100	313,650	268,820
Net Income							44,830			44,830
							201,100	201,100	313,650	313,650

Prob. 4-4B, Continued

2.

WILLIS COMPANY
Income Statement
For Year Ended June 30, 1994

Revenues:		
Fees earned	$199,600	
Rent income.......................................	1,500	
Total revenues..................................		$201,100
Operating expenses:		
Salaries and wages expense........................	$ 82,200	
Advertising expense	28,200	
Utilities expense.................................	19,000	
Repairs expense	11,500	
Depreciation expense—equipment..................	5,500	
Insurance expense	2,700	
Depreciation expense—building	1,620	
Supplies expense	1,500	
Miscellaneous expense.............................	4,050	
Total operating expenses........................		156,270
Net income		$ 44,830

3.

WILLIS COMPANY
Statement of Owner's Equity
For Year Ended June 30, 1994

G. E. Willis, capital, July 1, 1993		$163,700
Net income for year	$44,830	
Less withdrawals......................................	20,000	
Increase in owner's equity		24,830
G. E. Willis, capital, June 30, 1994.....................		$188,530

Prob. 4-4B, Concluded

4.

WILLIS COMPANY
Balance Sheet
June 30, 1994

Assets

Current assets:
Cash	$ 7,200	
Accounts receivable	7,700	
Prepaid insurance	700	
Supplies	450	
Total current assets		$ 16,050

Plant assets:
Land		$50,000	
Building	$137,500		
Less accumulated depreciation	53,320	84,180	
Equipment	$ 90,100		
Less accumulated depreciation	40,800	49,300	
Total plant assets			183,480
Total assets			$199,530

Liabilities

Current liabilities:
Accounts payable	$ 7,500	
Salaries and wages payable	2,000	
Unearned rent	1,500	
Total liabilities		$ 11,000

Owner's Equity

G. E. Willis, capital	188,530
Total liabilities and owner's equity	$199,530

5. $44,830 \div 201,100 = 22.3\%$

2.

LEE MACHINE REPAIRS
Work Sheet
For Year Ended December 31, 1994

Account Title	Trial Balance Dr.	Trial Balance Cr.	Adjustments Dr.	Adjustments Cr.	Adjusted Trial Balance Dr.	Adjusted Trial Balance Cr.	Income Statement Dr.	Income Statement Cr.	Balance Sheet Dr.	Balance Sheet Cr.
Cash	6,825				6,825				6,825	
Supplies	4,820			(a) 3,960	860				860	
Prepaid Insurance	2,000			(b) 1,050	950				950	
Equipment	32,200				32,200				32,200	
Accum. Depr.—Equipment		9,050		(c) 6,080		15,130				15,130
Trucks	42,000				42,000				42,000	
Accum. Depr.—Trucks		27,100		(d) 5,500		32,600				32,600
Accounts Payable		4,015				4,015				4,015
S.T. Lee, Capital		25,800				25,800				25,800
S.T. Lee, Drawing	18,000				18,000				18,000	
Service Revenue		99,950				99,950		99,950		
Wages Expense	37,925		(e) 700		38,625		38,625			
Rent Expense	9,600				9,600		9,600			
Truck Expense	9,350				9,350		9,350			
Miscellaneous Expense	3,195				3,195		3,195			
	165,915	165,915								
Supplies Expense			(a) 3,960		3,960		3,960			
Insurance Expense			(b) 1,050		1,050		1,050			
Depr. Expense—Equipment			(c) 6,080		6,080		6,080			
Depr. Expense—Trucks			(d) 5,500		5,500		5,500			
Wages Payable				(e) 700		700				700
			17,290	17,290	178,195	178,195	77,360	99,950	100,835	78,245
Net Income							22,590			22,590
							99,950	99,950	100,835	100,835

Prob. 4-5B, Continued

3.

LEE MACHINE REPAIRS
Income Statement
For Year Ended December 31, 1994

Service revenue		$99,950
Operating expenses:		
Wages expense	$38,625	
Rent expense	9,600	
Truck expense	9,350	
Depreciation expense—equipment	6,080	
Depreciation expense—trucks	5,500	
Supplies expense	3,960	
Insurance expense	1,050	
Miscellaneous expense	3,195	
Total operating expenses		77,360
Net income		$22,590

LEE MACHINE REPAIRS
Statement of Owner's Equity
For Year Ended December 31, 1994

S.T. Lee, capital, January 1, 1994		$25,800
Net income for the year	$22,590	
Less withdrawals	18,000	
Increase in owner's equity		4,590
S.T. Lee, capital, December 31, 1994		$30,390

Prob. 4-5B, Continued

LEE MACHINE REPAIRS
Balance Sheet
December 31, 1994

Assets

Current assets:
Cash .... $ 6,825
Supplies 860
Prepaid insurance....................................... 950
  Total current assets .... $ 8,635
Plant assets:
Equipment $32,200
  Less accumulated depreciation 15,130 $17,070
Trucks $42,000
  Less accumulated depreciation 32,600   9,400
    Total plant assets 26,470
Total assets $35,105

Liabilities

Current liabilities:
Accounts payable....................................... $ 4,015
Wages payable 700
Total liabilities....................................... $ 4,715

Owner's Equity

S.T. Lee, capital 30,390
Total liabilities and owner's equity..................... $35,105

1, 4, and 5

Cash   11

Date	Item	Post. Ref.	Dr.	Cr.	Balance Dr.	Cr.
1994						
Dec. 31	Balance	√	....	....	6,825	....

Supplies   13

Date	Item	Post. Ref.	Dr.	Cr.	Balance Dr.	Cr.
1994						
Dec. 31	Balance	√	....	....	4,820	....
31	Adjusting	26	......	3,960	860	....

Prob. 4-5B, Continued

Prepaid Insurance   **14**

		Post.			Balance	
Date	Item	Ref.	Dr.	Cr.	Dr.	Cr.
1994						
Dec. 31	Balance	√	....	....	2,000	....
31	Adjusting	26	....	1,050	950	....

Equipment   **16**

1994						
Dec. 31	Balance	√	....	....	32,200	....

Accumulated Depreciation—Equipment   **17**

1994						
Dec. 31	Balance	√	....	....	....	9,050
31	Adjusting	26	....	6,080	....	15,130

Trucks   **18**

1994						
Dec. 31	Balance	√	....	....	42,000	....

Accumulated Depreciation—Trucks   **19**

1994						
Dec. 31	Balance	√	....	....	....	27,100
31	Adjusting	26	....	5,500	....	32,600

Accounts Payable   **21**

1994						
Dec. 31	Balance	√	....	....	....	4,015

Wages Payable   **22**

1994						
Dec. 31	Adjusting	26	....	700	....	700

S.T. Lee, Capital   **31**

1994						
Dec. 31	Balance	√	....	....	....	25,800
31	Closing..........	27	....	22,590	....	48,390
31	Closing..........	27	18,000	....	....	30,390

Prob. 4-5B, Continued

S.T. Lee, Drawing 32

Date	Item	Post. Ref.	Dr.	Cr.	Balance Dr.	Balance Cr.
1994						
Dec. 31	Balance	√	......	......	18,000	......
31	Closing.................	27	......	18,000		

Income Summary 33

Date	Item	Post. Ref.	Dr.	Cr.	Balance Dr.	Balance Cr.
1994						
Dec. 31	Closing.................	26	......	99,950	......	99,950
31	Closing.................	26	77,360	......	......	22,590
31	Closing.................	27	22,590	......		

Service Revenue 41

Date	Item	Post. Ref.	Dr.	Cr.	Balance Dr.	Balance Cr.
1994						
Dec. 31	Balance	√	......	......	......	99,950
31	Closing.................	26	99,950	......		

Wages Expense 51

Date	Item	Post. Ref.	Dr.	Cr.	Balance Dr.	Balance Cr.
1994						
Dec. 31	Balance	√	......	......	37,925	......
31	Adjusting	26	700	......	38,625	......
31	Closing.................	26	......	38,625		

Supplies Expense 52

Date	Item	Post. Ref.	Dr.	Cr.	Balance Dr.	Balance Cr.
1994						
Dec. 31	Adjusting	26	3,960	......	3,960	......
31	Closing.................	26	......	3,960		

Rent Expense 53

Date	Item	Post. Ref.	Dr.	Cr.	Balance Dr.	Balance Cr.
1994						
Dec. 31	Balance	√	......	......	9,600	......
31	Closing.................	26	......	9,600		

Depreciation Expense—Equipment 54

Date	Item	Post. Ref.	Dr.	Cr.	Balance Dr.	Balance Cr.
1994						
Dec. 31	Adjusting	26	6,080	......	6,080	......
31	Closing.................	26	......	6,080		

Prob. 4-5B, Continued

Truck Expense   55

| | | | | | Balance | |
Date	Item	Post. Ref.	Dr.	Cr.	Dr.	Cr.
1994						
Dec. 31	Balance	√	......	......	9,350	......
31	Closing.................	26	......	9,350		

Depreciation Expense—Trucks   56

1994						
Dec. 31	Adjusting	26	5,500	......	5,500	.....
31	Closing.................	26	......	5,500		

Insurance Expense   57

1994						
Dec. 31	Adjusting	26	1,050	......	1,050	......
31	Closing.................	26	......	1,050		

Miscellaneous Expense   59

1994						
Dec. 31	Balance	√	......	......	3,195	......
31	Closing.................	26	......	3,195		

4.

Adjusting Entries	Post. Ref.	Debit	Credit
1994			
Dec. 31 Supplies Expense.........................	52	3,960	
Supplies.................................	13		3,960
31 Insurance Expense.........................	57	1,050	
Prepaid Insurance.........................	14		1,050
31 Depreciation Expense—Equipment	54	6,080	
Accumulated Depreciation—Equipment ..	17		6,080
31 Depreciation Expense—Trucks..............	56	5,500	
Accumulated Depreciation—Trucks	19		5,500
31 Wages Expense............................	51	700	
Wages Payable............................	22		700

Prob. 4-5B, Concluded

5.

Closing Entries	Post. Ref.	Debit	Credit
1994			
Dec. 31 Service Revenue.........................	41	99,950	
Income Summary........................	33		99,950
31 Income Summary...........................	33	77,360	
Wages Expense........................	51		38,625
Rent Expense..........................	53		9,600
Truck Expense.........................	55		9,350
Miscellaneous Expense...................	59		3,195
Supplies Expense......................	52		3,960
Insurance Expense......................	57		1,050
Depreciation Expense—Equipment........	54		6,080
Depreciation Expense—Trucks...........	56		5,500
31 Income Summary........................	33	22,590	
S.T. Lee, Capital	31		22,590
31 S.T. Lee, Capital	31	18,000	
S.T. Lee, Drawing	32		18,000

6.

LEE MACHINE REPAIRS
Post-Closing Trial Balance
December 31, 1994

	Debit	Credit
Cash..	6,825	
Supplies	860	
Prepaid Insurance....................................	950	
Equipment	32,200	
Accumulated Depreciation—Equipment....................		15,130
Trucks	42,000	
Accumulated Depreciation—Trucks		32,600
Accounts Payable.....................................		4,015
Wages Payable		700
S.T. Lee, Capital		30,390
	82,835	82,835

Mini-Case 4

1. A set of financial statements provides useful information concerning the economic condition of an enterprise. For example, the balance sheet describes the financial condition of the enterprise as of a given date and is useful in assessing the financial soundness and liquidity of an enterprise. The income statement describes the results of operations for a period and indicates the profitability of the enterprise. The statement of owner's equity describes the changes in the owner's interest in the enterprise for a period. Each of these statements is useful in evaluating whether to extend credit to the enterprise.

Mini-Case 4, Concluded

2. The following adjustments might be necessary before an accurate set of financial statements could be prepared:

   - No supplies expense is shown. The supplies account should be adjusted for the supplies used during the year.
   - No depreciation expense is shown for the trucks or equipment accounts. An adjusting entry should be prepared for depreciation expense on each of these assets.
   - An inquiry should be made as to whether any accrued expenses, such as wages or utilities, exist at the end of the year.
   - An inquiry should be made as to whether any prepaid expenses, such as rent or insurance, exist at the end of the year.
   - An inquiry should be made as to whether the owner withdrew any funds from the enterprise during the year. No drawing account is shown in the "Statement of Accounts."
   - The following items should be relabeled for greater clarity:

     Billings Due from Others–Accounts Receivable
     Amounts Owed to Others–Accounts Payable
     Investment in Business–Jean Wicks, Capital
     Other Expenses–Miscellaneous Expense

   Note to Instructors: The preceding items are not intended to include all adjustments that might exist in the Statement of Accounts. The possible adjustments listed include only items which have been covered in Chapters 1–4. For example, uncollectible accounts expense (discussed in Chapter 9) is not mentioned.

3. In general, the decision to extend a loan is based upon an assessment of the profitability and riskiness of the loan. Although the financial statements provide useful data for this purpose, other factors such as the following might also be significant:

   - The due date and payment terms of the loan.
   - Security for the loan. For example, whether Jean Wicks is willing to pledge personal assets in support of the loan will affect the riskiness of the loan.
   - The use to which the loan will be put. For example, if the loan is to purchase real estate (possibly for a future building site), the real estate could be used as security for the loan.
   - The projected profitability of the enterprise.

COMPREHENSIVE PROBLEM 1

1.

JOURNAL

Pages 1 and 2

Date	Description	Post. Ref.	Debit	Credit
19—				
Sept. 1	Cash	11	6,000	
	Accounts Receivable	12	1,000	
	Supplies	14	1,250	
	Office Equipment	18	6,200	
	Lance Fox, Capital	31		14,450
2	Prepaid Rent	15	2,400	
	Cash	11		2,400
2	Prepaid Insurance	16	1,800	
	Cash	11		1,800
4	Cash	11	2,500	
	Unearned Fees	23		2,500
4	Office Equipment	18	2,000	
	Accounts Payable	21		2,000
6	Cash	11	600	
	Accounts Receivable	12		600
9	Miscellaneous Expense	59	80	
	Cash	11		80
11	Accounts Payable	21	1,100	
	Cash	11		1,100
12	Accounts Receivable	12	1,200	
	Fees Earned	41		1,200
13	Salary Expense	51	400	
	Cash	11		400
17	Cash	11	2,100	
	Fees Earned	41		2,100
17	Supplies	14	950	
	Cash	11		950

Comp. Prob. 1, Continued

JOURNAL

Date	Description	Post. Ref.	Debit	Credit
19—				
Sept. 20	Accounts Receivable	12	1,100	
	Fees Earned	41		1,100
24	Cash	11	1,850	
	Fees Earned	41		1,850
27	Cash	11	1,200	
	Accounts Receivable	12		1,200
27	Salary Expense	51	400	
	Cash	11		400
30	Miscellaneous Expense...................	59	65	
	Cash	11		65
30	Miscellaneous Expense...................	59	140	
	Cash	11		140
30	Cash	11	850	
	Fees Earned	41		850
30	Accounts Receivable	12	500	
	Fees Earned	41		500
30	Lance Fox, Drawing......................	32	1,200	
	Cash	11		1,200

Comp. Prob. 1, Continued

2, 5, and 6

Cash 11

Date	Item	Post. Ref.	Debit	Credit	Balance Debit	Balance Credit
19—						
Sept. 1	....	1	6,000	......	6,000	......
2	....	1	.....	2,400	3,600	......
2	....	1	.....	1,800	1,800	......
4	....	1	2,500	......	4,300	......
6	....	1	600	......	4,900	......
9	....	1	.....	80	4,820	......
11	....	1	.....	1,100	3,720	......
13	....	1	.....	400	3,320	......
17	....	2	2,100	......	5,420	......
17	....	2	.....	950	4,470	......
24	....	2	1,850	......	6,320	......
27	....	2	1,200	......	7,520	......
27	....	2	.....	400	7,120	......
30	....	2	.....	65	7,055	......
30	....	2	.....	140	6,915	......
30	....	2	850	......	7,765	......
30	....	2	.....	1,200	6,565	......

Accounts Receivable 12

Date	Item	Post. Ref.	Debit	Credit	Balance Debit	Balance Credit
19—						
Sept. 1	....	1	1,000	......	1,000	......
6	....	1	.....	600	400	......
12	....	1	1,200	......	1,600	......
20	....	2	1,100	......	2,700	......
27	....	2	.....	1,200	1,500	......
30	....	2	500	......	2,000	......

Supplies 14

Date	Item	Post. Ref.	Debit	Credit	Balance Debit	Balance Credit
19—						
Sept. 1	....	1	1,250	......	1,250	......
17	....	2	950	......	2,200	......
30	....	3	.....	780	1,420	......

Comp. Prob. 1, Continued

Prepaid Rent

15

Date	Item	Post. Ref.	Debit	Credit	Balance Debit	Balance Credit
19—						
Sept. 2	....	1	2,400	......	2,400	......
30	....	3	.....	800	1,600	......

Prepaid Insurance

16

Date	Item	Post. Ref.	Debit	Credit	Balance Debit	Balance Credit
19—						
Sept. 2	....	1	1,800	......	1,800	......
30	....	3	.....	250	1,550	......

Office Equipment

18

Date	Item	Post. Ref.	Debit	Credit	Balance Debit	Balance Credit
19—						
Sept. 1	....	1	6,200	......	6,200	......
4	....	1	2,000	......	8,200	......

Accumulated Depreciation

19

Date	Item	Post. Ref.	Debit	Credit	Balance Debit	Balance Credit
19—						
Sept. 30	....	3	.....	750	....	750

Accounts Payable

21

Date	Item	Post. Ref.	Debit	Credit	Balance Debit	Balance Credit
19—						
Sept. 4	....	1	.....	2,000	....	2,000
11	....	1	1,100	......	....	900

Salaries Payable

22

Date	Item	Post. Ref.	Debit	Credit	Balance Debit	Balance Credit
19—						
Sept. 30	....	3	.....	100	....	100

Unearned Fees

23

Date	Item	Post. Ref.	Debit	Credit	Balance Debit	Balance Credit
19—						
Sept. 4	....	1	.....	2,500	....	2,500
30	....	3	1,400	......	....	1,100

Comp. Prob. 1, Continued

Lance Fox, Capital   31

Date	Item	Post. Ref.	Debit	Credit	Balance Debit	Balance Credit
19—						
Sept. 1	....	1	.....	14,450	....	14,450
30	....	4	.....	5,235	....	19,685
30	....	4	1,200	......	....	18,485

Lance Fox, Drawing   32

Date	Item	Post. Ref.	Debit	Credit	Balance Debit	Balance Credit
19—						
Sept. 30	....	2	1,200	......	1,200	......
30	....	4	.....	1,200	—	—

Income Summary   33

Date	Item	Post. Ref.	Debit	Credit	Balance Debit	Balance Credit
19—						
Sept. 30	....	4	.....	9,000	....	9,000
30	....	4	3,765	......	....	5,235
30	....	4	5,235	......	—	—

Fees Earned   41

Date	Item	Post. Ref.	Debit	Credit	Balance Debit	Balance Credit
19—						
Sept. 12	....	1	.....	1,200	....	1,200
17	....	2	.....	2,100	....	3,300
20	....	2	.....	1,100	....	4,400
24	....	2	.....	1,850	....	6,250
30	....	2		850	....	7,100
30	....	2		500	....	7,600
30	....	3	.....	1,400	....	9,000
30	....	4	9,000	......	—	—

Salary Expense   51

Date	Item	Post. Ref.	Debit	Credit	Balance Debit	Balance Credit
19—						
Sept. 13	....	1	400	......	400	......
27	....	2	400	......	800	......
30	....	3	100	......	900	......
30	....	4	.....	900	—	—

Comp. Prob. 1, Continued

Rent Expense   52

Date	Item	Post. Ref.	Debit	Credit	Balance Debit	Balance Credit
19—						
Sept. 30	....	3	800	.....	800	.....
30	....	4	.....	800	—	—

Supplies Expense   53

Date	Item	Post. Ref.	Debit	Credit	Balance Debit	Balance Credit
19—						
Sept. 30	....	3	780	.....	780	.....
30	....	4	.....	780	—	—

Depreciation Expense   54

Date	Item	Post. Ref.	Debit	Credit	Balance Debit	Balance Credit
19—						
Sept. 30	....	3	750	.....	750	.....
30	....	4	.....	750	—	—

Insurance Expense   55

Date	Item	Post. Ref.	Debit	Credit	Balance Debit	Balance Credit
19—						
Sept. 30	....	3	250	.....	250	.....
30	....	4	.....	250	—	—

Miscellaneous Expense   59

Date	Item	Post. Ref.	Debit	Credit	Balance Debit	Balance Credit
19—						
Sept. 9	....	1	80	.....	80	.....
30	....	2	65	.....	145	.....
30	....	2	140	.....	285	.....
30	....	4	.....	285	—	—

3.

Comp. Prob. 1, Continued

FOX CONSULTING
Work Sheet
For Month Ended September 30, 19—

Account Title	Trial Balance Dr.	Trial Balance Cr.	Adjustments Dr.	Adjustments Cr.	Adjusted Trial Balance Dr.	Adjusted Trial Balance Cr.	Income Statement Dr.	Income Statement Cr.	Balance Sheet Dr.	Balance Sheet Cr.
Cash	6,565				6,565				6,565	
Accounts Receivable	2,000				2,000				2,000	
Supplies	2,200			(b) 780	1,420				1,420	
Prepaid Rent	2,400			(e) 800	1,600				1,600	
Prepaid Insurance	1,800			(a) 250	1,550				1,550	
Office Equipment	8,200				8,200				8,200	
Accumulated Depr.				(c) 750		750				750
Accounts Payable		900				900				900
Salaries Payable				(d) 100		100				100
Unearned Fees		2,500	(f) 1,400			1,100				1,100
Lance Fox, Capital		14,450				14,450				14,450
Lance Fox, Drawing	1,200				1,200				1,200	
Fees Earned		7,600		(f) 1,400		9,000		9,000		
Salary Expense	800		(d) 100		900		900			
Rent Expense			(e) 800		800		800			
Supplies Expense			(b) 780		780		780			
Depreciation Expense			(c) 750		750		750			
Insurance Expense			(a) 250		250		250			
Miscellaneous Expense	285				285		285			
	25,450	25,450	4,080	4,080	26,300	26,300	3,765	9,000	22,535	17,300
Net Income							5,235			5,235
							9,000	9,000	22,535	22,535

Comp. Prob. 1, Continued

4.

FOX CONSULTING
Income Statement
For Month Ended September 30, 19—

Fees earned		$9,000
Operating expenses:		
Salary expense	$900	
Rent expense..	800	
Supplies expense	780	
Depreciation expense	750	
Insurance expense	250	
Miscellaneous expense.................................	285	
Total operating expenses................................		3,765
Net income		$5,235

FOX CONSULTING
Statement of Owner's Equity
For Month Ended September 30, 19—

Investment during month....................................		$14,450
Net income for the month	$5,235	
Less withdrawals..	1,200	
Increase in owner's equity		4,035
Lance Fox, capital, September 30, 19—		$18,485

Comp. Prob. 1, Continued

FOX CONSULTING
Balance Sheet
September 30, 19—

Assets

Current assets:		
Cash	$6,565	
Accounts receivable	2,000	
Supplies	1,420	
Prepaid rent	1,600	
Prepaid insurance.	1,550	
Total current assets		$13,135
Plant assets:		
Office equipment	$8,200	
Less accumulated depreciation	750	7,450
Total assets		$20,585

Liabilities

Current liabilities:		
Accounts payable.	$ 900	
Salaries payable	100	
Unearned fees	1,100	
Total liabilities.		$ 2,100

Owner's Equity

Lance Fox, capital		18,485
Total liabilities and owner's equity.		$20,585

5.

Adjusting Entries	Post. Ref.	Debit	Credit
19—			
Sept. 30 Insurance Expense	55	250	
Prepaid Insurance	16		250
30 Supplies Expense	53	780	
Supplies.	14		780
30 Depreciation Expense	54	750	
Accumulated Depreciation.	19		750
30 Salary Expense	51	100	
Salaries Payable.	22		100
30 Rent Expense.	52	800	
Prepaid Rent.	15		800
30 Unearned Fees.	23	1,400	
Fees Earned	41		1,400

Comp. Prob. 1, Concluded

6.

Closing Entries	Post. Ref.	Debit	Credit
19—			
Sept. 30 Fees Earned	41	9,000	
Income Summary	33		9,000
30 Income Summary	33	3,765	
Salary Expense	51		900
Rent Expense	52		800
Supplies Expense	53		780
Depreciation Expense	54		750
Insurance Expense	55		250
Miscellaneous Expense	59		285
30 Income Summary	33	5,235	
Lance Fox, Capital	31		5,235
30 Lance Fox, Capital	31	1,200	
Lance Fox, Drawing	32		1,200

7.

FOX CONSULTING
Post-Closing Trial Balance
September 30, 19—

	Debit	Credit
Cash	6,565	
Accounts Receivable	2,000	
Supplies	1,420	
Prepaid Rent	1,600	
Prepaid Insurance	1,550	
Office Equipment	8,200	
Accumulated Depreciation		750
Accounts Payable		900
Salaries Payable		100
Unearned Fees		1,100
Lance Fox, Capital		18,485
Totals	21,335	21,335

CHAPTER 5

DISCUSSION QUESTIONS

1. Merchandising enterprises acquire merchandise for resale to customers. It is the selling of merchandise, instead of a service, that makes the activities of a merchandising enterprise different from the activities of a service enterprise.

2. Gross profit is the excess of (net) sales over cost of merchandise sold.

3. $75,000 ($250,000 − $175,000)

4. $260,000 ($410,000 − $150,000)

5. Yes. Gross profit is the excess of (net) sales over cost of merchandise sold. A net loss arises when operating expenses exceed gross profit. Therefore an enterprise can earn a gross profit but incur operating expenses in excess of this gross profit and end up with a net loss.

6. Sales

7. Sales to customers who use bank credit cards are generally treated as cash sales. The credit card invoices representing these sales are deposited by the seller directly into the bank, along with the currency and checks received from customers. Sales made by the use of nonbank credit cards generally must be reported periodically to the card company before cash is received. Therefore, such sales create a receivable with the card company. In both cases, any service or collection fees charged by the bank or card company are debited to expense accounts.

8. The date of sale as shown by the date of the invoice or bill.

9. June 16

10. a. 1% discount allowed if paid within ten days of date of invoice; entire amount of invoice due within 60 days of date of invoice.
    b. Payment due within 30 days of date of invoice.
    c. Payment due by the end of the month in which the sale was made.

11. Sales Discounts

12. A credit memorandum issued by the seller of merchandise indicates the amount for which the buyer's account is to be credited (credit to Accounts Receivable) and the reason for the sales return or allowance.

13. Sales Returns and Allowances
    Sales Discounts

14. a. $4,950
    b. Sales Returns and Allowances .. 5,000
       Sales Discounts   50
       Cash.   4,950

15. 1. Sold merchandise on account, $10,000.
    2. Granted an allowance or accepted a return of merchandise, $500.
    3. Received balance due within discount period, $9,310. (Sale of $10,000, less return or allowance of $500, less discount of $190 [2% × $9,500].)

16. a. At the time of sale
    b. $200
    c. $212
    d. Sales Tax Payable

17. Purchases

18. Purchases Discounts

19. a. (Store) Equipment
    b. (Store) Equipment
    c. Purchases
    d. Office Supplies

20. a. $1,485 ($2,000 − $500 − $15 [$1,500 × 1%])
    b. Purchases Returns and Allowances
       Purchases Discounts

21. a. (1) Purchased merchandise on account, $5,000.
       (2) Paid transportation costs, $100.
       (3) An allowance or return of merchandise was granted by the creditor, $1,000.
       (4) Paid the balance due within the discount period, deducting discount, $80, and paying cash, $3,920.
    b. 2% ($80/$4,000)

22. A debit memorandum issued by the purchaser of merchandise indicates the amount for which the seller's account is to be debited (debit to Accounts Payable) and the reason for the purchases return or allowance.

23. a. The buyer
    b. The seller

24. a. $10,000
    b. $10,250

c. $100 (1% × $10,000)
d. $10,150

25. Offer B is lower than offer A. Details are as follows:

	A	B
List price	$5,000	$5,200
Less discount	100	52
	$4,900	$5,148
Transportation	275	
	$5,175	$5,148

26. a. $583,000 ($610,000 − $7,000 − $20,000)
b. $588,500 ($583,000 + $5,500)

27. a. debit
b. credit
c. debit
d. debit
e. credit
f. credit
g. debit

28. Periodic inventory system

29. Some companies charge gasoline station owners a processing or collection fee of 3 or 4 percent for processing credit card sales. As a result, it is often more economical for a gas station owner to offer cash discounts to induce customers to pay in cash rather than use credit cards.

ETHICS DISCUSSION CASE *Standards of Ethical Conduct for Management Accountants* requires management accountants to perform in a competent manner and to comply with relevant laws, regulations, and technical standards. If Kay Williams intentionally subtracted the discount with knowledge that the discount period had expired, she would have behaved in an unethical manner. Such behavior could eventually jeopardize Katz Company's buyer/supplier relationship with C. L. Allan Co.

EXERCISES

Ex. 5-1 a. $85,000 ($200,000 + $375,000 − $490,000)

b. No. If operating expenses are less than gross profit, there will be a net income. On the other hand, if operating expenses exceed gross profit, there will be a net loss.

Ex. 5-2

BRIDGES COMPANY
Income Statement
For Year Ended December 31, 19—

Sales	$210,000
Cost of merchandise sold	142,500
Gross profit	$ 67,500
Operating expenses	50,000
Net income	$ 17,500

Ex. 5-3 a. $9,500
b. $7,840
c. $4,950
d. $3,951
e. $1,275

Ex. 5-4
a.	Cash	12,500	
	Sales		12,500
b.	Accounts Receivable	10,000	
	Sales		10,000
c.	Cash	4,750	
	Sales		4,750
d.	Accounts Receivable	3,100	
	Sales		3,100
e.	Service Fee Expense	250	
	Cash		250
f.	Cash	2,910	
	Credit Card Collection Expense	190	
	Accounts Receivable		3,100

Ex. 5-5
a.	Accounts Receivable	5,300	
	Sales		5,000
	Sales Tax Payable		300
b.	Sales Tax Payable	1,650	
	Cash		1,650

Ex. 5-6 Yes. The accountant's method was acceptable, but the accounts would not reveal the amount of sales returns and allowances.

Ex. 5-7 May 5 Accounts Receivable..................... 10,000
                       Sales....................................   10,000

              5 Accounts Receivable.....................   120
                       Cash......................................   120

             10 Sales Returns and Allowances........... 1,000
                       Accounts Receivable...................   1,000
             15 Cash.................................... 8,940
                 Sales Discounts   180
                       Accounts Receivable...................   9,120

Ex. 5-8 a. Accounts Receivable........................ 7,500
                       Sales....................................   7,500

                Accounts Receivable........................   250
                       Cash......................................   250

        b. Sales Returns and Allowances.................   500
                 Accounts Receivable   500

        c. Cash... 7,180
            Sales Discounts   70
                 Accounts Receivable........................   7,250

Ex. 5-9 a. Purchases 7,500
            Transportation In   250
                 Accounts Payable   7,750

        b. Accounts Payable.............................   500
                 Purchases Returns and Allowances   500

        c. Accounts Payable............................. 7,250
                 Purchases Discounts...........................   70
                 Cash   7,180

Ex. 5-10 a. Purchases 6,000
             Transportation In   150
                 Accounts Payable.............................   6,150

        b. Accounts Payable.............................   500
                 Purchases Returns and Allowances   500

        c. Accounts Payable............................. 5,650
                 Purchases Discounts   55
                 Cash..   5,595

Ex. 5-11 a. Purchases 10,000
                  Accounts Payable   10,000

      b. Accounts Payable 10,000
                  Purchases Discounts   100
                  Cash   9,900

      ***c.** Accounts Payable   990
                  Purchases Discounts   10
                  Purchases Returns and Allowances   1,000

      d. Purchases   800
                  Purchases Discounts   8
                  Accounts Payable   792

      e. Cash   198
                  Accounts Payable   198

Note: The debit of $990 to Accounts Payable in entry (c) is the amount of
cash refund due from Craig Co. The $10 debit to Purchases Discounts reduces
the $100 discount recorded earlier to $90, which is equivalent to 1% of the net
purchase of $9,000 ($10,000 − $1,000). The credit of $792 to Accounts Payable
in entry (d) reduces the debit balance in the account to $198, which is the
amount of the cash refund in entry (e). The two sets of alternative entries below yield the same final results. For these alternatives, however, note that
the balances of the accounts receivable (accounts payable) and the purchases
discounts accounts are slightly inaccurate during the interim period.

Alternative One:

      c. Accounts Receivable 1,000
                  Purchases Returns and Allowances   1,000

      d. Purchases   800
                  Accounts Receivable   800

      e. Cash   198
                  Purchases Discounts   2
                  Accounts Receivable   200

Alternative Two:

      c. Accounts Payable 1,000
                  Purchases Returns and Allowances   1,000

      d. Purchases   800
                  Accounts Payable   800

      e. Cash   198
                  Purchases Discounts   2
                  Accounts Payable   200

Ex. 5-12 a. Purchases..................................... 15,000
        Accounts Payable........................... 15,000

    b. Accounts Receivable........................ 3,150
        Sales.................................... 3,000
        Sales Tax Payable......................... 150

    c. Accounts Payable........................... 15,000
        Purchases Discounts....................... 150
        Cash.................................... 14,850

    d. Sales Tax Payable.......................... 2,100
        Cash.................................... 2,100

Ex. 5-13 a. August 11
    b. August 31
    c. Discount of 1% on $15,000 $150.00
       Interest for 20 days at rate of 10% on
          $14,850 ($15,000 − $150)   82.50
       Savings affected by borrowing $ 67.50

Ex. 5-14 a. Purchases discounts, purchases returns and allowances
    b. Transportation in
    c. Merchandise available for sale
    d. Merchandise inventory (ending)

Ex. 5-15

Balance Sheet Accounts	Income Statement Accounts

Balance Sheet Accounts

100 Assets
   110 Cash
   111 Notes Receivable
   112 Accounts Receivable
   113 Interest Receivable
   114 Merchandise Inventory
   115 Store Supplies
   116 Office Supplies
   117 Prepaid Insurance
   120 Land
   123 Store Equipment
   124 Accumulated
        Depreciation—
        Store Equipment
   125 Office Equipment
   126 Accumulated
        Depreciation—
        Office Equipment

200 Liabilities
   210 Accounts Payable
   211 Salaries Payable
   212 Notes Payable

300 Owner's Equity
   310 C.C. Kline, Capital
   311 C.C. Kline, Drawing
   312 Income Summary

Income Statement Accounts

400 Revenues
   410 Sales
   411 Sales Returns and
        Allowances
   412 Sales Discounts

500 Expenses
   510 Purchases
   511 Purchases Returns and
        Allowances
   512 Purchases Discounts
   513 Transportation In
   520 Sales Salaries Expense
   521 Advertising Expense
   522 Depreciation Expense—
        Store Equipment
   523 Store Supplies Expense
   529 Miscellaneous Selling
        Expenses
   530 Office Salaries Expense
   531 Rent Expense
   532 Depreciation Expense—
        Office Equipment
   533 Insurance Expense
   534 Office Supplies Expense
   539 Miscellaneous
        Administrative Expense

600 Other Income
   610 Interest Income

700 Other Expense
   710 Interest Expense

Note: The order of some of the accounts within subclassifications is some-what arbitrary, as in accounts 115–117 and accounts 521–523. In a new enterprise, the order of magnitude of balances in such accounts is not determinable in advance. The magnitude may also vary from period to period.

WHAT'S WRONG WITH THIS?

1. The schedule should begin with the January 1, not the December 31 merchandise inventory.
2. Purchases returns and allowances and purchases discounts should be deducted from (not added to) purchases.

WHAT'S WRONG?, Concluded

3. The result of subtracting purchases returns and allowances and purchases discounts from purchases should be labeled "net purchases."
4. Transportation in should be added to net purchases to yield cost of merchandise purchased.
5. The merchandise inventory at December 31 should be deducted from merchandise available for sale to yield cost of merchandise sold.

A correct cost of merchandise sold section is as follows:

Cost of merchandise sold:

Merchandise inventory, January 1, 19—			$111,300
Purchases		$500,000	
Less: Purchases returns and allowances....	$12,500		
Purchases discounts.................	6,500	19,000	
Net purchases		$481,000	
Add transportation in.....................		2,400	
Cost of merchandise purchased..........			483,400
Merchandise available for sale.............			$594,700
Less merchandise inventory, December 31, 19—			105,000
Cost of merchandise sold			$489,700

PROBLEMS

Prob. 5-1A

July	1	Accounts Receivable	4,000	
		Sales		4,000
	1	Transportation Out	95	
		Cash		95
	2	Cash	630	
		Sales		600
		Sales Tax Payable		30
	3	Accounts Receivable	2,500	
		Sales		2,500
	5	Cash	1,260	
		Sales		1,200
		Sales Tax Payable		60
	8	Accounts Receivable	1,500	
		Sales		1,500

Prob. 5-1A, Concluded

11	Cash	3,920	
	Sales Discount	80	
	Accounts Receivable		4,000
12	Accounts Receivable	3,500	
	Sales		3,500
13	Accounts Receivable	6,500	
	Sales		6,500
15	Sales Returns and Allowances	500	
	Accounts Receivable		500
16	Accounts Receivable	10,000	
	Sales		10,000
18	Accounts Receivable	7,500	
	Sales		7,500
18	Accounts Receivable	85	
	Cash		85
23	Cash	5,940	
	Sales Discounts	60	
	Accounts Receivable		6,000
24	Sales Returns and Allowances	250	
	Accounts Receivable		250
26	Cash	9,410	
	Credit Card Collection Expense	590	
	Accounts Receivable		10,000
28	Cash	7,510	
	Sales Discounts	75	
	Accounts Receivable		7,585
30	Cash	4,000	
	Accounts Receivable		4,000
31	Transportation Out	770	
	Cash		770
Aug. 4	Credit Card Collection Expense	480	
	Cash		480
10	Sales Tax Payable	875	
	Cash		875
15	Cash	9,750	
	Accounts Receivable		9,750

Prob. 5-2A

July	1	Purchases	4,800	
		Accounts Payable		4,800
	3	Purchases	10,000	
		Transportation In	200	
		Accounts Payable		10,200
	5	Purchases	5,000	
		Accounts Payable		5,000
	8	Accounts Payable	1,000	
		Purchases Returns and Allowances		1,000
	13	Accounts Payable	10,200	
		Purchases Discounts		100
		Cash		10,100
	15	Accounts Payable	4,000	
		Purchases Discounts		80
		Cash		3,920
	18	Purchases	8,250	
		Accounts Payable		8,250
	18	Transportation In	220	
		Cash		220
	19	Purchases	4,500	
		Accounts Payable		4,500
	29	Accounts Payable	4,500	
		Purchases Discounts		90
		Cash		4,410
	31	Accounts Payable	4,800	
		Cash		4,800
	31	Accounts Payable	8,250	
		Cash		8,250

Prob. 5-3A

1.

Oct.	4	Accounts Receivable	10,000	
		Sales		10,000
	4	Transportation Out	600	
		Cash		600
	10	Accounts Receivable	15,000	
		Sales		15,000
	12	Sales Returns and Allowances	2,000	
		Accounts Receivable		2,000

Prob. 5-3A, Concluded

18	Accounts Receivable	18,000	
	Sales		18,000
18	Accounts Receivable	1,500	
	Cash		1,500
19	Cash	7,920	
	Sales Discounts	80	
	Accounts Receivable		8,000
28	Cash	19,140	
	Sales Discounts	360	
	Accounts Receivable		19,500
31	Cash	15,000	
	Accounts Receivable		15,000

2.

Oct.	4	Purchases	10,000	
		Accounts Payable		10,000
	10	Purchases	15,000	
		Accounts Payable		15,000
	12	Accounts Payable	2,000	
		Purchases Returns and Allowances		2,000
	14	Transportation In	1,200	
		Cash		1,200
	18	Purchases	18,000	
		Transportation In	1,500	
		Accounts Payable		19,500
	19	Accounts Payable	8,000	
		Purchases Discounts		80
		Cash		7,920
	28	Accounts Payable	19,500	
		Purchases Discounts		360
		Cash		19,140
	31	Accounts Payable	15,000	
		Cash		15,000

Prob. 5-4A

Nov.	3	Office Supplies	720	
		Cash		720
	5	Purchases	12,500	
		Accounts Payable		12,500
	6	Cash	2,950	
		Sales		2,950

Prob. 5-4A, Concluded

		Debit	Credit
7	Purchases...............................	6,400	
	Transportation In.......................	190	
	Accounts Payable.......................		6,590
7	Accounts Payable	2,500	
	Purchases Returns and Allowances		2,500
11	Accounts Receivable.......................	1,800	
	Sales		1,800
15	Accounts Payable	10,000	
	Cash...............................		9,900
	Purchases Discounts.....................		100
16	Accounts Receivable.......................	3,850	
	Sales		3,850
17	Accounts Payable	6,590	
	Cash...............................		6,462
	Purchases Discounts.....................		128
19	Purchases...............................	3,500	
	Cash...............................		3,500
21	Cash....................................	1,782	
	Sales Discounts	18	
	Accounts Receivable.......................		1,800
24	Accounts Receivable.......................	4,200	
	Sales		4,200
28	Cash....................................	3,660	
	Credit Card Collection Expense..................	190	
	Accounts Receivable.......................		3,850
30	Sales Returns and Allowances	2,700	
	Accounts Receivable.......................		2,700

Prob. 5-5A

2. and 3. JOURNAL Pages 12, 13 and 14

Date		Description	Post. Ref.	Debit	Credit
19—					
July	1	Rent Expense.............................	60	2,500	
		Cash	11		2,500
	3	Purchases	51	11,200	
		Accounts Payable	21		11,200
	5	Purchases	51	18,600	
		Accounts Payable	21		18,600

Prob. 5-5A, Continued

JOURNAL   **Pages 12, 13 and 14**

Date	Description	Post. Ref.	Debit	Credit
8	Accounts Receivable	12	12,300	
	Sales	41		12,300
9	Transportation In	54	450	
	Cash	11		450
10	Cash	11	14,750	
	Sales Discounts.	43	250	
	Accounts Receivable	12		15,000
11	Accounts Payable	21	16,980	
	Cash	11		16,700
	Purchases Discounts	53		280
14	Cash	11	9,500	
	Sales	41		9,500
15	Sales Returns and Allowances	42	800	
	Accounts Receivable	12		800
16	Sales Salaries Expense	55	3,400	
	Office Salaries Expense	59	1,100	
	Cash	11		4,500
17	Accounts Payable	21	12,950	
	Cash	11		12,750
	Purchases Discounts	53		200
18	Cash	11	9,500	
	Sales Discounts.	43	120	
	Accounts Receivable	12		9,620
21	Purchases	51	15,200	
	Accounts Payable	21		15,200
22	Advertising Expense	56	3,000	
	Cash	11		3,000
23	Cash	11	8,100	
	Sales	41		8,100
24	Accounts Payable	21	6,800	
	Purchases Returns and Allowances	52		6,800
25	Cash	11	4,600	
	Sales	41		4,600

Prob. 5-5A, Continued

| | | JOURNAL | | Pages 12, 13 and 14 | |

Date	Description	Post. Ref.	Debit	Credit
28	Accounts Receivable.....................	12	27,300	
	Sales......................................	41		27,300
28	Sales Returns and Allowances............	42	350	
	Cash......................................	11		350
29	Sales Salaries Expense...................	55	2,800	
	Office Salaries Expense	59	1,100	
	Cash......................................	11		3,900
30	Accounts Payable.........................	21	10,900	
	Cash......................................	11		10,900
31	Cash......................................	11	12,500	
	Accounts Receivable	12		12,500

1. and 3.

Cash

11

Date	Item	Post. Ref.	Dr.	Cr.	Balance Dr.	Balance Cr.
19—						
July 1	Balance..................	√	......	......	15,540	......
1	....	12	......	2,500	......	......
9	....	12	......	450	......	......
10	....	12	14,750	......	......	......
11	....	12	......	16,700	......	......
14	....	12	9,500	......	......	......
16	....	12	......	4,500	......	......
17	....	13	......	12,750	......	......
18	....	13	9,500	......	......	......
22	....	13	......	3,000	......	......
23	....	13	8,100	......	......	......
25	....	13	4,600	......	......	......
28	....	13	......	350	......	......
29	....	13	......	3,900	......	......
30	....	14	......	10,900	......	......
31	....	14	12,500	......	19,440	......

Prob. 5-5A, Continued

Accounts Receivable 12

Date	Item	Post. Ref.	Dr.	Cr.	Balance Dr.	Cr.
19—						
July 1	Balance...................	√	......	......	31,800	......
8	....	12	12,300	......	......	......
10	....	12	......	15,000	......	......
15	....	12	......	800	......	......
18	....	13	......	9,620	......	......
28	....	13	27,300	......	......	......
31	....	14	......	12,500	33,480	......

Merchandise Inventory 13

Date	Item	Post. Ref.	Dr.	Cr.	Balance Dr.	Cr.
19—						
July 1	Balance...................	√	......	......	82,600	......

Prepaid Insurance 14

Date	Item	Post. Ref.	Dr.	Cr.	Balance Dr.	Cr.
19—						
July 1	Balance...................	√	......	......	2,500	......

Store Supplies 15

Date	Item	Post. Ref.	Dr.	Cr.	Balance Dr.	Cr.
19—						
July 1	Balance...................	√	......	......	1,700	......

Accounts Payable 21

Date	Item	Post. Ref.	Dr.	Cr.	Balance Dr.	Cr.
19—						
July 1	Balance...................	√	......	......	......	28,300
3	....	12	......	11,200	......	......
5	....	12	......	18,600	......	......
11	....	12	16,980	......	......	......
17	....	13	12,950	......	......	......
21	....	13	......	15,200	......	......
24	....	13	6,800	......	......	......
30	....	14	10,900	......	......	25,670

Prob. 5-5A, Continued

C. Raleigh, Capital   31

Date	Item	Post. Ref.	Dr.	Cr.	Balance Dr.	Balance Cr.
19—						
July 1 Balance..................		√	......	......	......	105,840

C. Raleigh, Drawing   32

Income Summary   33

Sales   41

Date	Item	Post. Ref.	Dr.	Cr.	Balance Dr.	Balance Cr.
19—						
July 8		12	......	12,300	......	......
14		12	......	9,500	......	......
23		13	......	8,100	......	......
25		13	......	4,600	......	......
28		13	......	27,300	......	61,800

Sales Returns and Allowances   42

Date	Item	Post. Ref.	Dr.	Cr.	Balance Dr.	Balance Cr.
19—						
July 15		12	800	......	......	......
28		13	350	......	1,150	......

Sales Discounts   43

Date	Item	Post. Ref.	Dr.	Cr.	Balance Dr.	Balance Cr.
19—						
July 10		12	250	......	......	......
18		13	120	......	370	......

Purchases   51

Date	Item	Post. Ref.	Dr.	Cr.	Balance Dr.	Balance Cr.
19—						
July 3		12	11,200	......	......	......
5		12	18,600	......	......	......
21		13	15,200	......	45,000	......

Purchases Returns and Allowances   52

Date	Item	Post. Ref.	Dr.	Cr.	Balance Dr.	Balance Cr.
19—						
July 24		13	......	6,800	......	6,800

Prob. 5-5A, Continued

Purchases Discounts   53

Date	Item	Post. Ref.	Dr.	Cr.	Balance Dr.	Balance Cr.
19—						
July 11	....	12	......	280	......	......
17	....	13	......	200	......	480

Transportation In   54

Date	Item	Post. Ref.	Dr.	Cr.	Balance Dr.	Balance Cr.
19—						
July 9	....	12	450	......	450	......

Sales Salaries Expense   55

Date	Item	Post. Ref.	Dr.	Cr.	Balance Dr.	Balance Cr.
19—						
July 16	....	12	3,400	......	......	......
29	....	13	2,800	......	6,200	......

Advertising Expense   56

Date	Item	Post. Ref.	Dr.	Cr.	Balance Dr.	Balance Cr.
19—						
July 22	....	13	3,000	......	3,000	......

Store Supplies Expense   57

Miscellaneous Selling Expense   58

Office Salaries Expense   59

Date	Item	Post. Ref.	Dr.	Cr.	Balance Dr.	Balance Cr.
19—						
July 16	....	12	1,100	......	......	......
29	....	13	1,100	......	2,200	......

Rent Expense   60

Date	Item	Post. Ref.	Dr.	Cr.	Balance Dr.	Balance Cr.
19—						
July 1	....	12	2,500	......	2,500	......

Insurance Expense   61

Miscellaneous Administrative Expense   62

Prob. 5-5A, Concluded

4.

RALEIGH COMPANY
Trial Balance
July 31, 19—

Cash...	19,440	
Accounts Receivable.....................................	33,480	
Merchandise Inventory..................................	82,600	
Prepaid Insurance.......................................	2,500	
Store Supplies	1,700	
Accounts Payable..		25,670
C. Raleigh, Capital		105,840
C. Raleigh, Drawing.....................................		
Income Summary...		
Sales		61,800
Sales Returns and Allowances........................	1,150	
Sales Discounts	370	
Purchases...	45,000	
Purchases Returns and Allowances		6,800
Purchases Discounts....................................		480
Transportation In..	450	
Sales Salaries Expense.................................	6,200	
Advertising Expense.....................................	3,000	
Store Supplies Expense.................................		
Miscellaneous Selling Expense		
Office Salaries Expense.................................	2,200	
Rent Expense	2,500	
Insurance Expense.......................................		
Miscellaneous Administrative Expense................		
	200,590	200,590

Prob. 5-6A

1. Cost of merchandise sold:

Merchandise inventory, May 1, 1993................			$115,000
Purchases...................		$550,000	
Less: Purchases returns and allowances...........	$4,500		
Purchases discounts....	2,950	7,450	
Net purchases................		$542,550	
Add transportation in........		3,950	
Cost of merchandise purchased...............		546,500	
Merchandise available for sale		$661,500	
Less merchandise inventory, April 30, 1994..............		125,000	
Cost of merchandise sold...			$536,500

2. $134,125 ($670,625 − $536,500)
3. 20% ($134,125/$670,625)
4. The gross profit would be overstated by $20,000 because the cost of merchandise sold would be understated by $20,000.

Prob. 5-1B

May	1	Accounts Receivable............................	12,000	
		Sales..		12,000
	1	Transportation Out..............................	225	
		Cash..		225
	2	Cash..	742	
		Sales..		700
		Sales Tax Payable.............................		42
	3	Accounts Receivable............................	2,500	
		Sales..		2,500
	5	Cash..	1,272	
		Sales..		1,200
		Sales Tax Payable.............................		72
	8	Accounts Receivable............................	4,500	
		Sales..		4,500
	11	Cash..	11,880	
		Sales Discount................................	120	
		Accounts Receivable............................		12,000
	12	Accounts Receivable............................	2,500	
		Sales..		2,500

Prob. 5-1B, Concluded

13	Accounts Receivable	6,500	
	Sales		6,500
15	Sales Returns and Allowances	500	
	Accounts Receivable		500
16	Accounts Receivable	5,000	
	Sales		5,000
18	Accounts Receivable	7,500	
	Sales		7,500
18	Accounts Receivable	110	
	Cash		110
23	Cash	5,940	
	Sales Discounts	60	
	Accounts Receivable		6,000
24	Sales Returns and Allowances	250	
	Accounts Receivable		250
26	Cash	7,410	
	Credit Card Collection Expense	590	
	Accounts Receivable		8,000
28	Cash	7,535	
	Sales Discounts	75	
	Accounts Receivable		7,610
30	Cash	7,000	
	Accounts Receivable		7,000
31	Transportation Out	670	
	Cash		670
June 4	Credit Card Collection Expense	380	
	Cash		380
10	Sales Tax Payable	375	
	Cash		375
15	Cash	4,750	
	Accounts Receivable		4,750

Prob. 5-2B

May 1	Purchases	5,750	
	Accounts Payable		5,750
3	Purchases	10,000	
	Transportation In	250	
	Accounts Payable		10,250
5	Purchases	5,000	
	Accounts Payable		5,000
8	Accounts Payable	1,000	
	Purchases Returns and Allowances		1,000

Prob. 5-2B, Concluded

13	Accounts Payable	10,250	
	Purchases Discounts		200
	Cash		10,050
15	Accounts Payable	4,000	
	Purchases Discounts		40
	Cash		3,960
18	Purchases	8,250	
	Accounts Payable		8,250
18	Transportation In	220	
	Cash		220
19	Purchases	7,500	
	Accounts Payable		7,500
29	Accounts Payable	7,500	
	Purchases Discounts		150
	Cash		7,350
31	Accounts Payable	5,750	
	Cash		5,750
31	Accounts Payable	8,250	
	Cash		8,250

Prob. 5-3B

1.

April 3	Accounts Receivable	12,500	
	Sales		12,500
3	Accounts Receivable	600	
	Cash		600
8	Accounts Receivable	16,000	
	Sales		16,000
8	Transportation Out	800	
	Cash		800
11	Sales Returns and Allowances	4,000	
	Accounts Receivable		4,000
13	Cash	12,850	
	Sales Discounts	250	
	Accounts Receivable		13,100
23	Cash	11,880	
	Sales Discounts	120	
	Accounts Receivable		12,000
24	Accounts Receivable	8,000	
	Sales		8,000
30	Cash	8,000	
	Accounts Receivable		8,000

Prob. 5-3B, Concluded

2.

April	3	Purchases....................................	12,500	
		Transportation In..............................	600	
		Accounts Payable		13,100
	8	Purchases....................................	16,000	
		Accounts Payable		16,000
	11	Accounts Payable	4,000	
		Purchases Returns and Allowances.............		4,000
	13	Accounts Payable	13,100	
		Purchases Discounts...........................		250
		Cash..		12,850
	23	Accounts Payable	12,000	
		Purchases Discounts...........................		120
		Cash..		11,880
	24	Purchases....................................	8,000	
		Accounts Payable		8,000
	27	Transportation In..............................	300	
		Cash..		300
	30	Accounts Payable	8,000	
		Cash..		8,000

Prob. 5-4B

May	3	Purchases	4,000	
		Transportation In	120	
		Accounts Payable.............................		4,120
	5	Purchases	8,500	
		Accounts Payable.............................		8,500
	6	Accounts Receivable............................	2,800	
		Sales..		2,800
	8	Office Supplies	650	
		Cash		650
	10	Accounts Payable..............................	1,300	
		Purchases Returns and Allowances		1,300
	13	Accounts Payable..............................	4,120	
		Cash		4,040
		Purchases Discounts		80
	14	Purchases	10,500	
		Cash		10,500
	15	Accounts Payable..............................	7,200	
		Cash		7,128
		Purchases Discounts		72

Prob. 5-4B, Concluded

			Debit	Credit
16	Cash		2,744	
	Sales Discounts		56	
	Accounts Receivable			2,800
19	Accounts Receivable		2,450	
	Sales			2,450
22	Accounts Receivable		3,480	
	Sales			3,480
24	Cash		4,350	
	Sales			4,350
25	Sales Returns and Allowances		1,480	
	Accounts Receivable			1,480
31	Cash		2,310	
	Credit Card Collection Expense		140	
	Accounts Receivable			2,450

Prob. 5-5B

2. and 3.   JOURNAL   Pages 12, 13 and 14

Date	Description	Post. Ref.	Debit	Credit
19—				
June 1	Rent Expense	60	3,500	
	Cash	11		3,500
2	Purchases	51	12,500	
	Accounts Payable	21		12,500
4	Purchases	51	20,100	
	Accounts Payable	21		20,100
7	Accounts Receivable	12	16,000	
	Sales	41		16,000
9	Transportation In	54	525	
	Cash	11		525
10	Cash	11	9,800	
	Sales Discounts	43	200	
	Accounts Receivable	12		10,000
11	Accounts Payable	21	16,980	
	Cash	11		16,700
	Purchases Discounts	53		280
14	Cash	11	9,500	
	Sales	41		9,500
15	Sales Returns and Allowances	42	800	
	Accounts Receivable	12		800

Prob. 5-5B, Continued

		JOURNAL		Pages 12, 13 and 14	

Date	Description	Post. Ref.	Debit	Credit
16	Sales Salaries Expense	55	3,950	
	Office Salaries Expense..................	59	1,280	
	Cash..................................	11		5,230
17	Accounts Payable	21	13,000	
	Cash..................................	11		12,740
	Purchases Discounts...................	53		260
18	Cash	11	14,700	
	Sales Discounts	43	300	
	Accounts Receivable	12		15,000
21	Purchases............................	51	15,200	
	Accounts Payable	21		15,200
22	Advertising Expense	56	4,250	
	Cash..................................	11		4,250
23	Cash	11	11,600	
	Sales	41		11,600
24	Accounts Payable	21	2,200	
	Purchases Returns and Allowances......	52		2,200
25	Accounts Receivable	12	30,200	
	Sales	41		30,200
28	Cash	11	8,200	
	Sales	41		8,200
28	Sales Returns and Allowances	42	350	
	Cash..................................	11		350
29	Sales Salaries Expense	55	3,800	
	Office Salaries Expense..................	59	1,280	
	Cash..................................	11		5,080
30	Accounts Payable	21	10,900	
	Cash..................................	11		10,900
30	Cash	11	12,500	
	Accounts Receivable	12		12,500

Prob. 5-5B, Continued

1. and 3.

Cash 11

Date	Item	Post. Ref.	Dr.	Cr.	Balance Dr.	Cr.
19—						
June 1	Balance	√	......	......	19,940	......
1		12	......	3,500	......	......
9		12	......	525	......	......
10		12	9,800	......	......	......
11		12	......	16,700	......	......
14		12	9,500	......	......	......
16		12	......	5,230	......	......
17		13	......	12,740	......	......
18		13	14,700	......	......	......
22		13	......	4,250	......	......
23		13	11,600	......	......	......
28		13	8,200	......	......	......
28		13	......	350	......	......
29		13	......	5,080	......	......
30		14	......	10,900	......	......
30		14	12,500	......	26,965	......

Accounts Receivable 12

Date	Item	Post. Ref.	Dr.	Cr.	Balance Dr.	Cr.
19—						
June 1	Balance	√	......	......	32,350	......
7		12	16,000	......	......	......
10		12	......	10,000	......	......
15		12	......	800	......	......
18		13	......	15,000	......	......
25		13	30,200	......	......	......
30		14	......	12,500	40,250	......

Merchandise Inventory 13

Date	Item	Post. Ref.	Dr.	Cr.	Balance Dr.	Cr.
19—						
June 1	Balance	√	......	......	79,600	......

Prepaid Insurance 14

Date	Item	Post. Ref.	Dr.	Cr.	Balance Dr.	Cr.
19—						
June 1	Balance	√	......	......	4,050	......

Prob. 5-5B, Continued

Store Supplies   15

Date	Item	Post. Ref.	Dr.	Cr.	Balance Dr.	Balance Cr.
19—						
June 1	Balance...................	√	......	......	2,700	......

Accounts Payable   21

Date	Item	Post. Ref.	Dr.	Cr.	Balance Dr.	Balance Cr.
19—						
June 1	Balance...................	√	......	......	......	28,300
2	....	12	......	12,500	......	......
4	....	12	......	20,100	......	......
11	....	12	16,980	......	......	......
17	....	13	13,000	......	......	......
21	....	13	......	15,200	......	......
24	....	13	2,200	......	......	......
30	....	14	10,900	......	......	33,020

Art Evans, Capital   31

Date	Item	Post. Ref.	Dr.	Cr.	Balance Dr.	Balance Cr.
19—						
June 1	Balance...................	√	......	......	......	110,340

Art Evans, Drawing   32

Income Summary   33

Sales   41

Date	Item	Post. Ref.	Dr.	Cr.	Balance Dr.	Balance Cr.
19—						
June 7	....	12	......	16,000	......	......
14	....	12	......	9,500	......	......
23	....	13	......	11,600	......	......
25	....	13	......	30,200	......	......
28	....	13	......	8,200	......	75,500

Sales Returns and Allowances   42

Date	Item	Post. Ref.	Dr.	Cr.	Balance Dr.	Balance Cr.
19—						
June 15	....	12	800	......	......	......
28	....	13	350	......	1,150	......

Prob. 5-5B, Continued

Sales Discounts   43

Date	Item	Post. Ref.	Dr.	Cr.	Balance Dr.	Balance Cr.
19—						
June 10	....	12	200	......	......	......
18	....	13	300	......	500	......

Purchases   51

Date	Item	Post. Ref.	Dr.	Cr.	Balance Dr.	Balance Cr.
19—						
June 2	....	12	12,500	......	......	......
4	....	12	20,100	......	......	......
21	....	13	15,200	......	47,800	......

Purchases Returns and Allowances   52

Date	Item	Post. Ref.	Dr.	Cr.	Balance Dr.	Balance Cr.
19—						
June 24	....	13	......	2,200	......	2,200

Purchases Discounts   53

Date	Item	Post. Ref.	Dr.	Cr.	Balance Dr.	Balance Cr.
19—						
June 11	....	12	......	280	......	......
17	....	13	......	260	......	540

Transportation In   54

Date	Item	Post. Ref.	Dr.	Cr.	Balance Dr.	Balance Cr.
19—						
June 9	....	12	525	......	525	......

Sales Salaries Expense   55

Date	Item	Post. Ref.	Dr.	Cr.	Balance Dr.	Balance Cr.
19—						
June 16	....	12	3,950	......	......	......
29	....	13	3,800	......	7,750	......

Advertising Expense   56

Date	Item	Post. Ref.	Dr.	Cr.	Balance Dr.	Balance Cr.
19—						
June 22	....	13	4,250	......	4,250	......

Store Supplies Expense   57

Miscellaneous Selling Expense   58

Prob. 5-5B, Concluded

Office Salaries Expense   59

Date	Item	Post. Ref.	Dr.	Cr.	Balance Dr.	Balance Cr.
19—						
June 16	....	12	1,280	......	......	......
29	....	13	1,280	......	2,560	......

Rent Expense   60

Date	Item	Post. Ref.	Dr.	Cr.	Balance Dr.	Balance Cr.
19—						
June 1	....	12	3,500	......	3,500	......

Insurance Expense   61

Miscellaneous Administrative Expense   62

4.
EVANS COMPANY
Trial Balance
June 30, 19—

Cash	26,965	
Accounts Receivable	40,250	
Merchandise Inventory	79,600	
Prepaid Insurance	4,050	
Store Supplies	2,700	
Accounts Payable		33,020
Art Evans, Capital		110,340
Art Evans, Drawing		
Income Summary		
Sales		75,500
Sales Returns and Allowances	1,150	
Sales Discounts	500	
Purchases	47,800	
Purchases Returns and Allowances		2,200
Purchases Discounts		540
Transportation In	525	
Sales Salaries Expense	7,750	
Advertising Expense	4,250	
Store Supplies Expense		
Miscellaneous Selling Expense		
Office Salaries Expense	2,560	
Rent Expense	3,500	
Insurance Expense		
Miscellaneous Administrative Expense		
	221,600	221,600

Prob. 5-6B

1. Cost of merchandise sold:

Merchandise inventory, January 1, 1993			$ 92,500
Purchases		$475,000	
Less: Purchases returns and allowances	$7,250		
Purchases discounts	2,750	10,000	
Net purchases		$465,000	
Add transportation in		8,150	
Cost of merchandise purchased			473,150
Merchandise available for sale			$565,650
Less merchandise inventory, December 31, 1993			85,650
Cost of merchandise sold . . .			$480,000

2. $160,000 ($640,000 − $480,000)
3. 25% ($160,000/$640,000)
4. The gross profit would be understated by $10,000 because the cost of merchandise sold would be overstated by $10,000.

Mini-Case 5

1.

	19X3	19X2	19X1
Purchases	$20,400,000	$18,200,000	$16,300,000
Less purchases returns and allowances.	204,000	136,500	81,500
Net purchases	$20,196,000	$18,063,500	$16,218,500
Discount rate	× 2%	× 2%	× 2%
Purchases discounts	$ 403,920	$ 361,270	$ 324,370
Less interest earned on investments of excess cash	65,974*	68,842*	61,811*
Net savings.	$ 337,946	$ 292,428	$ 262,559

*COMPUTATIONS:	19X3	19X2	19X1
Net purchases	$20,196,000	$18,063,500	$16,218,500
Less amount of discount	403,920	361,270	324,370
Net amount required to pay invoices within discount period.	$19,792,080	$17,702,230	$15,894,130

Mini-Case 5, Concluded

Interest income forgone by paying within discount period:
19X1: $15,894,130 × 7% × 20/360 = $61,811
19X2: $17,702,230 × 7% × 20/360 = $68,842
19X3: $19,792,080 × 6% × 20/360 = $65,974

2. Net purchases [$20,196,000 + (15% × $20,196,000)]........ $23,225,400
   Less purchases discounts ($23,225,400 × 2%).............. 464,508

   Net amount required to pay invoices within
   discount period $22,760,892

   Purchases discounts .... $ 464,508
   Less interest ($22,760,892 × 11% × 20/360) 139,094
   Net savings.. $ 325,414

3. Other questions of concern would be why the purchases returns and allowances has increased so rapidly during the past two years and whether the transportation in costs are reasonable in comparison to industry standards. The purchases returns and allowances have increased from $81,500 (.5% of gross purchases) in 19X1 to $204,000 (1% of gross purchases) in 19X3. Valley Discount Stores might want to consider changing some suppliers due to the receipt of poor quality merchandise which must be returned. If the transportation in costs are high in comparison to industry standards, Valley Discount Stores might consider renegotiating shipping terms with its suppliers to obtain more favorable treatment.

CHAPTER 6

DISCUSSION QUESTIONS

1. Merchandise Inventory

2. Income Summary

3. a. Inventory of merchandise at January 1, beginning of the year

4. a. Merchandise Inventory
   b. Merchandise Inventory
   c. $205,000
   d. $187,500
   e. $125,000

5. Adjustments debit and credit, adjusted trial balance debit and credit, income statement credit, and balance sheet debit columns

6. Single-step form and multiple-step form

7. The primary characteristic of the multiple-step income statement is its many sections, subsections, and intermediate balances.

8. $1,199,900 ($1,250,000 − $10,100 − $40,000)

9. a. $805,000
   b. $715,000
   c. $280,000
   d. $90,000

10. Selling expenses are incurred directly and entirely in connection with the sale of merchandise. Administrative expenses are incurred in the administration or general operations of the business.

11. a. Selling expense, (3), (4), (8)
    b. Administrative expense, (2), (5), (6), (7)
    c. Other expense, (1)

12. The multiple-step form of income statement contains conventional groupings for revenues and expenses, with intermediate balances, before concluding with the net income balance. In the single-step form, the total of all expenses is deducted from the total of all revenues, without intermediate balances.

13. The major advantages of the single-step form of income statement are its simplicity and its emphasis on total revenues and total expenses as the determinants of net income. The major objection to the form is that such relationships as gross profit to sales and income from operations to sales are not as readily determinable as when the multiple-step form is used.

14. Revenues from sources other than the principal activity of the business are classified as other income.

15. a. net income
    b. owner's capital, end of period

16. The assets are listed on the left-hand side and the liabilities and owner's equity are listed on the right-hand side of the account form of balance sheet. In the report form, the assets, liabilities, and owner's equity are presented in a downward sequence, with the total assets equaling the total liabilities plus owner's equity.

17. c. Purchases
    d. Purchases Returns and Allowances
    e. Sales
    f. Sales Discounts
    h. Supplies Expense
    i. Salaries Expense

18. a. Accounts Payable
    b. Accumulated Depreciation
    c. Cash
    e. Equipment

19. a. foreign luxury-car dealer
    c. large retailer with computerized accounting system

20. a. Merchandise Inventory
    b. Merchandise Inventory

21. No. Adjusting entries are unnecessary because under the perpetual inventory system the amount of unsold merchandise on hand is continually reflected in the merchandise inventory account.

22. The Price Club relies on a large volume of sales and tight controls over purchasing and selling and general expenses. For example, warehouse clubs only buy "hot" selling items. These items are purchased in large quantities in order to obtain volume discounts. In addition, warehouse clubs carefully screen their members and accept only checks or cash in order to avoid processing expenses on credit cards. In addition, by monitoring members on a continuing basis, acceptance of bad checks is minimized.

ETHICS DISCUSSION CASE Both the single-step and the multiple-step income statement forms are widely accepted; therefore, D. L. McLain will not have behaved unethically if the single-step form is used.

EXERCISES

Ex. 6-1

Income Summary	145,000	
Merchandise Inventory		145,000
Merchandise Inventory	137,500	
Income Summary		137,500

Ex. 6-2

SIMONE COMPANY
Income Statement
For Year Ended December 31, 19—

Revenue from sales:			
Sales		$705,000	
Less: Sales returns and allowances	$ 8,700		
Sales discounts	6,500	15,200	
Net sales			$689,800
Cost of merchandise sold:			
Merchandise inventory, January 1, 19—		$ 55,000	
Purchases	$562,000		
Less: Purchases returns and allowances	$15,500		
Purchases discounts	8,000	23,500	
Net purchases		$538,500	
Add transportation in		12,500	
Cost of merchandise purchased		551,000	
Merchandise available for sale		$606,000	
Less merchandise inventory, December 31, 19—		57,500	
Cost of merchandise sold			548,500
Gross profit			$141,300

Ex. 6-3   a. Sales returns and allowances, sales discounts
          b. Purchases returns and allowances, purchases discounts
          c. Transportation in
          d. Merchandise available for sale
          e. Merchandise inventory (ending)
          f. Gross profit
          g. Selling expenses, administrative expenses
          h. Income from operations
          i. Other income, other expense

Ex. 6-4

a.	$162,000	e.	$355,000	i.	$575,000
b.	$25,000	f.	$210,000	j.	$7,000
c.	$60,000	g.	$15,000	k.	$720,000
d.	$585,000	h.	$240,000	l.	$95,000

Ex. 6-5

SOLAR PRODUCTS COMPANY
Income Statement
For Year Ended June 30, 1994

Revenues:		
Net sales...		$1,500,000
Rent income...		30,000
Total revenues...................................		$1,530,000
Expenses:		
Cost of merchandise sold	$925,000	
Selling expenses..................................	210,000	
Administrative expenses	145,000	
Interest expense..................................	27,500	
Total expenses..................................		1,307,500
Net income		$ 222,500

Ex. 6-6

a.

VINCENT COMPANY
Income Statement
For Year Ended December 31, 19—

Revenue from sales:			
Sales.......................		$1,275,000	
Less: Sales returns and			
allowances		$34,300	
Sales discounts		10,200	44,500
Net sales			$1,230,500
Cost of merchandise sold:			
Merchandise inventory,			
January 1, 19—............		$ 225,000	
Purchases		$850,000	
Less: Purchases returns and			
allowances	$12,000		
Purchases discounts....	8,000	20,000	
Net purchases		$830,000	
Add transportation in........		11,300	
Cost of merchandise			
purchased		841,300	
Merchandise available for sale		$1,066,300	
Less merchandise inventory,			
December 31, 19—.........		230,000	
Cost of merchandise sold...			836,300
Gross profit			$ 394,200
Operating expenses:			
Selling expenses.............		$ 132,700	
Administrative expenses		79,500	
Total operating expenses...			212,200
Income from operations........			$ 182,000
Other expense:			
Interest expense.............			2,500
Net income			$ 179,500

b. The major advantage of the multiple-step form of income statement is that relationships such as gross profit to sales are indicated. The major disadvantages are that it is more complex and the total revenues and expenses are not indicated, as is the case in the single-step income statement.

Ex. 6-7 **a.** Income Summary............................ 225,000
　　　　　　　　Merchandise Inventory...................   225,000

　　　　　　　Merchandise Inventory.................... 230,000
　　　　　　　　Income Summary.........................   230,000

　　　　　b. Sales.................................... 1,275,000
　　　　　　　Purchases Returns and Allowances......   12,000
　　　　　　　Purchases Discounts...................   8,000
　　　　　　　　Income Summary.....................   1,295,000

　　　　　　　Income Summary....................... 1,120,500
　　　　　　　　Sales Returns and Allowances   34,300
　　　　　　　　Sales Discounts......................   10,200
　　　　　　　　Purchases...........................   850,000
　　　　　　　　Transportation In   11,300
　　　　　　　　Selling Expenses....................   132,700
　　　　　　　　Administrative Expenses   79,500
　　　　　　　　Interest Expense....................   2,500

　　　　　　　Income Summary......................   179,500
　　　　　　　　N. L. Vincent, Capital.................   179,500

　　　　　　　N. L. Vincent, Capital..................   60,000
　　　　　　　　N. L. Vincent, Drawing...............   60,000

Ex. 6-8 Balance sheet items: a, b, d, e, f, i

Ex. 6-9 **a.** Accounts Receivable........................... 6,900
　　　　　　　　Sales.......................................   6,900

　　　　　　　Cost of Merchandise Sold....................   3,900
　　　　　　　　Merchandise Inventory.......................   3,900

　　　　　b. Sales Returns and Allowances.................   750
　　　　　　　Accounts Receivable.........................   750

　　　　　　　Merchandise Inventory........................   450
　　　　　　　　Cost of Merchandise Sold   450

　　　　　c. Cash... 6,027
　　　　　　　Sales Discounts   123
　　　　　　　Accounts Receivable........................   6,150

Ex. 6-10 a. Merchandise Inventory........................ 6,900
　　　　　　　Accounts Payable...........................   6,900

　　　　　b. Accounts Payable.............................   750
　　　　　　　Merchandise Inventory......................   750

　　　　　c. Accounts Payable............................. 6,150
　　　　　　　Cash..   6,027
　　　　　　　Merchandise Inventory......................   123

Ex 6-11 Mar. 31   Sales   637,500
                       Interest Income   5,000
                           Income Summary.....................   642,500

31   Income Summary   556,950
      Sales Discounts   11,200
      Sales Returns & Allowances..........   21,750
      Cost of Merchandise Sold...........   382,500
      Selling Expenses   95,600
      Administrative Expenses.............   42,300
      Interest Expense.....................   3,600

31   Income Summary   85,550
      C. F. Kelly, Capital...................   85,550

31   C. F. Kelly, Capital......................   15,000
      C. F. Kelly, Drawing   15,000

WHAT'S WRONG WITH THIS?

1. Sales returns and allowances and sales discounts should be deducted from (not added to) sales.
2. Sales returns and allowances and sales discounts should be deducted from sales to yield "net sales" (not gross sales).
3. Deduction of purchases returns and allowances and purchases discounts from purchases yields net purchases.
4. Addition of transportation in to net purchases would yield cost of merchandise purchased.
5. Deduction of cost of merchandise sold from net sales yields gross profit.
6. Deduction of total operating expenses from gross profit would yield income from operations (or operating income).
7. The final amount on the income statement should be labeled net income.

WHAT'S WRONG?, Concluded

A correct income statement would be as follows:

BAXTER COMPANY
Income Statement
For Year Ended December 31, 19—

Revenue from sales:			
Sales....................			$1,200,000
Less: Sales returns and allowances		$ 28,000	
Sales discounts		9,500	37,500
Net sales			$1,162,500
Cost of merchandise sold:			
Merchandise inventory, January 1, 19—...........			$ 200,000
Purchases	$850,000		
Less: Purchases returns and allowances	$15,000		
Purchases discounts....	10,000	25,000	
Net purchases		$825,000	
Add transportation in........		6,300	
Cost of merchandise purchased		831,300	
Merchandise available for sale		$1,031,300	
Less merchandise inventory, December 31, 19—........		230,000	
Cost of merchandise sold...			801,300
Gross profit			$ 361,200
Operating expenses:			
Selling expenses.............		$ 125,000	
Administrative expenses.....		87,200	
Total operating expenses...			212,200
Income from operations.......			$ 149,000
Other expense:			
Interest expense.............			7,500
Net income			$ 141,500

PROBLEMS

Prob. 6-1A

HORWITZ COMPANY
Work Sheet
For Year Ended April 30, 19—

Account Title	Trial Balance Dr.	Trial Balance Cr.	Adjustments Dr.	Adjustments Cr.	Adjusted Trial Balance Dr.	Adjusted Trial Balance Cr.	Income Statement Dr.	Income Statement Cr.	Balance Sheet Dr.	Balance Sheet Cr.
Cash	19,750				19,750				19,750	
Accounts Receivable	64,100				64,100				64,100	
Merchandise Inventory	87,150		(b) 90,000	(a) 87,150	90,000				90,000	
Prepaid Insurance	7,100			(c) 3,800	3,300				3,300	
Store Supplies	5,450			(d) 3,700	1,750				1,750	
Store Equipment	53,700				53,700				53,700	
Accum. Depr.—Store Equipment		15,180		(e) 11,500		26,680				26,680
Accounts Payable		26,800				26,800				26,800
Salaries Payable				(f) 2,350		2,350				2,350
J. A. Horwitz, Capital		144,020				144,020				144,020
J. A. Horwitz, Drawing	15,000				15,000				15,000	
Income Summary			(a) 87,150	(b) 90,000	87,150	90,000	87,150	90,000		
Sales		562,200				562,200		562,200		
Purchases	360,000				360,000		360,000			
Sales Salaries Expense	46,500		(f) 1,600		48,100		48,100			
Advertising Expense	15,800				15,800		15,800			
Depr. Expense—Store Equipment			(e) 11,500		11,500		11,500			
Store Supplies Expense			(d) 3,700		3,700		3,700			
Misc. Selling Expense	2,750				2,750		2,750			
Office Salaries Expense	30,000		(f) 750		30,750		30,750			
Rent Expense	24,000				24,000		24,000			
Heating and Lighting Expense	9,660				9,660		9,660			
Taxes Expense	5,100				5,100		5,100			
Insurance Expense			(c) 3,800		3,800		3,800			
Misc. Adm. Expense	2,140				2,140		2,140			
	748,200	748,200	198,500	198,500	852,050	852,050	604,450	652,200	247,600	199,850
Net Income							47,750			47,750
							652,200	652,200	247,600	247,600

This work sheet solution is applicable only if the alternate method of inventory recording presented in Appendix D is used.

Prob. 6-1A, Concluded

HORWITZ COMPANY
Work Sheet
For Year Ended April 30, 19—

Account Title	Trial Balance Dr.	Trial Balance Cr.	Adjustments Dr.	Adjustments Cr.	Adjusted Trial Balance Dr.	Adjusted Trial Balance Cr.	Income Statement Dr.	Income Statement Cr.	Balance Sheet Dr.	Balance Sheet Cr.
Cash	19,750				19,750				19,750	
Accounts Receivable	64,100				64,100				64,100	
Merchandise Inventory	87,150				87,150		87,150	90,000	90,000	
Prepaid Insurance	7,100			(a) 3,800	3,300				3,300	
Store Supplies	5,450			(b) 3,700	1,750				1,750	
Store Equipment	53,700				53,700				53,700	
Accum. Depr.—Store Equipment		15,180		(c) 11,500		26,680				26,680
Accounts Payable		26,800				26,800				26,800
Salaries Payable				(d) 2,350		2,350				2,350
J. A. Horwitz, Capital		144,020				144,020				144,020
J. A. Horwitz, Drawing	15,000				15,000				15,000	
Sales		562,200				562,200		562,200		
Purchases	360,000				360,000		360,000			
Sales Salaries Expense	46,500		(d) 1,600		48,100		48,100			
Advertising Expense	15,800				15,800		15,800			
Depr. Expense—Store Equipment			(c) 11,500		11,500		11,500			
Store Supplies Expense			(b) 3,700		3,700		3,700			
Misc. Selling Expense	2,750				2,750		2,750			
Office Salaries Expense	30,000		(d) 750		30,750		30,750			
Rent Expense	24,000				24,000		24,000			
Heating and Lighting Expense	9,660				9,660		9,660			
Taxes Expense	5,100				5,100		5,100			
Insurance Expense			(a) 3,800		3,800		3,800			
Misc. Adm. Expense	2,140				2,140		2,140			
	748,200	748,200	21,350	21,350	762,050	762,050	604,450	652,200	247,600	199,850
Net Income							47,750			47,750
							652,200	652,200	247,600	247,600

Prob. 6-2A

1.
MERZ COMPANY
Income Statement
For Year Ended January 31, 1994

Revenue from sales:			
Sales			$1,400,000
Less: Sales returns and allowances		$ 12,100	
Sales discounts		11,900	24,000
Net sales.................			$1,376,000
Cost of merchandise sold:			
Merchandise inventory, February 1, 1993			$ 125,000
Purchases..................		$1,100,000	
Less: Purchases returns and allowances	$24,600		
Purchases discounts...	15,400	40,000	
Net purchases		$1,060,000	
Add transportation in.......		15,000	
Cost of merchandise purchased...............			1,075,000
Merchandise available for sale......................			$1,200,000
Less merchandise inventory, January 31, 1994..........			100,000
Cost of merchandise sold .			1,100,000
Gross profit..................			$ 276,000

Prob. 6-2A, Continued

Operating expenses:

Selling expenses:			
Sales salaries expense.....	$ 123,200		
Advertising expense	22,800		
Depreciation expense— store equipment	6,400		
Miscellaneous selling expense..........	1,600		
Total selling expenses ...		$ 154,000	
Administrative expenses:			
Office salaries expense....	$ 31,150		
Rent expense	16,350		
Depreciation expense— office equipment........	12,700		
Insurance expense	3,900		
Office supplies expense ...	1,300		
Miscellaneous administrative expense..	1,600		
Total administrative expenses..............		67,000	
Total operating expenses....			221,000
Income from operations.......			$ 55,000
Other income:			
Interest income		$ 21,000	
Other expense:			
Interest expense		6,000	15,000
Net income			$ 70,000

2.

MERZ COMPANY
Statement of Owner's Equity
For Year Ended January 31, 1994

P.C. Merz, capital, February 1, 1993.....................		$391,000
Net income for the year...............................	$70,000	
Less withdrawals......................................	15,000	
Increase in owner's equity		55,000
P.C. Merz, capital, January 31, 1994		$446,000

Prob. 6-2A, Concluded

3.

MERZ COMPANY
Balance Sheet
January 31, 1994

Assets

Current assets:

Cash		$ 39,000
Notes receivable...........................		120,000
Accounts receivable		212,000
Merchandise inventory....................		100,000
Office supplies		5,600
Prepaid insurance..........................		3,400
Total current assets		$480,000

Plant assets:

Office equipment	$35,000		
Less accumulated depreciation	12,800	$ 22,200	
Store equipment...........................	$72,000		
Less accumulated depreciation	24,200	47,800	
Total plant assets			70,000
Total assets			$550,000

Liabilities

Current liabilities:

Accounts payable..........................		$ 45,600
Note payable (current portion)............		6,000
Salaries payable		2,400
Total current liabilities		$ 54,000

Long-term liabilities:

Note payable (final payment, 2004)	50,000
Total liabilities.............................	$104,000

Owner's Equity

P.C. Merz, capital..........................	446,000
Total liabilities and owner's equity..........	$550,000

4. **a.** The multiple-step form of income statement contains various sections for revenues and expenses, with intermediate balances, and concludes with net income. In the single-step form, the total of all expenses is deducted from the total of all revenues. There are no intermediate balances.

    b. In the report form of balance sheet, the assets, liabilities, and owner's equity are presented in that order in a downward sequence. In the account form, the assets are listed on the left-hand side and the liabilities and owner's equity are listed on the right-hand side.

Prob. 6-3A

1.

MERZ COMPANY
Income Statement
For Year Ended January 31, 1994

Revenues:		
Net sales....................................		$1,376,000
Interest income...............................		21,000
Total revenues................................		$1,397,000
Expenses:		
Cost of merchandise sold	$1,100,000	
Selling expenses..............................	154,000	
Administrative expenses.......................	67,000	
Interest expense..............................	6,000	
Total expenses...............................		1,327,000
Net income		$ 70,000

2.

MERZ COMPANY
Statement of Owner's Equity
For Year Ended January 31, 1994

P.C. Merz, capital, February 1, 1993....................		$391,000
Net income for the year...............................	$70,000	
Less withdrawals.....................................	15,000	
Increase in owner's equity		55,000
P.C. Merz, capital, January 31, 1994		$446,000

Prob. 6-3A, Concluded

3.

MERZ COMPANY
Balance Sheet
January 31, 1994

__Assets__

Current assets:
Cash		$ 39,000
Notes receivable		120,000
Accounts receivable		212,000
Merchandise inventory		100,000
Office supplies		5,600
Prepaid insurance		3,400
Total current assets		$480,000

Plant assets:
Office Equipment	$35,000		
Less accumulated depreciation	12,800	$ 22,200	
Store equipment	$72,000		
Less accumulated depreciation	24,200	47,800	
Total plant assets			70,000
Total assets			$550,000

__Liabilities__

Current liabilities:
Accounts payable	$45,600	
Note payable (current portion)	6,000	
Salaries payable	2,400	
Total current liabilities		$ 54,000

Long-term liabilities:
Note payable (final payment, 2004)		50,000
Total liabilities		$104,000

__Owner's Equity__

P.C. Merz, capital		446,000
Total liabilities and owner's equity		$550,000

Prob. 6-4A

1.

WATSON COMPANY
Work Sheet
For Year Ended March 31, 1994

Account Title	Trial Balance Dr.	Trial Balance Cr.	Adjustments Dr.	Adjustments Cr.	Adjusted Trial Balance Dr.	Adjusted Trial Balance Cr.	Income Statement Dr.	Income Statement Cr.	Balance Sheet Dr.	Balance Sheet Cr.
Cash	44,300				44,300				44,300	
Accounts Receivable	103,800				103,800				103,800	
Merchandise Inventory	235,500		(b) 260,000	(a) 235,500	260,000				260,000	
Prepaid Insurance	11,400			(c) 7,300	4,100				4,100	
Store Supplies	2,160			(d) 1,100	1,060				1,060	
Office Supplies	1,440			(e) 800	640				640	
Store Equipment	110,000				110,000				110,000	
Accum. Depr.—Store Equip.		33,600		(f) 9,750		43,350				43,350
Office Equipment	32,750				32,750				32,750	
Accum. Depr.—Office Equip.		14,400		(g) 3,600		18,000				18,000
Accounts Payable		60,700				60,700				60,700
Salaries Payable				(h) 4,500		4,500				4,500
Note Payable (final payment, 2005)		120,000				120,000				120,000
L. L. Watson, Capital		206,050				206,050				206,050
L. L. Watson, Drawing	20,000				20,000				20,000	
Income Summary			(a) 235,500	(b) 260,000	235,500	260,000	235,500	260,000		
Sales		900,000				900,000		900,000		
Sales Returns and Allowances	7,200				7,200		7,200			
Sales Discounts	4,200				4,200		4,200			
Purchases	600,000				600,000		600,000			
Purchases Returns and Allow.		15,000				15,000		15,000		
Purchases Discounts		7,800				7,800		7,800		
Transportation In	3,000				3,000		3,000			
Sales Salaries Expense	72,000		(h) 3,000		75,000		75,000			
Advertising Expense	25,000				25,000		25,000			
Depr. Expense—Store Equip.			(f) 9,750		9,750		9,750			
Store Supplies Expense			(d) 1,100		1,100		1,100			
Misc. Selling Expense	1,620				1,620		1,620			
Office Salaries Expense	50,000		(h) 1,500		51,500		51,500			
Rent Expense	15,000				15,000		15,000			
Insurance Expense			(c) 7,300		7,300		7,300			
Depr. Expense—Office Equip.			(g) 3,600		3,600		3,600			
Office Supplies Expense			(e) 800		800		800			
Misc. Administrative Expense	1,380				1,380		1,380			
Interest Expense	16,800				16,800		16,800			
	1,357,550	1,357,550	522,550	522,550	1,635,400	1,635,400	1,058,750	1,182,800	576,650	452,600
Net Income							124,050			124,050
							1,182,800	1,182,800	576,650	576,650

This work sheet solution is applicable only if the alternate method of inventory recording presented in Appendix D is used.

1.

Prob. 6-4A, Continued

WATSON COMPANY
Work Sheet
For Year Ended March 31, 1994

Account Title	Trial Balance Dr.	Trial Balance Cr.	Adjustments Dr.	Adjustments Cr.	Adjusted Trial Balance Dr.	Adjusted Trial Balance Cr.	Income Statement Dr.	Income Statement Cr.	Balance Sheet Dr.	Balance Sheet Cr.
Cash	44,300				44,300				44,300	
Accounts Receivable	103,800				103,800				103,800	
Merchandise Inventory	235,500				235,500		235,500			
Prepaid Insurance	11,400			(a) 7,300	4,100				4,100	
Store Supplies	2,160			(b) 1,100	1,060				1,060	
Office Supplies	1,440			(c) 800	640				640	
Store Equipment	110,000				110,000				110,000	
Accum. Depr.—Store Equip.		33,600		(d) 9,750		43,350				43,350
Office Equipment	32,750				32,750				32,750	
Accum. Depr.—Office Equip.		14,400		(e) 3,600		18,000				18,000
Accounts Payable		60,700				60,700				60,700
Salaries Payable				(f) 4,500		4,500				4,500
Note Payable (final payment, 2005)		120,000				120,000				120,000
L. L. Watson, Capital		206,050				206,050				206,050
L. L. Watson, Drawing	20,000				20,000				20,000	
Sales		900,000				900,000		900,000		
Sales Returns and Allowances	7,200				7,200		7,200			
Sales Discounts	4,200				4,200		4,200			
Purchases	600,000				600,000		600,000			
Purchases Returns and Allow.		15,000				15,000		15,000		
Purchases Discounts		7,800				7,800		7,800		
Transportation In	3,000				3,000		3,000			
Sales Salaries Expense	72,000		(f) 3,000		75,000		75,000			
Advertising Expense	25,000				25,000		25,000			
Depr. Expense—Store Equip.			(d) 9,750		9,750		9,750			
Store Supplies Expense			(b) 1,100		1,100		1,100			
Misc. Selling Expense	1,620				1,620		1,620			
Office Salaries Expense	50,000		(f) 1,500		51,500		51,500			
Rent Expense	15,000				15,000		15,000			
Insurance Expense			(a) 7,300		7,300		7,300			
Depr. Expense—Office Equip.			(e) 3,600		3,600		3,600			
Office Supplies Expense			(c) 800		800		800			
Misc. Administrative Expense	1,380				1,380		1,380			
Interest Expense	16,800				16,800		16,800			
	1,357,550	1,357,550	27,050	27,050	1,375,400	1,375,400	1,058,750	1,182,800	576,650	452,600
Net Income							124,050			124,050
							1,182,800	1,182,800	576,650	576,650

Prob. 6-4A, Continued

2.

WATSON COMPANY
Income Statement
For Year Ended March 31, 1994

Revenue from sales:			
Sales		$900,000	
Less: Sales returns and			
allowances	$ 7,200		
Sales discounts...........	4,200	11,400	
Net sales......................			$888,600
Cost of merchandise sold:			
Merchandise inventory,			
April 1, 1993		$235,500	
Purchases......................	$600,000		
Less: Purchases returns and			
allowances $15,000			
Purchases discounts........ 7,800	22,800		
Net purchases	$577,200		
Add transportation in............	3,000		
Cost of merchandise purchased		580,200	
Merchandise available for sale		$815,700	
Less merchandise inventory,			
March 31, 1994.................		260,000	
Cost of merchandise sold			555,700
Gross profit.........................			$332,900
Operating expenses:			
Selling expenses:			
Sales salaries expense..........	$ 75,000		
Advertising expense	25,000		
Depreciation expense—store			
equipment	9,750		
Store supplies expense.........	1,100		
Miscellaneous selling expense ..	1,620		
Total selling expenses		$112,470	
Administrative expenses:			
Office salaries expense.........	$ 51,500		
Rent expense	15,000		
Insurance expense	7,300		
Depreciation expense—office			
equipment	3,600		
Office supplies expense	800		
Miscellaneous			
administrative expense.......	1,380		
Total administrative expense .		79,580	
Total operating expenses........			192,050
Income from operations...........			$140,850

Prob. 6-4A, Continued

Other expense:

Interest expense	16,800
Net income	$124,050

3.
WATSON COMPANY
Statement of Owner's Equity
For Year Ended March 31, 1994

L. L. Watson, capital, April 1, 1993		$206,050
Net income for the year............................	$124,050	
Less withdrawals...................................	20,000	
Increase in owner's equity		104,050
L. L. Watson, capital, March 31, 1994.................		$310,100

Prob. 6-4A, Concluded

4.

WATSON COMPANY
Balance Sheet
March 31, 1994

Assets

Current assets:
Cash		$ 44,300
Accounts receivable		103,800
Merchandise inventory		260,000
Prepaid insurance		4,100
Store supplies		1,060
Office supplies		640
Total current assets		$413,900

Plant assets:
Store equipment	$110,000		
Less accumulated depreciation	43,350	$ 66,650	
Office equipment	$ 32,750		
Less accumulated depreciation	18,000	14,750	
Total plant assets			81,400
Total assets			$495,300

Liabilities

Current liabilities:
Accounts payable	$ 60,700	
Note payable (current portion)	12,000	
Salaries payable	4,500	
Total current liabilities		$ 77,200

Long-term liabilities:
Note payable (final payment, 2005)		108,000
Total liabilities		$185,200

Owner's Equity

L. L. Watson, capital		310,100
Total liabilities and owner's equity		$495,300

Prob. 6-5A

Oct. 31	Interest Receivable.............................	500	
	Interest Income..............................		500
31	Income Summary.............................	354,000	
	Merchandise Inventory.......................		354,000
31	Merchandise Inventory........................	335,000	
	Income Summary............................		335,000
31	Rent Expense................................	36,000	
	Prepaid Rent................................		36,000
31	Insurance Expense...........................	4,100	
	Prepaid Insurance...........................		4,100
31	Supplies Expense............................	960	
	Supplies....................................		960
31	Depreciation Expense—Store Equipment........	16,460	
	Accumulated Depreciation—Store Equipment .		16,460
31	Depreciation Expense—Office Equipment.......	5,180	
	Accumulated Depreciation—Office Equipment .		5,180
31	Sales Salaries Expense.......................	4,500	
	Sales Salaries Payable.......................		4,500

Prob. 6-6A

1.

GANT COMPANY
Work Sheet
For Year Ended December 31, 19—

Account Title	Trial Balance Dr.	Trial Balance Cr.	Adjustments Dr.	Adjustments Cr.	Adjusted Trial Balance Dr.	Adjusted Trial Balance Cr.	Income Statement Dr.	Income Statement Cr.	Balance Sheet Dr.	Balance Sheet Cr.
Cash	68,175				68,175				68,175	
Accounts Receivable	112,500				112,500				112,500	
Merchandise Inventory	180,000		(b) 220,000	(a) 180,000	220,000				220,000	
Prepaid Insurance	9,700			(c) 7,260	2,440				2,440	
Store Supplies	4,250			(d) 2,550	1,700				1,700	
Office Supplies	2,100			(e) 1,700	400				400	
Store Equipment	112,000				112,000				112,000	
Accum. Depr.—Store Equip.		40,300		(f) 9,500		49,800				49,800
Office Equipment	50,000				50,000				50,000	
Accum. Depr.—Office Equip.		17,200		(g) 4,800		22,000				22,000
Accounts Payable		66,700				66,700				66,700
Salaries Payable				(h) 3,900		3,900				3,900
Unearned Rent		1,200	(i) 800			400				400
Note Payable (final payment, 2000)		105,000				105,000				105,000
R. L. Gant, Capital		220,510				220,510				220,510
R. L. Gant, Drawing	40,000				40,000				40,000	
Income Summary			(a) 180,000	(b) 220,000	180,000	220,000	180,000	220,000		
Sales		995,000				995,000		995,000		
Sales Returns and Allowances	11,900				11,900		11,900			
Sales Discounts	7,100				7,100		7,100			
Purchases	635,000				635,000		635,000			
Purchases Returns and Allow.		10,100				10,100		10,100		
Purchases Discounts		4,900				4,900		4,900		
Transportation In	6,200				6,200		6,200			
Sales Salaries Expense	86,400		(h) 2,750		89,150		89,150			
Advertising Expense	30,000				30,000		30,000			
Depr. Expense—Store Equip.			(f) 9,500		9,500		9,500			
Store Supplies Expense			(d) 2,550		2,550		2,550			
Misc. Selling Expense	1,335				1,335		1,335			
Office Salaries Expense	54,000		(h) 1,150		55,150		55,150			
Rent Expense	36,000				36,000		36,000			
Insurance Expense			(c) 7,260		7,260		7,260			
Depr. Expense—Office Equip.			(g) 4,800		4,800		4,800			
Office Supplies Expense			(e) 1,700		1,700		1,700			
Misc. Adm. Expense	1,650				1,650		1,650			
Rent Income				(i) 800		800		800		
Interest Expense	12,600				12,600		12,600			
	1,460,910	1,460,910	430,510	430,510	1,699,110	1,699,110	1,091,895	1,230,800	607,215	468,310
Net Income							138,905			138,905
							1,230,800	1,230,800	607,215	607,215

This work sheet solution is applicable only if the alternative method of inventory recording presented in Appendix D is used.

1.

Prob. 6-6A, Continued

GANT COMPANY
Work Sheet
For Year Ended December 31, 19—

Account Title	Trial Balance Dr.	Trial Balance Cr.	Adjustments Dr.	Adjustments Cr.	Adjusted Trial Balance Dr.	Adjusted Trial Balance Cr.	Income Statement Dr.	Income Statement Cr.	Balance Sheet Dr.	Balance Sheet Cr.
Cash	68,175				68,175				68,175	
Accounts Receivable	112,500				112,500				112,500	
Merchandise Inventory	180,000				180,000		180,000	220,000	220,000	
Prepaid Insurance	9,700			(a) 7,260	2,440				2,440	
Store Supplies	4,250			(b) 2,550	1,700				1,700	
Office Supplies	2,100			(c) 1,700	400				400	
Store Equipment	112,000				112,000				112,000	
Accum. Depr.—Store Equip.		40,300		(d) 9,500		49,800				49,800
Office Equipment	50,000				50,000				50,000	
Accum. Depr.—Office Equip.		17,200		(e) 4,800		22,000				22,000
Accounts Payable		66,700				66,700				66,700
Salaries Payable				(f) 3,900		3,900				3,900
Unearned Rent		1,200	(g) 800			400				400
Note Payable (final payment, 2000)		105,000				105,000				105,000
R.L. Gant, Capital		220,510				220,510				220,510
R.L. Gant, Drawing	40,000				40,000				40,000	
Sales		995,000				995,000		995,000		
Sales Returns and Allowances	11,900				11,900		11,900			
Sales Discounts	7,100				7,100		7,100			
Purchases	635,000				635,000		635,000			
Purchases Returns and Allow.		10,100				10,100		10,100		
Purchases Discounts		4,900				4,900		4,900		
Transportation In	6,200				6,200		6,200			
Sales Salaries Expense	86,400		(f) 2,750		89,150		89,150			
Advertising Expense	30,000				30,000		30,000			
Depr. Expense—Store Equip.			(d) 9,500		9,500		9,500			
Store Supplies Expense			(b) 2,550		2,550		2,550			
Misc. Selling Expense	1,335				1,335		1,335			
Office Salaries Expense	54,000		(f) 1,150		55,150		55,150			
Rent Expense	36,000				36,000		36,000			
Insurance Expense			(a) 7,260		7,260		7,260			
Depr. Expense — Office Equip.			(e) 4,800		4,800		4,800			
Office Supplies Expense			(c) 1,700		1,700		1,700			
Misc. Adm. Expense	1,650				1,650		1,650			
Rent Income				(g) 800		800		800		
Interest Expense	12,600				12,600		12,600			
	1,460,910	1,460,910	30,510	30,510	1,479,110	1,479,110	1,091,895	1,230,800	607,215	468,310
Net Income							138,905			138,905
							1,230,800	1,230,800	607,215	607,215

Prob. 6-6A, Continued

2.

GANT COMPANY
Income Statement
For Year Ended December 31, 19—

Revenue from sales:			
Sales			$995,000
Less: Sales returns and			
allowances		$ 11,900	
Sales discounts...........		7,100	19,000
Net sales.......................			$976,000
Cost of merchandise sold:			
Merchandise inventory,			
January 1, 19—			$180,000
Purchases.......................	$635,000		
Less: Purchases returns and			
allowances	$10,100		
Purchases discounts........	4,900	15,000	
Net purchases		$620,000	
Add transportation in............		6,200	
Cost of merchandise purchased		626,200	
Merchandise available for sale		$806,200	
Less merchandise inventory,			
December 31, 19—		220,000	
Cost of merchandise sold			586,200
Gross profit........................			$389,800
Operating expenses:			
Selling expenses:			
Sales salaries expense..........		$ 89,150	
Advertising expense		30,000	
Depreciation expense—store			
equipment		9,500	
Store supplies expense........		2,550	
Miscellaneous selling expense ..		1,335	
Total selling expenses			$132,535
Administrative expenses:			
Office salaries expense.........		$ 55,150	
Rent expense		36,000	
Insurance expense		7,260	
Depreciation expense—office			
equipment		4,800	
Office supplies expense		1,700	
Misc. administrative expense...		1,650	
Total admin. expenses........			106,560
Total operating expenses........			239,095
Income from operations...........			$150,705

Prob. 6-6A, Continued

Other expense:		
Interest expense	$ 12,600	
Other income:		
Rent income	800	11,800
Net income		$138,905

3.

GANT COMPANY
Statement of Owner's Equity
For Year Ended December 31, 19—

R. L. Gant, capital, January 1, 19—		$220,510
Net income for the year............................	$138,905	
Less withdrawals....................................	40,000	
Increase in owner's equity		98,905
R. L. Gant, capital, December 31, 19—		$319,415

Prob. 6-6A, Continued

4.

GANT COMPANY
Balance Sheet
December 31, 19—

Assets

Current assets:

Cash	$ 68,175	
Accounts receivable	112,500	
Merchandise inventory	220,000	
Prepaid insurance	2,440	
Store supplies	1,700	
Office supplies	400	
Total current assets		$405,215

Plant assets:

Store equipment	$112,000		
Less accumulated depreciation	49,800	$ 62,200	
Office equipment	$ 50,000		
Less accumulated depreciation	22,000	28,000	
Total plant assets			90,200
Total assets			$495,415

Liabilities

Current liabilities:

Accounts payable	$ 66,700	
Note payable (current portion)	15,000	
Salaries payable	3,900	
Unearned rent	400	
Total current liabilities		$ 86,000

Long-term liabilities:

Note payable (final payment, 2000)		90,000
Total liabilities		$176,000

Owner's Equity

R. L. Gant, capital		319,415
Total liabilities and owner's equity		$495,415

Prob. 6-6A, Continued

5. Income Summary 180,000

    Merchandise Inventory   180,000

   Merchandise Inventory 220,000

    Income Summary   220,000

   Insurance Expense 7,260

    Prepaid Insurance   7,260

   Store Supplies Expense 2,550

    Store Supplies   2,550

   Office Supplies Expense 1,700

    Office Supplies   1,700

   Depreciation Expense—Store Equipment 9,500

    Accum. Depreciation—Store Equipment   9,500

   Depreciation Expense—Office Equipment 4,800

    Accum. Depreciation—Office Equipment   4,800

   Sales Salaries Expense 2,750

   Office Salaries Expense 1,150

    Salaries Payable   3,900

   Unearned Rent 800

    Rent Income   800

Prob. 6-6A, Continued

6. Sales.. 995,000
   Purchases Returns and Allowances 10,100
   Purchases Discounts 4,900
   Rent Income.................................... 800
     Income Summary   1,010,800

Income Summary.................................... 911,895
   Sales Returns and Allowances   11,900
   Sales Discounts.................................   7,100
   Purchases   635,000
   Transportation In   6,200
   Sales Salaries Expense   89,150
   Advertising Expense   30,000
   Depreciation Expense—Store Equipment.........   9,500
   Store Supplies Expense   2,550
   Miscellaneous Selling Expense...................   1,335
   Office Salaries Expense   55,150
   Rent Expense...................................   36,000
   Insurance Expense   7,260
   Depreciation Expense—Office Equipment   4,800
   Office Supplies Expense.........................   1,700
   Miscellaneous Administrative Expense   1,650
   Interest Expense   12,600

Income Summary................................... 138,905
   R. L. Gant, Capital..............................   138,905

R. L. Gant, Capital................................. 40,000
   R. L. Gant, Drawing   40,000

Prob. 6-6A, Continued

The following adjusting and closing entries are applicable only if the alternative method of inventory recording presented in Appendix D is used. This approach classifies the entries for beginning and ending merchandise inventory as closing entries rather than adjusting entries.

5. Insurance Expense 7,260
      Prepaid Insurance 7,260

   Store Supplies Expense 2,550
      Store Supplies 2,550

   Office Supplies Expense 1,700
      Office Supplies.................................... 1,700

   Depreciation Expense—Store Equipment 9,500
      Accum. Depreciation—Store Equipment 9,500

   Depreciation Expense—Office Equipment.......... 4,800
      Accum. Depreciation—Office Equipment......... 4,800

   Sales Salaries Expense 2,750
   Office Salaries Expense 1,150
      Salaries Payable................................... 3,900

   Unearned Rent 800
      Rent Income....................................... 800

Prob. 6-6A, Concluded

6.
Sales	995,000	
Merchandise Inventory	220,000	
Purchases Returns and Allowances	10,100	
Purchases Discounts	4,900	
Rent Income	800	
Income Summary		1,230,800
Income Summary	1,091,895	
Merchandise Inventory		180,000
Sales Returns and Allowances		11,900
Sales Discounts		7,100
Purchases		635,000
Transportation In		6,200
Sales Salaries Expense		89,150
Advertising Expense		30,000
Depreciation Expense—Store Equipment		9,500
Store Supplies Expense		2,550
Miscellaneous Selling Expense		1,335
Office Salaries Expense		55,150
Rent Expense		36,000
Insurance Expense		7,260
Depreciation Expense—Office Equipment		4,800
Office Supplies Expense		1,700
Miscellaneous Administrative Expense		1,650
Interest Expense		12,600
Income Summary	138,905	
R. L. Gant, Capital		138,905
R. L. Gant, Capital	40,000	
R. L. Gant, Drawing		40,000

Prob. 6-7A

Nov.	3	Office Supplies....................................	120	
		Cash...		120
	5	Merchandise Inventory	12,500	
		Accounts Payable................................		12,500
	6	Cash...	2,950	
		Sales		2,950
	6	Cost of Merchandise Sold.........................	1,450	
		Merchandise Inventory............................		1,450
	7	Merchandise Inventory	6,590	
		Accounts Payable................................		6,590
	7	Accounts Payable	2,500	
		Merchandise Inventory............................		2,500
	11	Accounts Receivable.............................	1,800	
		Sales		1,800
	11	Cost of Merchandise Sold.........................	880	
		Merchandise Inventory............................		880
	15	Accounts Payable	10,000	
		Cash...		9,900
		Merchandise Inventory............................		100
	16	Accounts Receivable.............................	3,850	
		Sales		3,850
	16	Cost of Merchandise Sold.........................	1,900	
		Merchandise Inventory............................		1,900
	17	Accounts Payable	6,590	
		Cash...		6,462
		Merchandise Inventory............................		128
	19	Merchandise Inventory	3,500	
		Cash...		3,500
	21	Cash...	1,782	
		Sales Discounts	18	
		Accounts Receivable.............................		1,800
	24	Accounts Receivable.............................	4,200	
		Sales		4,200
	24	Cost of Merchandise Sold.........................	2,025	
		Merchandise Inventory............................		2,025
	28	Cash...	3,660	
		Credit Card Collection Expense....................	190	
		Accounts Receivable.............................		3,850
	30	Sales Returns and Allowances	2,700	
		Accounts Receivable.............................		2,700
	30	Merchandise Inventory	1,310	
		Cost of Merchandise Sold.........................		1,310

Prob. 6-8A

IYER CO.
Work Sheet
For Year Ended July 31, 19—

Account Title	Trial Balance Dr.	Trial Balance Cr.	Adjustments Dr.	Adjustments Cr.	Adjusted Trial Balance Dr.	Adjusted Trial Balance Cr.	Income Statement Dr.	Income Statement Cr.	Balance Sheet Dr.	Balance Sheet Cr.
Cash	18,500				18,500				18,500	
Notes Receivable	50,000				50,000				50,000	
Accounts Receivable	53,340				53,340				53,340	
Merchandise Inventory	80,000				80,000				80,000	
Prepaid Insurance	4,200			(a) 1,060	3,140				3,140	
Store Supplies	2,100			(b) 1,280	820				820	
Store Equipment	154,200				154,200				154,200	
Accum. Depr.—Store Equip.		84,600		(c) 9,300		93,900				93,900
Accounts Payable		32,000				32,000				32,000
Salaries Payable				(d) 2,700		2,700				2,700
Unearned Rent		7,600	(e) 3,800			3,800				3,800
C. A. Iyer, Capital		241,640				241,640				241,640
C. A. Iyer, Drawing	26,000				26,000				26,000	
Sales		790,500				790,500		790,500		
Cost of Merchandise Sold	474,300				474,300		474,300			
Sales Salaries Expense	79,800		(d) 1,500		81,300		81,300			
Advertising Expense	34,850				34,850		34,850			
Depr. Expense—Store Equip.			(c) 9,300		9,300		9,300			
Store Supplies Expense			(b) 1,280		1,280		1,280			
Misc. Selling Expense	1,600				1,600		1,600			
Office Salaries Expense	83,700		(d) 1,200		84,900		84,900			
Rent Expense	45,000				45,000		45,000			
Heating and Lighting Exp	37,400				37,400		37,400			
Taxes Expense	7,850				7,850		7,850			
Insurance Expense			(a) 1,060		1,060		1,060			
Misc. Administrative Expense	3,500				3,500		3,500			
Rent Income				(e) 3,800		3,800		3,800		
	1,156,340	1,156,340	18,140	18,140	1,168,340	1,168,340	782,340	794,300	386,000	374,040
Net Income							11,960			11,960
							794,300	794,300	386,000	386,000

Prob. 6-9A

1.

SYCAMORE CO.
Work Sheet
For Year Ended April 30, 19—

Account Title	Trial Balance Dr.	Trial Balance Cr.	Adjustments Dr.	Adjustments Cr.	Adjusted Trial Balance Dr.	Adjusted Trial Balance Cr.	Income Statement Dr.	Income Statement Cr.	Balance Sheet Dr.	Balance Sheet Cr.
Cash	28,500				28,500				28,500	
Accounts Receivable	88,300				88,300				88,300	
Merchandise Inventory	105,200				105,200				105,200	
Prepaid Insurance	11,500			(a) 6,900	4,600				4,600	
Store Supplies	2,300			(b) 1,400	900				900	
Office Supplies	1,500			(c) 900	600				600	
Store Equipment	166,600				166,600				166,600	
Accum. Depr.—Store Equip.		68,000		(d) 8,100		76,100				76,100
Office Equipment	49,300				49,300				49,300	
Accum. Depr.—Office Equip.		12,000		(e) 3,000		15,000				15,000
Accounts Payable		29,500				29,500				29,500
Salaries Payable				(f) 4,700		4,700				4,700
Unearned Rent		2,400	(g) 1,600			800				800
Note Payable (due 1999)		100,000				100,000				100,000
D. B. Sycamore, Capital		136,100				136,100				136,100
D. B. Sycamore, Drawing	30,000				30,000				30,000	
Sales		760,000				760,000		760,000		
Sales Returns and Allowances	12,000				12,000		12,000			
Sales Discounts	7,500				7,500		7,500			
Cost of Merchandise Sold	456,300				456,300		456,300			
Sales Salaries Expense	64,000		(f) 3,500		67,500		67,500			
Advertising Expense	13,000				13,000		13,000			
Depr. Expense—Store Equip.			(d) 8,100		8,100		8,100			
Store Supplies Expense			(b) 1,400		1,400		1,400			
Misc. Selling Expense	4,400				4,400		4,400			
Office Salaries Expense	31,000		(f) 1,200		32,200		32,200			
Rent Expense	24,000				24,000		24,000			
Depr. Expense—Office Equip.			(e) 3,000		3,000		3,000			
Insurance Expense			(a) 6,900		6,900		6,900			
Office Supplies Expense			(c) 900		900		900			
Misc. Administrative Expense	1,100				1,100		1,100			
Rent Income				(g) 1,600		1,600		1,600		
Interest Expense	11,500				11,500		11,500			
	1,108,000	1,108,000	26,600	26,600	1,123,800	1,123,800	649,800	761,600	474,000	362,200
Net Income							111,800			111,800
							761,600	761,600	474,000	474,000

Prob. 6-9A, Concluded

2.

SYCAMORE CO.
Income Statement
For Year Ended April 30, 19—

Revenues:		
Net sales..		$740,500
Rent income..		1,600
Total revenues		$742,100
Expenses:		
Cost of merchandise sold	$456,300	
Selling expenses	94,400	
Administrative expenses...........................	68,100	
Interest expense	11,500	
Total expenses		630,300
Net income..		$111,800

3.

Apr. 30	Sales...		760,000	
	Rent Income..................................		1,600	
	Income Summary			761,600
30	Income Summary...............................		649,800	
	Sales Returns and Allowances			12,000
	Sales Discounts..............................			7,500
	Cost of Merchandise Sold			456,300
	Sales Salaries Expense			67,500
	Advertising Expense			13,000
	Depreciation Expense—Store Equipment........			8,100
	Store Supplies Expense			1,400
	Miscellaneous Selling Expense.................			4,400
	Office Salaries Expense			32,200
	Rent Expense.................................			24,000
	Depreciation Expense—Office Equipment			3,000
	Insurance Expense			6,900
	Office Supplies Expense.......................			900
	Miscellaneous Administrative Expense			1,100
	Interest Expense..............................			11,500
30	Income Summary...............................		111,800	
	D.B. Sycamore, Capital			111,800
30	D.B. Sycamore, Capital.........................		30,000	
	D.B. Sycamore, Drawing.......................			30,000

Prob. 6-1B

R. FERN COMPANY
Work Sheet
For Year Ended August 31, 19—

Account Title	Trial Balance Dr.	Trial Balance Cr.	Adjustments Dr.	Adjustments Cr.	Adjusted Trial Balance Dr.	Adjusted Trial Balance Cr.	Income Statement Dr.	Income Statement Cr.	Balance Sheet Dr.	Balance Sheet Cr.
Cash	17,760				17,760				17,760	
Accounts Receivable	53,340				53,340				53,340	
Merchandise Inventory	121,400		(b) 100,000	(a) 121,400	100,000				100,000	
Prepaid Insurance	2,480			(c) 1,560	920				920	
Store Supplies	2,120			(d) 1,600	520				520	
Store Equipment	166,200				166,200				166,200	
Accum. Depr.—Store Equipment		84,600		(e) 9,300		93,900				93,900
Accounts Payable		32,000				32,000				32,000
Salaries Payable				(f) 2,700		2,700				2,700
R. Fern, Capital		199,550				199,550				199,550
R. Fern, Drawing	16,000				16,000				16,000	
Income Summary			(a) 121,400	(b) 100,000	121,400	100,000	121,400	100,000		
Sales		790,500				790,500		790,500		
Purchases	513,700				513,700		513,700			
Sales Salaries Expense	82,800		(f) 1,500		84,300		84,300			
Advertising Expense	23,300				23,300		23,300			
Depr. Expense—Store Equipment			(e) 9,300		9,300		9,300			
Store Supplies Expense			(d) 1,600		1,600		1,600			
Misc. Selling Expense	1,600				1,600		1,600			
Office Salaries Expense	52,200		(f) 1,200		53,400		53,400			
Rent Expense	25,000				25,000		25,000			
Heating and Lighting Expense	17,400				17,400		17,400			
Taxes Expense	7,850				7,850		7,850			
Insurance Expense			(c) 1,560		1,560		1,560			
Misc. Adm. Expense	3,500				3,500		3,500			
	1,106,650	1,106,650	236,560	236,560	1,218,650	1,218,650	863,910	890,500	354,740	328,150
Net Income							26,590			26,590
							890,500	890,500	354,740	354,740

This work sheet solution is applicable only if the alternate method of inventory recording presented in Appendix D is used.

Prob. 6-1B, Concluded

R. FERN COMPANY
Work Sheet
For Year Ended August 31, 19—

Account Title	Trial Balance Dr.	Trial Balance Cr.	Adjustments Dr.	Adjustments Cr.	Adjusted Trial Balance Dr.	Adjusted Trial Balance Cr.	Income Statement Dr.	Income Statement Cr.	Balance Sheet Dr.	Balance Sheet Cr.
Cash	17,760				17,760				17,760	
Accounts Receivable	53,340				53,340				53,340	
Merchandise Inventory	121,400				121,400		121,400	100,000	100,000	
Prepaid Insurance	2,480			(a) 1,560	920				920	
Store Supplies	2,120			(b) 1,600	520				520	
Store Equipment	166,200				166,200				166,200	
Accum. Depr.—Store Equipment		84,600		(c) 9,300		93,900				93,900
Accounts Payable		32,000				32,000				32,000
Salaries Payable				(d) 2,700		2,700				2,700
R. Fern, Capital		199,550				199,550				199,550
R. Fern, Drawing	16,000				16,000				16,000	
Sales		790,500				790,500		790,500		
Purchases	513,700				513,700		513,700			
Sales Salaries Expense	82,800		(d) 1,500		84,300		84,300			
Advertising Expense	23,300				23,300		23,300			
Depr. Expense—Store Equipment			(c) 9,300		9,300		9,300			
Store Supplies Expense			(b) 1,600		1,600		1,600			
Misc. Selling Expense	1,600				1,600		1,600			
Office Salaries Expense	52,200		(d) 1,200		53,400		53,400			
Rent Expense	25,000				25,000		25,000			
Heating and Lighting Expense	17,400				17,400		17,400			
Taxes Expense	7,850				7,850		7,850			
Insurance Expense			(a) 1,560		1,560		1,560			
Misc. Adm. Expense	3,500				3,500		3,500			
	1,106,650	1,106,650	15,160	15,160	1,118,650	1,118,650	863,910	890,500	354,740	328,150
Net Income							26,590			26,590
							890,500	890,500	354,740	354,740

Prob. 6-2B

1.

KILGORE COMPANY
Income Statement
For Year Ended November 30, 1994

Revenue from sales:			
Sales			$1,000,000
Less: Sales returns and			
allowances		$ 9,000	
Sales discounts		8,500	17,500
Net sales....................			$982,500
Cost of merchandise sold:			
Merchandise inventory,			
December 1, 1993			$ 90,000
Purchases.....................		$790,000	
Less: Purchases returns and			
allowances	$16,200		
Purchases discounts......	3,800	20,000	
Net purchases		$770,000	
Add transportation in.........		10,300	
Cost of merchandise			
purchased.................			780,300
Merchandise available for sale ..			$ 870,300
Less merchandise inventory,			
November 30, 1994...........			100,000
Cost of merchandise sold			770,300
Gross profit.....................			$212,200

Prob. 6-2B, Continued

Operating expenses:
Selling expenses:

Sales salaries expense........	$ 88,000	
Advertising expense	16,300	
Depreciation expense—store equipment	4,600	
Miscellaneous selling expense..................	1,000	
Total selling expenses		$ 109,900

Administrative expenses:

Office salaries expense.......	$ 30,900	
Rent expense	12,150	
Depreciation expense—office equipment...........	3,700	
Insurance expense	2,750	
Office supplies expense	900	
Miscellaneous administrative expense..................	1,150	
Total administrative expenses.................		51,550
Total operating expenses.......		161,450
Income from operations..........		$ 50,750

Other income:

Interest income	$ 5,400	
Other expense:		
Interest expense	3,660	1,740
Net income		$ 52,490

2.
KILGORE COMPANY
Statement of Owner's Equity
For Year Ended November 30, 1994

S.T. Kilgore, capital, December 1, 1993..................		$294,010
Net income for the year...............................	$52,490	
Less withdrawals.....................................	25,000	
Increase in owner's equity		27,490
S.T. Kilgore, capital, November 30, 1994		$321,500

Prob. 6-2B, Concluded

3.   **KILGORE COMPANY**
                                         Balance Sheet
                                       November 30, 1994

Assets

Current assets:

Cash	$105,000	
Notes receivable............................	50,000	
Accounts receivable	92,000	
Merchandise inventory....................	100,000	
Office supplies	1,600	
Prepaid insurance..........................	6,800	
Total current assets		$355,400

Plant assets:

Office equipment..........................	$24,000	
Less accumulated depreciation	10,800	$ 13,200
Store equipment...........................	$40,500	
Less accumulated depreciation	18,900	21,600
Total plant assets		34,800
Total assets		$390,200

Liabilities

Current liabilities:

Accounts payable.........................	$ 32,000	
Note payable (current portion).............	3,500	
Salaries payable	1,700	
Total current liabilities		$ 37,200

Long-term liabilities:

Note payable (final payment, 2004)		31,500
Total liabilities..............................		$ 68,700

Owner's Equity

S.T. Kilgore, capital		321,500
Total liabilities and owner's equity..........		$390,200

4. a. The multiple-step form of income statement contains various sections for revenues and expenses, with intermediate balances, and concludes with net income. In the single-step form, the total of all expenses is deducted from the total of all revenues. There are no intermediate balances.

    b. In the report form of balance sheet, the assets, liabilities, and owner's equity are presented in that order in a downward sequence. In the account form, the assets are listed on the left-hand side and the liabilities and owner's equity are listed on the right-hand side.

Prob. 6-3B

1.

KILGORE COMPANY
Income Statement
For Year Ended November 30, 1994

Revenues:		
Net sales...................................		**$982,500**
Interest income............................		**5,400**
Total revenues.........................		**$987,900**
Expenses:		
Cost of merchandise sold	$770,300	
Selling expenses..........................	109,900	
Administrative expenses	51,550	
Interest expense..........................	3,660	
Total expenses.......................		935,410
Net income		**$ 52,490**

2.

KILGORE COMPANY
Statement of Owner's Equity
For Year Ended November 30, 1994

S.T. Kilgore, capital, December 1, 1993.................		**$294,010**
Net income for the year..............................	$52,490	
Less withdrawals....................................	25,000	
Increase in owner's equity		27,490
S.T. Kilgore, capital, November 30, 1994		**$321,500**

Prob. 6-3B, Concluded

3.

KILGORE COMPANY
Balance Sheet
November 30, 1994

Assets

Current assets:

Cash		$105,000	
Notes receivable		50,000	
Accounts receivable		92,000	
Merchandise inventory		100,000	
Office supplies		1,600	
Prepaid insurance		6,800	
Total current assets			$355,400

Plant assets:

Office equipment	$24,000		
Less accumulated depreciation	10,800	$ 13,200	
Store equipment	$40,500		
Less accumulated depreciation	18,900	21,600	
Total plant assets			34,800
Total assets			$390,200

Liabilities

Current liabilities:

Accounts payable	$32,000		
Note payable (current portion)	3,500		
Salaries payable	1,700		
Total current liabilities		$ 37,200	

Long-term liabilities:

Note payable (final payment, 2004)		31,500	
Total liabilities		$ 68,700	

Owner's Equity

S.T. Kilgore, capital		321,500	
Total liabilities and owner's equity		$390,200	

Prob. 6-4B

1.

WATSON COMPANY
Work Sheet
For Year Ended March 31, 1994

Account Title	Trial Balance Dr.	Trial Balance Cr.	Adjustments Dr.	Adjustments Cr.	Adjusted Trial Balance Dr.	Adjusted Trial Balance Cr.	Income Statement Dr.	Income Statement Cr.	Balance Sheet Dr.	Balance Sheet Cr.
Cash	44,300				44,300				44,300	
Accounts Receivable	103,800				103,800				103,800	
Merchandise Inventory	235,500		(b) 260,000	(a) 235,500	260,000				260,000	
Prepaid Insurance	11,400			(c) 7,300	4,100				4,100	
Store Supplies	2,160			(d) 1,100	1,060				1,060	
Office Supplies	1,440			(e) 800	640				640	
Store Equipment	110,000				110,000				110,000	
Accum. Depr.—Store Equip.		33,600		(f) 9,750		43,350				43,350
Office Equipment	32,750				32,750				32,750	
Accum. Depr.—Office Equip.		14,400		(g) 3,600		18,000				18,000
Accounts Payable		60,700				60,700				60,700
Salaries Payable				(h) 4,500		4,500				4,500
Note Payable (final payment, 2005)		120,000				120,000				120,000
L. L. Watson, Capital		206,050				206,050				206,050
L. L. Watson, Drawing	20,000				20,000				20,000	
Income Summary			(a) 235,500	(b) 260,000	235,500	260,000	235,500	260,000		
Sales		900,000				900,000		900,000		
Sales Returns and Allowances	7,200				7,200		7,200			
Sales Discounts	4,200				4,200		4,200			
Purchases	600,000				600,000		600,000			
Purchases Returns and Allow.		15,000				15,000		15,000		
Purchases Discounts		7,800				7,800		7,800		
Transportation In	3,000				3,000		3,000			
Sales Salaries Expense	72,000		(h) 3,000		75,000		75,000			
Advertising Expense	25,000				25,000		25,000			
Depr. Expense—Store Equip.			(f) 9,750		9,750		9,750			
Store Supplies Expense			(d) 1,100		1,100		1,100			
Misc. Selling Expense	1,620				1,620		1,620			
Office Salaries Expense	50,000		(h) 1,500		51,500		51,500			
Rent Expense	15,000				15,000		15,000			
Insurance Expense			(c) 7,300		7,300		7,300			
Depr. Expense—Office Equip.			(g) 3,600		3,600		3,600			
Office Supplies Expense			(e) 800		800		800			
Misc. Administrative Expense	1,380				1,380		1,380			
Interest Expense	16,800				16,800		16,800			
	1,357,550	1,357,550	522,550	522,550	1,635,400	1,635,400	1,058,750	1,182,800	576,650	452,600
Net Income							124,050			124,050
							1,182,800	1,182,800	576,650	576,650

This work sheet solution is applicable only if the alternate method of inventory recording presented in Appendix D is used.

1.

Prob. 6-4B, Continued

WATSON COMPANY
Work Sheet
For Year Ended March 31, 1994

Account Title	Trial Balance Dr.	Trial Balance Cr.	Adjustments Dr.	Adjustments Cr.	Adjusted Trial Balance Dr.	Adjusted Trial Balance Cr.	Income Statement Dr.	Income Statement Cr.	Balance Sheet Dr.	Balance Sheet Cr.
Cash	44,300				44,300				44,300	
Accounts Receivable	103,800				103,800				103,800	
Merchandise Inventory	235,500				235,500		235,500	260,000	260,000	
Prepaid Insurance	11,400			(a) 7,300	4,100				4,100	
Store Supplies	2,160			(b) 1,100	1,060				1,060	
Office Supplies	1,440			(c) 800	640				640	
Store Equipment	110,000				110,000				110,000	
Accum. Depr.—Store Equip.		33,600		(d) 9,750		43,350				43,350
Office Equipment	32,750				32,750				32,750	
Accum. Depr.—Office Equip.		14,400		(e) 3,600		18,000				18,000
Accounts Payable		60,700				60,700				60,700
Salaries Payable				(f) 4,500		4,500				4,500
Note Payable (final payment, 2005)		120,000				120,000				120,000
L. L. Watson, Capital		206,050				206,050				206,050
L. L. Watson, Drawing	20,000				20,000				20,000	
Sales		900,000				900,000		900,000		
Sales Returns and Allowances	7,200				7,200		7,200			
Sales Discounts	4,200				4,200		4,200			
Purchases	600,000				600,000		600,000			
Purchases Returns and Allow.		15,000				15,000		15,000		
Purchases Discounts		7,800				7,800		7,800		
Transportation In	3,000				3,000		3,000			
Sales Salaries Expense	72,000		(f) 3,000		75,000		75,000			
Advertising Expense	25,000				25,000		25,000			
Depr. Expense—Store Equip.			(d) 9,750		9,750		9,750			
Store Supplies Expense			(b) 1,100		1,100		1,100			
Misc. Selling Expense	1,620				1,620		1,620			
Office Salaries Expense	50,000		(f) 1,500		51,500		51,500			
Rent Expense	15,000				15,000		15,000			
Insurance Expense			(a) 7,300		7,300		7,300			
Depr. Expense—Office Equip.			(e) 3,600		3,600		3,600			
Office Supplies Expense			(c) 800		800		800			
Misc. Administrative Expense	1,380				1,380		1,380			
Interest Expense	16,800				16,800		16,800			
	1,357,550	1,357,550	27,050	27,050	1,375,400	1,375,400	1,058,750	1,182,800	576,650	452,600
Net Income							124,050			124,050
							1,182,800	1,182,800	576,650	576,650

Prob. 6-4B, Continued

2.

WATSON COMPANY
Income Statement
For Year Ended March 31, 1994

Revenue from sales:			
Sales			$900,000
Less: Sales returns and			
allowances		$ 7,200	
Sales discounts...........		4,200	11,400
Net sales......................			$888,600
Cost of merchandise sold:			
Merchandise inventory,			
April 1, 1993			$235,500
Purchases........................		$600,000	
Less: Purchases returns and			
allowances	$15,000		
Purchases discounts........	7,800	22,800	
Net purchases		$577,200	
Add transportation in............		3,000	
Cost of merchandise purchased			580,200
Merchandise available for sale			$815,700
Less merchandise inventory,			
March 31, 1994.................			260,000
Cost of merchandise sold			555,700
Gross profit........................			$332,900
Operating expenses:			
Selling expenses:			
Sales salaries expense..........		$ 75,000	
Advertising expense		25,000	
Depreciation expense—store			
equipment		9,750	
Store supplies expense.........		1,100	
Miscellaneous selling expense ..		1,620	
Total selling expenses			$112,470
Administrative expenses:			
Office salaries expense.........		$ 51,500	
Rent expense		15,000	
Insurance expense		7,300	
Depreciation expense—office			
equipment		3,600	
Office supplies expense		800	
Miscellaneous			
administrative expense.......		1,380	
Total administrative expenses			79,580
Total operating expenses.........			192,050
Income from operations............			$140,850

Prob. 6-4B, Continued

Other expense:
Interest expense   16,800
Net income $124,050

3.   **WATSON COMPANY**
                          Statement of Owner's Equity
                          For Year Ended March 31, 1994

L. L. Watson, capital, April 1, 1993		$206,050
Net income for the year.	$124,050	
Less withdrawals.	20,000	
Increase in owner's equity		104,050
L. L. Watson, capital, March 31, 1994.		$310,100

Prob. 6-4B, Concluded

4.

WATSON COMPANY
Balance Sheet
March 31, 1994

Assets

Current assets:

Cash	$ 44,300	
Accounts receivable	103,800	
Merchandise inventory	260,000	
Prepaid insurance	4,100	
Store supplies	1,060	
Office supplies	640	
Total current assets		$413,900

Plant assets:

Store equipment	$110,000		
Less accumulated depreciation	43,350	$ 66,650	
Office equipment	$ 32,750		
Less accumulated depreciation	18,000	14,750	
Total plant assets			81,400
Total assets			$495,300

Liabilities

Current liabilities:

Accounts payable	$ 60,700	
Note payable (current portion)	10,000	
Salaries payable	4,500	
Total current liabilities		$ 75,200

Long-term liabilities:

Note payable (final payment, 2005)		110,000
Total liabilities		$185,200

Owner's Equity

L. L. Watson, capital		310,100
Total liabilities and owner's equity		$495,300

Prob. 6-5B

Nov. 30	Interest Receivable	600	
	Interest Income		600
30	Income Summary	260,500	
	Merchandise Inventory		260,500
30	Merchandise Inventory	241,650	
	Income Summary		241,650
30	Rent Expense	33,600	
	Prepaid Rent		33,600
30	Insurance Expense	11,500	
	Prepaid Insurance		11,500
30	Supplies Expense	2,040	
	Supplies		2,040
30	Depreciation Expense—Store Equipment	11,800	
	Accumulated Depreciation—Store Equipment		11,800
30	Depreciation Expense—Office Equipment	5,180	
	Accumulated Depreciation—Office Equipment		5,180
30	Sales Salaries Expense	4,500	
	Sales Salaries Payable		4,500

Prob. 6-6B

1.

DIETZ COMPANY
Work Sheet
For Year Ended December 31, 19—

Account Title	Trial Balance Dr.	Trial Balance Cr.	Adjustments Dr.	Adjustments Cr.	Adjusted Trial Balance Dr.	Adjusted Trial Balance Cr.	Income Statement Dr.	Income Statement Cr.	Balance Sheet Dr.	Balance Sheet Cr.
Cash	59,575				59,575				59,575	
Accounts Receivable	116,100				116,100				116,100	
Merchandise Inventory	180,000		(b) 220,000	(a) 180,000	220,000				220,000	
Prepaid Insurance	10,600			(c) 6,760	3,840				3,840	
Store Supplies	3,750			(d) 1,950	1,800				1,800	
Office Supplies	1,700			(e) 1,200	500				500	
Store Equipment	115,000				115,000				115,000	
Accum. Depr.—Store Equip.		40,300		(f) 9,500		49,800				49,800
Office Equipment	52,000				52,000				52,000	
Accum. Depr.—Office Equip.		17,200		(g) 4,800		22,000				22,000
Accounts Payable		66,700				66,700				66,700
Salaries Payable				(h) 4,600		4,600				4,600
Unearned Rent		1,200	(i) 800			400				400
Note Payable (final payment, 2000)		105,000				105,000				105,000
N. L. Dietz, Capital		220,510				220,510				220,510
N. L. Dietz, Drawing	40,000				40,000				40,000	
Income Summary			(a) 180,000	(b) 220,000	180,000	220,000	180,000	220,000		
Sales		997,500				997,500		997,500		
Sales Returns and Allow.	15,500				15,500		15,500			
Sales Discounts	6,000				6,000		6,000			
Purchases	637,500				637,500		637,500			
Purchases Returns and Allow.		11,500				11,500		11,500		
Purchases Discounts		6,000				6,000		6,000		
Transportation In	6,200				6,200		6,200			
Sales Salaries Expense	86,400		(h) 3,050		89,450		89,450			
Advertising Expense	29,450				29,450		29,450			
Depr. Expense—Store Equip.			(f) 9,500		9,500		9,500			
Store Supplies Expense			(d) 1,950		1,950		1,950			
Misc. Selling Expense	1,885				1,885		1,885			
Office Salaries Expense	60,000		(h) 1,550		61,550		61,550			
Rent Expense	30,000				30,000		30,000			
Insurance Expense			(c) 6,760		6,760		6,760			
Depr. Expense—Office Equip.			(g) 4,800		4,800		4,800			
Office Supplies Expense			(e) 1,200		1,200		1,200			
Misc. Adm. Expense	1,650				1,650		1,650			
Rent Income				(i) 800		800		800		
Interest Expense	12,600				12,600		12,600			
	1,465,910	1,465,910	429,610	429,610	1,704,810	1,704,810	1,095,995	1,235,800	608,815	469,010
Net Income							139,805			139,805
							1,235,800	1,235,800	608,815	608,815

This work sheet solution is applicable only if the alternative method of inventory recording presented in Appendix D is used.

Prob. 6-6B, Continued

DIETZ COMPANY
Work Sheet
For Year Ended December 31, 19—

Account Title	Trial Balance Dr.	Trial Balance Cr.	Adjustments Dr.	Adjustments Cr.	Adjusted Trial Balance Dr.	Adjusted Trial Balance Cr.	Income Statement Dr.	Income Statement Cr.	Balance Sheet Dr.	Balance Sheet Cr.
Cash	59,575				59,575				59,575	
Accounts Receivable	116,100				116,100				116,100	
Merchandise Inventory	180,000				180,000		180,000	220,000	220,000	
Prepaid Insurance	10,600			(a) 6,760	3,840				3,840	
Store Supplies	3,750			(b) 1,950	1,800				1,800	
Office Supplies	1,700			(c) 1,200	500				500	
Store Equipment	115,000				115,000				115,000	
Accum. Depr.—Store Equip.		40,300		(d) 9,500		49,800				49,800
Office Equipment	52,000				52,000				52,000	
Accum. Depr.—Office Equip.		17,200		(e) 4,800		22,000				22,000
Accounts Payable		66,700				66,700				66,700
Salaries Payable				(f) 4,600		4,600				4,600
Unearned Rent		1,200	(g) 800			400				400
Note Payable (final payment, 2000)		105,000				105,000				105,000
N.L. Dietz, Capital		220,510				220,510				220,510
N.L. Dietz, Drawing	40,000				40,000				40,000	
Sales		997,500				997,500		997,500		
Sales Returns and Allow.	15,500				15,500		15,500			
Sales Discounts	6,000				6,000		6,000			
Purchases	637,500				637,500		637,500			
Purchases Returns and Allow.		11,500				11,500		11,500		
Purchases Discounts		6,000				6,000		6,000		
Transportation In	6,200				6,200		6,200			
Sales Salaries Expense	86,400		(f) 3,050		89,450		89,450			
Advertising Expense	29,450				29,450		29,450			
Depr. Expense—Store Equip.			(d) 9,500		9,500		9,500			
Store Supplies Expense			(b) 1,950		1,950		1,950			
Misc. Selling Expense	1,885				1,885		1,885			
Office Salaries Expense	60,000		(f) 1,550		61,550		61,550			
Rent Expense	30,000				30,000		30,000			
Insurance Expense			(a) 6,760		6,760		6,760			
Depr. Expense—Office Equip.			(e) 4,800		4,800		4,800			
Office Supplies Expense			(c) 1,200		1,200		1,200			
Misc. Adm. Expense	1,650				1,650		1,650			
Rent Income				(g) 800		800		800		
Interest Expense	12,600				12,600		12,600			
	1,465,910	1,465,910	29,610	29,610	1,484,810	1,484,810	1,095,995	1,235,800	608,815	469,010
Net Income							139,805			139,805
							1,235,800	1,235,800	608,815	608,815

Prob. 6-6B, Continued

2.

DIETZ COMPANY
Income Statement
For Year Ended December 31, 19—

Revenue from sales:			
Sales		$997,500	
Less: Sales returns and			
allowances	$ 15,500		
Sales discounts..........	6,000	21,500	
Net sales......................			$976,000
Cost of merchandise sold:			
Merchandise inventory,			
January 1, 19—		$180,000	
Purchases......................	$637,500		
Less: Purchases returns and			
allowances	$11,500		
Purchases discounts........	6,000	17,500	
Net purchases	$620,000		
Add transportation in............	6,200		
Cost of merchandise purchased		626,200	
Merchandise available for sale		$806,200	
Less merchandise inventory,			
December 31, 19—		220,000	
Cost of merchandise sold			586,200
Gross profit........................			$389,800
Operating expenses:			
Selling expenses:			
Sales salaries expense..........	$ 89,450		
Advertising expense	29,450		
Depreciation expense—store			
equipment	9,500		
Store supplies expense.........	1,950		
Miscellaneous selling expense ..	1,885		
Total selling expenses		$132,235	
Administrative expenses:			
Office salaries expense.........	$ 61,550		
Rent expense	30,000		
Insurance expense	6,760		
Depreciation expense—office			
equipment	4,800		
Office supplies expense	1,200		
Miscellaneous administrative			
expense......................	1,650		
Total admin. expenses........		105,960	
Total operating expenses........			238,195
Income from operations...........			$151,605

Prob. 6-6B, Continued

Other expense:		
Interest expense	$ 12,600	
Other income:		
Rent income	800	11,800
Net income		$139,805

3.

DIETZ COMPANY
Statement of Owner's Equity
For Year Ended December 31, 19—

N. L. Dietz, capital, January 1, 19—		$220,510
Net income for the year.............................	$139,805	
Less withdrawals....................................	40,000	
Increase in owner's equity		99,805
N. L. Dietz, capital, December 31, 19—...............		$320,315

Prob. 6-6B, Continued

4.

DIETZ COMPANY
Balance Sheet
December 31, 19—

Assets

Current assets:

Cash	$ 59,575	
Accounts receivable	116,100	
Merchandise inventory	220,000	
Prepaid insurance	3,840	
Store supplies	1,800	
Office supplies	500	
Total current assets		$401,815

Plant assets:

Store equipment	$115,000		
Less accumulated depreciation	49,800	$ 65,200	
Office equipment	$ 52,000		
Less accumulated depreciation	22,000	30,000	
Total plant assets			95,200
Total assets			$497,015

Liabilities

Current liabilities:

Accounts payable	$ 66,700	
Note payable (current portion)	15,000	
Salaries payable	4,600	
Unearned rent	400	
Total current liabilities		$ 86,700

Long-term liabilities:

Note payable (final payment, 2000)	90,000
Total liabilities	$176,700

Owner's Equity

N. L. Dietz, capital	320,315
Total liabilities and owner's equity	$497,015

Prob. 6-6B, Continued

5. Income Summary 180,000
        Merchandise Inventory 180,000
    Merchandise Inventory 220,000
        Income Summary 220,000
    Insurance Expense 6,760
        Prepaid Insurance 6,760
    Store Supplies Expense 1,950
        Store Supplies 1,950
    Office Supplies Expense 1,200
        Office Supplies 1,200
    Depreciation Expense—Store Equipment 9,500
        Accum. Depreciation—Store Equipment 9,500
    Depreciation Expense—Office Equipment 4,800
        Accum. Depreciation—Office Equipment 4,800
    Sales Salaries Expense 3,050
    Office Salaries Expense 1,550
        Salaries Payable 4,600
    Unearned Rent 800
        Rent Income 800

Prob. 6-6B, Continued

6. Sales 997,500
   Purchases Returns and Allowances 11,500
   Purchases Discounts 6,000
   Rent Income 800
     Income Summary 1,015,800

   Income Summary 915,995
     Sales Returns and Allowances 15,500
     Sales Discounts 6,000
     Purchases 637,500
     Transportation In 6,200
     Sales Salaries Expense 89,450
     Advertising Expense 29,450
     Depreciation Expense—Store Equipment 9,500
     Store Supplies Expense 1,950
     Miscellaneous Selling Expense 1,885
     Office Salaries Expense 61,550
     Rent Expense 30,000
     Insurance Expense 6,760
     Depreciation Expense—Office Equipment 4,800
     Office Supplies Expense 1,200
     Miscellaneous Administrative Expense 1,650
     Interest Expense 12,600

   Income Summary 139,805
     N. L. Dietz, Capital 139,805

   N. L. Dietz, Capital 40,000
     N. L. Dietz, Drawing 40,000

Prob. 6-6B, Continued

The following adjusting and closing entries are applicable only if the alternative method of inventory recording presented in Appendix D is used. This approach classifies the entries for beginning and ending merchandise inventory as closing entries rather than adjusting entries.

5.

Insurance Expense	6,760	
Prepaid Insurance		6,760
Store Supplies Expense	1,950	
Store Supplies		1,950
Office Supplies Expense	1,200	
Office Supplies		1,200
Depreciation Expense—Store Equipment	9,500	
Accum. Depreciation—Store Equipment		9,500
Depreciation Expense—Office Equipment	4,800	
Accum. Depreciation—Office Equipment		4,800
Sales Salaries Expense	3,050	
Office Salaries Expense	1,550	
Salaries Payable		4,600
Unearned Rent	800	
Rent Income		800

Prob. 6-6B, Concluded

6. Sales 997,500
   Merchandise Inventory 220,000
   Purchases Returns and Allowances 11,500
   Purchases Discounts 6,000
   Rent Income 800
      Income Summary 1,235,800

   Income Summary 1,095,995
      Merchandise Inventory 180,000
      Sales Returns and Allowances 15,500
      Sales Discounts 6,000
      Purchases 637,500
      Transportation In 6,200
      Sales Salaries Expense 89,450
      Advertising Expense 29,450
      Depreciation Expense—Store Equipment 9,500
      Store Supplies Expense 1,950
      Miscellaneous Selling Expense 1,885
      Office Salaries Expense 61,550
      Rent Expense 30,000
      Insurance Expense 6,760
      Depreciation Expense—Office Equipment 4,800
      Office Supplies Expense 1,200
      Miscellaneous Administrative Expense 1,650
      Interest Expense 12,600

   Income Summary 139,805
      N. L. Dietz, Capital 139,805

   N. L. Dietz, Capital 40,000
      N. L. Dietz, Drawing 40,000

Prob. 6-7B

May	3	Merchandise Inventory	4,120	
		Accounts Payable		4,120
	5	Merchandise Inventory	8,500	
		Accounts Payable		8,500
	6	Accounts Receivable	2,800	
		Sales		2,800
	6	Cost of Merchandise Sold	1,125	
		Merchandise Inventory		1,125
	8	Office Supplies	150	
		Cash		150
	10	Accounts Payable	1,300	
		Merchandise Inventory		1,300
	13	Accounts Payable	4,120	
		Cash		4,040
		Merchandise Inventory		80
	14	Merchandise Inventory	10,500	
		Cash		10,500
	15	Accounts Payable	7,200	
		Cash		7,128
		Merchandise Inventory		72
	16	Cash	2,744	
		Sales Discounts	56	
		Accounts Receivable		2,800
	19	Accounts Receivable	2,450	
		Sales		2,450
	19	Cost of Merchandise Sold	980	
		Merchandise Inventory		980
	22	Accounts Receivable	3,480	
		Sales		3,480
	22	Cost of Merchandise Sold	1,400	
		Merchandise Inventory		1,400
	24	Cash	4,350	
		Sales		4,350
	24	Cost of Merchandise Sold	1,750	
		Merchandise Inventory		1,750
	25	Sales Returns and Allowances	1,480	
		Accounts Receivable		1,480
	25	Merchandise Inventory	600	
		Cost of Merchandise Sold		600
	31	Cash	2,310	
		Credit Card Collection Expense	140	
		Accounts Receivable		2,450

MARDEN COMPANY
Work Sheet
For Year Ended June 30, 19—

Account Title	Trial Balance Dr.	Trial Balance Cr.	Adjustments Dr.	Adjustments Cr.	Adjusted Trial Balance Dr.	Adjusted Trial Balance Cr.	Income Statement Dr.	Income Statement Cr.	Balance Sheet Dr.	Balance Sheet Cr.
Cash	15,100				15,100				15,100	
Notes Receivable	50,000				50,000				50,000	
Accounts Receivable	67,600				67,600				67,600	
Merchandise Inventory	91,700				91,700				91,700	
Prepaid Insurance	5,800			(a) 3,800	2,000				2,000	
Store Supplies	4,950			(b) 4,080	870				870	
Store Equipment	50,500				50,500				50,500	
Accum. Depr.—Store Equipment		30,130		(c) 10,500		40,630				40,630
Accounts Payable		26,800				26,800				26,800
Salaries Payable				(d) 4,250		4,250				4,250
Unearned Rent		4,600	(e) 3,800			800				800
L. Marden, Capital		169,870				169,870				169,870
L. Marden, Drawing	15,000				15,000				15,000	
Sales		600,500				600,500		600,500		
Cost of Merchandise Sold	360,300				360,300		360,300			
Sales Salaries Expense	61,500		(d) 2,600		64,100		64,100			
Advertising Expense	25,800				25,800		25,800			
Depr. Expense—Store Equip.			(c) 10,500		10,500		10,500			
Store Supplies Expense			(b) 4,080		4,080		4,080			
Misc. Selling Expense	3,750				3,750		3,750			
Office Salaries Expense	39,000		(d) 1,650		40,650		40,650			
Rent Expense	24,000				24,000		24,000			
Heating and Lighting Expense	9,660				9,660		9,660			
Taxes Expense	5,100				5,100		5,100			
Insurance Expense			(a) 3,800		3,800		3,800			
Misc. Administrative Expense	2,140				2,140		2,140			
Rent Income				(e) 3,800		3,800		3,800		
	831,900	831,900	26,430	26,430	846,650	846,650	553,880	604,300	292,770	242,350
Net Income							50,420			50,420
							604,300	604,300	292,770	292,770

Prob. 6-9B

MCNAIR COMPANY
Work Sheet
For Year Ended October 31, 19—

Account Title	Trial Balance Dr.	Cr.	Adjustments Dr.	Cr.	Adjusted Trial Balance Dr.	Cr.	Income Statement Dr.	Cr.	Balance Sheet Dr.	Cr.
Cash	14,400				14,400				14,400	
Accounts Receivable	86,300				86,300				86,300	
Merchandise Inventory	108,400				108,400				108,400	
Prepaid Insurance	10,500			(a) 7,600	2,900				2,900	
Store Supplies	3,800			(b) 2,200	1,600				1,600	
Office Supplies	1,200			(c) 750	450				450	
Store Equipment	159,600				159,600				159,600	
Accum. Depr.—Store Equip.		53,000		(d) 10,500		63,500				63,500
Office Equipment	47,300				47,300				47,300	
Accum. Depr.—Office Equip.		12,000		(e) 3,800		15,800				15,800
Accounts Payable		30,500				30,500				30,500
Salaries Payable				(f) 4,100		4,100				4,100
Unearned Rent		2,400	(g) 1,600			800				800
Note Payable (due 1999)		80,000				80,000				80,000
A.C. McNair, Capital		149,200				149,200				149,200
A.C. McNair, Drawing	29,000				29,000				29,000	
Sales		820,000				820,000		820,000		
Sales Returns and Allowances	7,000				7,000		7,000			
Sales Discounts	8,500				8,500		8,500			
Cost of Merchandise Expense	515,000				515,000		515,000			
Sales Salaries Expense	70,000		(f) 3,200		73,200		73,200			
Advertising Expense	28,000				28,000		28,000			
Depr. Expense—Store Equip.			(d) 10,500		10,500		10,500			
Store Supplies Expense			(b) 2,200		2,200		2,200			
Misc. Selling Expense	2,400				2,400		2,400			
Office Salaries Expense	35,000		(f) 900		35,900		35,900			
Rent Expense	10,000				10,000		10,000			
Depr. Expense—Office Equip.			(e) 3,800		3,800		3,800			
Insurance Expense			(a) 7,600		7,600		7,600			
Office Supplies Expense			(c) 750		750		750			
Misc. Administrative Expense	1,100				1,100		1,100			
Rent Income				(g) 1,600		1,600		1,600		
Interest Expense	9,600				9,600		9,600			
	1,147,100	1,147,100	30,550	30,550	1,165,500	1,165,500	715,550	821,600	449,950	343,900
Net Income							106,050			106,050
							821,600	821,600	449,950	449,950

Prob. 6-9B, Concluded

2.

MCNAIR COMPANY
Income Statement
For Year Ended October 31, 19—

Revenues:		
Net sales..		$804,500
Rent income.......................................		1,600
Total revenues..................................		$806,100
Expenses:		
Cost of merchandise sold	$515,000	
Selling expenses.................................	116,300	
Administrative expenses.........................	59,150	
Interest expense.................................	9,600	
Total expenses................................		700,050
Net income		$106,050

3.

Oct. 31	Sales.......................................	820,000	
	Rent Income..................................	1,600	
	Income Summary		821,600
31	Income Summary	715,550	
	Sales Returns and Allowances		7,000
	Sales Discounts..............................		8,500
	Cost of Merchandise Sold		515,000
	Sales Salaries Expense		73,200
	Advertising Expense		28,000
	Depreciation Expense—Store Equipment		10,500
	Store Supplies Expense		2,200
	Miscellaneous Selling Expense		2,400
	Office Salaries Expense		35,900
	Rent Expense................................		10,000
	Depreciation Expense—Office Equipment		3,800
	Insurance Expense		7,600
	Office Supplies Expense......................		750
	Miscellaneous Administrative Expense		1,100
	Interest Expense		9,600
31	Income Summary	106,050	
	A.C. McNair, Capital.........................		106,050
31	A.C. McNair, Capital	29,000	
	A.C. McNair, Drawing		29,000

Mini-Case 6

1.

BROOKS VIDEO COMPANY
Income Statement
For Year Ended May 31, 1994

Revenue from sales:			
Sales			$308,200
Less sales returns and allowances.................			1,200
Net sales........................			$307,000
Cost of merchandise sold:			
Merchandise inventory, June 1, 1993		$ 44,800	
Purchases.........................		$231,600	
Less: Purchases returns and allowances.................	$3,820		
Purchases discounts.........	2,480	6,300	
Net purchases		$225,300	
Add transportation in.............		7,100	
Cost of merchandise purchased .		232,400	
Merchandise available for sale.....		$277,200	
Less merchandise inventory, May 31, 1994...................		62,300	
Cost of merchandise sold			214,900
Gross profit........................			$ 92,100

Mini-Case 6, Continued

Operating expenses:
  Selling expenses:

Sales salaries expense............	$ 20,200	
Transportation out..............	14,160	
Advertising expense	6,940	
Depreciation expense—store equipment	2,160	
Store supplies expense..........	1,600	
Miscellaneous selling expense ...	1,020	
Total selling expenses		$ 46,080

Administrative expenses:

Office salaries expense..........	$ 9,400	
Heating and lighting expense....	5,750	
Insurance expense	4,050	
Depreciation expense—building .	2,880	
Depreciation expense—office equipment	1,260	
Office supplies expense	840	
Miscellaneous administrative expense......................	600	
Total administrative expenses....................	24,780	
Total operating expenses.........		70,860
Income from operations............		$ 21,240

Other expense:

Interest expense	$ 6,000	
Other income:		
Interest income	500	5,500
Net income		$ 15,740

BROOKS VIDEO COMPANY
Statement of Owner's Equity
For Year Ended May 31, 1994

D. Brooks, capital, June 1, 1993.........................		$130,760
Net income for the year................................	$15,740	
Less withdrawals......................................	15,000	
Increase in owner's equity		740
D. Brooks, capital, May 31, 1994		$131,500

Mini-Case 6, Continued

BROOKS VIDEO COMPANY
Balance Sheet
May 31, 1994

Assets

Current assets:			
Cash		$15,100	
Notes receivable		5,000	
Accounts receivable		25,600	
Merchandise inventory		62,300	
Supplies		1,820	
Prepaid insurance		1,680	
Total current assets			$111,500
Plant assets:			
Land		$30,000	
Building	$58,900		
Less accumulated depreciation	5,760	53,140	
Office equipment	$ 6,300		
Less accumulated depreciation	2,520	3,780	
Store equipment	$12,800		
Less accumulated depreciation	4,320	8,480	
Total plant assets			95,400
Total assets			$206,900

Liabilities

Current liabilities:		
Accounts payable	$13,800	
Salaries payable	1,600	
Total current liabilities		$ 15,400
Long-term liabilities:		
Note payable (due in 2002)		60,000
Total liabilities		$ 75,400

Owner's Equity

D. Brooks, capital	131,500
Total liabilities and owner's equity	$206,900

Mini-Case 6, Continued

2.

BROOKS VIDEO COMPANY
Projected Income Statement
For Year Ended May 31, 1995

Revenues:		
Net sales (a)		$337,700
Interest income		500
Total revenues		$338,200
Expenses:		
Cost of merchandise sold (b)	$236,390	
Selling expenses (c)	32,182	
Administrative expenses (d)...........................	24,924	
Interest expense	6,000	
Total expenses.....................................		299,496
Net income		$ 38,704

Notes:

(a)	Projected net sales [$307,000 + (10% × $307,000)].....		$337,700
(b)	Projected cost of merchandise sold		
	($337,700 × 70%).................................		$236,390
(c)	Total selling expenses for year ended May 31, 1994 ...		$ 46,080
	Add: Increase in store supplies expense		
	($1,600 × 10%)................................	$160	
	Increase in miscellaneous selling expense		
	($1,020 × 10%)................................	102	262
	Less transportation out expenses		(14,160)
	Projected total selling expenses		$ 32,182
(d)	Total administrative expenses for year ended		
	May 31, 1994...		$ 24,780
	Add: Increase in office supplies expense		
	($840 × 10%)	$ 84	
	Increase in miscellaneous administrative expense		
	($600 × 10%)	60	144
	Projected total administrative expenses		$ 24,924

3. **a.** Yes. The proposed change will increase net income from $15,740 to $38,704, a change of $22,964.

  b. Possible concerns related to the proposed changes include the following:

   The primary concern is with the accuracy of the estimates used for projecting the effects of the proposed changes. If the increase in sales does not materialize, Brooks Video Company could incur significant costs of carrying excess inventory stocked in anticipation of increasing sales. At the same time it is incurring these additional inventory costs, cash collections from customers will be reduced by the amount of the discounts. This could create a liquidity problem for Brooks Video Company.

Mini-Case 6, Concluded

Another concern arises from the proposed change in shipping terms so as to eliminate all shipments of merchandise FOB destination, thereby eliminating transportation out expenses. Brooks Video Company assumes that this change will have no effect on sales. However, some (perhaps a significant number) customers may object to this change and may seek other vendors with more favorable shipping terms. Hence, an unanticipated *decline* in sales could occur because of this change.

As with any business decision, risks (concerns) such as those mentioned above must be thoroughly considered before final action is taken.

COMPREHENSIVE PROBLEM 2

2.   JOURNAL   Pages 20 and 21

Date		Description	Post. Ref.	Debit	Credit
1994					
May	1	Rent Expense.............................	531	2,500	
		Cash	110		2,500
	1	Notes Receivable	111	10,000	
		Accounts Receivable	112		10,000
	2	Purchases	510	22,000	
		Accounts Payable	210		22,000
	3	Transportation In	513	860	
		Cash	110		860
	4	Purchases	510	16,200	
		Accounts Payable	210		16,200
	5	Accounts Receivable......................	112	8,500	
		Sales.................................	410		8,500
	8	Cash	110	14,900	
		Accounts Receivable	112		14,900
	10	Cash	110	18,300	
		Sales.................................	410		18,300
	11	Accounts Payable.........................	210	13,000	
		Purchases Discounts	512		200
		Cash	110		12,800
	12	Accounts Payable.........................	210	22,000	
		Purchases Discounts	512		440
		Cash	110		21,560
	13	Sales Returns and Allowances.............	411	1,000	
		Accounts Receivable	112		1,000
	14	Advertising Expense......................	521	2,000	
		Cash	110		2,000
	15	Cash	110	7,350	
		Sales Discounts.........................	412	150	
		Accounts Receivable	112		7,500
	18	Sales Salaries Expense....................	520	1,500	
		Office Salaries Expense	530	500	
		Cash	110		2,000
	18	Cash	110	28,500	
		Sales Discounts.........................	412	400	
		Accounts Receivable	112		28,900

Comp. Prob. 2, Continued

Date	Description	Post. Ref.	Debit	Credit
1994				
May 19	Purchases	510	6,400	
	Cash	110		6,400
19	Accounts Payable..........................	210	13,400	
	Purchases Discounts	512		250
	Cash	110		13,150
20	Accounts Receivable......................	112	16,000	
	Sales..................................	410		16,000
21	Accounts Receivable......................	112	600	
	Cash	110		600
21	Purchases	510	15,000	
	Accounts Payable	210		15,000
22	Accounts Payable..........................	210	16,200	
	Cash	110		16,200
24	Accounts Payable..........................	210	3,000	
	Purchases Returns and Allowances	511		3,000
25	Sales Returns and Allowances.............	411	400	
	Cash	110		400
27	Sales Salaries Expense....................	520	1,200	
	Office Salaries Expense	530	400	
	Cash	110		1,600
28	Accounts Receivable......................	112	24,700	
	Sales..................................	410		24,700
29	Store Supplies............................	117	350	
	Cash	110		350
30	Cash	110	16,440	
	Sales Discounts.........................	412	160	
	Accounts Receivable	112		16,600
31	Accounts Payable.........................	210	12,000	
	Purchases Discounts	512		120
	Cash	110		11,880
31	Accounts Receivable......................	112	17,400	
	Sales..................................	410		17,400
31	Purchases	510	19,700	
	Accounts Payable........................	210		19,700

JOURNAL   **Pages 21 and 22**

Comp. Prob. 2, Continued

6. and 7.   JOURNAL   **Pages 23 and 24**

Date	Description	Post. Ref.	Debit	Credit
	Adjusting Entries			
1994				
May 31	Interest Receivable......................	113	100	
	Interest Income	611		100
31	Income Summary......................	312	123,900	
	Merchandise Inventory	115		123,900
31	Merchandise Inventory..................	115	134,150	
	Income Summary	312		134,150
31	Insurance Expense.....................	532	2,250	
	Prepaid Insurance	116		2,250
31	Store Supplies Expense	523	2,150	
	Store Supplies	117		2,150
31	Depreciation Expense	522	8,860	
	Accumulated Depreciation—Store Equip.	124		8,860
31	Sales Salaries Expense	520	400	
	Office Salaries Expense	530	140	
	Salaries Payable	211		540
	Closing Entries			
1994				
May 31	Sales.................................	410	826,500	
	Purchases Returns and Allowances	511	24,600	
	Purchases Discounts	512	6,770	
	Interest Income........................	611	100	
	Income Summary	312		857,970
31	Income Summary.......................	312	819,120	
	Sales Returns and Allowances	411		15,000
	Sales Discounts.......................	412		5,910
	Purchases	510		619,300
	Transportation In	513		6,260
	Sales Salaries Expense	520		77,500
	Advertising Expense	521		20,000
	Depreciation Expense	522		8,860
	Store Supplies Expense	523		2,150
	Miscellaneous Selling Expense.........	529		2,800
	Office Salaries Expense	530		30,440
	Rent Expense..........................	531		27,000
	Insurance Expense	532		2,250
	Miscellaneous Administrative Expense .	539		1,650

Comp. Prob. 2, Continued

JOURNAL

Date	Description	Post. Ref.	Debit	Credit
1994				
May 31	Income Summary........................	312	49,100	
	F. L. Oliver, Capital	310		49,100
31	F. L. Oliver, Capital	310	4,500	
	F. L. Oliver, Drawing...................	311		4,500

1, 3, 6, and 7.

Cash   **110**

					Balance	
Date	Item	Post. Ref.	Dr.	Cr.	Dr.	Cr.
1994						
May 1	Balance..............	√	......	......	39,160	......
1	....	20	......	2,500	......	......
3	....	20	......	860	......	......
8	....	20	14,900	......		
10	....	20	18,300	......		
11	....	20	......	12,800	......	......
12	....	20	......	21,560	......	......
14	....	21	......	2,000	......	......
15	....	21	7,350	......		
18	....	21	......	2,000	......	......
18	....	21	28,500	......		
19	....	21	......	6,400	......	......
19	....	21	......	13,150	......	......
21	....	21	......	600	......	......
22	....	22	......	16,200	......	......
25	....	22	......	400	......	......
27	....	22	......	1,600	......	......
29	....	22	......	350	......	......
30	....	22	16,440	......	......	......
31	....	22	......	11,880	32,350	......

Notes Receivable   **111**

1994						
May 1	....	20	10,000	......	10,000	......

Comp. Prob. 2, Continued

Accounts Receivable

Date	Item	Post. Ref.	Dr.	Cr.	Balance Dr.	Balance Cr.
1994						
May 1	Balance..............	√	....	....	60,220	......
1	....	20	....	10,000	....	......
5	....	20	8,500	....	....	......
8	....	20	....	14,900	....	......
13	....	21	....	1,000	....	......
15	....	21	....	7,500	....	......
18	....	21	....	28,900	....	......
20	....	21	16,000	....	....	......
21	....	21	600	....	....	......
28	....	22	24,700	....	....	......
30	....	22	....	16,600	....	......
31	....	22	17,400	....	48,520	......

112

Interest Receivable

Date	Item	Post. Ref.	Dr.	Cr.	Balance Dr.	Balance Cr.
1994						
May 31	Adjusting...........	23	100	....	100	......

113

Merchandise Inventory

Date	Item	Post. Ref.	Dr.	Cr.	Balance Dr.	Balance Cr.
1993						
June 1	Balance..............	√	....	....	123,900	....
1994						
May 31	Adjusting...........	23	....	123,900	....	....
31	Adjusting...........	23	134,150	....	134,150	....

115

Prepaid Insurance

Date	Item	Post. Ref.	Dr.	Cr.	Balance Dr.	Balance Cr.
1994						
May 1	Balance..............	√	....	....	3,750	......
31	Adjusting...........	23	....	2,250	1,500	......

116

Store Supplies

Date	Item	Post. Ref.	Dr.	Cr.	Balance Dr.	Balance Cr.
1994						
May 1	Balance..............	√	....	....	2,550	......
29	....	22	350	....	2,900	......
31	Adjusting...........	23	....	2,150	750	......

117

Comp. Prob. 2, Continued

Store Equipment   123

| | | | Post. | | | Balance | |
Date	Item		Ref.	Dr.	Cr.	Dr.	Cr.
1994							
May 1	Balance............		√	......	....	44,300	......

Accumulated Depreciation—Store Equipment   124

1994							
May 1	Balance............		√	....	....	....	12,600
31	Adjusting...........		23	....	8,860	....	21,460

Accounts Payable   210

1994							
May 1	Balance............		√	......	....	....	38,500
2	....		20	....	22,000	....	....
4	....		20	....	16,200	....	....
11	....		20	13,000	......	....	....
12	....		20	22,000	......	....	....
19	....		21	13,400	......	....	....
21	....		21	....	15,000	....	....
22	....		22	16,200	......	....	....
24	....		22	3,000	......	....	....
31	....		22	12,000	......	....	....
31	....		22	....	19,700	....	31,800

Salaries Payable   211

1994							
May 31	Adjusting...........		23	....	540	....	540

F. L. Oliver, Capital   310

1993							
June 1	Balance............		√	....	....	....	173,270
1994							
May 31	Closing............		24	....	49,100	....	....
31	Closing............		24	4,500	....	....	217,870

F. L. Oliver, Drawing   311

1994							
May 1	Balance............		√	....	....	4,500	......
31	Closing............		24	....	4,500	—	—

Comp. Prob. 2, Continued

Income Summary   312

Date	Item	Post. Ref.	Dr.	Cr.	Balance Dr.	Balance Cr.
1994						
May 31	Adjusting............	23	123,900	....	....	....
31	Adjusting............	23	....	134,150	....	....
31	Closing.............	24	....	857,970	....	....
31	Closing.............	24	819,120	....	....	....
31	Closing.............	24	49,100	....	—	—

Sales   410

Date	Item	Post. Ref.	Dr.	Cr.	Balance Dr.	Balance Cr.
1994						
May 1	Balance..............	√	....	....	....	741,600
5	....	20	....	8,500	....	....
10	....	20	....	18,300	....	....
20	....	21	....	16,000	....	....
28	....	22	....	24,700	....	....
31	....	22	....	17,400	....	826,500
31	Closing.............	24	826,500	....	—	—

Sales Returns and Allowances   411

Date	Item	Post. Ref.	Dr.	Cr.	Balance Dr.	Balance Cr.
1994						
May 1	Balance..............	√	....	....	13,600	....
13	....	21	1,000	....	....	....
25	....	22	400	....	15,000	....
31	Closing.............	24	....	15,000	—	—

Sales Discounts   412

Date	Item	Post. Ref.	Dr.	Cr.	Balance Dr.	Balance Cr.
1994						
May 1	Balance..............	√	....	....	5,200	....
15	....	21	150	....	....	....
18	....	21	400	....	....	....
30	....	22	160	....	5,910	....
31	Closing.............	24	....	5,910	—	—

Comp. Prob. 2, Continued

Purchases   510

Date	Item	Post. Ref.	Dr.	Cr.	Balance Dr.	Balance Cr.
1994						
May 1	Balance.............	√	....	....	540,000	......
2	....	20	22,000	....	....	......
4	....	20	16,200	....	....	......
19	....	21	6,400	....	....	......
21	....	21	15,000	....	....	......
31	....	22	19,700	....	619,300	......
31	Closing.............	24	....	619,300	—	—

Purchases Returns and Allowances   511

Date	Item	Post. Ref.	Dr.	Cr.	Balance Dr.	Balance Cr.
1994						
May 1	Balance.............	√	....	....	....	21,600
24	....	22	....	3,000	....	24,600
31	Closing.............	24	24,600	....	—	—

Purchases Discounts   512

Date	Item	Post. Ref.	Dr.	Cr.	Balance Dr.	Balance Cr.
1994						
May 1	Balance.............	√	....	....	....	5,760
11	....	20	....	200	....	......
12	....	20	....	440	....	......
19	....	21	....	250	....	......
31	....	22	....	120	....	6,770
31	Closing.............	24	6,770	....	—	—

Transportation In   513

Date	Item	Post. Ref.	Dr.	Cr.	Balance Dr.	Balance Cr.
1994						
May 1	Balance.............	√	....	....	5,400	......
3	....	20	860	....	6,260	......
31	Closing.............	24	....	6,260	—	—

Sales Salaries Expense   520

Date	Item	Post. Ref.	Dr.	Cr.	Balance Dr.	Balance Cr.
1994						
May 1	Balance.............	√	....	....	74,400	......
18	....	21	1,500	....	....	......
27	....	22	1,200	....	77,100	......
31	Adjusting...........	23	400	....	77,500	......
31	Closing.............	24	....	77,500	—	—

Comp. Prob. 2, Continued

Advertising Expense   521

Date		Item	Post. Ref.	Dr.	Cr.	Balance Dr.	Balance Cr.
1994							
May	1	Balance.............	√	....	....	18,000	....
	14	....	21	2,000	....	20,000	....
	31	Closing.............	24	....	20,000	—	—

Depreciation Expense   522

Date		Item	Post. Ref.	Dr.	Cr.	Balance Dr.	Balance Cr.
1994							
May	31	Adjusting...........	23	8,860	....	8,860	....
	31	Closing.............	24	....	8,860	—	—

Store Supplies Expense   523

Date		Item	Post. Ref.	Dr.	Cr.	Balance Dr.	Balance Cr.
1994							
May	31	Adjusting...........	23	2,150	....	2,150	....
	31	Closing.............	24	....	2,150	—	—

Miscellaneous Selling Expense   529

Date		Item	Post. Ref.	Dr.	Cr.	Balance Dr.	Balance Cr.
1994							
May	1	Balance.............	√	....	....	2,800	....
	31	Closing.............	24	....	2,800	—	—

Office Salaries Expense   530

Date		Item	Post. Ref.	Dr.	Cr.	Balance Dr.	Balance Cr.
1994							
May	1	Balance.............	√	....	....	29,400	....
	18	....	21	500	....	....	....
	27	....	22	400	....	30,300	....
	31	Adjusting...........	23	140	....	30,440	....
	31	Closing.............	24	....	30,440	—	—

Rent Expense   531

Date		Item	Post. Ref.	Dr.	Cr.	Balance Dr.	Balance Cr.
1994							
May	1	Balance.............	√	....	....	24,500	....
	1	....	20	2,500	....	27,000	....
	31	Closing.............	24	....	27,000	—	—

Comp. Prob. 2, Continued

Insurance Expense 532

| Date | Item | Post. Ref. | Dr. | Cr. | Balance | |
					Dr.	Cr.
1994						
May 31	Adjusting............	23	2,250	....	2,250	....
31	Closing...............	24	....	2,250	—	—

Miscellaneous Administrative Expense 539

1994						
May 1	Balance..............	√	....	....	1,650	....
31	Closing..............	24	....	1,650	—	—

Interest Income 611

1994						
May 31	Adjusting............	23	....	100	....	100
31	Closing..............	24	100	....	—	—

Comp. Prob. 2, Continued

4.

OLIVER COMPANY
Work Sheet
For Year Ended May 31, 1994

Account Title	Trial Balance Dr.	Trial Balance Cr.	Adjustments Dr.	Adjustments Cr.	Adjusted Trial Balance Dr.	Adjusted Trial Balance Cr.	Income Statement Dr.	Income Statement Cr.	Balance Sheet Dr.	Balance Sheet Cr.
Cash	32,350				32,350				32,350	
Notes Receivable	10,000				10,000				10,000	
Accounts Receivable	48,520				48,520				48,520	
Interest Receivable			(a) 100		100				100	
Merchandise Inventory	123,900		(c) 134,150	(b) 123,900	134,150				134,150	
Prepaid Insurance	3,750			(d) 2,250	1,500				1,500	
Store Supplies	2,900			(e) 2,150	750				750	
Store Equipment	44,300				44,300				44,300	
Accum. Depreciation		12,600		(f) 8,860		21,460				21,460
Accounts Payable		31,800				31,800				31,800
Salaries Payable				(g) 540		540				540
F.L. Oliver, Capital		173,270				173,270				173,270
F.L. Oliver, Drawing	4,500				4,500				4,500	
Income Summary			(b) 123,900	(c) 134,150	123,900	134,150	123,900	134,150		
Sales		826,500				826,500		826,500		
Sales Returns and Allowances	15,000				15,000		15,000			
Sales Discounts	5,910				5,910		5,910			
Purchases	619,300				619,300		619,300			
Purch. Returns and Allow.		24,600				24,600		24,600		
Purchases Discounts		6,770				6,770		6,770		
Transportation In	6,260				6,260		6,260			
Sales Salaries Expense	77,100		(g) 400		77,500		77,500			
Advertising Expense	20,000				20,000		20,000			
Depreciation Expense			(f) 8,860		8,860		8,860			
Store Supplies Expense			(e) 2,150		2,150		2,150			
Misc. Selling Expense	2,800				2,800		2,800			
Office Salaries Expense	30,300		(g) 140		30,440		30,440			
Rent Expense	27,000				27,000		27,000			
Insurance Expense			(d) 2,250		2,250		2,250			
Misc. Adm. Expense	1,650				1,650		1,650			
Interest Income				(a) 100		100		100		
	1,075,540	1,075,540	271,950	271,950	1,219,190	1,219,190	943,020	992,120	276,170	227,070
Net Income							49,100			49,100
							992,120	992,120	276,170	276,170

Comp. Prob. 2, Continued

5.   **OLIVER COMPANY**
                              Income Statement
                        For Year Ended May 31, 1994

Revenue from sales:		
Sales		$826,500
Less: Sales returns and		
allowances	$ 15,000	
Sales discounts..........	5,910	20,910
Net sales......................		$805,590
Cost of merchandise sold:		
Merchandise inventory,		
June 1, 1993		$123,900
Purchases.....................	$619,300	
Less: Purchases returns and		
allowances	$24,600	
Purchases discounts........	6,770	31,370
Net purchases	$587,930	
Add transportation in............	6,260	
Cost of merchandise purchased		594,190
Merchandise available for sale		$718,090
Less merchandise inventory,		
May 31, 1994..................		134,150
Cost of merchandise sold		583,940
Gross profit........................		$221,650
Operating expenses:		
Selling expenses:		
Sales salaries expense..........	$ 77,500	
Advertising expense	20,000	
Depreciation expense	8,860	
Store supplies expense.........	2,150	
Miscellaneous selling expense ..	2,800	
Total selling expenses		$111,310
Administrative expenses:		
Office salaries expense..........	$ 30,440	
Rent expense	27,000	
Insurance expense	2,250	
Miscellaneous administrative		
expense......................	1,650	
Total administrative expenses		61,340
Total operating expenses........		172,650
Income from operations............		$ 49,000
Other income:		
Interest income		100
Net income		$ 49,100

Comp. Prob. 2, Continued

OLIVER COMPANY
Statement of Owner's Equity
For Year Ended May 31, 1994

F. L. Oliver, capital, June 1, 1993		$173,270
Net income for the year	$49,100	
Less withdrawals	4,500	
Increase in owner's equity		44,600
F. L. Oliver, capital, May 31, 1994		$217,870

OLIVER COMPANY
Balance Sheet
May 31, 1994

Assets

Current assets:		
Cash	$ 32,350	
Notes receivable	10,000	
Accounts receivable	48,520	
Interest receivable	100	
Merchandise inventory	134,150	
Prepaid insurance	1,500	
Store supplies	750	
Total current assets		$227,370
Plant assets:		
Store equipment	$ 44,300	
Less accumulated depreciation	21,460	
Total plant assets		22,840
Total assets		$250,210

Liabilities

Current liabilities:		
Accounts payable	$ 31,800	
Salaries payable	540	
Total liabilities		$ 32,340

Owner's Equity

F. L. Oliver, capital		217,870
Total liabilities and owner's equity		$250,210

Comp. Prob. 2, Concluded

8.

OLIVER COMPANY
Post-Closing Trial Balance
May 31, 1994

Cash	32,350	
Notes Receivable	10,000	
Accounts Receivable	48,520	
Interest Receivable	100	
Merchandise Inventory	134,150	
Prepaid Insurance	1,500	
Store Supplies	750	
Store Equipment	44,300	
Accumulated Depreciation		21,460
Accounts Payable		31,800
Salaries Payable		540
F. L. Oliver, Capital		217,870
Total	271,670	271,670

CHAPTER 7

DISCUSSION QUESTIONS

1. The accounting system is an information system because it provides information for management's use in conducting the affairs of the business and in reporting to owners, creditors, and others. It includes the entire network of communications used by an enterprise.

2. Internal controls are the detailed procedures used by management to direct operations, protect assets, and provide reasonable assurance that the business's objectives are achieved.

3. The objective of systems analysis is the determination of informational needs, the sources of such information, and the deficiencies in procedures and data processing methods currently employed.

4. A *Systems Manual* contains the forms, records, procedures, processing methods, and reports used by an enterprise.

5. The three elements of the internal control structure are (1) the accounting system, (2) the control procedures, and (3) the control environment. The accounting system is an integral part of the internal control structure because it provides the information needed by management to plan and direct operations in order to achieve enterprise goals. The control procedures are those policies and procedures established to provide reasonable assurance that enterprise goals will be achieved. The control environment is the overall attitude toward and awareness of the importance of control by employees.

6. The knowledge that job rotation is practiced and one employee may perform another's job at a later date tends to discourage deviations from prescribed procedures. Also, rotation helps to disclose any irregularities that may occur.

7. Vesting complete control over a sequence of related operations in one individual presents opportunities for inefficiency, errors, and fraud. The control over a sequence of operations should be divided so that the work of each employee is automatically checked by another employee in the normal course of work. A system functioning in this manner helps prevent errors and inefficiency. Fraud is unlikely without collusion between two or more employees.

8. To reduce the possibility of errors and embezzlement, the functions of operations and accounting should be separated. Thus, one employee should not be responsible for handling cash receipts (operations) and maintaining the accounts receivable records (accounting).

9. Responsibility for related operations, such as responsibility for cash receipts and approving sales returns and allowances, should be separated to decrease the possibility of inefficiency, errors, and fraud. For example, an employee handling cash could take it and cover the fraud by recording a sales return or allowance in the accounting records.

10. No. Combining the responsibility for related operations, such as combining the functions of purchasing, receiving, and storing of merchandise, increases the possibility of errors and fraud.

11. No. Combining the responsibility for related operations (such as combining the maintenance of personnel records and timekeeping, preparation of payroll records, and distribution of payroll checks), increases the possibility of errors and fraud.

12. The control procedure requiring that responsibility for a sequence of related operations be divided among different persons is violated in this situation. This weakness in the internal control may permit irregularities. For example, the ticket seller, while acting as ticket taker, could take the admission ticket, fail to dispose of it, and later resell it.

13. The responsibility for maintaining the accounting records should be separated from the responsibility for operations so that the accounting records can serve as an independent check on operations.

14. The use of a fidelity bond insures a company against losses caused by fraud on the part of employees who are entrusted with company assets, and it serves as a psychological deterrent to the misuse of assets.

15. Internal auditors, who should be independent of the employees responsible for operations, periodically review and evaluate the internal control structure to determine that the internal control procedures are being effectively applied. They report weaknesses and recommend changes to correct them.

16. a. Subsidiary ledger
    b. Controlling account

17. The major advantages of the use of special journals are substantial savings in record keeping expenses and a reduction of record keeping errors.

18. a. Cash receipts journal
    b. Sales journal

19. a. 250
    b. None

20. a. 250
    b. 1

21. a. The subsidiary ledger will not agree with the controlling account and the general ledger will be out of balance.
    b. A diagonal line should be inserted in the Posting Reference column immediately after the credit is recorded in the general journal. This calls attention to the necessity for two postings.

22. a. That the credit has been posted to the appropriate account receivable in the subsidiary ledger (and needs no further attention).
    b. That the credit to Sales needs no further attention (the column total will be posted).

23. a. Cash receipts journal
    b. Cash receipts journal
    c. Cash receipts journal
    d. Sales journal
    e. Cash receipts journal
    f. Cash receipts journal
    g. General journal
    h. General journal
    i. General journal
    j. General journal

24. a. Purchases
    b. Purchases
    c. Store Equipment
    d. Store Supplies
    e. Purchases
    f. Store Equipment
    g. Prepaid Insurance
    h. Office Equipment
    i. Purchases

25. a. Sometime following the end of the current month, one of two things may happen: (1) an overdue notice will be received from Hoffman Co., and/or (2) a letter will be received from Hoffer Co., informing the buyer of the overpayment. (It is also possible that the error will be discovered at the time of making payment if the original invoice is inspected at the time the check is being written.)
    b. The schedule of accounts payable would not agree with the balance of the accounts payable account. The error might also be discovered at the time the invoice is paid.

c. The creditor will call the attention of the debtor to the unpaid balance of $1,000.
d. The error will become evident during the verification process at the end of the month. The total debits in the purchases journal will be less than the total credits by $2,000.

26. a. The error will not cause the trial balance totals to be unequal.
    b. The sum of the balances in the creditors ledger will not agree with the balance of the accounts payable account in the general ledger.

27. When the equality of the debits and the credits in the cash payments journal is verified at the end of the month, a discrepancy of $10 will be discovered.

28. a. Cash payments journal
    b. Purchases journal
    c. Cash payments journal
    d. General journal
    e. Purchases journal
    f. Cash payments journal

29. a. (1) Accounts Receivable, Dr.
           Sales, Cr.
       (2) Cost of Merchandise Sold, Dr.
           Merchandise Inventory, Cr.
    b. Accounts receivable and merchandise inventory subsidiary ledgers.

30. A primary weakness that contributed to the occurrence and the size of the fraud was the easy accessibility of the programmers to the computer and the computer tapes containing the insurance policies. This allowed several of the computer programmers to add bogus policies to the real policies. In a strong system of internal control, access to accounting records (such as computer tapes) and to the computer should be strictly controlled. In this way, a system of checks and balances will exist among the computer programmers, the librarian controlling access to the computer files, and the computer operators. An additional weakness in the Equity Funding system of internal control was the lack of an effective independent review program utilizing internal auditors. This contributed to the failure to discover the fraud until it had grown to a magnitude of billions of dollars.

ETHICS DISCUSSION CASE It would be unethical for Ann Godwin to utilize Cardenas Co.'s journal and subsidiary ledger formats without prior permission from its management. The *Standards of Ethical Conduct for Management Accountants* requires management accountants to refrain from disclosing information acquired in the course of their work, except when authorized.

EXERCISES

Ex. 7-1 a. **Agree.** Susan has made one employee responsible for the cash drawer in accordance with the internal control principle of assignment of responsibility.

           b. **Disagree.** It is commendable that Susan has given the employee a specific responsibility and is holding that employee accountable for it. However, after the cashier has counted the cash, another employee (or perhaps Susan) should remove the cash register tape and compare the amount on the tape with the cash in the drawer. Also, Susan's standard of no mistakes may encourage the cashiers to overcharge a few customers in order to cover any possible shortages in the cash drawer.

           c. **Disagree.** Stealing is a serious issue. An employee who can justify taking a box of potato chips can probably justify "borrowing" cash from the cash register.

Ex. 7-2 a. The sales clerks could steal money by writing phony refunds and pocketing the cash supposedly refunded to these fictitious customers.

           b. 1. Fashions Now suffers from inadequate separation of responsibilities for related operations, since the clerks issue refunds and restock all merchandise. In addition, there is a lack of proofs and security measures, since the supervisors authorize returns two hours after they are issued.

               2. A store credit for any merchandise returned without a receipt would reduce the possibility of theft of cash. In this case, a clerk could only issue a phony store credit rather than taking money from the cash register. A store credit is not as tempting as cash. In addition, sales clerks could only use a few store credits to purchase merchandise for themselves without management getting suspicious.

                    An advantage of issuing a store credit for returns without a receipt is that the possibility of stealing cash is reduced. The store will also lose less revenue if customers must choose other store merchandise instead of getting a cash refund. The overall level of returns/exchanges may be reduced, since customers will not return an acceptable gift simply because they need cash more than the gift. The policy will also reduce the "cash drain" during the weeks immediately following the holidays, allowing Fashions Now to keep more of its money earning interest or to use that cash to purchase spring merchandise or pay creditors.

                    A disadvantage of issuing a store credit for returns without a receipt is that pre-holiday sales might drop as gift-givers realize that the return policy has tightened. After the holidays, customers wishing to return items for cash refunds may be frustrated when they learn the store policy

Ex. 7-2, Continued

has changed. The ill will may reduce future sales. It may take longer to explain the new policy and fill out the paperwork for a store credit, lengthening lines at the return counter after the holidays. Sales clerks will need to be trained to apply the new policy and write up a store credit. Sales clerks also will need to be trained to handle the redemption of the store credit on future merchandise purchases.

3. The potential for abuse in the cash refund system could be eliminated if clerks were required to get a supervisor's authorization for a refund before giving the customer the cash. The supervisor should only authorize the refund after seeing both the customer and the merchandise that is being returned.

    An alternative would be to use security measures that would detect a sales clerk attempting to ring up a refund and remove cash when a customer is not present at the sales desk. These security measures could include cameras or additional security personnel discreetly monitoring the sales desk.

Ex. 7-3 Subsidiary ledger account: (a), (b), (c), (d)
Two general ledger accounts: (e)

Ex. 7-4 General ledger account: (a)
General ledger account and subsidiary ledger account: (b)

Ex. 7-5 a, b, and c.

Accounts Receivable

Nov. 30	4,035	Nov. 21	500
3,535			

Environmental Safety Co.		Smith and Smith	
Nov. 1	1,500	Nov. 20	1,100

Greenberg Co.		Envirolab	
Nov. 10	795	Nov. 21	500	Nov. 27	640
295			

Ex. 7-5, Concluded

d.

J. A. BACH CO.
Schedule of Accounts Receivable
November 30, 19—

Environmental Safety Co.	$1,500
Greenberg Co.	295
Smith and Smith	1,100
Envirolab	640
Total accounts receivable	$3,535

Ex. 7-6 Sept. 3 Sale of merchandise on account; posted from sales journal.
            9 Return, allowance granted, or correction of error related to sale of September 3; posted from general journal.
           13 Receipt of cash for balance due; posted from cash receipts journal.

Ex. 7-7 1. General ledger account: (c), (h), (i), (j), (k), (l)
            2. Subsidiary ledger account: (a), (b), (d), (e), (f), (g)
            3. No posting required: (m)

Ex. 7-8 1. General ledger account: (b), (c), (e), (f), (g), (i), (k), (l), (m)
            2. Subsidiary ledger account: (a), (d), (h)
            3. No posting required: (j)

Ex. 7-9 July 6 Purchase of merchandise or other commodities on account; posted from purchases journal.
            10 Return, allowance, or correction of error related to purchase of July 6; posted from general journal.
            16 Payment of balance owed; posted from cash payments journal.

Ex. 7-10 a. Two errors were made in balancing the accounts in the subsidiary ledger:
            (1) The C. D. Cali Co. transaction of October 25 should have resulted in a balance of $3,000 instead of $2,000.
            (2) The Taber Supply transaction of October 7 should have resulted in a balance of $13,150 instead of $13,050, and the account balance at October 31 should have been $7,200 instead of $7,100.

Ex. 7-10, Concluded

b.   **SYPEK COMPANY**
                                      Schedule of Accounts Payable
                                             October 31, 19—

C. D. Cali Co.	$ 3,000
Cutler and Powell	7,500
C. D. Greer and Son	10,750
Taber Supply	7,200
L. L. Weiss Co.	2,750
Total accounts payable	$31,200

Ex. 7-11 Sales journal: (c), (i)
Cash receipts journal: (a), (d), (j), (l)
Purchases journal: (h), (m)
Cash payments journal: (b), (f), (n), (p)
General journal: (e), (g), (k), (o)

Ex. 7-12

July 5	Accounts Payable—Mathews Equipment Co.	4,000	
	Equipment		4,000
8	Sales Returns and Allowances	900	
	Accounts Receivable—R. D. Sharp Co.		900
12	Accounts Payable—L. L. Linke Co.	1,100	
	Purchases Returns and Allowances		1,100
19	Sales Returns and Allowances	220	
	Accounts Receivable—C. C. Palmer		220
24	Notes Receivable	5,000	
	Accounts Receivable—JMB Co.		5,000

WHAT'S WRONG WITH THIS?

1. The Sales Discounts column is for debits (not credits).
2. The Other Accounts column is for credits (not debits).
3. A better order of columns, as corrected by 1 and 2, would be to place the Other Accounts Cr. column to the left of the Sales Cr. column.

A recommended and corrected cash receipts journal is as follows:

CASH RECEIPTS JOURNAL   PAGE

DATE	ACCOUNT CREDITED	POST. REF.	OTHER ACCOUNTS CR.	SALES CR.	ACCOUNTS REC. CR.	SALES DISCOUNTS DR.	CASH DR.

PROBLEMS

Prob. 7-1A

1. and 2. SALES JOURNAL Page 1

Date	Invoice No.	Account Debited	Post. Ref.	Accts. Rec. Dr. Sales Cr.
19—				
May 21	1	Boritz Co........................	✓	1,200
22	2	Stark Co.	✓	2,750
24	3	Morris Co.	✓	3,175
27	4	C. D. Walters Co.................	✓	2,500
28	5	A. Udall Co......................	✓	1,500
30	6	Stark Co.	✓	2,925
31	7	Morris Co.	✓	995
31				15,045
				(113) (411)

JOURNAL Page 1

Date	Description	Post. Ref.	Debit	Credit
19—				
May 25	Sales Returns and Allowances...............	412	100	
	Accounts Receivable—Boritz Co.	113/✓		100
28	Sales Returns and Allowances...............	412	150	
	Accounts Receivable—Stark Co.	113/✓		150
30	Sales Returns and Allowances...............	412	75	
	Accounts Receivable—C. D. Walters Co. ...	113/✓		75

2. GENERAL LEDGER

Accounts Receivable 113

Date	Item	Post. Ref.	Dr.	Cr.	Balance Dr.	Balance Cr.
19—						
May 25	....	J1	......	100	.....	......
28	....	J1	......	150	.....	......
30	....	J1	......	75	.....	......
31	....	S1	15,045	......	14,720	......

Prob. 7-1A, Continued

Sales   **411**

Date	Item	Post. Ref.	Dr.	Cr.	Balance Dr.	Balance Cr.
19— May 31	....	S1	......	15,045	.....	15,045

Sales Returns and Allowances   **412**

Date	Item	Post. Ref.	Dr.	Cr.	Balance Dr.	Balance Cr.
19— May 25	....	J1	100	......	.....	......
28	....	J1	150	......	.....	......
30	....	J1	75	......	325	......

1.   ACCOUNTS RECEIVABLE LEDGER

Boritz Co.

Date	Item	Post. Ref.	Dr.	Cr.	Bal.
19— May 21	....	S1	1,200	.....	1,200
25	....	J1	....	100	1,100

Morris Co.

Date	Item	Post. Ref.	Dr.	Cr.	Bal.
19— May 24	....	S1	3,175	.....	3,175
31	....	S1	995	.....	4,170

Stark Co.

Date	Item	Post. Ref.	Dr.	Cr.	Bal.
19— May 22	....	S1	2,750	.....	2,750
28	....	J1	....	150	2,600
30	....	S1	2,925	.....	5,525

A. Udall Co.

Date	Item	Post. Ref.	Dr.	Cr.	Bal.
19— May 28	....	S1	1,500	.....	1,500

Prob. 7-1A, Concluded

C. D. Walters Co.

Date	Item	Post. Ref.	Dr.	Cr.	Bal.
19—					
May 27	....	S1	2,500	....	2,500
30	....	J1	....	75	2,425

3. a. $14,720
    b. $14,720

4. The single money column in the sales journal can be replaced with three columns for (1) Accounts Receivable Dr., (2) Sales Cr., and (3) Sales Tax Payable Cr.

Prob. 7-2A

1. and 2.   JOURNAL   **Page 21**

Date	Description	Post. Ref.	Debit	Credit
19—				
July 15	Sales Returns and Allowances...............	412	75	
	Accounts Receivable—C. D. Martin Co.....	113/√		75
30	Sales Returns and Allowances...............	412	110	
	Accounts Receivable—G. A. Carr Co.......	113/√		110
31	Notes Receivable	112	2,500	
	Accounts Receivable—Ignacio and Co.....	113/√		2,500

1. and 3.   SALES JOURNAL   **Page 34**

Date	Invoice No.	Account Debited	Post. Ref.	Accts. Rec. Dr. Sales Cr.
19—				
July 2	710	Ignacio and Co....................	√	4,250
6	711	Janet Rowe Co.	√	1,500
10	712	C. D. Martin Co.	√	2,975
12	713	R. C. Fellows Co..................	√	5,800
17	714	C. D. Martin Co.	√	970
23	715	Janet Rowe Co.	√	3,100
27	716	G. A. Carr Co.	√	2,150
28	717	Ignacio and Co....................	√	2,750
31				23,495
				(113) (411)

Prob. 7-2A, Continued

1, 2, and 3.   CASH RECEIPTS JOURNAL   Page 37

Date	Account Credited	Post. Ref.	Other Accts. Cr.	Sales Cr.	Accts. Rec. Cr.	Sales Disc. Dr.	Cash Dr.
19—							
July 1	C. D. Martin Co.......	√	......	.....	6,000	120	5,880
3	Notes Receivable	112	10,000	.....	......	.....	10,300
	Interest Income	811	300	.....	......	.....	......
7	Janet Rowe Co.......	√	......	.....	6,500	130	6,370
8	R. C. Fellows Co.	√	......	.....	2,200	.....	2,200
16	Sales................	√	......	4,610	......	.....	4,610
19	Equipment...........	121	1,000	.....	......	.....	1,000
20	C. D. Martin Co.......	√	......	.....	2,900	58	2,842
22	R. C. Fellows Co.	√	......	.....	5,800	116	5,684
27	Office Supplies	114	40	.....	......	.....	40
31	Ignacio and Co.	√	......	.....	1,750	.....	1,750
31	Sales................	√	......	4,150	......	.....	4,150
31			11,340	8,760	25,150	424	44,826
			(√)	(411)	(113)	(413)	(111)

1.   ACCOUNTS RECEIVABLE LEDGER

G. A. Carr Co.

Date	Item	Post. Ref.	Dr.	Cr.	Balance
19—					
July 27	....	S34	2,150	.....	2,150
30	....	J21	.....	110	2,040

R. C. Fellows Co.

Date	Item	Post. Ref.	Dr.	Cr.	Balance
19—					
June 10	....	S33	2,200	.....	2,200
July 8	....	CR37	.....	2,200	—
12	....	S34	5,800	.....	5,800
22	....	CR37	.....	5,800	—

Ignacio and Co.

Date	Item	Post. Ref.	Dr.	Cr.	Balance
19—					
July 2	....	S34	4,250	.....	4,250
28	....	S34	2,750	.....	7,000
31	....	CR37	.....	1,750	5,250
31	....	J21	.....	2,500	2,750

Prob. 7-2A, Continued

C.D. Martin Co.

Date	Item	Post. Ref.	Dr.	Cr.	Balance
19—					
June 21	....	S33	6,000	.....	6,000
July 1	....	CR37	.....	6,000	—
10	....	S34	2,975	.....	2,975
15	....	J21	.....	75	2,900
17	....	S34	970	.....	3,870
20	....	CR37	.....	2,900	970

Janet Rowe Co.

Date	Item	Post. Ref.	Dr.	Cr.	Balance
19—					
June 28	....	S33	6,500	.....	6,500
July 6	....	S34	1,500	.....	8,000
7	....	CR37	.....	6,500	1,500
23	....	S34	3,100	.....	4,600

2. and 3.   GENERAL LEDGER

Cash   111

Date	Item	Post. Ref.	Dr.	Cr.	Balance Dr.	Balance Cr.
19—						
July 1	Balance..................	✓	......	......	16,657	....
31	....	CR37	44,826	......	61,483	....

Notes Receivable   112

Date	Item	Post. Ref.	Dr.	Cr.	Balance Dr.	Balance Cr.
19—						
July 1	Balance..................	✓	......	......	20,000	....
3	....	CR37	......	10,000	......	....
31	....	J21	2,500	......	12,500	....

Accounts Receivable   113

Date	Item	Post. Ref.	Dr.	Cr.	Balance Dr.	Balance Cr.
19—						
July 1	Balance..................	✓	......	......	14,700	....
15	....	J21	......	75	......	....
30	....	J21	......	110	......	....
31	....	J21	......	2,500	......	....
31	....	S34	23,495	......	......	....
31	....	CR37	......	25,150	10,360	....

Prob. 7-2A, Continued

Office Supplies 114

Date	Item	Post. Ref.	Dr.	Cr.	Balance Dr.	Balance Cr.
19—						
July 1	Balance................	√	......	......	410	......
27	....	CR37	......	40	370	......

Equipment 121

Date	Item	Post. Ref.	Dr.	Cr.	Balance Dr.	Balance Cr.
19—						
July 1	Balance................	√	......	......	22,610	......
19	....	CR37	......	1,000	21,610	......

Sales 411

Date	Item	Post. Ref.	Dr.	Cr.	Balance Dr.	Balance Cr.
19—						
July 1	Balance................	√	......	......	......	186,125
31	....	S34	......	23,495	......	......
31	....	CR37	......	8,760	......	218,380

Sales Returns and Allowances 412

Date	Item	Post. Ref.	Dr.	Cr.	Balance Dr.	Balance Cr.
19—						
July 1	Balance................	√	......	......	1,770	......
15	....	J21	75	......	......	......
30	....	J21	110	......	1,955	......

Sales Discounts 413

Date	Item	Post. Ref.	Dr.	Cr.	Balance Dr.	Balance Cr.
19—						
July 1	Balance................	√	......	......	910	......
31	....	CR37	424	......	1,334	......

Interest Income 811

Date	Item	Post. Ref.	Dr.	Cr.	Balance Dr.	Balance Cr.
19—						
July 1	Balance................	√	......	......	......	325
3	....	CR37	......	300	......	625

Prob. 7-2A, Concluded

4.

UNISAC CO.
Schedule of Accounts Receivable
July 31, 19

G. A. Carr Co..	$ 2,040
Ignacio and Co..	2,750
C. D. Martin Co..	970
Janet Rowe Co.	4,600
Total accounts receivable	$10,360

Prob. 7-3A

3, 4, and 5   **SALES JOURNAL**   **Page 40**

Date	Invoice No.	Account Debited	Post. Ref.	Accts. Rec. Dr. Sales Cr.
19—				
June 15	√	Total Forwarded.................	√	25,350
15	793	Towers Co.......................	√	4,425
19	794	Halloway Co.	√	7,500
20	795	Ross and Son	√	2,975
24	796	Halloway Co.	√	4,950
28	797	F. G. Black Co.	√	2,100
30				47,300
				(113) (411)

JOURNAL   **Page 27**

Date	Description	Post. Ref.	Debit	Credit
19—				
June 24	Sales Returns and Allowances	412	275	
	Accounts Receivable—Towers Co.........	113/√		275
30	Sales Returns and Allowances..............	412	250	
	Accounts Receivable—F. G. Black Co.	113/√		250

Prob. 7-3A, Continued

CASH RECEIPTS JOURNAL   Page 36

Date	Account Credited	Post. Ref.	Other Accts. Cr.	Sales Cr.	Accts. Rec. Cr.	Sales Disc. Dr.	Cash Dr.
19—							
June 15	Totals Forwarded ..	√	3,467	13,470	22,600	366	39,171
16	F.G. Black Co......	√	.....	.....	8,900	178	8,722
23	Halloway Co........	√	.....	.....	9,825	.....	9,825
24	Notes Receivable...	112	1,500	.....	.....	.....	1,560
	Interest Income	811	60	.....	.....	.....	.....
25	Towers Co.	√	.....	.....	4,150	83	4,067
28	Halloway Co.......	√	.....	.....	7,500	150	7,350
30	Sales	√	.....	8,155	.....	.....	8,155
30			5,027	21,625	52,975	777	78,850
			(√)	(411)	(113)	(413)	(111)

2. and 4.   ACCOUNTS RECEIVABLE LEDGER

F.G. Black Co.

Date	Item	Post. Ref.	Dr.	Cr.	Balance
19—					
June 15	....	√	.....	.....	8,900
16	....	CR36	.....	8,900	—
28	....	S40	2,100	.....	2,100
30	....	J27	.....	250	1,850

Halloway Co.

Date	Item	Post. Ref.	Dr.	Cr.	Balance
19—					
June 15	....	√	.....	.....	9,825
19	....	S40	7,500	.....	17,325
23	....	CR36	.....	9,825	7,500
24	....	S40	4,950	.....	12,450
28	....	CR36	.....	7,500	4,950

Ross and Son

Date	Item	Post. Ref.	Dr.	Cr.	Balance
19—					
June 20	....	S40	2,975	.....	2,975

Prob. 7-3A, Continued

Towers Co.

Date	Item	Post. Ref.	Dr.	Cr.	Balance
19—					
June 15	....	S40	4,425	.....	4,425
24	....	J27	.....	275	4,150
25	....	CR36	.....	4,150	—

1. and 5.   GENERAL LEDGER

Cash   **111**

					Balance	
Date	Item	Post. Ref.	Dr.	Cr.	Dr.	Cr.
19—						
June 1	Balance	✓	......	......	13,705	......
30	....	CR36	78,850	......	92,555	......

Notes Receivable   **112**

19—						
June 1	Balance	✓	......	......	7,500	......
24	....	CR36	......	1,500	6,000	......

Accounts Receivable   **113**

19—						
June 1	Balance	✓	......	......	15,975	......
24	....	J27	......	275	15,700	......
30	....	J27	......	250	15,450	......
30	....	S40	47,300	......	62,750	......
30	....	CR36	......	52,975	9,775	......

Sales   **411**

19—						
June 30	....	S40	......	47,300	.....	47,300
30	....	CR36	......	21,625	.....	68,925

Sales Returns and Allowances   **412**

19—						
June 24	....	J27	275	......	275	......
30	....	J27	250	......	525	......

Prob. 7-3A, Concluded

Sales Discounts 413

Date	Item	Post. Ref.	Dr.	Cr.	Balance Dr.	Balance Cr.
19—						
June 30	....	CR36	777	......	777	......

Interest Income 811

Date	Item	Post. Ref.	Dr.	Cr.	Balance Dr.	Balance Cr.
19—						
June 24	....	CR36	......	60	.....	60

6. The subsidiary ledger is in agreement with the controlling account. Both have balances of $9,775.

Prob. 7-4A

3. and 4.

Page 30

PURCHASES JOURNAL

Date	Account Credited	Post. Ref.	Accounts Payable Cr.	Purchases Dr.	Store Supplies Dr.	Office Supplies Dr.	Other Accounts Dr. Account	Post. Ref.	Amount
19— May 1	Yu Co.	✓	6,150.50	6,150.50					
4	O'Grady Co.	✓	9,250.00	9,250.00					
9	Tyler Supply	✓	175.30			175.30			
13	Yu Co.	✓	4,370.50	4,370.50					
14	Diamond Equipment Co.	✓	5,500.00				Office Equipment	122	5,500.00
17	James Co.	✓	3,100.00	3,100.00					
20	Craig Co.	✓	1,130.30	1,130.30					
24	Tyler Supply	✓	325.00		325.00				
29	James Co.	✓	475.15	475.15					
31	Tyler Supply	✓	210.50			210.50			
31			30,687.25 (211)	24,476.45 (511)	325.00 (114)	385.80 (115)			5,500.00 (✓)

Page 17

JOURNAL

Date	Description	Post. Ref.	Debit	Credit
19— May 5	Accounts Payable—Yu Co.	211/✓	200.00	
	Purchases Returns and Allowances	512		200.00
19	Accounts Payable—Tyler Supply	211/✓	22.50	
	Office Supplies	115		22.50
27	Accounts Payable—O'Grady Co.	211/✓	500.00	
	Purchases Returns and Allowances	512		500.00

Prob. 7-4A, Continued

2. and 3.   ACCOUNTS PAYABLE LEDGER

Craig Co.

Date	Item	Post. Ref.	Dr.	Cr.	Bal.
19—					
May 1	Balance	√	.....	....	2,177.70
20	....	P30	.....	1,130.30	3,308.00

Diamond Equipment Co.

Date	Item	Post. Ref.	Dr.	Cr.	Bal.
19—					
May 14	....	P30	.....	5,500.00	5,500.00

James Co.

Date	Item	Post. Ref.	Dr.	Cr.	Bal.
19—					
May 1	Balance	√	.....	....	4,550.25
17	....	P30	.....	3,100.00	7,650.25
29	....	P30	.....	475.15	8,125.40

O'Grady Co.

Date	Item	Post. Ref.	Dr.	Cr.	Bal.
19—					
May 1	Balance	√	.....	....	5,484.35
4	....	P30	.....	9,250.00	14,734.35
27	....	J17	500.00	....	14,234.35

Tyler Supply

Date	Item	Post. Ref.	Dr.	Cr.	Bal.
19—					
May 9	....	P30	.....	175.30	175.30
19	....	J17	22.50	....	152.80
24	....	P30	.....	325.00	477.80
31	....	P30	.....	210.50	688.30

Yu Co.

Date	Item	Post. Ref.	Dr.	Cr.	Bal.
19—					
May 1	....	P30	.....	6,150.50	6,150.50
5	....	J17	200.00	....	5,950.50
13	....	P30	.....	4,370.50	10,321.00

Prob. 7-4A, Concluded

1. and 4.   GENERAL LEDGER

Store Supplies   114

Date	Post. Ref.	Dr.	Cr.	Balance Dr.	Balance Cr.
19—					
May 1	✓	....	....	460.00	....
31	P30	325.00	....	785.00	....

Office Supplies   115

Date	Post. Ref.	Dr.	Cr.	Balance Dr.	Balance Cr.
19—					
May 1 Balance.......	✓	....	....	327.40	....
19	J17	....	22.50	304.90	....
31	P30	385.80	....	690.70	....

Office Equipment   122

Date	Post. Ref.	Dr.	Cr.	Balance Dr.	Balance Cr.
19—					
May 1 Balance.......	✓	....	....	32,500.00	....
14	P30	5,500.00	....	38,000.00	....

Accounts Payable   211

Date	Post. Ref.	Dr.	Cr.	Balance Dr.	Balance Cr.
19—					
May 1 Balance.......	✓	....	....	....	12,212.30
5	J17	200.00	....	....	....
19	J17	22.50	....	....	....
27	J17	500.00	....	....	....
31	P30	....	30,687.25	....	42,177.05

Purchases   511

Date	Post. Ref.	Dr.	Cr.	Balance Dr.	Balance Cr.
19—					
May 1 Balance.......	✓	....	....	89,917.40	....
31	P30	24,476.45	....	114,393.85	....

Purchases Returns and Allowances   512

Date	Post. Ref.	Dr.	Cr.	Balance Dr.	Balance Cr.
19—					
May 1 Balance.......	✓	....	....	....	2,170.10
5	J17	....	200.00	....	....
27	J17	....	500.00	....	2,870.10

5. a. $42,177.05
    b. $42,177.05

Prob. 7-5A

1, 2, and 3

PURCHASES JOURNAL

Page 1

Date	Account Credited	Post. Ref.	Accounts Payable Cr.	Purchases Dr.	Store Supplies Dr.	Office Supplies Dr.	Other Accounts Dr. Account	Post. Ref.	Amount
19—									
June 16	Harper Equipment Co.	√	7,250	.....	.....	.....	Office Equipment	123	7,250
16	Hernandez Clothing Co.	√	15,500	15,500	.....	.....	....	.....	.....
18	Carter Clothing	√	9,720	9,720	.....	.....	....	.....	.....
19	Adams Co.	√	2,150	2,150	.....	.....	....	.....	.....
27	Adams Co.	√	1,610	1,610	.....	.....	....	.....	.....
30	Harper Equipment Co.	√	1,725	.....	150	75	Store Equipment.	121	1,500
30	Hernandez Clothing Co.	√	6,200	6,200	.....	.....	....	.....	.....
30			44,155	35,180	150	75			8,750
			(211)	(511)	(116)	(117)			(√)

Prob. 7-5A, Continued   Page 1

CASH PAYMENTS JOURNAL

Date	Ck. No.	Account Debited	Post. Ref.	Other Accounts Dr.	Accounts Payable Dr.	Purchases Discounts Cr.	Cash Cr.
19—							
June 16	1	Rent Expense	712	900	.....	.....	900
17	2	Store Supplies	116	410	.....	.....	700
		Office Supplies	117	290	.....	.....	—
23	3	Harper Equipment Co.	√	.....	7,250	.....	7,250
24	4	Hernandez Clothing Co.	√	.....	15,500	155	15,345
25	5	Sales Returns and Allowances	412	215	.....	.....	215
26	6	Carter Clothing	√	.....	9,000	180	8,820
30	7	Adams Co.	√	.....	1,685	.....	1,685
30	8	Sales Salaries Expense	611	1,775	.....	.....	1,775
30				3,590	33,435	335	36,690
				(√)	(211)	(513)	(111)

Prob. 7-5A, Continued

1. and 2.   JOURNAL   **Page 1**

Date	Description	Post. Ref.	Debit	Credit
19—				
June 20	Accounts Payable—Carter Clothing	211/√	720	
	Purchases Returns and Allowances.......	512		720
23	Accounts Payable—Adams Co..............	211/√	465	
	Purchases Returns and Allowances.......	512		465
30	Accounts Payable—Harper Equipment Co...	211/√	75	
	Office Equipment.......................	123		75

1.   ACCOUNTS PAYABLE LEDGER

Adams Co.

Date	Item	Post. Ref.	Dr.	Cr.	Balance
19—					
June 19	....	P1	......	2,150	2,150
23	....	J1	465	......	1,685
27	....	P1	......	1,610	3,295
30	....	CP1	1,685	......	1,610

Carter Clothing

Date	Item	Post. Ref.	Dr.	Cr.	Balance
19—					
June 18	....	P1	......	9,720	9,720
20	....	J1	720	......	9,000
26	....	CP1	9,000	......	—

Harper Equipment Co.

Date	Item	Post. Ref.	Dr.	Cr.	Balance
19—					
June 16	....	P1	......	7,250	7,250
23	....	CP1	7,250	......	—
30	....	P1	......	1,725	1,725
30	....	J1	75	......	1,650

Hernandez Clothing Co.

Date	Item	Post. Ref.	Dr.	Cr.	Balance
19—					
June 16	....	P1	......	15,500	15,500
24	....	CP1	15,500	......	—
30	....	P1	......	6,200	6,200

Prob. 7-5A, Continued

2. and 3.   **GENERAL LEDGER**

Cash   111

Date	Item	Post. Ref.	Dr.	Cr.	Balance Dr.	Balance Cr.
19—						
June 30		CP1	......	36,690	.....	36,690

Store Supplies   116

Date	Item	Post. Ref.	Dr.	Cr.	Balance Dr.	Balance Cr.
19—						
June 17		CP1	410	......	.....	......
30		P1	150	......	560	......

Office Supplies   117

Date	Item	Post. Ref.	Dr.	Cr.	Balance Dr.	Balance Cr.
19—						
June 17		CP1	290	......	.....	......
30		P1	75	......	365	......

Store Equipment   121

Date	Item	Post. Ref.	Dr.	Cr.	Balance Dr.	Balance Cr.
19—						
June 30		P1	1,500	......	1,500	......

Office Equipment   123

Date	Item	Post. Ref.	Dr.	Cr.	Balance Dr.	Balance Cr.
19—						
June 16		P1	7,250	......	.....	......
30		J1	......	75	7,175	......

Accounts Payable   211

Date	Item	Post. Ref.	Dr.	Cr.	Balance Dr.	Balance Cr.
19—						
June 20		J1	720	......	.....	......
23		J1	465	......	.....	......
30		J1	75	......	.....	......
30		P1	......	44,155	.....	......
30		CP1	33,435	......	.....	9,460

Sales Returns and Allowances   412

Date	Item	Post. Ref.	Dr.	Cr.	Balance Dr.	Balance Cr.
19—						
June 25		CP1	215	......	215	......

Prob. 7-5A, Concluded

Purchases   511

Date	Item	Post. Ref.	Dr.	Cr.	Balance Dr.	Balance Cr.
19—						
June 30	....	P1	35,180	......	35,180	......

Purchases Returns and Allowances   512

Date	Item	Post. Ref.	Dr.	Cr.	Balance Dr.	Balance Cr.
19—						
June 20	....	J1	......	720	.....	......
23	....	J1	......	465	.....	1,185

Purchases Discounts   513

Date	Item	Post. Ref.	Dr.	Cr.	Balance Dr.	Balance Cr.
19—						
June 30	....	CP1	......	335	.....	335

Sales Salaries Expense   611

Date	Item	Post. Ref.	Dr.	Cr.	Balance Dr.	Balance Cr.
19—						
June 30	....	CP1	1,775	......	1,775	......

Rent Expense   712

Date	Item	Post. Ref.	Dr.	Cr.	Balance Dr.	Balance Cr.
19—						
June 16	....	CP1	900	......	900	......

4.

FASHION CLOTHIERS CO.
Schedule of Accounts Payable
June 30, 19—

Adams Co.	$1,610
Harper Equipment Co.	1,650
Hernandez Clothing Co.	6,200
Total accounts payable	$9,460

2, 3, and 4

Prob. 7-6A

Page 37

PURCHASES JOURNAL

Date	Account Credited	Post. Ref.	Accounts Payable Cr.	Purchases Dr.	Store Supplies Dr.	Office Supplies Dr.	Other Accounts Dr. Account	Other Accounts Dr. Post. Ref.	Other Accounts Dr. Amount
19—									
July 2	Bidwell Co.	✓	2,590	2,590	.....	.....			.....
3	Glass Equipment Co.	✓	9,600	.....	.....	.....	Equipment	121	9,600
17	Bone Enterprises	✓	7,920	7,920	.....	.....			.....
19	Moore Supply Co.	✓	445	.....	248	197			.....
24	Howell Co.	✓	5,419	5,127	292	.....			.....
31			25,974	15,637	540	197			9,600
			(211)	(511)	(115)	(116)			(✓)

CASH RECEIPTS JOURNAL

Page 42

Date	Account Credited	Post. Ref.	Other Accounts Cr.	Sales Cr.	Accounts Receivable Cr.	Sales Discounts Dr.	Cash Dr.
19—							
July 6	Powell Co.	✓	.....	.....	2,800	28	2,772
10	Sax Manufacturing Co.	✓	.....	.....	7,375	.....	7,375
12	W. Cox Co.	✓	.....	.....	1,700	17	1,683
16	Sales	✓	.....	21,520	.....	.....	21,520
18	Purchases Returns and Allowances	512	790	.....	.....	.....	790
25	Powell Co.	✓	.....	.....	2,800	.....	2,800
31	Sales	✓	.....	18,150	.....	.....	18,150
31			790	39,670	14,675	45	55,090
			(✓)	(411)	(113)	(413)	(111)

Prob. 7-6A, Continued

2. and 4. SALES JOURNAL Page 35

Date	Invoice No.	Account Debited	Post. Ref.	Accts. Rec. Dr. Sales Cr.
19—				
July 5	940	W. Cox Co.............................	√	1,700
9	941	Collins Co.	√	8,500
11	942	Joy Co.	√	3,120
23	943	Sax Manufacturing Co.	√	8,172
25	944	Collins Co.	√	4,650
31				26,142
				(113) (411)

2, 3, and 4. CASH PAYMENTS JOURNAL Page 34

Date	Check No.	Account Debited	Post. Ref.	Other Accts. Dr.	Accts. Pay. Dr.	Purch. Disc. Cr.	Cash Cr.
19—							
July 1	610	Rent Expense	712	1,400	......	.....	1,400
6	611	Misc. Selling Expense	619	310	......	.....	310
10	612	Howell Co..........	√	......	9,500	95	9,405
10	613	Bone Enterprises...	√	......	2,120	.....	2,120
11	614	Porter Co..........	√	......	705	.....	705
13	615	Bidwell Co.	√	......	2,300	46	2,254
16	616	Purchases..........	511	2,725	......	.....	2,725
18	617	Misc. Adm. Expense	719	238	......	.....	238
20	618	Advertising Expense	612	1,850	......	.....	1,850
26	619	Glass Equipment Co.	√	......	9,600	.....	9,600
27	620	D. D. Miles, Drawing	312	3,500	......	.....	3,500
30	621	Sales Salaries Expense	611	9,100	......	.....	12,900
		Office Salaries Expense	711	3,800	......	.....	......
31	622	Transportation In ..	514	930	......	.....	930
31				23,853	24,225	141	47,937
				(√)	(211)	(513)	(111)

Prob. 7-6A, Continued

2. and 3.   JOURNAL   **Page 31**

Date	Description	Post. Ref.	Debit	Credit
19—				
July 9	Accounts Payable—Bidwell Co..............	211/√	290	
	Purchases Returns and Allowances	512		290
13	Sales Returns and Allowances..............	412	320	
	Accounts Receivable—Joy Co.............	113/√		320

1, 3, and 4   GENERAL LEDGER

Cash   **111**

Date	Item	Post. Ref.	Dr.	Cr.	Balance Dr.	Balance Cr.
19—						
July 1	Balance	√	......	......	9,850	......
31	....	CR42	55,090	......	......	......
31	....	CP34	......	47,937	17,003	......

Accounts Receivable   **113**

Date	Item	Post. Ref.	Dr.	Cr.	Balance Dr.	Balance Cr.
19—						
July 1	Balance	√	......	......	12,975	......
13	....	J31	......	320	......	......
31	....	S35	26,142	......	......	......
31	....	CR42	......	14,675	24,122	......

Merchandise Inventory   **114**

Date	Item	Post. Ref.	Dr.	Cr.	Balance Dr.	Balance Cr.
19—						
July 1	Balance	√	......	......	35,500	......

Store Supplies   **115**

Date	Item	Post. Ref.	Dr.	Cr.	Balance Dr.	Balance Cr.
19—						
July 1	Balance	√	......	......	545	......
31	....	P37	540	......	1,085	......

Office Supplies   **116**

Date	Item	Post. Ref.	Dr.	Cr.	Balance Dr.	Balance Cr.
19—						
July 1	Balance	√	......	......	360	......
31	....	P37	197	......	557	......

Prob. 7-6A, Continued

Prepaid Insurance   117

Date	Item	Post. Ref.	Dr.	Cr.	Balance Dr.	Balance Cr.
19—						
July 1	Balance	✓	......	......	2,100	......

Equipment   121

Date	Item	Post. Ref.	Dr.	Cr.	Balance Dr.	Balance Cr.
19—						
July 1	Balance	✓	......	......	47,250	......
3	....	P37	9,600	......	56,850	......

Accumulated Depreciation   122

Date	Item	Post. Ref.	Dr.	Cr.	Balance Dr.	Balance Cr.
19—						
July 1	Balance	✓	......	......		22,250

Accounts Payable   211

Date	Item	Post. Ref.	Dr.	Cr.	Balance Dr.	Balance Cr.
19—						
July 1	Balance	✓	......	......	......	13,530
9	....	J31	290	......	......	......
31	....	P37	......	25,974	......	......
31	....	CP34	24,225	......	......	14,989

D. D. Miles, Capital   311

Date	Item	Post. Ref.	Dr.	Cr.	Balance Dr.	Balance Cr.
19—						
July 1	Balance	✓	......	......		72,800

D. D. Miles, Drawing   312

Date	Item	Post. Ref.	Dr.	Cr.	Balance Dr.	Balance Cr.
19—						
July 27	....	CP34	3,500	......	3,500	......

Sales   411

Date	Item	Post. Ref.	Dr.	Cr.	Balance Dr.	Balance Cr.
19—						
July 31	....	S35	......	26,142	......	......
31	....	CR42	......	39,670	......	65,812

Sales Returns and Allowances   412

Date	Item	Post. Ref.	Dr.	Cr.	Balance Dr.	Balance Cr.
19—						
July 13	....	J31	320	......	320	......

Prob. 7-6A, Continued

Sales Discounts 413

| | | Post. | | | Balance | |
Date	Item	Ref.	Dr.	Cr.	Dr.	Cr.
19—						
July 31	....	CR42	45	......	45	......

Purchases 511

19—						
July 16	....	CP34	2,725	......	......	......
31	....	P37	15,637	......	18,362	......

Purchases Returns and Allowances 512

19—						
July 9	....	J31	......	290	......	......
18	....	CR42	......	790	......	1,080

Purchases Discounts 513

19—						
July 31	....	CP34	......	141	......	141

Transportation In 514

19—						
July 31	....	CP34	930	......	930	......

Sales Salaries Expense 611

19—						
July 30	....	CP34	9,100	......	9,100	......

Advertising Expense 612

19—						
July 20	....	CP34	1,850	......	1,850	......

Miscellaneous Selling Expense 619

19—						
July 6	....	CP34	310	......	310	......

Office Salaries Expense 711

19—						
July 30	....	CP34	3,800	......	3,800	......

Prob. 7-6A, Concluded

Rent Expense   712

Date	Item	Post. Ref.	Dr.	Cr.	Balance Dr.	Balance Cr.
19—						
July 1	....	CP34	1,400	......	1,400	......

Miscellaneous Administrative Expense   719

Date	Item	Post. Ref.	Dr.	Cr.	Balance Dr.	Balance Cr.
19—						
July 18	....	CP34	238	......	238	......

5.

MILES COMPANY
Trial Balance
July 31, 19—

	Dr.	Cr.
Cash	17,003	
Accounts Receivable	24,122	
Merchandise Inventory	35,500	
Store Supplies	1,085	
Office Supplies	557	
Prepaid Insurance	2,100	
Equipment	56,850	
Accumulated Depreciation		22,250
Accounts Payable		14,989
D.D. Miles, Capital		72,800
D.D. Miles, Drawing	3,500	
Sales		65,812
Sales Returns and Allowances	320	
Sales Discounts	45	
Purchases	18,362	
Purchases Returns and Allowances		1,080
Purchases Discounts		141
Transportation In	930	
Sales Salaries Expense	9,100	
Advertising Expense	1,850	
Miscellaneous Selling Expense	310	
Office Salaries Expense	3,800	
Rent Expense	1,400	
Miscellaneous Administrative Expense	238	
	177,072	177,072

6. Total of accounts receivable ledger: $24,122
Total of accounts payable ledger: $14,989

Prob. 7-7A

Page 1

3. and 4.

SALES JOURNAL

Date	Invoice No.	Account Debited	Post. Ref.	Accts. Rec. Dr.	Sales Cr.	Sales Tax Payable Cr.
19—						
May 18	1	JMC Co.	√	1,575	1,500	75
20	2	Reese Co.	√	3,465	3,300	165
22	3	Innis Co.	√	3,780	3,600	180
27	4	D. L. Victor Co.	√	2,940	2,800	140
28	5	Tyson Co.	√	525	500	25
30	6	Reese Co.	√	1,890	1,800	90
31	7	Innis Co.	√	2,625	2,500	125
31				16,800	16,000	800
				(113)	(411)	(215)

Prob. 7-7A, Continued

JOURNAL   Page 1

Date	Description	Post. Ref.	Debit	Credit
19—				
May 23	Sales Returns and Allowances..............	412	300	
	Sales Tax Payable...........................	215	15	
	Accounts Receivable—JMC Co............	113/√		315
28	Sales Returns and Allowances..............	412	100	
	Sales Tax Payable...........................	215	5	
	Accounts Receivable—Reese Co.	113/√		105
30	Sales Returns and Allowances..............	412	200	
	Sales Tax Payable...........................	215	10	
	Accounts Receivable—D. L. Victor Co......	113/√		210

1. and 4.   GENERAL LEDGER

Accounts Receivable   113

Date	Item	Post. Ref.	Dr.	Cr.	Balance Dr.	Balance Cr.
19—						
May 23	....	J1	......	315	.....	......
28	....	J1	......	105	.....	......
30	....	J1	......	210	.....	......
31	....	S1	16,800	......	16,170	......

Sales Tax Payable   215

Date	Item	Post. Ref.	Dr.	Cr.	Balance Dr.	Balance Cr.
19—						
May 23	....	J1	15	......	.....	......
28	....	J1	5	......	.....	......
30	....	J1	10	......	.....	......
31	....	S1	......	800	.....	770

Sales   411

Date	Item	Post. Ref.	Dr.	Cr.	Balance Dr.	Balance Cr.
19—						
May 31	....	S1	......	16,000	.....	16,000

Sales Returns and Allowances   412

Date	Item	Post. Ref.	Dr.	Cr.	Balance Dr.	Balance Cr.
19—						
May 23	....	J1	300	......	.....	......
28	....	J1	100	......	.....	......
30	....	J1	200	......	600	......

Prob. 7-7A, Concluded

2. and 3.   ACCOUNTS RECEIVABLE LEDGER

JMC Co.

Date	Item	Post. Ref.	Dr.	Cr.	Bal.
19—					
May 18	....	S1	1,575	.....	1,575
23	....	J1	....	315	1,260

Innis Co.

Date	Item	Post. Ref.	Dr.	Cr.	Bal.
19—					
May 22	....	S1	3,780	.....	3,780
31	....	S1	2,625	.....	6,405

Reese Co.

Date	Item	Post. Ref.	Dr.	Cr.	Bal.
19—					
May 20	....	S1	3,465	.....	3,465
28	....	J1	....	105	3,360
30	....	S1	1,890	.....	5,250

Tyson Co.

Date	Item	Post. Ref.	Dr.	Cr.	Bal.
19—					
May 28	....	S1	525	.....	525

D. L. Victor Co.

Date	Item	Post. Ref.	Dr.	Cr.	Bal.
19—					
May 27	....	S1	2,940	.....	2,940
30	....	J1	....	210	2,730

3. a. $16,170
    b. $16,170

Prob. 7-1B

1. and 2.   **SALES JOURNAL**   **Page 1**

Date	Invoice No.	Account Debited	Post. Ref.	Accts. Rec. Dr. Sales Cr.
19—				
May 18	1	JMC Co.............................	√	1,500
20	2	Reese Co..........................	√	3,250
22	3	Innis Co...........................	√	3,375
27	4	D. L. Victor Co.	√	3,125
28	5	Tyson Co..........................	√	500
30	6	Reese Co..........................	√	1,800
31	7	Innis Co...........................	√	1,495
31				15,045
				(113) (411)

JOURNAL   **Page 1**

Date	Description	Post. Ref.	Debit	Credit
19—				
May 23	Sales Returns and Allowances..............	412	250	
	Accounts Receivable—JMC Co............	113/√		250
28	Sales Returns and Allowances..............	412	150	
	Accounts Receivable—Reese Co...........	113/√		150
30	Sales Returns and Allowances..............	412	200	
	Accounts Receivable—D. L. Victor Co......	113/√		200

2.   **GENERAL LEDGER**

Accounts Receivable   **113**

Date	Item	Post. Ref.	Dr.	Cr.	Balance Dr.	Balance Cr.
19—						
May 23	....	J1	......	250	.....	......
28	....	J1	......	150	.....	......
30	....	J1	......	200	.....	......
31	....	S1	15,045	......	14,445	......

Sales   **411**

Date	Item	Post. Ref.	Dr.	Cr.	Balance Dr.	Balance Cr.
19—						
May 31	....	S1	......	15,045	.....	15,045

Prob. 7-1B, Continued

Sales Returns and Allowances   **412**

Date	Item	Post. Ref.	Dr.	Cr.	Balance Dr.	Cr.
19—						
May 23	....	J1	250	......	.....	......
28	....	J1	150	......	.....	......
30	....	J1	200	......	600	......

1. ACCOUNTS RECEIVABLE LEDGER

JMC Co.

Date	Item	Post. Ref.	Dr.	Cr.	Bal.
19—					
May 18	....	S1	1,500	.....	1,500
23	....	J1	....	250	1,250

Innis Co.

Date	Item	Post. Ref.	Dr.	Cr.	Bal.
19—					
May 22	....	S1	3,375	.....	3,375
31	....	S1	1,495	.....	4,870

Reese Co.

Date	Item	Post. Ref.	Dr.	Cr.	Bal.
19—					
May 20	....	S1	3,250	.....	3,250
28	....	J1	....	150	3,100
30	....	S1	1,800	.....	4,900

Tyson Co.

Date	Item	Post. Ref.	Dr.	Cr.	Bal.
19—					
May 28	....	S1	500	.....	500

D. L. Victor Co.

Date	Item	Post. Ref.	Dr.	Cr.	Bal.
19—					
May 27	....	S1	3,125	.....	3,125
30	....	J1	....	200	2,925

3. a. $14,445
  b. $14,445

Prob. 7-1B, Concluded

4. The single money column in the sales journal can be replaced with three columns for (1) Accounts Receivable Dr., (2) Sales Cr., and (3) Sales Tax Payable Cr.

Prob. 7-2B

1. and 2.   JOURNAL   **Page 21**

Date	Description	Post. Ref.	Debit	Credit
19—				
July 15	Sales Returns and Allowances..............	412	75	
	Accounts Receivable—C. D. Martin Co.....	113/√		75
30	Sales Returns and Allowances..............	412	110	
	Accounts Receivable—G. A. Carr Co.......	113/√		110
31	Notes Receivable	112	2,500	
	Accounts Receivable—Ignacio and Co.....	113/√		2,500

1. and 3.   SALES JOURNAL   **Page 34**

Date	Invoice No.	Account Debited	Post. Ref.	Accts. Rec. Dr. Sales Cr.
19—				
July 2	710	Ignacio and Co.	√	4,250
6	711	Janet Rowe Co.	√	1,500
10	712	C. D. Martin Co.	√	2,975
12	713	R. C. Fellows Co.....................	√	5,800
17	714	C. D. Martin Co.	√	970
23	715	Janet Rowe Co.	√	3,100
27	716	G. A. Carr Co.	√	2,150
28	717	Ignacio and Co....................	√	2,750
31				23,495
				(113) (411)

Prob. 7-2B, Continued

1, 2, and 3.   **CASH RECEIPTS JOURNAL**   **Page 37**

Date	Account Credited	Post. Ref.	Other Accts. Cr.	Sales Cr.	Accts. Rec. Cr.	Sales Disc. Dr.	Cash Dr.
19—							
July 1	C. D. Martin Co.....	√	......	......	6,000	60	5,940
3	Notes Receivable ..	112	20,000	......	......	...	20,200
	Interest Income	811	200	......	......	...	......
8	Janet Rowe Co.....	√	......	......	6,500	65	6,435
10	R. C. Fellows Co. ...	√	......	......	2,200	...	2,200
15	Sales.............	√	......	14,915	......	...	14,915
19	Equipment	121	1,250	......	......		1,250
20	C. D. Martin Co.....	√	......	......	2,900	29	2,871
22	R. C. Fellows Co. ...	√	......	......	5,800	58	5,742
28	Office Supplies	114	50	......	......	...	50
31	Ignacio and Co.....	√	......	......	1,750	...	1,750
31	Sales.............	√	......	16,100	......	...	16,100
31			21,500	31,015	25,150	212	77,453
			(√)	(411)	(113)	(413)	(111)

1.   ACCOUNTS RECEIVABLE LEDGER

G. A. Carr Co.

Date	Item	Post. Ref.	Dr.	Cr.	Balance
19—					
July 27	....	S34	2,150	.....	2,150
30	....	J21	.....	110	2,040

R. C. Fellows Co.

Date	Item	Post. Ref.	Dr.	Cr.	Balance
19—					
June 10	....	S33	2,200	.....	2,200
July 10	....	CR37	.....	2,200	—
12	....	S34	5,800	.....	5,800
22	....	CR37	.....	5,800	—

Ignacio and Co.

Date	Item	Post. Ref.	Dr.	Cr.	Balance
19—					
July 2	....	S34	4,250	.....	4,250
28	....	S34	2,750	.....	7,000
31	....	CR37	.....	1,750	5,250
31	....	J21	.....	2,500	2,750

Prob. 7-2B, Continued

C. D. Martin Co.

Date	Item	Post. Ref.	Dr.	Cr.	Balance
19—					
June 21	....	S33	6,000	.....	6,000
July 1	....	CR37	.....	6,000	—
10	....	S34	2,975	.....	2,975
15	....	J21	.....	75	2,900
17	....	S34	970	.....	3,870
20	....	CR37	.....	2,900	970

Janet Rowe Co.

Date	Item	Post. Ref.	Dr.	Cr.	Balance
19—					
June 28	....	S33	6,500	.....	6,500
July 6	....	S34	1,500	.....	8,000
8	....	CR37	.....	6,500	1,500
23	....	S34	3,100	.....	4,600

2. and 3.   GENERAL LEDGER

Cash   111

Date	Item	Post. Ref.	Dr.	Cr.	Balance Dr.	Balance Cr.
19—						
July 1	Balance..................	√	......	......	16,657	....
31	....	CR37	77,453	......	94,110	....

Notes Receivable   112

Date	Item	Post. Ref.	Dr.	Cr.	Balance Dr.	Balance Cr.
19—						
July 1	Balance..................	√	......	......	20,000	....
3	....	CR37	......	20,000	......	....
31	....	J21	2,500	......	2,500	....

Accounts Receivable   113

Date	Item	Post. Ref.	Dr.	Cr.	Balance Dr.	Balance Cr.
19—						
July 1	Balance..................	√	......	......	14,700	....
15	....	J21	......	75	......	....
30	....	J21	......	110	......	....
31	....	J21	......	2,500	......	....
31	....	S34	23,495	......	......	....
31	....	CR37	......	25,150	10,360	....

Prob. 7-2B, Continued

Office Supplies   114

Date	Item	Post. Ref.	Dr.	Cr.	Balance Dr.	Balance Cr.
19—						
July 1	Balance.................	√	......	......	410	....
28	....	CR37	......	50	360	....

Equipment   121

Date	Item	Post. Ref.	Dr.	Cr.	Balance Dr.	Balance Cr.
19—						
July 1	Balance.................	√	......	......	22,610	....
19	....	CR37	......	1,250	21,360	....

Sales   411

Date	Item	Post. Ref.	Dr.	Cr.	Balance Dr.	Balance Cr.
19—						
July 1	Balance.................	√	......	......	......	186,125
31	....	S34	......	23,495	......	
31	....	CR37	......	31,015	......	240,635

Sales Returns and Allowances   412

Date	Item	Post. Ref.	Dr.	Cr.	Balance Dr.	Balance Cr.
19—						
July 1	Balance.................	√	......	......	1,770	....
15	....	J21	75	......	......	....
30	....	J21	110	......	1,955	....

Sales Discounts   413

Date	Item	Post. Ref.	Dr.	Cr.	Balance Dr.	Balance Cr.
19—						
July 1	Balance.................	√	......	......	910	....
31	....	CR37	212	......	1,122	....

Interest Income   811

Date	Item	Post. Ref.	Dr.	Cr.	Balance Dr.	Balance Cr.
19—						
July 1	Balance.................	√	......	......	......	325
3	....	CR37	......	200	......	525

Prob. 7-2B, Concluded

4.

DORAN CO.
Schedule of Accounts Receivable
July 31, 19—

G. A. Carr Co..	$ 2,040
Ignacio and Co...	2,750
C. D. Martin Co..	970
Janet Rowe Co.	4,600
Total accounts receivable	$10,360

Prob. 7-3B

3, 4, and 5   SALES JOURNAL   Page 40

Date	Invoice No.	Account Debited	Post. Ref.	Accts. Rec. Dr. Sales Cr.
19—				
June 15	√	Total Forwarded	√	25,350
15	717	Towers Co......................	√	6,100
17	718	Halloway Co.	√	7,700
18	719	Ross and Son	√	2,600
24	720	Halloway Co.	√	7,000
29	721	F. G. Black Co.	√	8,500
30				57,250
				(113) (411)

JOURNAL   Page 27

Date	Description	Post. Ref.	Debit	Credit
19—				
June 22	Sales Returns and Allowances	412	200	
	Accounts Receivable—Towers Co.........	113/√		200
30	Sales Returns and Allowances	412	150	
	Accounts Receivable—F. G. Black Co.	113/√		150

Prob. 7-3B, Continued

CASH RECEIPTS JOURNAL   Page 36

Date	Account Credited	Post. Ref.	Other Accts. Cr.	Sales Cr.	Accts. Rec. Cr.	Sales Disc. Dr.	Cash Dr.
19—							
June 15	Totals Forwarded ..	√	3,467	13,470	22,600	366	39,171
16	F.G. Black Co.......	√	.....	......	8,900	89	8,811
21	Halloway Co........	√	.....	......	9,825	.....	9,825
24	Notes Receivable...	112	1,000	......	......	.....	1,050
	Interest Income	811	50	......	......	.....	......
25	Towers Co.	√	.....	......	5,900	59	5,841
27	Halloway Co.......	√	.....	......	7,700	77	7,623
30	Sales	√	.....	11,750	......	.....	11,750
30			4,517	25,220	54,925	591	84,071
			(√)	(411)	(113)	(413)	(111)

2. and 4.   ACCOUNTS RECEIVABLE LEDGER

F.G. Black Co.

Date	Item	Post. Ref.	Dr.	Cr.	Balance
19—					
June 15	....	√	.....	.....	8,900
16	....	CR36	.....	8,900	—
29	....	S40	8,500	.....	8,500
30	....	J27	.....	150	8,350

Halloway Co.

Date	Item	Post. Ref.	Dr.	Cr.	Balance
19—					
June 15	....	√	.....	.....	9,825
17	....	S40	7,700	.....	17,525
21	....	CR36	.....	9,825	7,700
24	....	S40	7,000	.....	14,700
27	....	CR36	.....	7,700	7,000

Ross and Son

Date	Item	Post. Ref.	Dr.	Cr.	Balance
19—					
June 18	....	S40	2,600	.....	2,600

Prob. 7-3B, Continued

Towers Co.

Date	Item	Post. Ref.	Dr.	Cr.	Balance
19—					
June 15	....	S40	6,100	.....	6,100
22	....	J27	.....	200	5,900
25	....	CR36	.....	5,900	—

1. and 5.   GENERAL LEDGER

Cash   **111**

					Balance	
Date	Item	Post. Ref.	Dr.	Cr.	Dr.	Cr.
19—						
June 1	Balance	√	......	......	13,705	......
30	....	CR36	84,071	......	97,776	......

Notes Receivable   **112**

Date	Item	Post. Ref.	Dr.	Cr.	Dr.	Cr.
19—						
June 1	Balance	√	......	......	7,500	......
24	....	CR36	......	1,000	6,500	......

Accounts Receivable   **113**

Date	Item	Post. Ref.	Dr.	Cr.	Dr.	Cr.
19—						
June 1	Balance	√	......	......	15,975	......
22	....	J27	......	200	15,775	......
30	....	J27	......	150	15,625	......
30	....	S40	57,250	......	72,875	......
30	....	CR36	......	54,925	17,950	......

Sales   **411**

Date	Item	Post. Ref.	Dr.	Cr.	Dr.	Cr.
19—						
June 30	....	S40	......	57,250	.....	57,250
30	....	CR36	......	25,220	.....	82,470

Sales Returns and Allowances   **412**

Date	Item	Post. Ref.	Dr.	Cr.	Dr.	Cr.
19—						
June 22	....	J27	200	......	200	......
30	....	J27	150	......	350	......

Prob. 7-3B, Concluded

Sales Discounts   413

| | | Post. | | | Balance | |
| | | | | | | |
Date	Item	Ref.	Dr.	Cr.	Dr.	Cr.
19—						
June 30	....	CR36	591	......	591	......

Interest Income   811

| | | | | | | |
Date	Item	Post. Ref.	Dr.	Cr.	Dr.	Cr.
19—						
June 24	....	CR36	......	50	.....	50

6. The subsidiary ledger is in agreement with the controlling account. Both have balances of $17,950.

Prob. 7-4B

3. and 4.

Page 30

PURCHASES JOURNAL

Date	Account Credited	Post. Ref.	Accounts Payable Cr.	Purchases Dr.	Store Supplies Dr.	Office Supplies Dr.	Other Accounts Dr. Account	Post. Ref.	Amount
19—									
May 1	Wong Co.	√	6,085.20	6,085.20					
3	Lane Co.	√	11,552.50	11,552.50					
8	Tyler Supply	√	175.30			175.30			
12	Wong Co.	√	4,060.50	4,060.50					
13	Gregg Equipment Co.	√	11,900.00				Office Equipment	122	11,900.00
15	James Co.	√	3,100.00	3,100.00					
19	Eber Co.	√	2,500.00	2,500.00					
23	Tyler Supply	√	325.00		325.00				
26	James Co.	√	475.15	475.15					
30	Tyler Supply	√	375.10			375.10			
31			40,548.75	27,773.35	325.00	550.40			11,900.00
			(211)	(511)	(114)	(115)			(√)

JOURNAL

Page 17

Date	Description	Post. Ref.	Debit	Credit
19—				
May 4	Accounts Payable—Wong Co.	211/√	200.00	
	Purchases Returns and Allowances	512		200.00
18	Accounts Payable—Tyler Supply	211/√	22.50	
	Office Supplies	115		22.50
26	Accounts Payable—Lane Co.	211/√	500.00	
	Purchases Returns and Allowances	512		500.00

Prob. 7-4B, Continued

2. and 3.   ACCOUNTS PAYABLE LEDGER

Eber Co.

Date	Item	Post. Ref.	Dr.	Cr.	Bal.
19—					
May 1	Balance	√	......	....	3,150.00
19	....	P30	......	2,500.00	5,650.00

Gregg Equipment Co.

19—					
May 13	....	P30	......	11,900.00	11,900.00

James Co.

19—					
May 1	Balance	√	......	....	4,020.75
15	....	P30	......	3,100.00	7,120.75
26	....	P30	......	475.15	7,595.90

Lane Co.

19—					
May 1	Balance	√	......	....	4,684.35
3	....	P30	......	11,552.50	16,236.85
26	....	J17	500.00	....	15,736.85

Tyler Supply

19—					
May 8	....	P30	......	175.30	175.30
18	....	J17	22.50	....	152.80
23	....	P30	......	325.00	477.80
30	....	P30	......	375.10	852.90

Wong Co.

19—					
May 1	....	P30	......	6,085.20	6,085.20
4	....	J17	200.00	....	5,885.20
12	....	P30	......	4,060.50	9,945.70

Prob. 7-4B, Concluded

1. and 4.   **GENERAL LEDGER**

Store Supplies   114

Date		Post. Ref.	Dr.	Cr.	Balance Dr.	Cr.
19—						
May 1	Balance.......	√	....	....	603.50	....
31	....	P30	325.00	....	928.50	....

Office Supplies   115

19—						
May 1	Balance.......	√	....	....	295.00	....
18	....	J17	....	22.50	....	....
31	....	P30	550.40	....	822.90	....

Office Equipment   122

19—						
May 1	Balance.......	√	....	....	29,700.00	....
13	....	P30	11,900.00	....	41,600.00	....

Accounts Payable   211

19—						
May 1	Balance.......	√	....	....	....	11,855.10
4	....	J17	200.00	....	....	....
18	....	J17	22.50	....	....	....
26	....	J17	500.00	....	....	....
31	....	P30	....	40,548.75	....	51,681.35

Purchases   511

19—						
May 1	Balance.......	√	....	....	102,150.50	....
31	....	P30	27,773.35	....	129,923.85	....

Purchases Returns and Allowances   512

19—						
May 1	Balance.......	√	....	....	....	3,050.25
4	....	J17	....	200.00	....	....
26	....	J17	....	500.00	....	3,750.25

5. a. $51,681.35
     b. $51,681.35

1, 2, and 3

Prob. 7-5B

PURCHASES JOURNAL

Page 1

Date	Account Credited	Post. Ref.	Accounts Payable Cr.	Purchases Dr.	Store Supplies Dr.	Office Supplies Dr.	Other Accounts Dr.		
							Account	Post. Ref.	Amount
19—									
Mar. 16	Harper Equipment Co.	✓	9,900	.....	...	...	Store Equipment	121	9,900
17	Carter Clothing	✓	3,250	3,250					
19	Hernandez Clothing Co.	✓	5,920	5,920					
20	Adams Co.	✓	4,600	4,600	...	...			...
28	Adams Co.	✓	5,250	5,250					
30	Harper Equipment Co.	✓	3,602	.....	110	42	Office Equipment	123	3,450
30	Carter Clothing	✓	1,200	1,200	...	...			...
31			33,722	20,220	110	42			13,350
			(211)	(511)	(116)	(117)			(√)

Prob. 7-5B, Continued

Page 1

CASH PAYMENTS JOURNAL

Date	Ck. No.	Account Debited	Post. Ref.	Other Accounts Dr.	Accounts Payable Dr.	Purchases Discounts Cr.	Cash Cr.
19—							
Mar. 16	1	Rent Expense	712	1,000			1,000
18	2	Store Supplies	116	140			215
		Office Supplies	117	75			—
24	3	Harper Equipment Co.	✓		9,900		9,900
26	4	Carter Clothing	✓		3,250	65	3,185
28	5	Sales Returns and Allowances	412	65			65
28	6	Hernandez Clothing Co.	✓		5,700	114	5,586
30	7	Adams Co.	✓		4,300	43	4,257
31	8	Store Supplies	116	170			170
31	9	Sales Salaries Expense	611	2,200			2,200
				3,650	23,150	222	26,578
				(✓)	(211)	(513)	(111)

Prob. 7-5B, Continued

1. and 2.   JOURNAL   Page 1

Date	Description	Post. Ref.	Debit	Credit
19—				
Mar. 22	Accounts Payable—Hernandez Clothing Co..	211/√	220	
	Purchases Returns and Allowances.......	512		220
25	Accounts Payable—Adams Co..............	211/√	300	
	Purchases Returns and Allowances.......	512		300
31	Accounts Payable—Harper Equipment Co...	211/√	50	
	Office Equipment.......................	123		50

1.   ACCOUNTS PAYABLE LEDGER

Adams Co.

Date	Item	Post. Ref.	Dr.	Cr.	Bal.
19—					
Mar. 20	....	P1	.....	4,600	4,600
25	....	J1	300	.....	4,300
28	....	P1	.....	5,250	9,550
30	....	CP1	4,300	.....	5,250

Carter Clothing

Date	Item	Post. Ref.	Dr.	Cr.	Bal.
19—					
Mar. 17	....	P1	.....	3,250	3,250
26	....	CP1	3,250	.....	—
30	....	P1	.....	1,200	1,200

Harper Equipment Co.

Date	Item	Post. Ref.	Dr.	Cr.	Bal.
19—					
Mar. 16	....	P1	.....	9,900	9,900
24	....	CP1	9,900	.....	—
30	....	P1	.....	3,602	3,602
31	....	J1	50	.....	3,552

Hernandez Clothing Co.

Date	Item	Post. Ref.	Dr.	Cr.	Bal.
19—					
Mar. 19	....	P1	.....	5,920	5,920
22	....	J1	220	.....	5,700
28	....	CP1	5,700	.....	—

Prob. 7-5B, Continued

2. and 3.   GENERAL LEDGER

Cash   111

Date	Item	Post. Ref.	Dr.	Cr.	Balance Dr.	Balance Cr.
19—						
Mar. 31	....	CP1	......	26,578	.....	26,578

Store Supplies   116

Date	Item	Post. Ref.	Dr.	Cr.	Balance Dr.	Balance Cr.
19—						
Mar. 18	....	CP1	140	......	.....	......
31	....	CP1	170	......	.....	......
31	....	P1	110	......	420	......

Office Supplies   117

Date	Item	Post. Ref.	Dr.	Cr.	Balance Dr.	Balance Cr.
19—						
Mar. 18	....	CP1	75	......	.....	......
31	....	P1	42	......	117	......

Store Equipment   121

Date	Item	Post. Ref.	Dr.	Cr.	Balance Dr.	Balance Cr.
19—						
Mar. 16	....	P1	9,900	......	9,900	......

Office Equipment   123

Date	Item	Post. Ref.	Dr.	Cr.	Balance Dr.	Balance Cr.
19—						
Mar. 30	....	P1	3,450	......	.....	......
31	....	J1	......	50	3,400	......

Accounts Payable   211

Date	Item	Post. Ref.	Dr.	Cr.	Balance Dr.	Balance Cr.
19—						
Mar. 22	....	J1	220	......	.....	......
25	....	J1	300	......	.....	......
31	....	J1	50	......	.....	......
31	....	P1	......	33,722	.....	......
31	....	CP1	23,150	......	.....	10,002

Prob. 7-5B, Concluded

Sales Returns and Allowances 412

Date	Item	Post. Ref.	Dr.	Cr.	Balance Dr.	Balance Cr.
19— Mar. 28	....	CP1	65	......	65	......

Purchases 511

Date	Item	Post. Ref.	Dr.	Cr.	Balance Dr.	Balance Cr.
19— Mar. 31	....	P1	20,220	......	20,220	......

Purchases Returns and Allowances 512

Date	Item	Post. Ref.	Dr.	Cr.	Balance Dr.	Balance Cr.
19— Mar. 22	....	J1	......	220	......	......
25	....	J1	......	300	......	520

Purchases Discounts 513

Date	Item	Post. Ref.	Dr.	Cr.	Balance Dr.	Balance Cr.
19— Mar. 31	....	CP1	......	222	......	222

Sales Salaries Expense 611

Date	Item	Post. Ref.	Dr.	Cr.	Balance Dr.	Balance Cr.
19— Mar. 31	....	CP1	2,200	......	2,200	......

Rent Expense 712

Date	Item	Post. Ref.	Dr.	Cr.	Balance Dr.	Balance Cr.
19— Mar. 16	....	CP1	1,000	......	1,000	......

4.
CARR CO.
Schedule of Accounts Payable
March 31, 19—

Adams Co.	$ 5,250
Carter Clothing	1,200
Harper Equipment Co.	3,552
Total accounts payable	$10,002

2, 3, and 4

Prob. 7-6B

PURCHASES JOURNAL   Page 37

Date	Account Credited	Post. Ref.	Accounts Payable Cr.	Purchases Dr.	Store Supplies Dr.	Office Supplies Dr.	Other Accounts Dr.		
							Account	Post. Ref.	Amount
19—									
July 2	Mann Co.	✓	7,500	.....	.....	.....	Equipment.....	121	7,500
2	Evans Co.	✓	4,250	4,250	.....	.....			.....
18	Davis Enterprises	✓	6,420	6,420	.....	.....			.....
21	Cass Supply Co.	✓	420	.....	225	195			.....
24	Frank Co.	✓	4,300	4,170	130	.....			.....
31			22,890	14,840	355	195			7,500
			(211)	(511)	(115)	(116)			(✓)

CASH RECEIPTS JOURNAL   Page 42

Date	Account Credited	Post. Ref.	Other Accounts Cr.	Sales Cr.	Accounts Receivable Cr.	Sales Discounts Dr.	Cash Dr.
19—							
July 7	Owens Co.	✓	.....	.....	2,500	25	2,475
9	Baker Manufacturing Co.	✓	.....	.....	7,500	75	7,425
12	Black Co.	✓	.....	.....	775	.....	775
15	Sales	✓	.....	23,750	.....	.....	23,750
19	Purchases Returns and Allowances	512	90	.....	.....	.....	90
25	Owens Co.	✓	.....	.....	3,000	30	2,970
31	Sales	✓	.....	26,150	.....	.....	26,150
31			90	49,900	13,775	130	63,635
			(✓)	(411)	(113)	(413)	(111)

Prob. 7-6B, Continued

2. and 4. <div style="text-align:center">SALES JOURNAL</div> **Page 35**

Date	Invoice No.	Account Debited	Post. Ref.	Accts. Rec. Dr. Sales Cr.
19—				
July 3	832	Black Co.	√	1,975
8	833	Kane Co..........................	√	5,000
12	834	Owens Co.........................	√	3,500
23	835	Baker Manufacturing Co.	√	1,950
25	836	Jackson Co.......................	√	3,290
31				15,715
				(113) (411)

2, 3, and 4. <div style="text-align:center">CASH PAYMENTS JOURNAL</div> **Page 34**

Date	Check No.	Account Debited	Post. Ref.	Other Accts. Dr.	Accts. Pay. Dr.	Purch. Disc. Cr.	Cash Cr.
19—							
July 1	920	Rent Expense	712	2,000	......	.....	2,000
7	921	Misc. Selling Expense	619	190	......	.....	190
9	922	Frank Co.	√	......	9,500	190	9,310
10	923	Davis Enterprises ..	√	......	3,100	.....	3,100
12	924	Ross Co............	√	......	930	.....	930
15	925	Evans Co...........	√	......	4,000	80	3,920
15	926	Purchases..........	511	2,250	......	.....	2,250
19	927	Misc. Adm. Expense	719	145	......	.....	145
22	928	Advertising Expense	612	945	......	.....	945
29	929	Mann Co...........	√	......	7,500	.....	7,500
30	930	D. D. Miles, Drawing	312	3,000	......	.....	3,000
31	931	Sales Salaries Expense	611	11,100	......	.....	15,600
		Office Salaries Expense	711	4,500	......	.....	......
31	932	Transportation In ..	514	465	......	.....	465
31				24,595	25,030	270	49,355
				(√)	(211)	(513)	(111)

Prob. 7-6B, Continued

2. and 3.   JOURNAL   Page 31

Date	Description	Post. Ref.	Debit	Credit
19—				
July 7	Accounts Payable—Evans Co.	211/√	250	
	Purchases Returns and Allowances	512		250
14	Sales Returns and Allowances.	412	500	
	Accounts Receivable—Owens Co.	113/√		500

1, 3, and 4   GENERAL LEDGER

Cash   **111**

Date	Item	Post. Ref.	Dr.	Cr.	Balance Dr.	Balance Cr.
19—						
July 1	Balance	√	. . . . . .	. . . . . .	9,850	. . . . . .
31	. . . .	CR42	63,635	. . . . . .		. . . . . .
31	. . . .	CP34	. . . . . .	49,355	24,130	. . . . . .

Accounts Receivable   **113**

Date	Item	Post. Ref.	Dr.	Cr.	Balance Dr.	Balance Cr.
19—						
July 1	Balance	√	. . . . . .	. . . . . .	12,975	. . . . . .
14	. . . .	J31	. . . . . .	500	. . . . . .	. . . . . .
31	. . . .	S35	15,715	. . . . . .	. . . . . .	. . . . . .
31	. . . .	CR42	. . . . . .	13,775	14,415	. . . . . .

Merchandise Inventory   **114**

Date	Item	Post. Ref.	Dr.	Cr.	Balance Dr.	Balance Cr.
19—						
July 1	Balance	√	. . . . . .	. . . . . .	35,500	. . . . . .

Store Supplies   **115**

Date	Item	Post. Ref.	Dr.	Cr.	Balance Dr.	Balance Cr.
19—						
July 1	Balance	√	. . . . . .	. . . . . .	545	. . . . . .
31	. . . .	P37	355	. . . . . .	900	. . . . . .

Office Supplies   **116**

Date	Item	Post. Ref.	Dr.	Cr.	Balance Dr.	Balance Cr.
19—						
July 1	Balance	√	. . . . . .	. . . . . .	360	. . . . . .
31	. . . .	P37	195	. . . . . .	555	. . . . . .

Prob. 7-6B, Continued

Prepaid Insurance 117

Date	Item	Post. Ref.	Dr.	Cr.	Balance Dr.	Cr.
19—						
July 1	Balance	√	......	......	2,100	......

Equipment 121

Date	Item	Post. Ref.	Dr.	Cr.	Balance Dr.	Cr.
19—						
July 1	Balance	√	......	......	47,250	......
2	....	P37	7,500	......	54,750	......

Accumulated Depreciation 122

Date	Item	Post. Ref.	Dr.	Cr.	Balance Dr.	Cr.
19—						
July 1	Balance	√	......	......	......	22,250

Accounts Payable 211

Date	Item	Post. Ref.	Dr.	Cr.	Balance Dr.	Cr.
19—						
July 1	Balance	√	......	......	......	13,530
7	....	J31	250	......	......	......
31	....	P37	......	22,890	......	......
31	....	CP34	25,030	......	......	11,140

D. D. Miles, Capital 311

Date	Item	Post. Ref.	Dr.	Cr.	Balance Dr.	Cr.
19—						
July 1	Balance	√	......	......	......	72,800

D. D. Miles, Drawing 312

Date	Item	Post. Ref.	Dr.	Cr.	Balance Dr.	Cr.
19—						
July 30	....	CP34	3,000	......	3,000	......

Sales 411

Date	Item	Post. Ref.	Dr.	Cr.	Balance Dr.	Cr.
19—						
July 31	....	S35	......	15,715	......	......
31	....	CR42	......	49,900	......	65,615

Sales Returns and Allowances 412

Date	Item	Post. Ref.	Dr.	Cr.	Balance Dr.	Cr.
19—						
July 14	....	J31	500	......	500	......

Prob. 7-6B, Continued

Sales Discounts 413

Date	Item	Post. Ref.	Dr.	Cr.	Balance Dr.	Balance Cr.
19—						
July 31	....	CR42	130	......	130	......

Purchases 511

Date	Item	Post. Ref.	Dr.	Cr.	Balance Dr.	Balance Cr.
19—						
July 15	....	CP34	2,250	......	......	......
31	....	P37	14,840	......	17,090	......

Purchases Returns and Allowances 512

Date	Item	Post. Ref.	Dr.	Cr.	Balance Dr.	Balance Cr.
19—						
July 7	....	J31	......	250	......	......
19	....	CR42	......	90	......	340

Purchases Discounts 513

Date	Item	Post. Ref.	Dr.	Cr.	Balance Dr.	Balance Cr.
19—						
July 31	....	CP34	......	270	......	270

Transportation In 514

Date	Item	Post. Ref.	Dr.	Cr.	Balance Dr.	Balance Cr.
19—						
July 31	....	CP34	465	......	465	......

Sales Salaries Expense 611

Date	Item	Post. Ref.	Dr.	Cr.	Balance Dr.	Balance Cr.
19—						
July 31	....	CP34	11,100	......	11,100	......

Advertising Expense 612

Date	Item	Post. Ref.	Dr.	Cr.	Balance Dr.	Balance Cr.
19—						
July 22	....	CP34	945	......	945	......

Miscellaneous Selling Expense 619

Date	Item	Post. Ref.	Dr.	Cr.	Balance Dr.	Balance Cr.
19—						
July 7	....	CP34	190	......	190	......

Office Salaries Expense 711

Date	Item	Post. Ref.	Dr.	Cr.	Balance Dr.	Balance Cr.
19—						
July 31	....	CP34	4,500	......	4,500	......

Prob. 7-6B, Concluded

Rent Expense   712

Date	Item	Post. Ref.	Dr.	Cr.	Balance Dr.	Balance Cr.
19— July 1	....	CP34	2,000	......	2,000	......

Miscellaneous Administrative Expense   719

Date	Item	Post. Ref.	Dr.	Cr.	Balance Dr.	Balance Cr.
19— July 19	....	CP34	145	......	145	......

5.

MILES COMPANY
Trial Balance
July 31, 19—

	Dr.	Cr.
Cash...	24,130	
Accounts Receivable.............................	14,415	
Merchandise Inventory...........................	35,500	
Store Supplies	900	
Office Supplies.................................	555	
Prepaid Insurance...............................	2,100	
Equipment	54,750	
Accumulated Depreciation		22,250
Accounts Payable................................		11,140
D. D. Miles, Capital............................		72,800
D. D. Miles, Drawing	3,000	
Sales		65,615
Sales Returns and Allowances....................	500	
Sales Discounts	130	
Purchases.......................................	17,090	
Purchases Returns and Allowances		340
Purchases Discounts.............................		270
Transportation In...............................	465	
Sales Salaries Expense..........................	11,100	
Advertising Expense.............................	945	
Miscellaneous Selling Expense	190	
Office Salaries Expense.........................	4,500	
Rent Expense	2,000	
Miscellaneous Administrative Expense............	145	
	172,415	172,415

6. Total of accounts receivable ledger: $14,415
   Total of accounts payable ledger: $11,140

Prob. 7-7B

Page 1

3. and 4.

SALES JOURNAL

Date	Invoice No.	Account Debited	Post. Ref.	Accts. Rec. Dr.	Sales Cr.	Sales Tax Payable Cr.
19—						
May 21	1	Boritz Co.	✓	1,272	1,200	72
22	2	Stark Co.	✓	2,915	2,750	165
24	3	Morris Co.	✓	3,286	3,100	186
27	4	C. D. Walters Co.	✓	2,650	2,500	150
28	5	A. Udall Co.	✓	1,590	1,500	90
30	6	Stark Co.	✓	3,074	2,900	174
31	7	Morris Co.	✓	1,060	1,000	60
31				15,847	14,950	897
				(113)	(411)	(215)

Prob. 7-7B, Continued

		Post.		
Date	Description	Ref.	Debit	Credit

JOURNAL Page 1

		Post. Ref.	Debit	Credit
19—				
May 25	Sales Returns and Allowances..............	412	100	
	Sales Tax Payable.........................	215	6	
	Accounts Receivable—Boritz Co.	113/√		106
28	Sales Returns and Allowances..............	412	150	
	Sales Tax Payable.........................	215	9	
	Accounts Receivable—Stark Co...........	113/√		159
30	Sales Returns and Allowances..............	412	200	
	Sales Tax Payable.........................	215	12	
	Accounts Receivable—C. D. Walters Co. ...	113/√		212

1. and 4.   GENERAL LEDGER

Accounts Receivable   113

		Post.			Balance	
Date	Item	Ref.	Dr.	Cr.	Dr.	Cr.
19—						
May 25	....	J1	......	106	.....	......
28	....	J1	......	159	.....	......
30	....	J1	......	212	.....	......
31	....	S1	15,847	......	15,370	......

Sales Tax Payable   215

		Post.			Balance	
19—						
May 25	....	J1	6	......	.....	......
28	....	J1	9	......	.....	......
30	....	J1	12	......	.....	......
31	....	S1	......	897	.....	870

Sales   411

		Post.			Balance	
19—						
May 31	....	S1	......	14,950	.....	14,950

Prob. 7-7B, Concluded

Sales Returns and Allowances

412

Date	Item	Post. Ref.	Dr.	Cr.	Balance Dr.	Balance Cr.
19—						
May 25	....	J1	100	......	.....	......
28	....	J1	150	......	.....	......
30	....	J1	200	......	450	......

2. and 3.   ACCOUNTS RECEIVABLE LEDGER

Boritz Co.

Date	Item	Post. Ref.	Dr.	Cr.	Bal.
19—					
May 21	....	S1	1,272	.....	1,272
25	....	J1	....	106	1,166

Morris Co.

Date	Item	Post. Ref.	Dr.	Cr.	Bal.
19—					
May 24	....	S1	3,286	.....	3,286
31	....	S1	1,060	.....	4,346

Stark Co.

Date	Item	Post. Ref.	Dr.	Cr.	Bal.
19—					
May 22	....	S1	2,915	.....	2,915
28	....	J1	....	159	2,756
30	....	S1	3,074	.....	5,830

A. Udall Co.

Date	Item	Post. Ref.	Dr.	Cr.	Bal.
19—					
May 28	....	S1	1,590	.....	1,590

C.D. Walters Co.

Date	Item	Post. Ref.	Dr.	Cr.	Bal.
19—					
May 27	....	S1	2,650	.....	2,650
30	....	J1	....	212	2,438

3. a. $15,370
   b. $15,370

Mini-Case 7

1. Special journals are used to reduce the processing time and expense to record transactions. A special journal is usually created when a specific type of transaction occurs frequently enough that the use of the traditional 2-column journal becomes cumbersome. The frequency of transactions for Creative Jewelers would probably justify the following special journals:

> Purchases Journal
> Cash Payment Journal
> Sales Journal
> Cash Receipts Journal

Instructor's Note: The number and nature of the special journals to be established for Creative Jewelers involves judgment. Differences of opinion may exist as to whether all the preceding special journals are necessary or cost-efficient. Instructors may wish to use this time to comment further on the costs of establishing special journals and the potential benefits of reducing the processing time to record transactions.

2.

PURCHASES JOURNAL   PAGE

DATE	ACCOUNT CREDITED	POST. REF.	ACCOUNTS PAYABLE CR.	NOTES PAYABLE CR.	PURCHASES DR.	STORE SUPPLIES DR.	OFFICE SUPPLIES DR.	OTHER ACCOUNTS DR.		
								ACCOUNT	POST. REF.	AMOUNT

Note: The Notes Payable Cr. column is included because approximately 10% of all purchases on account involve the issuance of notes.

SALES JOURNAL   PAGE

DATE	INVOICE NO.	ACCOUNT DEBITED	POST. REF.	ACCTS. REC. DEBIT	SALES CREDIT	SALES TAX PAYABLE CREDIT

Note: The Sales Tax Payable column is included because all intrastate sales are subject to a 6% sales tax, which is collected by Creative Jewelers. The sales tax must then be periodically remitted to the state or local governing unit.

Mini-Case 7, Concluded

3. Creative Jewelers should maintain subsidiary ledgers for accounts receivable and accounts payable. A subsidiary ledger could also be established for notes payable. Alternatively, a notes payable register such as illustrated below could be used instead of a subsidiary notes payable ledger.* Regardless of whether a subsidiary ledger or register is established for notes payable, it is important that Creative Jewelers maintain accurate records of the notes payable outstanding, their terms, and their due dates.

Page 3   (left page)   NOTES PAYABLE REGISTER

Date Issued	No.	Payable To	Payable At	Date of Note
19—				
Jan. 9	34	A. J. Gainer Co..............	Union National Bank	1-9
26	35	L. Young & Co.	Belford State Bank	1-26
Feb. 23	36	Franz Distributors	City National Bank	2-23
Mar. 16	37	Spritz Jewelers.............	Tudor State Bank	3-16
25	38	Roberts Co.	Belford State Bank	3-25

(right page)   Page 3

Time	J	F	M	A	M	J	J	A	S	O	N	D	Face	Rate of Int.	Dis-position
30 days	·	8	·	·	·	·	·	·	·	·	·	·	10,000	10%	Pd. 2/8
60 days	·	·	27	·	·	·	·	·	·	·	·	·	9,000	....	Pd. 3/27
90 days	·	·	·	·	24	·	·	·	·	·	·	·	16,000	10%	....
30 days	·	·	·	15	·	·	·	·	·	·	·	·	10,000	....	....
90 days	·	·	·	·	·	23	·	·	·	·	·	·	2,500	12%	....

*Note to Instructors: The notes payable register has not been presented in this chapter. However, instructors may find its presentation useful in enhancing student understanding of the nature of special records. Instructors may also wish to point out to students that accounting systems must be tailored to the individual needs of each enterprise.

4, 5, and 6

COMPREHENSIVE PROBLEM 3

PURCHASES JOURNAL

Date	Account Credited	Post. Ref.	Accounts Payable Cr.	Purchases Dr.	Store Supplies Dr.	Office Supplies Dr.	Other Accounts Dr. Account	Post. Ref.	Amount
19—									
Jan. 2	Dane Co.	✓	2,250	2,250					
2	Lee Equipment Co.	✓	3,700				Equipment	121	3,700
17	Collins Enterprises	✓	6,420	6,420					
21	Bunn Supply Co.	✓	385		215	170			
24	Easterly Co.	✓	3,235	3,125	110				
31			15,990	11,795	325	170			3,700
			(211)	(511)	(115)	(116)			(✓)

CASH RECEIPTS JOURNAL

Date	Account Credited	Post. Ref.	Other Accounts Cr.	Sales Cr.	Accounts Receivable Cr.	Sales Discounts Dr.	Cash Dr.
19—							
Jan. 7	Nichols Co.	✓			2,800	56	2,744
9	Baker Manufacturing Co.	✓			9,800	196	9,604
12	C. Block Co.	✓			775		775
15	Sales	✓		18,942			18,942
18	Purchases Returns and Allowances	512	75				75
25	Nichols Co.	✓			3,000	60	2,940
31	Sales	✓		19,250			19,250
31			75	38,192	16,375	312	54,330
			(✓)	(411)	(113)	(413)	(111)

Comp. Prob. 3, Continued

4. and 6.   **SALES JOURNAL**   **Page 29**

Date	Invoice No.	Account Debited	Post. Ref.	Accts. Rec. Dr. Sales Cr.
19—				
Jan. 3	942	C. Block Co....................	√	1,320
8	943	Jackson Co.....................	√	5,000
10	944	Nichols Co.	√	3,225
23	945	Baker Manufacturing Co.	√	1,950
25	946	Jackson Co.....................	√	3,290
31				14,785
				(113) (411)

4, 5, and 6.   **CASH PAYMENTS JOURNAL**   **Page 28**

Date	Check No.	Account Debited	Post. Ref.	Other Accts. Dr.	Accts. Pay. Dr.	Purch. Disc. Cr.	Cash Cr.
19—							
Jan. 2	810	Rent Expense	712	1,500	......	....	1,500
7	811	Misc. Selling Expense	619	205	......	....	205
9	812	Easterly Co.......	√	......	9,500	190	9,310
10	813	Collins Enterprises	√	......	2,120	....	2,120
11	814	Peak Co..........	√	......	705	....	705
15	815	Dane Co..........	√	......	2,100	42	2,058
15	816	Purchases........	511	1,250	......	....	1,250
18	817	Misc. Adm. Expense	719	130	......	....	130
22	818	Advertising Expense	612	610	......	....	610
26	819	Lee Equipment Co.	√	......	3,700	....	3,700
29	820	Purchases........	511	2,500	......	....	2,500
30	821	Sales Salaries Expense	611	9,600	......	....	13,400
		Office Salaries Expense	711	3,800	......	....	......
31	822	Purchases........	511	390	......	....	390
31				19,985	18,125	232	37,878
				(√)	(211)	(513)	(111)

Comp. Prob. 3, Continued

4. and 5.

JOURNAL

Page 25

Date	Description	Post. Ref.	Debit	Credit
19—				
Jan. 8	Accounts Payable—Dane Co.	211/√	150	
	Purchases Returns and Allowances	512		150
14	Sales Returns and Allowances.............	412	225	
	Accounts Receivable—Nichols Co.	113/√		225

1, 5, and 6

GENERAL LEDGER

Cash

111

					Balance	
Date	Item	Post. Ref.	Dr.	Cr.	Dr.	Cr.
19—						
Jan. 1	Balance	√	......	......	9,100	....
31	....	CR36	54,330	......	......	....
31	....	CP28	......	37,878	25,552	....

Accounts Receivable

113

19—						
Jan. 1	Balance	√	......	......	16,200	....
14	....	J25	......	225	......	....
31	....	S29	14,785	......	......	....
31	....	CR36	......	16,375	14,385	....

Merchandise Inventory

114

19—						
Jan. 1	Balance	√	......	......	31,500	....

Store Supplies

115

19—						
Jan. 1	Balance	√	......	......	410	....
31	....	P31	325	......	735	....

Office Supplies

116

19—						
Jan. 1	Balance	√	......	......	225	....
31	....	P31	170	......	395	....

Comp. Prob. 3, Continued

Prepaid Insurance   **117**

Date	Item	Post. Ref.	Dr.	Cr.	Balance Dr.	Balance Cr.
19— Jan. 1	Balance	✓	......	......	2,100	....

Equipment   **121**

Date	Item	Post. Ref.	Dr.	Cr.	Balance Dr.	Balance Cr.
19— Jan. 1	Balance	✓	......	......	40,650	....
2		P31	3,700	......	44,350	....

Accumulated Depreciation   **122**

Date	Item	Post. Ref.	Dr.	Cr.	Balance Dr.	Balance Cr.
19— Jan. 1	Balance	✓	......	......	......	12,350

Accounts Payable   **211**

Date	Item	Post. Ref.	Dr.	Cr.	Balance Dr.	Balance Cr.
19— Jan. 1	Balance	✓	......	......	......	12,325
8		J25	150	......	......	....
31		P31	......	15,990	......	....
31		CP28	18,125	......	......	10,040

D. L. Redman, Capital   **311**

Date	Item	Post. Ref.	Dr.	Cr.	Balance Dr.	Balance Cr.
19— Jan. 1	Balance	✓	......	......	......	75,510

D. L. Redman, Drawing   **312**

Sales   **411**

Date	Item	Post. Ref.	Dr.	Cr.	Balance Dr.	Balance Cr.
19— Jan. 31		S29	......	14,785	......	....
31		CR36	......	38,192	......	52,977

Sales Returns and Allowances   **412**

Date	Item	Post. Ref.	Dr.	Cr.	Balance Dr.	Balance Cr.
19— Jan. 14		J25	225	......	225	....

Sales Discounts   **413**

Date	Item	Post. Ref.	Dr.	Cr.	Balance Dr.	Balance Cr.
19— Jan. 31		CR36	312	......	312	....

Comp. Prob. 3, Continued

Purchases   511

Date	Item	Post. Ref.	Dr.	Cr.	Balance Dr.	Cr.
19—						
Jan. 15	....	CP28	1,250	......	......	....
29	....	CP28	2,500	......	......	....
31	....	CP28	390	......	......	....
31	....	P31	11,795	......	15,935	....

Purchases Returns and Allowances   512

Date	Item	Post. Ref.	Dr.	Cr.	Balance Dr.	Cr.
19—						
Jan. 8	....	J25	......	150	......	....
18	....	CR36	......	75	......	225

Purchases Discounts   513

Date	Item	Post. Ref.	Dr.	Cr.	Balance Dr.	Cr.
19—						
Jan. 31	....	CP28	......	232	......	232

Sales Salaries Expense   611

Date	Item	Post. Ref.	Dr.	Cr.	Balance Dr.	Cr.
19—						
Jan. 30	....	CP28	9,600	......	9,600	....

Advertising Expense   612

Date	Item	Post. Ref.	Dr.	Cr.	Balance Dr.	Cr.
19—						
Jan. 22	....	CP28	610	......	610	....

Miscellaneous Selling Expense   619

Date	Item	Post. Ref.	Dr.	Cr.	Balance Dr.	Cr.
19—						
Jan. 7	....	CP28	205	......	205	....

Office Salaries Expense   711

Date	Item	Post. Ref.	Dr.	Cr.	Balance Dr.	Cr.
19—						
Jan. 30	....	CP28	3,800	......	3,800	....

Rent Expense   712

Date	Item	Post. Ref.	Dr.	Cr.	Balance Dr.	Cr.
19—						
Jan. 2	....	CP28	1,500	......	1,500	....

Comp. Prob. 3, Continued

Miscellaneous Administrative Expense   719

Date	Item	Post. Ref.	Dr.	Cr.	Balance Dr.	Balance Cr.
19—						
Jan. 18	....	CP28	130	......	130	....

2. and 4.   ACCOUNTS RECEIVABLE LEDGER

Baker Manufacturing Co.

Date	Item	Post. Ref.	Debit	Credit	Balance
19—					
Jan. 1	Balance	√	.....	....	9,800
9	....	CR36	.....	9,800	—
23	....	S29	1,950	....	1,950

C. Block Co.

Date	Item	Post. Ref.	Debit	Credit	Balance
19—					
Jan. 1	Balance	√	.....	....	775
3	....	S29	1,320	....	2,095
12	....	CR36	.....	775	1,320

Jackson Co.

Date	Item	Post. Ref.	Debit	Credit	Balance
19—					
Jan. 8	....	S29	5,000	....	5,000
25	....	S29	3,290	....	8,290

Nichols Co.

Date	Item	Post. Ref.	Debit	Credit	Balance
19—					
Jan. 1	Balance	√	.....	....	2,800
7	....	CR36	.....	2,800	—
10	....	S29	3,225	....	3,225
14	....	J25	.....	225	3,000
25	....	CR36	.....	3,000	.....

Wilson and Son

Date	Item	Post. Ref.	Debit	Credit	Balance
19—					
Jan. 1	Balance	√	.....	....	2,825

Comp. Prob. 3, Continued

3. and 4.   ACCOUNTS PAYABLE LEDGER

Bunn Supply Co.

Date	Item	Post. Ref.	Debit	Credit	Balance
19—					
Jan. 21	....	P31	.....	385	385

Collins Enterprises

Date	Item	Post. Ref.	Debit	Credit	Balance
19—					
Jan. 1	Balance	✓	.....	....	2,120
10	....	CP28	2,120	....	—
17	....	P31	.....	6,420	6,420

Dane Co.

Date	Item	Post. Ref.	Debit	Credit	Balance
19—					
Jan. 2	....	P31	.....	2,250	2,250
8	....	J25	150	....	2,100
15	....	CP28	2,100	....	—

Easterly Co.

Date	Item	Post. Ref.	Debit	Credit	Balance
19—					
Jan. 1	Balance	✓	.....	....	9,500
9	....	CR28	9,500	....	—
24	....	P31	.....	3,235	3,235

Lee Equipment Co.

Date	Item	Post. Ref.	Debit	Credit	Balance
19—					
Jan. 2	....	P31	.....	3,700	3,700
26	....	CP28	3,700	....	—

Peak Co.

Date	Item	Post. Ref.	Debit	Credit	Balance
19—					
Jan. 1	Balance	✓	.....	....	705
11	....	CP28	705	....	—

Comp. Prob. 3, Concluded

7.
REDMAN SUPPLY CO.
Trial Balance
January 31, 19—

Cash	25,552	
Accounts Receivable	14,385	
Merchandise Inventory	31,500	
Store Supplies	735	
Office Supplies	395	
Prepaid Insurance	2,100	
Equipment	44,350	
Accumulated Depreciation		12,350
Accounts Payable		10,040
D. L. Redman, Capital		75,510
Sales		52,977
Sales Returns and Allowances	225	
Sales Discounts	312	
Purchases	15,935	
Purchases Returns and Allowances		225
Purchases Discounts		232
Sales Salaries Expense	9,600	
Advertising Expense	610	
Miscellaneous Selling Expense	205	
Office Salaries Expense	3,800	
Rent Expense	1,500	
Miscellaneous Administrative Expense	130	
	151,334	151,334

8.
REDMAN SUPPLY CO.
Schedule of Accounts Receivable
January 31, 19—

Baker Manufacturing Co.	$ 1,950.00
C. Block Co.	1,320.00
Jackson Co.	8,290.00
Wilson and Son	2,825.00
Total accounts receivable	$14,385.00

REDMAN SUPPLY CO.
Schedule of Accounts Payable
January 31, 19—

Bunn Supply Co.	$ 385.00
Collins Enterprises	6,420.00
Easterly Co.	3,235.00
Total accounts payable	$10,040.00

CHAPTER 8

DISCUSSION QUESTIONS

1. A great many transactions affect cash and it is the asset most susceptible to improper diversion and use because of its high value in relation to its mass and its ease of transfer among parties. For these reasons, the control of cash often warrants special attention.

2. The drawer is the party that signs the check and the payee is the party to whose order the check is drawn.

3. Remittance advice

4. The Cash in Bank balance and bank statement balance are likely to differ because of (1) delay by bank or depositor in recording transactions or (2) errors by bank or depositor in recording transactions.

5. The purpose of the bank reconciliation is to determine the reasons for the difference between the balance according to the depositor's records and the balance according to the bank statement, and to correct those items representing errors in recording that may have been made by the bank or by the depositor.

6. a. Additions made by the bank to the depositor's balance.

7. Accounts Receivable should be debited and Cash in Bank credited.

8. a. Addition to the balance per bank: (1), (4)
   b. Deduction from the balance per bank: (3)
   c. Addition to the balance per depositor's records: (2), (5)
   d. Deduction from the balance per depositor's records: (6), (7)

9. (2), (5), (6), (7)

10. a. The salesclerks should not have access to the cash register tapes.
    b. The cash register tapes should be locked in the cash register and the key retained by the cashier. An employee of the cashier's office should remove the cash register tape, record the total on the memorandum form, and note discrepancies.

11. a. The remittance advices should not be sent to the cashier.
    b. The remittance advices should be sent directly to the accounting department by the mailroom.

12. a. Cash Short and Over
    b. Cash shortages are debited to this account.

13. Other income section

14. A voucher is a special form on which are recorded pertinent data about an obligation and the particulars of its payment.

15. The three documents supporting the liability are: vendor's invoice, purchase order, and receiving report. The invoice should be compared with the receiving report to determine that the items billed have been received and with the purchase order to verify quantities, prices, and terms.

16. a. Accounts Payable is a controlling account.
    b. There is a subsidiary creditors ledger, but it is not in the form that has been employed in earlier chapters of the textbook. The unpaid voucher file is the subsidiary ledger.

17. After payment, vouchers and supporting documents can be run through a canceling machine to prevent reuse.

18. The prenumbering of checks and the paying of all obligations by check are desirable elements of internal control, although the proper use of a petty cash fund for small cash disbursements would be useful and would not weaken the system. The fundamental weakness in internal control is the failure to separate the responsibility for the maintenance of the accounting records (bookkeeping) from the responsibility for operations (payment of obligations).

19. a. In the unpaid voucher file, the vouchers should be filed by the due dates so that each voucher can be paid when due.
    b. In the paid voucher file, the vouchers should be filed in numerical order so that they can be easily located when needed.

20. A principal advantage of recording purchases at the net amount is that the cost of failure to take cash discounts is recorded in a discounts lost account. Another advantage is that merchandise purchased is recorded initially at the net price; thus, no later adjustments to cost are necessary.

21. a. (1) $4,900 (2) $5,000
    b. (1) $4,900 (2) $4,900

22. Payments of small amounts by check often result in delay, annoyance, and excessive expense of maintaining records and processing the payments. For these reasons, small cash payments are made from a petty cash fund.

23. a. Petty cash account
    b. Various expense and asset accounts as indicated by a summary of expenditures

24. The fund should be replenished as of the last day of the period. It is the simplest means of recording the $407 of expenditures in the appropriate accounts and restoring the amount of the petty cash to the amount shown in the ledger account.

25. a. Cash equivalents are highly liquid investments of excess cash.
    b. Cash and cash equivalents are usually reported as one amount in the Current Asset section of the balance sheet.

26. a. A compensating balance is the minimum cash balance that must be maintained in the checking account.

    b. The details of the compensating balance are reported in notes to the financial statements.

27. Electronic funds transfer is a payment system that uses computerized electronic impulses rather than paper (money, checks, etc.) to effect a cash transaction.

28. The fundamental principle of control over cash, violated by Perini Corporation, was the necessity of safeguarding the blank prenumbered checks. This allowed someone to forge the checks. *Note to Instructor:* This case was originally reported in *The Wall Street Journal* in 1971 and has never been solved. In addition, because of weaknesses in Perini's controls, the insurance companies bonding Perini's employees and the banks involved disclaimed responsibility for the amount of the forged checks.

ETHICS DISCUSSION CASE Acceptable business and professional conduct requires Jane Ellet to notify the bank of the error. *Note to Instructor:* Individuals may be criminally prosecuted for knowingly using funds that are erroneously credited to their bank accounts.

EXERCISES

Ex. 8-1

C.C. DAVIDSON
Bank Reconciliation
February 28, 19—

Cash balance according to bank statement	$9,100.50
Add deposit in transit, not recorded by bank	780.40
	$9,880.90
Deduct outstanding checks	4,111.20
Adjusted balance	$5,769.70
Cash balance according to depositor's records	$5,530.20
Add error in recording check	270.00
	$5,800.20
Deduct bank service charges	30.50
Adjusted balance	$5,769.70

Ex. 8-2

Cash in Bank	270.00	
Accounts Payable		270.00
Miscellaneous Administrative Expense	30.50	
Cash in Bank		30.50

Ex. 8-3

Cash in Bank	5,075.00	
Notes Receivable		5,000.00
Interest Income		75.00

Ex. 8-4

Cash	7,155.20	
Cash Short and Over	5.50	
Sales		7,160.70

Ex. 8-5 Strength: (b), (c), (f), (g)
Weakness: (a), (d), (e)

Ex. 8-6 Bob's Burgers suffers from a failure to separate responsibilities for related operations.

Bob's Burgers could stop this theft by limiting the drive-through clerk to taking customer orders, entering them on the cash register, accepting the customers' payments, returning customers' change, and handing customers their orders that another employee has assembled. By making another employee responsible for filling orders, the drive-through clerk must enter the orders on the cash register. This will produce a printed receipt or an entry on a computer screen at the food bin area, specifying the items that must be assembled to fill each order. Once the drive-through clerk has entered the sale on the cash register, the clerk cannot steal the customer's payment because the clerk's cash drawer will not balance at the

Ex. 8-6, Concluded

end of the shift. This change also makes the drive-through more efficient and could reduce the time it takes to service a drive-through customer.

If another employee cannot be added, the weakness in internal control could be improved with more thorough supervision. The restaurant manager should be directed to keep a watchful eye on the drive-through area in order to detect when a clerk takes an order without ringing up the sale.

Ex. 8-7 The use of the voucher system is appropriate, the essentials of which are outlined below. (Although the invoices could be used instead of vouchers, the latter more satisfactorily provide for account distribution, signatures, and other significant data.)

1. Each voucher should be approved for payment by a designated official only after completion of the following verifications: (a) that prices, quantities, terms, etc., on the invoice are in accordance with the provisions of the purchase order, (b) that all quantities billed have been received in good condition, and (c) that all arithmetic details are correct.

2. The file for unpaid vouchers should be composed of 31 compartments, one for each day of the month. Each voucher should be filed in the compartment representing the last day of the discount period or the due date if the invoice is not subject to a cash discount.

3. Each day, the vouchers should be removed from the appropriate section of the file and checks issued by the disbursing official. If the bank balance is insufficient to pay all of the vouchers, those that remain unpaid should be refiled according to the date when payment should next be considered.

4. At the time of payment, all vouchers and supporting documents should be stamped or perforated "paid" to prevent their resubmission for payment. They should then be filed in numerical sequence for future reference.

Ex. 8-8 To deter the embezzlement scheme described, NDT must separate responsibilities for related operations. As in the past, all service requisitions should be submitted to the Purchasing Department. After receiving the service request, Purchasing should complete a Service Verification form, stating what service has been ordered and the name of the company that will provide the service. This form should be delivered via intercompany mail to the person responsible for verifying that the service was performed. This person should be someone who has first-hand knowledge of whether the service has been performed. This person, who must be someone other than the manager requesting the service, should fill in the date and time the

Ex. 8-8, Concluded

service was received and sign the form. In addition, the vendor providing the service should sign the form before leaving the premises. When completed, the Service Verification form should be forwarded to the Accounting Department. Accounting will authorize payment of the vendor's invoice after the Service Verification form has been compared with the invoice.

Ex. 8-9

Voucher Register

May	1	Purchases	2,000.00	
		Accounts Payable		2,000.00

Voucher Register

	5	Purchases	1,500.00	
		Accounts Payable		1,500.00

Check Register

	14	Accounts Payable	1,500.00	
		Cash in Bank		1,470.00
		Purchases Discounts		30.00

Voucher Register

	17	Purchases	2,500.00	
		Accounts Payable		2,500.00

Check Register

	26	Accounts Payable	2,500.00	
		Cash in Bank		2,450.00
		Purchases Discounts		50.00

Voucher Register

	30	Store Supplies	67.50	
		Office Supplies	41.25	
		Miscellaneous Administrative Expense	36.10	
		Miscellaneous Selling Expense	27.05	
		Accounts Payable		171.90

Check Register

	30	Accounts Payable	171.90	
		Cash in Bank		171.90

Check Register

	31	Accounts Payable	2,000.00	
		Cash in Bank		2,000.00

Ex. 8-10 July 7 Purchases 4,950.00

 Accounts Payable 4,950.00

 15 Purchases 2,450.00

 Accounts Payable 2,450.00

 25 Accounts Payable 2,450.00

 Cash in Bank 2,450.00

 Aug. 6 Accounts Payable 4,950.00

 Discounts Lost 50.00

 Cash in Bank 5,000.00

Ex. 8-11 a. Petty Cash 150.00

 Accounts Payable 150.00

 b. Accounts Payable 150.00

 Cash in Bank 150.00

 c. Office Supplies 52.15

 Miscellaneous Selling Expense 50.60

 Miscellaneous Administrative Expense 28.70

 Cash Short and Over 1.25

 Accounts Payable 132.70

 d. Accounts Payable 132.70

 Cash in Bank 132.70

Ex. 8-12 a. Cash on Hand 500.00

 Accounts Payable 500.00

 b. Accounts Payable 500.00

 Cash in Bank 500.00

 c. Cash in Bank 4,656.50

 Sales 4,655.30

 Cash Short and Over 1.20

WHAT'S WRONG WITH THIS?

1. The heading should be for April 30 and not for Month Ended April 30.
2. In deducting the outstanding checks in the balance per bank statement section, the adjusted balance is incorrectly determined to be $9,801.02 instead of $9,798.02.
3. Service charges should be deducted in the balance per depositor's records section.
4. The error in recording the April 15 deposit of $497 as $479 should be added in the balance per depositor's records section.

What's Wrong?, Concluded

A correct bank reconciliation would be as follows:

WRIGHT COMPANY
Bank Reconciliation
April 30, 19—

Cash balance according to bank statement		$10,767.76
Add deposit of April 29, not recorded by bank		510.06
		$11,277.82
Deduct outstanding checks:		
No. 721	$ 345.95	
739	172.75	
743	359.60	
744	601.50	1,479.80
Adjusted balance		$ 9,798.02
Cash balance according to depositor's records		$ 7,491.32
Add: Proceeds of note collected by bank:		
Principal	$2,500.00	
Interest	75.00 $2,575.00	
Error in recording April 15 deposit of $497 as $479	18.00	2,593.00
		$10,084.32
Deduct: Check returned because of insufficient funds	$ 266.80	
Service charges	19.50	286.30
Adjusted balance		$ 9,798.02

PROBLEMS

Prob. 8-1A

1.

A.C. FORREST CO.
Bank Reconciliation
June 30, 19—

Cash balance according to bank statement		$31,016.30
Add: Deposit of June 30, not recorded by bank	$6,917.75	
Bank error in charging check for $550 instead		
of $55	495.00	7,412.75
		$38,429.05
Deduct outstanding checks		15,391.50
Adjusted balance		$23,037.55
Cash balance according to depositor's records		$20,100.30
Add proceeds of note collected by bank, including		
$145 interest....................................		3,045.00
		$23,145.30
Deduct: Error in recording check	$ 72.00	
Bank service charges	35.75	107.75
Adjusted balance		$23,037.55

2. Cash in Bank......................................	3,045.00	
Notes Receivable.................................		2,900.00
Interest Income		145.00
Accounts Payable	72.00	
Miscellaneous Administrative Expense	35.75	
Cash in Bank.................................		107.75

Prob. 8-2A

1.

SORTER CORPORATION
Bank Reconciliation
April 30, 19—

Cash balance according to bank statement		$10,867.76
Add deposit of April 29, not recorded by bank......................................		510.06
		$11,377.82
Deduct outstanding checks:		
No. 736	$ 345.95	
755	172.75	
758	359.60	
759	601.50	1,479.80
Adjusted balance		$ 9,898.02
Cash balance according to depositor's records*		$ 7,591.32
Add: Proceeds of note collected by bank:		
Principal...........................	$2,500.00	
Interest...........................	125.00	$2,625.00
Error in recording April 17 deposit .	18.00	2,643.00
		$10,234.32
Deduct: Check returned because of insufficient funds.............	$ 291.90	
Service charges................	44.40	336.30
Adjusted balance		$ 9,898.02
*Balance per cash in bank account, April 1..............................		$ 8,317.40
Add April receipts, per cash receipts journal................................		7,679.58
Deduct April disbursements, per check register.............................		(8,405.66)
		$ 7,591.32

2.

Cash in Bank......................................	2,643.00	
Notes Receivable................................		2,500.00
Interest Income		125.00
Sales..		18.00
Accounts Receivable	291.90	
Miscellaneous Administrative Expense	44.40	
Cash in Bank......................................		336.30

3. $9,898.02

4. The error of $90 in the canceled check should be added to the "balance according to bank statement" on the bank reconciliation. The canceled check should be presented to the bank, with a request that the bank balance be corrected.

Prob. 8-3A

1. and 2.

Page 30   (left page)   **VOUCHER REGISTER**

	Date	Vou. No.	Payee	Date Paid	Ck. No.	Accounts Payable Cr.	Purchases Dr.	Office Supplies Dr.
	19—							
1	May 25	√	Amounts forwarded	√	√	40,805.60	34,070.00	285.00
2	26	617	Victor Co...........	...	...	5,000.00	5,000.00	.....
3	26	618	United Auto Insurance Co.	5-26	755	1,975.00	....	.....
4	27	619	Gleason Co..........	...	...	2,250.00	2,250.00	.....
5	27	620	Marine National Bank	5-27	756	10,200.00	....	.....
6			....	...	...	....	....	.....
7	28	621	Lakewood Gazette ..	5-28	757	630.00	....	.....
8	29	622	Petty Cash..........	5-29	758	189.05	....	57.40
9	31					61,049.65	41,320.00	342.40
						(210)		

(right page)   Page 30

	Advertising Expense Dr.	Delivery Expense Dr.	Misc. Selling Expense Dr.	Misc. Admin. Expense Dr.	Other Accounts Dr. Account	Post. Ref.	Amount
1	210.00	194.50	91.10	99.75	....	√	5,855.25
2	......	......	......	......			....
3	......	......	......	......	Prepaid Insurance..	....	1,975.00
4	......	......	......	......	....	....	....
5	......	......	......	......	Notes Payable	....	10,000.00
6	......	......	......	......	Interest Expense...	....	200.00
7	630.00	......	......	......	....	....	....
8	20.55	40.10	31.95	39.05	....	....	....
9	860.55	234.60	123.05	138.80	....	....	18,030.25

Prob. 8-3A, Continued

1. and 2. CHECK REGISTER Page 27

Date	Ck. No.	Payee	Vou. No.	Accounts Payable Dr.	Purchases Discounts Cr.	Cash in Bank Cr.
19—						
1 May 25	√	Amounts forwarded	√	48,395.20	427.50	47,967.70
2 26	754	Lowe Co.	611	3,000.00	60.00	2,940.00
3 26	755	United Auto Insurance Co.	618	1,975.00	......	1,975.00
4 27	756	Marine National Bank	620	10,200.00	......	10,200.00
5 28	757	Lakewood Gazette	621	630.00	......	630.00
6 29	758	Petty Cash	622	189.05	......	189.05
7 31	759	Marcus Co.	614	1,550.00	......	1,550.00
				65,939.25	487.50	65,451.75
				(210)		

2.

Accounts Payable 210

Date	Item	Post. Ref.	Dr.	Cr.	Balance Dr.	Balance Cr.
19—						
May 1	Balance	√	....	....	....	24,089.60
31	....	VR30	....	61,049.65	....	85,139.25
31	....	CR27	65,939.25	....	....	19,200.00

3. MIDLER CO.
Schedule of Unpaid Vouchers
May 31, 19—

600	Armo Co.	$	950.00
610	C. Wellington and Daughter Co.		4,550.00
611	Griffen Co.		6,450.00
617	Victor Co.		5,000.00
619	Gleason Co.		2,250.00
			$19,200.00

Prob. 8-3A, Concluded

4.

MIDLER CO.
Bank Reconciliation
May 31, 19—

Cash balance according to bank statement		$23,565.10
Deduct outstanding checks:		
No. 699	$ 290.00	
755	1,975.00	
759	1,550.00	3,815.00
Adjusted balance		$19,750.10
Cash balance according to depositor's records		$19,930.00
Deduct: NSF check from Ann Franks	$ 150.00	
Bank service charges	29.90	179.90
Adjusted balance		$19,750.10

JOURNAL   **Page 19**

Date	Description	Post. Ref.	Debit	Credit
19—				
May 31	Accounts Receivable—Ann Franks	. . . .	150.00	
	Miscellaneous Administrative Expense	. . . .	29.90	
	Cash in Bank	. . . .		179.90

Prob. 8-4A

19—

May	2	Petty Cash	200.00	
		Cash on Hand	500.00	
		Accounts Payable		700.00
	2	Accounts Payable	700.00	
		Cash in Bank		700.00
	4	Advances to Salespersons Fund	1,000.00	
		Accounts Payable		1,000.00
	4	Accounts Payable	1,000.00	
		Cash in Bank		1,000.00
	17	Cash in Bank	3,973.20	
		Cash Short and Over		2.60
		Sales		3,970.60
	29	Store Supplies	21.50	
		Transportation In	36.00	
		Office Supplies	85.05	
		Miscellaneous Administrative Expense	38.55	
		Accounts Payable		181.10
	29	Accounts Payable	181.10	
		Cash in Bank		181.10
	30	Cash in Bank	4,051.60	
		Cash Short and Over	3.90	
		Sales		4,055.50
	31	Travel Expenses	841.10	
		Accounts Payable		841.10
	31	Accounts Payable	841.10	
		Cash in Bank		841.10

Prob. 8-5A

Page 1

1. and 3.

VOUCHER REGISTER

Date	Vou. No.	Payee	Date Paid	Ck. No.	Accounts Payable Cr.	Pur- chases Dr.	Store Supplies Dr.	Office Supplies Dr.	Other Accounts Dr. Account	Post. Ref.	Amt.
19—											
May 22	1	Carr Co.	5-31	4	5,000	5,000	...	...		...	...
22	2	Walter Company	5-23	1	250	...	...	250		...	...
23	3	Dwyer Co.	...	:	7,500	7,500	...	...		...	...
25	4	Bunker Co.	5-25	2	490	...	490	...		...	...
27	5	Reese Co.	...	:	9,500	9,500	...	...		...	...
28	6	Andrews Office Equip. Co.	...	:	6,500	...	...	...	Office Equipment	...	6,500
30	7	Flash Express	5-30	3	60	...	...	...	Transportation In	...	60
31					29,300	22,000	490	250			6,560
					(211)						

Prob. 8-5A, Concluded

2. and 3.   CHECK REGISTER   Page 1

Date	Ck. No.	Payee	Vou. No.	Accounts Payable Dr.	Purchases Discounts Cr.	Cash in Bank Cr.
19—						
May 23	1	Walter Company.......	2	250	....	250
25	2	Bunker Co.	4	490	....	490
30	3	Flash Express	7	60	....	60
31	4	Carr Co...............	1	5,000	50	4,950
31				5,800	50	5,750
				(211)		

3.

Accounts Payable   211

Date	Item	Post. Ref.	Dr.	Cr.	Balance Dr.	Balance Cr.
19—						
May 31	....	VR1	.....	29,300	.....	29,300
31	....	CR1	5,800	......	.....	23,500

4.   KELLER COMPANY
                        Schedule of Unpaid Vouchers
                            May 31, 19—

3	Dwyer Co...	$ 7,500
5	Reese Co.	9,500
6	Andrews Office Equipment Co...............................	6,500
		$23,500

Prob. 8-6A

Page 66

2. and 4.

VOUCHER REGISTER

Date	Vou. No.	Payee	Date Paid	Ck. No.	Accounts Payable Cr.	Purchases Dr.	Store Supplies Dr.	Office Supplies Dr.	Other Accounts Dr. Account	Post. Ref.	Amt.
19—											
June 1	723	Marshall Co.	6-11	693	4,800	4,800	...	...		...	.....
2	724	LCS Co.	6-2	690	400	...	...	400		...	.....
6	725	Walls Co.	6-16	697	750	750	...	...		...	.....
7	726	Mann Supply	6-7	692	105	...	105	...		...	.....
9	727	Ramos Co.	6-19	698	1,250	1,250	...	...		...	.....
12	728	Ace Express	6-12	694	52	...	...	...	Delivery Expense	...	52
15	729	S & C Bank	6-15	696	7,140	...	...	...	Notes Payable	...	7,000
									Interest Expense	...	140
18	730	Duncan Office Co.	...	...	2,250	...	...	...	Office Equipment	...	2,250
19	731	Ross & Co.	6-29	701	950	950	...	...		...	.....
23	732	L.M. Carr Co.	6-23	699	2,200	...	...	...	Store Equipment	...	2,200
25	733	Thomas Co.	...	...	3,450	3,450	...	...		...	.....
30	734	Petty Cash	6-30	702	170	...	55	47	Misc. Selling Expense	...	38
									Misc. Administrative Exp.	...	30
30					23,517	11,200	160	447			11,710
					(205)						

Prob. 8-6A, Concluded

1. and 4.

Accounts Payable 205

Date	Item	Post. Ref.	Dr.	Cr.	Balance Dr.	Balance Cr.
19—						
June 1	Balance	√	......	....	.....	7,250
30	....	VR66	......	23,517	.....	30,767
30	....	CR59	25,067	......	.....	5,700

3. and 4.   CHECK REGISTER   Page 59

Date	Ck. No.	Payee	Vou. No.	Accounts Payable Dr.	Purchases Discounts Cr.	Cash in Bank Cr.
19—						
June 2	690	LCS Co.	724	400	...	400
3	691	Iris Co.	714	3,000	30	2,970
7	692	Mann Supply	726	105	...	105
11	693	Marshall Co.	723	4,800	48	4,752
12	694	Ace Express	728	52	...	52
12	695	Reese Co.............	696	2,500	...	2,500
15	696	S & C Bank	729	7,140	...	7,140
16	697	Walls Co.	725	750	15	735
19	698	Ramos Co.............	727	1,250	25	1,225
23	699	L. M. Carr Co.	732	2,200	...	2,200
28	700	Horst Co..............	720	1,750	...	1,750
29	701	Ross & Co.	731	950	19	931
30	702	Petty Cash	734	170	...	170
30				25,067	137	24,930
				(205)		

5.   STANLEY CO.
                  Schedule of Unpaid Vouchers
                        June 30, 19—

730	Duncan Office Co...	$2,250
733	Thomas Co...	3,450
		$5,700

Prob. 8-1B

1.

R.O. DIBBLE CO.
Bank Reconciliation
May 31, 19—

Cash balance according to bank statement		$19,391.40
Add deposit of May 31, not recorded by bank		4,215.50
		$23,606.90
Deduct: Outstanding checks	$5,950.00	
Bank error in charging check for $36 instead of $63	27.00	5,977.00
Adjusted balance		$17,629.90
Cash balance according to depositor's records		$14,460.00
Add: Proceeds of note collected by bank, including $120 interest	$3,120.00	
Error in recording check	90.00	3,210.00
		$17,670.00
Deduct bank service charges		40.10
Adjusted balance		$17,629.90

2.

Cash in Bank..	3,210.00	
Notes Receivable.................................		3,000.00
Interest Income		120.00
Accounts Payable		90.00
Miscellaneous Administrative Expense	40.10	
Cash in Bank...................................		40.10

Prob. 8-2B

1.

RUNDLE COMPANY
Bank Reconciliation
July 31, 19—

Cash balance according to bank statement		$12,275.54
Add deposit of July 30, not recorded by bank		677.05
		$12,952.59
Deduct outstanding checks:		
No. 602	$ 85.50	
628	737.70	
634	103.30	926.50
Adjusted balance		$12,026.09
Cash balance according to depositor's records*		$ 7,195.59
Add proceeds of note collected by bank:		
Principal	$5,000.00	
Interest	100.00	5,100.00
		$12,295.59
Deduct: Check returned because of insufficient		
funds....................................	$ 225.40	
Service charges...........................	34.10	
Error in recording Check No. 619..........	10.00	269.50
Adjusted balance		$12,026.09
*Balance per cash in bank account, July 1		$ 9,578.00
Add July receipts, per cash receipts journal		6,232.60
Deduct July disbursements, per check register ..		(8,615.01)
Balance per cash in bank account, July 31.......		$ 7,195.59

2.

Cash in Bank.......................................	5,100.00	
Notes Receivable................................		5,000.00
Interest Income		100.00
Accounts Receivable	225.40	
Miscellaneous Administrative Expense	34.10	
Accounts Payable	10.00	
Cash in Bank.......................................		269.50

3. $12,026.09

4. The error of $100 in the canceled check should be added to the "balance according to bank statement" on the bank reconciliation. The canceled check should be presented to the bank, with a request that the bank balance be corrected.

Prob. 8-3B

1. and 2.

Page 30   (left page)   **VOUCHER REGISTER**

	Date	Vou. No.	Payee	Date Paid	Ck. No.	Accounts Payable Cr.	Purchases Dr.	Office Supplies Dr.
	19—							
1	May 25	√	Amounts forwarded	√	√	40,805.60	34,070.00	285.00
2	26	635	Fox Co.	...	...	10,000.00	10,000.00	.....
3	27	636	Acme Auto Ins. Co.	5-27	617	1,584.00	....	.....
4	27	637	Solo Co.	...	...	2,500.00	2,500.00	.....
5	28	638	Castle National Bank	5-28	618	4,200.00	....	.....
6			....	...	...	....	....	.....
7	29	639	Royal News	5-29	620	350.00	....	.....
8	31	640	Petty Cash	5-31	621	179.90	....	42.50
9						59,619.50	46,570.00	327.50
						(210)		

(right page)   **Page 30**

	Advertising Expense Dr.	Delivery Expense Dr.	Misc. Selling Expense Dr.	Misc. Admin. Expense Dr.	Other Accounts Dr. Account	Post. Ref.	Amount
1	210.00	194.50	91.10	99.75	....	√	5,855.25
2	......	......	......	......	....	....	....
3	......	......	......	......	Prepaid Insurance	....	1,584.00
4	......	......	......	......	....	....	....
5	......	......	......	......	Notes Payable	....	4,000.00
6	......	......	......	......	Interest Expense	....	200.00
7	350.00	......	......	......	....	....	....
8	31.45	22.50	47.22	36.23	....	....	....
9	591.45	217.00	138.32	135.98			11,639.25

Prob. 8-3B, Continued

1. and 2.   CHECK REGISTER   Page 27

	Date	Ck. No.	Payee	Vou. No.	Accounts Payable Dr.	Purchases Discounts Cr.	Cash in Bank Cr.
	19—						
1	May 25	√	Amounts forwarded	√	48,395.20	427.50	47,967.70
2	26	616	Booker Co...............	623	3,000.00	30.00	2,970.00
3	27	617	Acme Auto Ins. Co.....	636	1,584.00	......	1,584.00
4	28	618	Castle National Bank...	638	4,200.00	......	4,200.00
5	28	619	Henry Stevens Co......	631	1,550.00	31.00	1,519.00
6	29	620	Royal News............	639	350.00	......	350.00
7	31	621	Petty Cash.............	640	179.90	......	179.90
8	31				59,259.10	488.50	58,770.60
					(210)		

2.

Accounts Payable   210

Date	Item	Post. Ref.	Dr.	Cr.	Balance Dr.	Balance Cr.
19—						
May 1	Balance.......	√	....	....	....	24,089.60
31	....	VR30	....	59,619.50	....	83,709.10
31	....	CR27	59,259.10	....	....	24,450.00

3.

MIDLER CO.
Schedule of Unpaid Vouchers
May 31, 19—

600	Armo Co.	$ 950.00
610	C. Wellington and Daughter Co.	4,550.00
611	Griffen Co.	6,450.00
635	Fox Co.	10,000.00
637	Solo Co.	2,500.00
		$24,450.00

Prob. 8-3B, Concluded

4.

MIDLER CO.
Bank Reconciliation
May 31, 19—

Cash balance according to bank statement		$21,443.50
Deduct outstanding checks:		
No. 600	$ 375.00	
617	1,584.00	
619	1,519.00	
620	350.00	3,828.00
Adjusted balance		$17,615.50
Cash balance according to depositor's records		$18,075.50
Deduct NSF check from Vernon Co.		460.00
Adjusted balance		$17,615.50

JOURNAL   **Page 19**

Date	Description	Post. Ref.	Debit	Credit
19—				
May 31	Accounts Receivable—Vernon Co.	....	460.00	
	Cash in Bank	....		460.00

Prob. 8-4B

19—				
June	**1**	Petty Cash...................................	250.00	
		Cash on Hand................................	500.00	
		Accounts Payable		750.00
	1	Accounts Payable	750.00	
		Cash in Bank..............................		750.00
	3	Advances to Salespersons Fund..............	1,000.00	
		Accounts Payable		1,000.00
	4	Accounts Payable	1,000.00	
		Cash in Bank..............................		1,000.00
	15	Cash in Bank................................	2,998.20	
		Cash Short and Over		2.60
		Sales		2,995.60
	26	Store Supplies	26.50	
		Transportation In	35.00	
		Office Supplies	75.95	
		Miscellaneous Administrative Expense	62.05	
		Accounts Payable		199.50
	26	Accounts Payable	199.50	
		Cash in Bank..............................		199.50
	30	Cash in Bank................................	3,005.60	
		Cash Short and Over	3.90	
		Sales		3,009.50
	30	Travel Expenses.............................	828.00	
		Accounts Payable		828.00
	30	Accounts Payable	828.00	
		Cash in Bank..............................		828.00

Prob. 8-5B

Page 1

1. and 3.

VOUCHER REGISTER

Date	Vou. No.	Payee	Date Paid	Ck. No.	Accounts Payable Cr.	Purchases Dr.	Store Supplies Dr.	Office Supplies Dr.	Other Accounts Dr. — Account	Post. Ref.	Amt.
19—											
June 21	1	Polk Co.	6-30	4	9,500	9,500	…	…			…
22	2	Newton Supplies Co.	6-23	1	620	…	…	620			…
23	3	C. Masters and Son	…	2	5,100	5,100	…	…			…
25	4	Rudd Co.	6-25		375	…	375	…			…
27	5	Ramos Co.	…		4,500	4,500	…	…			…
28	6	Hoffman Office Equip. Co.	…		6,500	…	…	…	Office Equipment		6,500
30	7	Ace Express	6-30	3	65	…	…	…	Transportation In		65
					26,660	19,100	375	620			6,565
					(211)						

Prob. 8-5B, Concluded

2. and 3.

CHECK REGISTER

Page 1

Date	Ck. No.	Payee	Vou. No.	Accounts Payable Dr.	Purchases Discounts Cr.	Cash in Bank Cr.
19—						
June 23	1	Newton Supplies Co..	2	620	. . .	620
25	2	Rudd Co.	4	375	. . .	375
30	3	Ace Express	7	65	. . .	65
30	4	Polk Co.	1	9,500	95	9,405
30				10,560	95	10,465
				(211)		

3.

Accounts Payable

211

Date	Item	Post. Ref.	Dr.	Cr.	Balance Dr.	Balance Cr.
19—						
June 30	. . . .	VR1	. . . . . .	26,660	. . . . .	26,660
30	. . . .	CR1	10,560	. . . . . .	. . . . .	16,100

4.

BUCKINGHAM COMPANY
Schedule of Unpaid Vouchers
June 30, 19—

3	C. Masters and Son.	$ 5,100
5	Ramos Co.	4,500
6	Hoffman Office Equipment Co.	6,500
		$16,100

Prob. 8-6B

Page 66

2. and 4.

VOUCHER REGISTER

Date	Vou. No.	Payee	Date Paid	Ck. No.	Accounts Payable Cr.	Purchases Dr.	Store Supplies Dr.	Office Supplies Dr.	Other Accounts Dr. Account	Post. Ref.	Other Accounts Dr. Amt.
19—											
June 3	518	Sheer Fashions	6-3	390	9,500	9,500	...	...	......	...	
4	519	R and M Supply	6-14	395	110		110	...	......	...	
5	520	Barr Co.	6-15	396	1,250	1,250	...	...	......	...	
8	521	C.C. Glass Co.	6-18	397	900	900	...	...	......	...	
13	522	Second National Bank	6-13	394	20,500				Notes Payable	...	20,000
							...	...	Interest Expense	...	500
15	523	Roberts Supply	...	...	13,950				Office Equipment	...	13,950
20	524	Sax Printers	6-20	398	215			215	......	...	
22	525	Bach Sportswear	...	...	1,250	1,250			......	...	
25	526	The Blouse Shop	...	...	1,900	1,900			......	...	
28	527	Eastman Co.	...	...	550	550			......	...	
30	528	Parkhill Motors	6-30	399	30,000				Delivery Equipment	...	30,000
30	529	Petty Cash	6-30	400	175		49	50	Misc. Selling Expense	...	39
									Misc. Admin. Expense	...	37
30					80,300	15,350	159	265			64,526
					(205)						

Prob. 8-6B, Concluded

1. and 4.

Accounts Payable 205

Date		Item	Post. Ref.	Dr.	Cr.	Balance Dr.	Balance Cr.
19—							
June	1	Balance	✓	......	......	.....	17,250
	30	....	VR66	......	80,300	.....	97,550
	30	....	CR59	79,900	......	.....	17,650

3. and 4.　　　　CHECK REGISTER　　　　Page 59

Date		Ck. No.	Payee	Vou. No.	Accounts Payable Dr.	Purchases Discounts Cr.	Cash in Bank Cr.
19—							
June	3	390	Sheer Fashions........	518	9,500	. . .	9,500
	8	391	Down Co.............	510	9,000	90	8,910
	10	392	RX Shoes............	498	3,500	. . .	3,500
	13	393	Hill Co.	500	4,750	. . .	4,750
	13	394	Second National Bank	522	20,500	. . .	20,500
	14	395	R and M Supply......	519	110	. . .	110
	15	396	Barr Co.	520	1,250	25	1,225
	18	397	C.C. Glass Co.	521	900	18	882
	20	398	Sax Printers	524	215	. . .	215
	30	399	Parkhill Motors	528	30,000	. . .	30,000
	30	400	Petty Cash	529	175	. . .	175
	30				79,900	133	79,767
					(205)		

5.　　　　MILNER CLOTHIERS
Schedule of Unpaid Vouchers
June 30, 19—

523	Roberts Supply	$13,950
525	Bach Sportswear..	1,250
526	The Blouse Shop	1,900
527	Eastman Co.	550
		$17,650

Mini-Case 8

1. There are several methods which could be used to determine how much the cashier has stolen. The method described below is based upon the preparation of a bank reconciliation as illustrated in this chapter. Because of the theft of the undeposited receipts, the bank reconciliation adjusted balances will not agree. The difference between the adjusted balances is the estimate of the amount stolen by the cashier.

CRIER & COMPANY
Bank Reconciliation
July 31, 19—

Balance according to bank statement................		$18,704.95
Add undeposited cash receipts on hand		4,425.00
		$23,129.95
Deduct outstanding checks:		
No. 470	$950.20	
479	510.00	
490	616.50	
996	227.40	
997	720.00	
999	351.50	3,375.60
Adjusted balance		$19,754.35
Balance according to depositor's records..............		$21,931.05
Add note collected by bank, with interest.............		5,150.00
Adjusted balance		$27,081.05
Adjusted balance according to depositor's records.....		$27,081.05
Adjusted balance according to bank statement........		19,754.35
Amount stolen by cashier		$ 7,326.70

Note to Instructors: The amount stolen by the cashier could also be computed directly from the cashier-prepared bank reconciliation as follows:

Outstanding checks omitted from the bank reconciliation prepared by the cashier:		
No. 470	$950.20	
479	510.00	
490	616.50	$ 2,076.70
Unrecorded note plus interest incorrectly recorded on the bank reconciliation prepared by the cashier......		5,150.00
Addition error in the total of the outstanding checks in the bank reconciliation prepared by the cashier* ..		100.00
		$ 7,326.70

*Note: The cashier has altered the adding machine tape so that the total is not correct.

Mini-Case 8, Concluded

2. The cashier attempted to conceal the theft by preparing an incorrect bank reconciliation. Specifically, the cashier (1) omitted outstanding checks on July 31 totaling $2,076.70, (2) added the list of outstanding checks shown on the bank reconciliation incorrectly, so that the total is misstated by $100, and (3) incorrectly handled the treatment of the note and interest collected by the bank.

3. **a.** Two major weaknesses in internal controls, which allowed the cashier to steal the undeposited cash receipts, are as follows:

- Undeposited cash receipts were kept on hand for a two-day period, July 30 and 31. This large amount of undeposited cash receipts allowed the cashier to steal the cash without arousing suspicion that any cash was missing.

- The cashier prepared the bank reconciliation. This allowed the cashier to conceal the theft temporarily.

b. Two recommendations which would improve internal controls, so that similar types of thefts of undeposited cash receipts could be prevented, are the following:

- All cash receipts should be deposited daily. This would reduce the risk of significant cash losses. In addition, any missing cash would be more easily detected.

- The bank reconciliation should be prepared by an independent individual who does not handle cash or the accounting records. One possibility would be for the owner of Crier & Company to prepare the reconciliation.

Note to Instructor: In addition to the above recommendations, Crier & Company should be counseled that it is standard practice for any disgruntled employees, fired employees, or employees who have announced quitting dates to be removed from sensitive positions (such as the cashier position), so that company assets or records will not be jeopardized. Finally, checks which have been outstanding for long periods of time (such as Nos. 470, 479, and 490) should be voided (with stop-payment instructions given to the bank) and re-entered in the cash records. This establishes control over these items and prevents their misuse.

CHAPTER 9

DISCUSSION QUESTIONS

1. The advantages of a claim evidenced by a note are (1) the debt is acknowledged, (2) the payment terms are specified, (3) it is a stronger claim in the event of court action, and (4) it is usually more readily transferable to a creditor in settlement of a debt or to a bank for cash.

2. Trade receivables are notes and accounts receivable that originate from sales transactions.

3. (a) Current assets (b) Investments

4. The principle of separation of operations and accounting is violated. (Note to Instructor: This weakness in internal control may permit embezzlement. For example, the accounts receivable clerk may misappropriate cash receipts and cover the misappropriation by a process called lapping. In lapping, the cash receipts from one account are taken and the cash received on a subsequent account is used to cover the shortage. The receipts on another account are then used to cover the shortage in this latter customer's account, etc. This lapping generally continues until the records are falsified to correct for the shortage, the cash is returned by the clerk, or the embezzlement is discovered.)

5. a. Stevens Company
   b. Notes Receivable

6. The interest will amount to $1,000 only if the note is payable one year from the date it was created. The usual practice is to state the interest rate in terms of an annual rate, rather than in terms of the period covered by the note.

7. a. $5,000
   b. $112.50
   c. $5,112.50
   d. July 30

8. $30 ($3,600 × 10% × 30/360)

9. a. $5,000
   b. $5,075
   c. June 19
   d. 40 days
   e. $5,018.61
   f. $18.61 interest income
   g. $5,075, plus any protest fee

10. a. Yes
    b. The contingent liability expires when the note is paid by the maker or on the due date of the note (September 5), whichever occurs first.

11. $37,500

12. Accounts Receivable 6,120
        Notes Receivable..............   6,000
        Interest Income...............   120

13. Accounts Receivable 8,135
        Cash   8,135

14. 1. Sale on account
    2. Correction of the sale (or a return or allowance if a separate account for such is not used).
    3. Note received from customer on account.
    4. Note discounted, receiving less than the face value.
    5. Paid liability for discounted note dishonored, and charged it to customer.
    6. Payment received from customer for dishonored note plus interest earned after due date.

15. The allowance method

16. Contra asset, credit balance

17. Uncollectible Accounts
        Expense.................... 5,900
        Allowance for Doubtful
            Accounts..............   5,900

18. a. $189,000 ($201,250 − $12,250)
    b. $189,000 ($200,250 − $11,250)

19. 1. The percentage rate used is excessive in relationship to the volume of accounts written off as uncollectible; hence, the balance in the allowance account is excessive.
    2. A substantial volume of old uncollectible accounts is still being carried in the accounts receivable account.

20. a. Allowance for Doubtful
        Accounts 750
            Accounts Receivable   750
    b. Uncollectible Accounts
        Expense.................... 750
            Accounts Receivable   750

21. Estimate based on analysis of receivables

22. Current assets

23. $202,750 (cost of $210,000 less allowance for decline to market of $7,250)

24. a. Hotel accounts and notes receivable:
    $3,256,000 ÷ $75,796,000 = 4.3%

362 top left, Chapter 9 top right.

b. Casino accounts receivable:
$6,654,000 ÷ $26,334,000 = 25.3%

c. Casino operations experience greater bad debt risk, since it is difficult to control the credit worthiness of customers entering the casino. In addition, individuals who may have adequate credit worthiness may overextend themselves and lose more than they can afford if they get caught up in the excitement of gambling.

ETHICS DISCUSSION CASE It is acceptable business conduct to use either the 360-day or the 365-day year for computation of interest. Therefore, Andrew Wilson is behaving in an ethical manner. By computing interest using a 365-day year for depository accounts (payables), Andrew is minimizing interest expense to the bank. By computing interest using a 360-day year for loans (receivables), Andrew is maximizing interest income to the bank. However, Andrew should also consider the potential customer ill will that may be created by such a one-sided policy.

EXERCISES

Ex. 9-1 a. Appropriate. Salespersons should not be responsible for approving credit.

b. Appropriate. A promissory note is a formal credit instrument that is frequently used for credit periods over 60 days.

c. Inappropriate. Since Simpson has a large number of credit sales supported by promissory notes, a notes receivable ledger should be maintained. Failure to maintain a subsidiary ledger when there are a significant number of notes receivable transactions violates the internal control principle that mandates proofs and security measures. Maintaining a note receivable ledger will allow Simpson to operate more efficiently and will increase the chance that Simpson will detect accounting errors related to the notes receivables. (The total of the accounts in the notes receivable ledger must match the balance of notes receivable in the general ledger.)

d. Inappropriate. The principle of proper separation of duties is violated. The accounts receivable clerk is responsible for too many related operations. The clerk also has both custody of assets (cash receipts) and does the accounting for those assets (records customer receipts in the subsidiary ledger).

e. Appropriate. The functions of maintaining the accounts receivable account in the general ledger should be performed by someone other than the accounts receivable clerk.

Ex. 9-2 The first error, posting the customer's receipt to the wrong account, will be detected when John Redman receives his next bill. Redman's bill will not show credit for his $50 payment. Once Redman realizes that he did pay the bill but did not get credit for the payment, he will contact Milford Florists and complain. Redman will have a canceled check to prove that payment was made.

The second error, forgetting to post a $250 credit sale, will be detected when the total of all accounts in the accounts receivable ledger is compared to the balance of Accounts Receivable in the general ledger.

Ex. 9-3

	Due Date	Interest
a.	April 10	$ 37.50
b.	July 19	100.00
c.	Aug. 13	250.00
d.	Sept. 7	375.00
e.	Nov. 8	700.00

Ex. 9-4 a. August 8

b. $10,225

c. (1) Notes Receivable 10,000
Accounts Receivable—Wallace Company   10,000

(2) Cash 10,225
Notes Receivable.........................   10,000
Interest Income   225

Ex. 9-5 Dec. 1 Notes Receivable......................... 10,000
Accounts Receivable—Barr Co.........   10,000

31 Interest Receivable   100
Interest Income.........................   100

31 Interest Income...........................   100
Income Summary.....................   100

Ex. 9-6 a. $20,600

b. 90 days

c. $515 ($20,600 × 90/360 × 10%)

d. $20,085 ($20,600 − $515)

e. Cash.. 20,085
Notes Receivable   20,000
Interest Income.............................   85

Ex. 9-7 March 1 Notes Receivable 40,000
Accounts Receivable—Sutcliffe Co...   40,000

16 Cash................................... 40,086
Notes Receivable   40,000
Interest Income.....................   86
[$800 − ($40,800 × 45/360 × 14%) = $86]

April 30 Accounts Receivable—Sutcliffe Co..... 40,850
Cash..............................   40,850

June 29 Cash................................... 41,667
Accounts Receivable—Sutcliffe Co...   40,850
Interest Income......................   817
[$40,850 × 60/360 × 12% = $817]

Ex. 9-8 July   1 Notes Receivable 20,000

                        Accounts Receivable—Grace Co.   20,000

          10 Notes Receivable 12,000

                        Accounts Receivable—O'Neil Co.   12,000

          31 Accounts Receivable—Grace Co. 20,200

                        Notes Receivable   20,000

                        Interest Income......................   200

    Sep.   9 Accounts Receivable—O'Neil Co. 12,240

                        Notes Receivable   12,000

                        Interest Income......................   240

    Oct. 14 Cash 20,705

                        Accounts Receivable—Grace Co.   20,200

                        Interest Income......................   505

                        ($20,200 × 75/360 × 12% = $505)

          30 Allowance for Doubtful Accounts...... 12,240

                        Accounts Receivable—O'Neil Co.   12,240

Ex. 9-9 a. (1) $15,500   (2) $14,250

          b. (1) $23,250   (2) $21,500

Ex. 9-10 Feb.   9 Accounts Receivable—B.C. Burr 5,500

                        Sales   5,500

    Aug. 19 Cash 2,500

                  Allowance for Doubtful Accounts 3,000

                        Accounts Receivable—B.C. Burr.........   5,500

    Dec. 30 Accounts Receivable—B.C. Burr 3,000

                        Allowance for Doubtful Accounts   3,000

          30 Cash 3,000

                        Accounts Receivable—B.C. Burr.........   3,000

Ex. 9-11 Jan. 11 Accounts Receivable—John Lang 3,000

                        Sales   3,000

    June   1 Cash 2,000

                  Uncollectible Accounts Expense 1,000

                        Accounts Receivable—John Lang   3,000

    Dec. 10 Accounts Receivable—John Lang 1,000

                        Uncollectible Accounts Expense   1,000

          10 Cash 1,000

                        Accounts Receivable—John Lang   1,000

Ex. 9-12 The temporary securities would be reported in the Current Assets section of the balance sheet at a cost of $166,000, less an allowance for decline to market price of $3,400, to yield a carrying amount of $162,600. The unrealized loss of $3,400 is included in the determination of net income and reported as a separate item on the income statement.

WHAT'S WRONG WITH THIS?

1. Marketable equity securities (temporary investments in equity securities) are carried at lower of cost or market. Therefore, there should be no allowance to increase marketable equity securities above cost.
2. The allowance for doubtful accounts should be deducted from accounts receivable.

A corrected partial balance sheet would be as follows:

LANE COMPANY
Balance Sheet
December 31, 19—

Assets

Current assets:		
Cash.....................................		$ 95,000
Marketable equity securities..............		460,000
Notes receivable		250,000
Accounts receivable	$445,000	
Less allowance for doubtful accounts....	15,000	430,000
Interest receivable........................		9,000

PROBLEMS

Prob. 9-1A

Jan. 15	Notes Receivable	10,000	
	Cash		10,000
Feb. 1	Accounts Receivable—Bryant and Son	6,000	
	Sales		6,000
20	Accounts Receivable—C. D. Connors Co.	7,500	
	Sales		7,500
Mar. 2	Cash	7,425	
	Sales Discounts	75	
	Accounts Receivable—C. D. Connors Co.		7,500
3	Notes Receivable	6,000	
	Accounts Receivable—Bryant and Son		6,000
Apr. 15	Notes Receivable	10,000	
	Cash	250	
	Notes Receivable		10,000
	Interest Income		250
May 2	Cash	6,120	
	Notes Receivable		6,000
	Interest Income		120
July 10	Accounts Receivable—Song Yu and Co.	30,000	
	Sales		30,000
14	Cash	10,300	
	Notes Receivable		10,000
	Interest Income		300
Aug. 9	Notes Receivable	30,000	
	Accounts Receivable—Song Yu and Co.		30,000
Sep. 8	Cash	30,243	
	Notes Receivable		30,000
	Interest Income		243
	[$600 − ($30,600 × 30/360 × 14%) = $243]		
Oct. 8	Accounts Receivable—Song Yu and Co.	30,600	
	Cash		30,600
28	Cash	30,804	
	Accounts Receivable—Song Yu and Co.		30,600
	Interest Income		204
	($30,600 × 20/360 × 12% = $204)		

Prob. 9-2A

1.

Note	(a) Due Date	(b) Interest Due at Maturity
(1)	Nov. 30	$100
(2)	Nov. 10	100
(3)	Jan. 26	217
(4)	Jan. 7	160
(5)	Feb. 9	264
(6)	Jan. 25	180

2.

Note	(a) Maturity Value	(b) Discount Period	(c) Discount	(d) Proceeds	(e) Interest Expense* or Interest Income
(1)	$ 6,100.00	45 days	$ 91.50	$ 6,008.50	$ 8.50
(2)	10,100.00	20 days	78.56	10,021.44	21.44
(3)	6,417.00	30 days	64.17	6,352.83	152.83
(4)	8,160.00	45 days	163.20	7,996.80	3.20*

3.

Note (2) Cash...............................	10,021.44	
Interest Income		21.44
Notes Receivable....................		10,000.00
Note (4) Cash...............................	7,996.80	
Interest Expense	3.20	
Notes Receivable....................		8,000.00

4. Dec. 31 Interest Receivable........................... 118.00

Interest Income 118.00

$14,400 × 20/360 × 11% = $ 88
$18,000 × 5/360 × 12% = 30
Total $118

Prob. 9-3A

April	1	Notes Receivable...............................	7,500	
		Accounts Receivable........................		7,500
	11	Notes Receivable...............................	30,000	
		Accounts Receivable........................		30,000
May	16	Notes Receivable...............................	24,000	
		Accounts Receivable........................		24,000
	21	Notes Receivable...............................	12,000	
		Accounts Receivable........................		12,000
	31	Cash...	7,675	
		Notes Receivable............................		7,500
		Interest Income		175
June	20	Cash...	12,120	
		Notes Receivable............................		12,000
		Interest Income		120
	26	Notes Receivable...............................	9,000	
		Accounts Receivable........................		9,000
July	15	Cash...	24,520	
		Notes Receivable............................		24,000
		Interest Income		520
	26	Cash...	9,090	
		Notes Receivable............................		9,000
		Interest Income		90
Aug.	9	Cash...	31,200	
		Notes Receivable............................		30,000
		Interest Income		1,200

Prob. 9-4A

1. and 2.

Allowance for Doubtful Accounts   115

Date	Item	Dr.	Cr.	Balance Dr.	Balance Cr.
19—					
Jan. 1	Balance	......	......	.....	29,050
Feb. 1	....	2,000	......	.....	27,050
May 17	....	......	675	.....	27,725
June 9	....	7,250	......	.....	20,475
Oct. 30	....	......	2,500	.....	22,975
Dec. 31	....	19,250	......	.....	3,725
31	....	......	28,975	.....	32,700

Prob. 9-4A, Concluded

Income Summary   313

Date	Item	Dr.	Cr.	Balance Dr.	Balance Cr.
19—					
Dec. 31	....	28,975	......	28,975	......

Uncollectible Accounts Expense   718

Date	Item	Dr.	Cr.	Balance Dr.	Balance Cr.
19—					
Dec. 31	....	28,975	......	28,975	......
31	....	......	28,975	—	—

2.

	19—		Dr.	Cr.
	Feb. 1	Cash...	6,000	
		Allowance for Doubtful Accounts.............	2,000	
		Accounts Receivable—Nixon Co.		8,000
	May 17	Accounts Receivable—Barbara Lyman	675	
		Allowance for Doubtful Accounts...........		675
	17	Cash...	675	
		Accounts Receivable—Barbara Lyman		675
	June 9	Allowance for Doubtful Accounts.............	7,250	
		Accounts Receivable—Larkin Co............		7,250
	Oct. 30	Accounts Receivable—Viscano Co.	2,500	
		Allowance for Doubtful Accounts...........		2,500
	30	Cash...	2,500	
		Accounts Receivable—Viscano Co.		2,500
	Dec. 31	Allowance for Doubtful Accounts.............	19,250	
		Accounts Receivable—Davis Co.............		3,950
		Nance Co.............		4,600
		Powell Distributors ..		6,500
		J. J. Stevens.........		4,200
	31	Uncollectible Accounts Expense...............	28,975	
		Allowance for Doubtful Accounts...........		28,975
	31	Income Summary.............................	28,975	
		Uncollectible Accounts Expense		28,975

3. $662,300 ($695,000 − $32,700)

4. a. $30,000 ($4,000,000 × .0075)
   b. $33,725 ($30,000 + $3,725)
   c. $661,275 ($695,000 − $33,725)

Prob. 9-5A

1.

Uncollectible Accounts Expense

Year	Expense Actually Reported	Expense Based on Estimate	Increase in Amount of Expense	Balance of Allowance Account, End of Year
1st	$2,000	$4,000	$2,000	$ 2,000
2d	2,950	6,000	3,050	5,050
3d	4,700	8,500	3,800	8,850
4th	6,000	9,000	3,000	11,850

2. Yes. The actual write-offs of accounts originating in the first two years are reasonably close to the expense that would have been charged to those years on the basis of 1% of sales. The total write-off of receivables originating in the first year amounted to $4,200, as compared with uncollectible accounts expense, based on the percentage of sales, of $4,000. For the second year, the comparable amounts were $5,750 and $6,000.

Prob. 9-6A

1.

CHEN COMPANY
Income Statement
For Year Ended December 31, 19—

Revenue from sales:		
Sales...	$805,000	
Less sales discounts	6,500	
Net sales		$798,500
Cost of merchandise sold		520,000
Gross profit		$278,500
Operating expenses:		
Selling expenses..................................	$110,500	
Administrative expenses	73,500	
Total operating expenses.........................		184,000
Income from operations		$ 94,500
Other income:		
Interest income...................................	$ 6,100	
Other expense:		
Unrealized loss from decline to market of		
marketable equity securities	1,100	5,000
Net income		$ 99,500

Prob. 9-6A, Concluded

2.

CHEN COMPANY
Statement of Owner's Equity
For Year Ended December 31, 19—

C. Chen, capital, January 1, 19—		$455,900
Net income for year	$99,500	
Less withdrawals	60,000	
Increase in owner's equity		39,500
C. Chen, capital, December 31, 19—		$495,400

3.

CHEN COMPANY
Balance Sheet
December 31, 19—

Assets

Current assets:			
Cash		$ 29,500	
Marketable equity securities	$ 60,000		
Less allowance for decline to market	1,100	58,900	
Notes receivable		40,000	
Accounts receivable	$ 57,500		
Less allowance for doubtful accounts	1,500	56,000	
Merchandise inventory		74,200	
Office supplies		5,600	
Prepaid insurance		5,200	
Total current assets			$269,400
Plant assets:			
Land		$ 65,000	
Building	$335,000		
Less accumulated depreciation	175,000	160,000	
Office equipment	$ 79,750		
Less accumulated depreciation	49,750	30,000	
Total plant assets			255,000
Total assets			$524,400

Liabilities

Current liabilities:		
Accounts payable	$ 26,100	
Salaries payable	2,900	
Total liabilities		$ 29,000

Owner's Equity

C. Chen, capital		495,400
Total liabilities and owner's equity		$524,400

Prob. 9-1B

19—

Jan.	31	Accounts Receivable—Perras Co..................	10,000	
		Sales		10,000
Mar.	2	Notes Receivable..............................	10,000	
		Accounts Receivable—Perras Co...............		10,000
May	1	Cash..	10,200	
		Notes Receivable		10,000
		Interest Income...............................		200
June	1	Accounts Receivable—Kohl's	5,000	
		Sales		5,000
	5	Notes Receivable..............................	9,000	
		Cash..		9,000
	11	Cash..	4,900	
		Sales Discounts	100	
		Accounts Receivable—Kohl's		5,000
July	5	Notes Receivable..............................	9,000	
		Cash..	105	
		Notes Receivable		9,000
		Interest Income...............................		105
Sep.	3	Cash..	9,210	
		Notes Receivable		9,000
		Interest Income...............................		210
	4	Accounts Receivable—Alice Gow	4,000	
		Sales		4,000
Oct.	4	Notes Receivable..............................	4,000	
		Accounts Receivable—Alice Gow...............		4,000
Nov.	3	Cash..	4,046	
		Notes Receivable		4,000
		Interest Income...............................		46
		[$80 − ($4,080 × 30/360 × 10%) = $46]		
Dec.	3	Accounts Receivable—Alice Gow	4,080	
		Cash..		4,080
	18	Cash..	4,097	
		Accounts Receivable—Alice Gow...............		4,080
		Interest Income...............................		17
		($4,080 × 15/360 × 10% = $17)		

Prob. 9-2B

1.

Note	(a) Due Date	(b) Interest Due at Maturity
(1)	April 30	$300
(2)	July 9	240
(3)	Oct. 9	750
(4)	Nov. 30	550
(5)	Feb. 9	360
(6)	Jan. 15	390

2.

Note	(a) Maturity Value	(b) Discount Period	(c) Discount	(d) Proceeds	(e) Interest Expense* or Interest Income
(1)	$15,300	40 days	$170	$15,130	$130
(2)	12,240	50 days	255	11,985	15*
(3)	30,750	60 days	615	30,135	135
(4)	20,550	60 days	411	20,139	139

3. Note (2) Cash.................................... 11,985.00
           Interest Expense 15.00
               Notes Receivable.................... 12,000.00

   Note (3) Cash.................................... 30,135.00
               Interest Income 135.00
               Notes Receivable.................... 30,000.00

4. Dec. 31 Interest Receivable........................... 315.00
               Interest Income 315.00

$18,000 × 20/360 × 12% = $120
$36,000 × 15/360 × 13% = 195
                Total $315

Prob. 9-3B

			Dr.	Cr.
Apr.	1	Notes Receivable...........................	30,000	
		Accounts Receivable.........................		30,000
	21	Notes Receivable...........................	18,000	
		Accounts Receivable.........................		18,000
May	16	Notes Receivable...........................	12,000	
		Accounts Receivable.........................		12,000
	21	Notes Receivable...........................	10,800	
		Accounts Receivable.........................		10,800
	31	Cash....................................	30,600	
		Notes Receivable........................		30,000
		Interest Income		600
June	20	Cash....................................	10,917	
		Notes Receivable........................		10,800
		Interest Income		117
	21	Notes Receivable...........................	7,000	
		Accounts Receivable.........................		7,000
July	20	Cash....................................	18,630	
		Notes Receivable........................		18,000
		Interest Income		630
	21	Cash....................................	7,070	
		Notes Receivable........................		7,000
		Interest Income		70
Aug.	14	Cash....................................	12,450	
		Notes Receivable........................		12,000
		Interest Income		450

Prob. 9-4B

1. and 2.

Allowance for Doubtful Accounts 115

Date		Item	Dr.	Cr.	Balance Dr.	Balance Cr.
19—						
Jan.	1	Balance	......	......	.....	17,955
Feb.	1	....	......	1,025	.....	18,980
	28	....	8,500	......	.....	10,480
May	7	....	2,000	......	.....	8,480
July	29	....	......	625	.....	9,105
Dec.	30	....	6,205	......	.....	2,900
	31	....	......	12,300	.....	15,200

Prob. 9-4B, Concluded

Income Summary   313

				Balance	
				---	---
Date	Item	Dr.	Cr.	Dr.	Cr.
19—					
Dec. 31	....	12,300	......	12,300	......

Uncollectible Accounts Expense   718

19—					
Dec. 31	....	12,300	......	12,300	......
31	....	......	12,300	—	—

2. 19—

Feb.	1	Accounts Receivable—Nancy Boyle...........	1,025	
		Allowance for Doubtful Accounts...........		1,025
	1	Cash.......................................	1,025	
		Accounts Receivable—Nancy Boyle.........		1,025
	28	Allowance for Doubtful Accounts.............	8,500	
		Accounts Receivable—D'Arrigo Co.		8,500
May	7	Cash.......................................	3,000	
		Allowance for Doubtful Accounts.............	2,000	
		Accounts Receivable—C. D. Clark Co.		5,000
July	29	Accounts Receivable—Louis Jaeger	625	
		Allowance for Doubtful Accounts...........		625
	29	Cash.......................................	625	
		Accounts Receivable—Louis Jaeger		625
Dec.	30	Allowance for Doubtful Accounts.............	6,205	
		Accounts Receivable—Boyd Co.		1,050
		Engel Co.............		1,760
		Loach Furniture......		2,775
		Briana Parker		620
Dec.	31	Uncollectible Accounts Expense..............	12,300	
		Allowance for Doubtful Accounts...........		12,300
	31	Income Summary.............................	12,300	
		Uncollectible Accounts Expense		12,300

3. $320,300 ($335,500 − $15,200)

4. a. $12,500 ($2,500,000 × .005)
   b. $15,400 ($12,500 + $2,900)
   c. $320,100 ($335,500 − $15,400)

Prob. 9-5B

1. **Uncollectible Accounts Expense**

Year	Expense Actually Reported	Expense Based on Estimate	Increase in Amount of Expense	Balance of Allowance Account, End of Year
1st	$2,600	$6,000	$3,400	$3,400
2d	3,500	7,000	3,500	6,900
3d	7,600	8,500	900	7,800
4th	8,550	9,500	950	8,750

2. Yes. The actual write-offs of accounts originating in the first two years are reasonably close to the expense that would have been charged to those years on the basis of 1% of sales. The total write-off of receivables originating in the first year amounted to $5,750, as compared with uncollectible accounts expense, based on the percentage of sales, of $6,000. For the second year, the comparable amounts were $7,250 and $7,000.

Prob. 9-6B

1.
LANDSBURG COMPANY
Income Statement
For Year Ended December 31, 19—

Revenue from sales:		
Sales....................................	$935,000	
Less sales discounts	8,500	
Net sales......................................		$926,500
Cost of merchandise sold		610,000
Gross profit......................................		$316,500
Operating expenses:		
Selling expenses...................................	$137,250	
Administrative expenses...........................	82,250	
Total operating expenses.........................		219,500
Income from operations		$ 97,000
Other income:		
Interest income..................................	$ 5,100	
Other expense:		
Unrealized loss from decline to market of marketable equity securities	2,400	2,700
Net income		$ 99,700

Prob. 9-6B, Concluded

2.   **LANDSBURG COMPANY**
                          Statement of Owner's Equity
                       For Year Ended December 31, 19—

G. M. Landsburg, capital, January 1, 19—		$603,400
Net income for year	$99,700	
Less withdrawals......................................	75,000	
Increase in owner's equity		24,700
G. M. Landsburg, capital, December 31, 19—		$628,100

3.   **LANDSBURG COMPANY**
                                 Balance Sheet
                              December 31, 19—

Assets

Current assets:			
Cash			$ 40,500
Marketable equity securities	$ 75,000		
Less allowance for decline to market ...	2,400	72,600	
Notes receivable.........................		50,000	
Accounts receivable	$ 88,000		
Less allowance for doubtful accounts ...	8,400	79,600	
Merchandise inventory...................		95,100	
Office supplies		5,500	
Prepaid insurance........................		7,000	
Total current assets...................			$350,300
Plant assets:			
Land......................................		$ 80,000	
Building..................................	$363,000		
Less accumulated depreciation	162,500	200,500	
Office equipment........................	$ 79,750		
Less accumulated depreciation	47,250	32,500	
Total plant assets			313,000
Total assets			$663,300

Liabilities

Current liabilities:		
Accounts payable.......................		$ 29,250
Salaries payable		5,950
Total liabilities........................		$ 35,200

Owner's Equity

G. M. Landsburg, capital		628,100
Total liabilities and owner's equity.........		$663,300

Mini-Case 9

1.

Year	Addition to Allowance for Doubtful Accounts	Accounts Written Off During Year
1990	$30,000	$24,000 ($30,000 − $ 6,000)
1991	33,500	29,500 ($ 6,000 + $33,500 − $10,000)
1992	31,000	26,500 ($10,000 + $31,000 − $14,500)
1993	27,500	22,500 ($14,500 + $27,500 − $19,500)

2. a. The estimate of 1/2 of 1% of credit sales may be too large, since the Allowance for Doubtful Accounts has steadily increased each year. The increasing balance of the Allowance for Doubtful Accounts may also be due to the failure to write off a large number of uncollectible accounts. These possibilities could be evaluated by examining the accounts in the subsidiary ledger for collectibility and comparing the result with the balance in Allowance for Doubtful Accounts.

Note to Instructors: Since the amount of credit sales has been fairly uniform over the years, the increase cannot be explained by an expanding volume of sales.

b. The balance of Allowance for Doubtful Accounts that should exist at December 31, 1993, can only be determined after all attempts have been made to collect the receivables on hand at December 31, 1993. However, the account balances at December 31, 1993, could be analyzed, perhaps using an aging schedule, to determine a reasonable amount of allowance and to determine accounts that should be written off. Also, past write-offs of uncollectible accounts could be analyzed in depth in order to develop a reasonable percentage for future adjusting entries, based on past history. Caution, however, must be exercised in using historical percentages. Specifically, inquiries should be made to determine whether any significant changes between prior years and the current year may have occurred, which might reduce the accuracy of the historical data. For example, a recent change in credit-granting policies or changes in the general economy (entering a recessionary period, for example) could reduce the usefulness of analyzing historical data.

Based upon the preceding analyses, a recommendation to decrease the annual rate charged as an expense may be in order (perhaps Harding's is experiencing a lower rate of uncollectibles than is the industry average), or perhaps a change to the "estimate based on analysis of receivables" method may be appropriate.

CHAPTER 10

DISCUSSION QUESTIONS

1. The inventory at the end of one period becomes the inventory for the beginning of the following period. Thus, if inventory is misstated at the end of a period, the net income for that period and the following period will be misstated.

2. (a) Gross profit for the year was overstated by $10,000. (b) Merchandise inventory and owner's equity were overstated by $10,000.

3. (a) Gross profit for the following year will be understated by $10,000. (b) None.

4. To protect inventory from customer theft, retailers use two-way mirrors, cameras, security guards, locked display cabinets, and inventory tags that set off an alarm if the inventory is removed from the store.

5. The perpetual inventory system provides the more effective means of controlling inventories, since the inventory account is updated for each purchase and sale. A perpetual record of the amount of inventory is maintained. This assists managers in determining when to reorder inventory items.

6. The receiving report should be reconciled to the initial purchase order and the vendor's invoice before recording or paying for inventory purchases. This procedure will verify that the inventory received matches the type and quantity of inventory ordered. It also verifies that the vendor's invoice is charging the company for the actual quantity of inventory received at the agreed price.

7. An employee should present a requisition form signed by an authorized manager before receiving inventory items from the company's warehouse.

8. A physical inventory should be taken periodically to test the accuracy of the perpetual records.

9. (a) When merchandise is shipped (b) When merchandise is delivered to the buyer

10. Midland Company. Since the merchandise was shipped FOB shipping point, title passed to Midland Company when it was shipped and should be reported in Midland Company's financial statements at December 31, the end of the fiscal year.

11. Manufacturer's

12. First-in, first-out (fifo) and last-in, first-out (lifo)

13. Lifo

14. No, they are not techniques for determining physical quantities. The terms refer to cost flow assumptions, which affect the determination of the cost prices assigned to items in the inventory.

15. No, the term refers to the flow of costs rather than the items remaining in the inventory. The inventory cost is composed of the earliest acquisitions costs rather than the most recent acquisitions costs.

16. (a) Last-in, first-out (lifo) method (b) First-in, first-out (fifo) method (c) Average cost method

17. a. $65
    b. $50
    c. $58

18. (a) Fifo (b) Lifo (c) Fifo (d) Lifo

19. Fifo

20. Lifo. In periods of rising prices, the use of lifo will result in the lowest net income and thus the lowest income tax expense.

21. Yes. The inventory method may be changed for a valid reason. The effect of any change in method and the reason for the change should be fully disclosed in the financial statements for the period in which the change occurred.

22. The balance of the subsidiary ledger accounts under the perpetual inventory system

23. Market means the cost to replace the merchandise on the inventory date.

24. $400

25. Net realizable value (estimated selling price less any direct costs of disposition, such as sales commissions)

26. By a notation next to "merchandise inventory" on the balance sheet or in a footnote to the financial statements

27. $325,000 ($500,000 × 65%)

28. Inventories estimated by the gross profit method are useful in preparing interim statements and in

establishing an estimate of the cost of merchandise destroyed by fire or other casualties.

29. a. $1,237,426,000 ($911,995,000 + $325,431,000)
     b. $352,232,000 ($311,944,000 − $285,143,000 + $325,431,000)

ETHICS DISCUSSION CASE Since the title to merchandise shipped FOB shipping point passes to the buyer when the merchandise is shipped, the shipments made before midnight, December 31, 1993, should properly be recorded as sales for the fiscal year ending December 31, 1993. Hence, Betty Arnett is behaving in an ethical manner. However, Betty should realize that recording these sales in 1993 precludes them from being recognized as sales in 1994. Thus, accelerating the shipment of orders to increase sales of one period will have the effect of decreasing sales of the next period.

EXERCISES

Ex. 10-1 Switching to a perpetual inventory system will strengthen Amis Hardware's internal controls over inventory, since the store managers will be able to keep track of how much of each item is on hand. This should minimize shortages of good-selling items and excess inventories of poor-selling items.

On the other hand, switching to a perpetual inventory system will not eliminate the need to take a physical inventory count. A physical inventory must be taken to verify the accuracy of the inventory records in a perpetual inventory system. In addition, a physical inventory count is needed to detect shortages of inventory due to damage or theft.

Ex. 10-2 a. Appropriate. The inventory tags will protect the inventory from customer theft.

b. Inappropriate. The internal control principle of using security measures to protect the inventory is violated if the stockroom is not locked.

c. Inappropriate. Good internal controls include using a voucher system to account for inventory purchases. Under a voucher system, a receiving report should be prepared after all inventory items received have been counted and inspected. Inventory purchased should only be recorded and paid for after reconciling the receiving report, the initial purchase order, and the vendor's invoice.

Ex. 10-3 a. $1,860 (30 units at $41 plus 15 units at $42)

b. $1,760 (40 units at $39 plus 5 units at $40)

c. $1,822.50 (45 units at $40.50)

Ex. 10-4

		Cost	
	Inventory Method	Merchandise Inventory	Merchandise Sold
a.	Fifo	$1,375	$2,495
b.	Lifo	1,210	2,660
c.	Average cost	1,290	2,580

Cost of merchandise available for sale:

15 units at $60	$ 900
10 units at $62	620
20 units at $65	1,300
15 units at $70	1,050
60 units (at average cost of $64.50)	$3,870

Ex. 10-4, Concluded

a. **First-in, first-out:**
   Merchandise inventory:
15 units at $70	$1,050
5 units at $65	325
20 units	$1,375

   Merchandise sold:
$3,870 − $1,375	$2,495

b. **Last-in, first-out:**
   Merchandise inventory:
15 units at $60	$ 900
5 units at $62	310
20 units	$1,210

   Merchandise sold:
$3,870 − $1,210	$2,660

c. **Average cost:**
   Merchandise inventory:
20 units at $64.50	$1,290

   Merchandise sold:
$3,870 − $1,290	$2,580

Ex. 10-5

Commodity E29

Date	Purchases Quantity	Purchases Unit Cost	Purchases Total Cost	Cost of Merchandise Sold Quantity	Cost of Merchandise Sold Unit Cost	Cost of Merchandise Sold Total Cost	Inventory Quantity	Inventory Unit Cost	Inventory Total Cost
Jan. 1							15	45	675
6				5	45	225	10	45	450
9	15	47	705				10 15	45 47	450 705
15				10 8	45 47	450 376	7	47	329
22				3	47	141	4	47	188
30	10	48	480				4 10	47 48	188 480

Ex. 10-6

Commodity A40										
	Purchases			Cost of Merchandise Sold			Inventory			
Date	Quantity	Unit Cost	Total Cost	Quantity	Unit Cost	Total Cost	Quantity	Unit Cost	Total Cost	
May 1							30	30	900	
4	20	31	620				30	30	900	
							20	31	620	
11				15	31	465	30	30	900	
							5	31	155	
17				5	31	155	25	30	750	
				5	30	150				
20	15	32	480				25	30	750	
							15	32	480	
27				10	32	320	25	30	750	
							5	32	160	

Ex. 10-7

Commodity	Inventory Quantity	Unit Cost Price	Unit Market Price	Total Cost	Total Lower of C or M
43B	8	$340	$350	$ 2,720	$ 2,720
19H	17	110	105	1,870	1,785
33P	12	275	260	3,300	3,120
90R	35	60	65	2,100	2,100
45T	20	95	100	1,900	1,900
Total				$11,890	$11,625

Ex. 10-8 The merchandise inventory would appear in the Current Assets section, as follows: Merchandise inventory—at lower of fifo, cost ($11,890) or market...$11,625

Ex. 10-9

	Cost	Retail
Merchandise inventory, June 1	$244,500	$370,500
Purchases in June (net)	164,700	249,500
Merchandise available for sale	$409,200	$620,000

Ratio of cost to retail price: $\dfrac{\$409,200}{\$620,000} = 66\%$

Sales for June (net)		259,000
Merchandise inventory, June 30, at retail price		$361,000
Merchandise inventory, June 30, at estimated cost ($361,000 × 66%)		$238,260

Ex. 10-10

a.

Merchandise inventory, Jan. 1		$172,250
Purchases (net), Jan. 1–March 20		212,250
Merchandise available for sale		$384,500
Sales (net), Jan. 1–March 20	$380,000	
Less estimated gross profit ($380,000 × 40%)	152,000	
Estimated cost of merchandise sold		228,000
Estimated merchandise inventory, March 20		$156,500

b. The gross profit method is useful for estimating inventories for monthly or quarterly financial statements. It is also useful in estimating the cost of merchandise destroyed by fire or other disaster.

WHAT'S WRONG WITH THIS?

1. When an error is discovered affecting the prior period, it should be corrected. In this case, the capital account could be debited and Merchandise Inventory credited for $50,000.
2. Since the ending inventory of 1993 became the beginning inventory of 1994, the income of both years would be misstated by equal but opposite amounts. In this case, failure to correct the beginning inventory for 1994, by itself, would understate 1994 net income by $50,000.
3. Understating the ending inventory of 1994 by $50,000, by itself, would understate 1994 net income by $50,000.
4. The combination of 2 and 3 would result in an understatement of net income of 1994 by $100,000. Thus the 1993 net income would be overstated by $50,000, the 1994 net income would be understated by $100,000, and if not corrected, 1995 net income would be overstated by $50,000.

PROBLEMS

Prob. 10-1A

1.

EDWARDS COMPANY
Income Statements
For Years Ended December 31, 1994 and 1993

	1994	1993
Net sales.........................	$900,000	$850,000
Cost of merchandise sold:		
Merchandise inventory, January 1	$ 85,000	$ 70,000
Cost of merchandise purchased.	640,000	610,000
Merchandise available for sale ..	$725,000	$680,000
Less merchandise inventory, December 31	75,000	85,000
Cost of merchandise sold.....	650,000	595,000
Gross profit	$250,000	$255,000
Operating expenses	190,000	185,000
Net income	$ 60,000	$ 70,000

2. a. Understated $10,000
   b. None

Prob. 10-2A

1. (c) Purchases.. 4,250
      Accounts Payable   4,250

(d) Sales 9,500
      Accounts Receivable   9,500

(e) Accounts Receivable 1,250
      Sales   1,250

2.   Merchandise Inventory Corrections

Preliminary inventory		$205,000
Additions:		
(b)	$1,500	
(d)	6,500	8,000
		$213,000
Deductions:		
(a)	$3,500	
(f)	8,500	12,000
Corrected inventory.................................		$201,000

3.   POOLE ENTERPRISES
                       Income Statement
            For Year Ended December 31, 19—

Sales (net)		$988,500*
Cost of merchandise sold:		
Merchandise inventory, January 1, 19—..........	$190,000	
Purchases (net)	699,250**	
Merchandise available for sale	$889,250	
Less merchandise inventory, December 31, 19—..	201,000	
Cost of merchandise sold.....................		688,250
Gross profit..		$300,250
Operating expenses		202,250
Net income		$ 98,000

* $996,750 − (d) $9,500 + (e) $1,250 = $988,500
**$695,000 + (c) $4,250 = $699,250

Prob. 10-3A

1. First-In, First-Out Method

Model	Quantity	Unit Cost	Total Cost
B91	5	$155	$ 775
F10	3	225	675
H21	2	536	1,072
	1	530	530
J39	6	542	3,252
	2	549	1,098
P80	6	225	1,350
	2	222	444
T15	4	321	1,284
	1	316	316
V11	2	230	460
Total..................................			$11,256

2. Last-In, First-Out Method

Model	Quantity	Unit Cost	Total Cost
B91	5	$150	$ 750
F10	3	210	630
H21	2	520	1,040
	1	530	530
J39	6	520	3,120
	2	531	1,062
P80	8	213	1,704
T15	5	305	1,525
V11	2	220	440
Total..................................			$10,801

3. Average Cost Method

Model	Quantity	Unit Cost	Total Cost
B91	5	$153	$ 765
F10	3	216	648
H21	3	529	1,587
J39	8	534	4,272
P80	8	218	1,744
T15	5	312	1,560
V11	2	225	450
Total..................................			$11,026

Prob. 10-3A, Concluded

4. a. During periods of rising prices, such as shown for House of Television, the lifo method will result in a lesser amount of net income than the other two methods. Hence, for House of Television, the lifo method would be preferred for the current year, since it would result in a lesser amount of income tax.

    b. During periods of declining prices, the fifo method will result in a lesser amount of net income and would be preferred for income tax purposes during such periods.

Prob. 10-4A

1.

Commodity 37D

Date	Purchases			Cost of Merchandise Sold			Inventory		
	Quantity	Unit Cost	Total Cost	Quantity	Unit Cost	Total Cost	Quantity	Unit Cost	Total Cost
April 1							9	220	1,980
5	25	225	5,625				9 25	220 225	1,980 5,625
12				9 1	220 225	1,980 225	24	225	5,400
22				6	225	1,350	18	225	4,050
May 4	10	230	2,300				18 10	225 230	4,050 2,300
6				8	225	1,800	10 10	225 230	2,250 2,300
21				5	225	1,125	5 10	225 230	1,125 2,300
28	15	235	3,525				5 10 15	225 230 235	1,125 2,300 3,525
June 5				5 4	225 230	1,125 920	6 15	230 235	1,380 3,525
13				6 4	230 235	1,380 940	11	235	2,585
19	10	240	2,400				11 10	235 240	2,585 2,400
26				8	235	1,880	3 10	235 240	705 2,400

Prob. 10-4A, Continued
4.

Commodity 37D

Date	Purchases			Cost of Merchandise Sold			Inventory		
	Quantity	Unit Cost	Total Cost	Quantity	Unit Cost	Total Cost	Quantity	Unit Cost	Total Cost
April 1							9	220	1,980
5	25	225	5,625				9	220	1,980
							25	225	5,625
12				10	225	2,250	9	220	1,980
							15	225	3,375
22				6	225	1,350	9	220	1,980
							9	225	2,025
May 4	10	230	2,300				9	220	1,980
							9	225	2,025
							10	230	2,300
6				8	230	1,840	9	220	1,980
							9	225	2,025
							2	230	460
21				2	230	460	9	220	1,980
				3	225	675	6	225	1,350
28	15	235	3,525				9	220	1,980
							6	225	1,350
							15	235	3,525
June 5				9	235	2,115	9	220	1,980
							6	225	1,350
							6	235	1,410
13				6	235	1,410	9	220	1,980
				4	225	900	2	225	450
19	10	240	2,400				9	220	1,980
							2	225	450
							10	240	2,400
26				8	240	1,920	9	220	1,980
							2	225	450
							2	240	480

Prob. 10-4A, Concluded

2. Accounts Receivable 17,375

    Sales 17,375

  Cost of Merchandise Sold 12,725

    Merchandise Inventory 12,725

3. $4,650 ($17,375 − $12,725)

Prob. 10-5A

Inventory Sheet
December 31, 19—

Description	Inventory Quantity		Unit Cost Price	Unit Market Price	Total Cost	Total Lower of C or M
A71	40	20	$ 60	$ 57	$ 1,200	$ 1,140
		20	59		1,180	1,140
C22	15		190	200	2,850	2,850
D82	20	15	145	140	2,175	2,100
		5	142		710	700
E34	110		25	26	2,750	2,750
F17	18	6	550	550	3,300	3,300
		12	540		6,480	6,480
J19	70		16	15	1,120	1,050
K41	5		400	390	2,000	1,950
P21	400		6	6	2,400	2,400
R72	100	70	17	17	1,190	1,190
		30	16		480	480
T15	6	5	250	240	1,250	1,200
		1	260		260	240
V55	600		10	10	6,000	6,000
AC2	80		45	44	3,600	3,520
BB7	10	5	410	425	2,050	2,050
		5	400		2,000	2,000
BD1	150	100	20	18	2,000	1,800
		50	19		950	900
CC1	40		15	15	600	600
EB2	60	40	29	30	1,160	1,160
		20	28		560	560
FF7	35		28	27	980	945
GE4	9	6	690	700	4,140	4,140
		3	700		2,100	2,100
					$55,485	$54,745

Prob. 10-6A

1. a. Income Summary 90,200
     Merchandise Inventory 90,200

    Merchandise Inventory 84,600
     Income Summary 84,600

b. Operating Expenses................................ 1,725
    Allowance for Doubtful Accounts 1,725

c. Operating Expenses................................ 5,500
    Accumulated Depreciation—Equipment........... 5,500

2. (a)

WORDEN SALES
Income Statement
For Year Ended December 31, 19—

Sales		$535,700
Cost of merchandise sold:		
Merchandise inventory, January 1, 19—	$ 90,200	
Purchases	395,800	
Merchandise available for sale	$486,000	
Less merchandise inventory, December 31, 19—	84,600	
Cost of merchandise sold		401,400
Gross profit		$134,300
Operating expenses		62,400
Income from operations		$ 71,900
Other income:		
Rent income	$ 1,200	
Other expense:		
Interest expense	1,100	100
Net income		$ 72,000

2. (b)

WORDEN SALES
Statement of Owner's Equity
For Year Ended December 31, 19—

Robert Worden, capital, January 1, 19—		$ 71,750
Net income for the year	$72,000	
Less withdrawals	36,000	
Increase in owner's equity		36,000
Robert Worden, capital, December 31, 19—		$107,750

Prob. 10-6A, Concluded

2. (c)

WORDEN SALES
Balance Sheet
December 31, 19—

Assets

Current assets:

Cash		$17,900
Accounts receivable	$29,500	
Less allowance for doubtful accounts	2,000	27,500
Merchandise inventory—at lower of cost (first-in, first-out method) or market		84,600
Total current assets		$130,000
Plant assets:		
Equipment	$30,000	
Less accumulated depreciation	17,750	
Total plant assets		12,250
Total assets		$142,250

Liabilities

Current liabilities:

Accounts payable	$24,500	
Notes payable	10,000	
Total liabilities		$ 34,500

Owner's Equity

Robert Worden, capital	107,750
Total liabilities and owner's equity	$142,250

Prob. 10-7A

1.   **WRIGHT CO.**

	Cost	Retail
Merchandise inventory, January 1,	$377,100	$579,100
Purchases................................ $186,600		
Less purchases discounts 2,100		
Net purchases....................	184,500	298,400
Merchandise available for sale	$561,600	$877,500

Ratio of cost to retail price: $\dfrac{\$561,600}{\$877,500} = 64\%$

Sales		$340,500
Less sales returns and allowances		5,500
Net sales.........................		335,000
Merchandise inventory, January 31, at retail		$542,500
Merchandise inventory, January 31, at estimated cost ($542,500 × 64%)		$347,200

2. a.   **C. F. JONES CO.**

Merchandise inventory, July 1..................		$517,900
Purchases	$425,500	
Less purchases discounts	3,600	
Net purchases..................................		421,900
Merchandise available for sale..................		$939,800
Sales	$570,250	
Less sales returns and allowances..............	5,250	
Net sales	$565,000	
Less estimated gross profit ($565,000 × 35%) ...	197,750	
Estimated cost of merchandise sold.............		367,250
Estimated merchandise inventory, August 31 ...		$572,550

b. Estimated merchandise inventory, August 31		$572,550
Physical inventory count, August 31		565,000
Estimated loss due to theft or damage, July 1–August 31		$ 7,550

Prob. 10-1B

1.
GROSS COMPANY
Income Statements
For Years Ended December 31, 1994 and 1993

	1994	1993
Net sales.............................	$950,000	$900,000
Cost of merchandise sold:		
Merchandise inventory,		
January 1	$ 75,000	$ 80,000
Cost of merchandise purchased.	670,000	640,000
Merchandise available for sale ..	$745,000	$720,000
Less merchandise inventory,		
December 31	85,000	75,000
Cost of merchandise sold.....	660,000	645,000
Gross profit	$290,000	$255,000
Operating expenses	190,000	185,000
Net income	$100,000	$ 70,000

2. a. Overstated $10,000
   b. None

Prob. 10-2B

1. (c) Purchases....................................... 3,000
       Accounts Payable   3,000

(d) Sales 10,000
    Accounts Receivable   10,000

(e) Accounts Receivable 1,250
    Sales   1,250

2.
Merchandise Inventory Corrections

Preliminary inventory		$245,000
Additions:		
(b)	$1,500	
(d)	6,500	8,000
		$253,000
Deductions:		
(a)	$5,000	
(f)	8,500	13,500
Corrected inventory.................................		$239,500

Prob. 10-2B, Concluded

3.

E. BANKS ENTERPRISES
Income Statement
For Year Ended December 31, 19—

Sales (net)		$977,000*
Cost of merchandise sold:		
Merchandise inventory, January 1, 19—..........	$230,000	
Purchases (net)	698,000**	
Merchandise available for sale	$928,000	
Less merchandise inventory, December 31, 19—..	239,500	
Cost of merchandise sold.....................		688,500
Gross profit		$288,500
Operating expenses		202,250
Net income		$ 86,250

  *$985,750 − (d) $10,000 + (e) $1,250 = $977,000
**$695,000 + (c) $3,000 = $698,000

Prob. 10-3B

1. First-In, First-Out Method

Model	Quantity	Unit Cost	Total Cost
A37	10	$266	$2,660
	2	260	520
E15	8	99	792
	2	89	178
L10	3	130	390
O18	6	92	552
	2	85	170
K72	4	275	1,100
S91	7	180	1,260
	1	175	175
V17	2	205	410
	3	200	600
Total............................			$8,807

Prob. 10-3B, Concluded

2. Last-In, First-Out Method

Model	Quantity	Unit Cost	Total Cost
A37	6	$238	$1,428
	4	250	1,000
	2	260	520
E15	6	77	462
	4	82	328
L10	2	108	216
	1	110	110
O18	8	88	704
K72	2	250	500
	2	260	520
S91	5	160	800
	3	170	510
V17	4	150	600
	1	200	200
Total............................			$7,898

3. Average Cost Method

Model	Quantity	Unit Cost	Total Cost
A37	12	$256	$3,072
E15	10	88	880
L10	3	121	363
O18	8	87	696
K72	4	267	1,068
S91	8	172	1,376
V17	5	181	905
Total..........................			$8,360

4. **a.** During periods of rising prices, such as shown for A-1 Television, the lifo method will result in a lesser amount of net income than the other two methods. Hence, for A-1 Television, the lifo method would be preferred for the current year, since it would result in a lesser amount of income tax.

    b. During periods of declining prices, the fifo method will result in a lesser amount of net income and would be preferred for income tax purposes during such periods.

Prob. 10-4B

1.

Soybeans

Date	Purchases			Cost of Merchandise Sold			Inventory		
	Quantity	Unit Cost	Total Cost	Quantity	Unit Cost	Total Cost	Quantity	Unit Cost	Total Cost
July 1							25,000	6.10	152,500
10	75,000	6.15	461,250				25,000	6.10	152,500
							75,000	6.15	461,250
15				25,000	6.10	152,500	65,000	6.15	399,750
				10,000	6.15	61,500			
25				30,000	6.15	184,500	35,000	6.15	215,250
Aug. 8				10,000	6.15	61,500	25,000	6.15	153,750
12	50,000	6.20	310,000				25,000	6.15	153,750
							50,000	6.20	310,000
17				25,000	6.15	153,750	40,000	6.20	248,000
				10,000	6.20	62,000			
28				20,000	6.20	124,000	20,000	6.20	124,000
Sep. 5	60,000	6.10	366,000				20,000	6.20	124,000
							60,000	6.10	366,000
17				20,000	6.20	124,000	40,000	6.10	244,000
				20,000	6.10	122,000			
20	30,000	6.00	180,000				40,000	6.10	244,000
							30,000	6.00	180,000
30				40,000	6.10	244,000	25,000	6.00	150,000
				5,000	6.00	30,000			

Prob. 10-4B, Continued

4.

Soybeans

Date	Purchases Quantity	Purchases Unit Cost	Purchases Total Cost	COMS Quantity	COMS Unit Cost	COMS Total Cost	Inventory Quantity	Inventory Unit Cost	Inventory Total Cost
July 1							25,000	6.10	152,500
10	75,000	6.15	461,250				25,000	6.10	152,500
							75,000	6.15	461,250
15				35,000	6.15	215,250	25,000	6.10	152,500
							40,000	6.15	246,000
25				30,000	6.15	184,500	25,000	6.10	152,500
							10,000	6.15	61,500
Aug. 8				10,000	6.15	61,500	25,000	6.10	152,500
12	50,000	6.20	310,000				25,000	6.10	152,500
							50,000	6.20	310,000
17				35,000	6.20	217,000	25,000	6.10	152,500
							15,000	6.20	93,000
28				15,000	6.20	93,000	20,000	6.10	122,000
				5,000	6.10	30,500			
Sep. 5	60,000	6.10	366,000				20,000	6.10	122,000
							60,000	6.10	366,000
17				40,000	6.10	244,000	40,000	6.10	244,000
20	30,000	6.00	180,000				40,000	6.10	244,000
							30,000	6.00	180,000
30				30,000	6.00	180,000	25,000	6.10	152,500
				15,000	6.10	91,500			

Prob. 10-4B, Concluded

2. Accounts Receivable............................ 1,516,000

    Sales....................................... 1,516,000

  Cost of Merchandise Sold 1,319,750

    Merchandise Inventory 1,319,750

3. $196,250

Prob. 10-5B

Inventory Sheet
December 31, 19—

Description	Inventory Quantity		Unit Cost Price	Unit Market Price	Total Cost	Total Lower of C or M
A71	40	20	$ 60	$ 57	$ 1,200	$ 1,140
		20	59		1,180	1,140
C22	15		210	200	3,150	3,000
D82	20	10	145	140	1,450	1,400
		10	142		1,420	1,400
E34	110		25	26	2,750	2,750
F17	18	10	560	550	5,600	5,500
		8	570		4,560	4,400
J19	70		15	15	1,050	1,050
K41	5		380	390	1,900	1,900
P21	400		6	6	2,400	2,400
R72	100	80	17	17	1,360	1,360
		20	18		360	340
T15	6	5	250	240	1,250	1,200
		1	260		260	240
V55	600		9	10	5,400	5,400
AC2	80		45	44	3,600	3,520
BB7	10	5	420	425	2,100	2,100
		5	425		2,125	2,125
BD1	150	100	20	18	2,000	1,800
		50	19		950	900
CC1	40		16	15	640	600
EB2	60	50	29	30	1,450	1,450
		10	28		280	280
FF7	35		26	27	910	910
GE4	9	5	710	700	3,550	3,500
		4	715		2,860	2,800
					$55,755	$54,605

Prob. 10-6B

1. a. Income Summary 85,200

      Merchandise Inventory   85,200

      Merchandise Inventory 89,600

      Income Summary   89,600

  b. Operating Expenses................................ 1,900

      Allowance for Doubtful Accounts   1,900

  c. Operating Expenses................................ 6,800

      Accumulated Depreciation—Equipment...........   6,800

2. (a)

BOYD IMPORTS
Income Statement
For Year Ended December 31, 19—

Sales		$850,200
Cost of merchandise sold:		
Merchandise inventory, January 1, 19—..............	$ 85,200	
Purchases	705,800	
Merchandise available for sale	$791,000	
Less merchandise inventory, December 31, 19—.....	89,600	
Cost of merchandise sold.........................		701,400
Gross profit		$148,800
Operating expenses		71,900
Income from operations..................................		$ 76,900
Other income:		
Rent income...	$ 1,200	
Other expense:		
Interest expense......................................	1,100	100
Net income		$ 77,000

2. (b)

BOYD IMPORTS
Statement of Owner's Equity
For Year Ended December 31, 19—

P. L. Boyd, capital, January 1, 19—......................		$ 86,675
Net income for the year.................................	$77,000	
Less withdrawals...	40,000	
Increase in owner's equity		37,000
P. L. Boyd, capital, December 31, 19—..................		$123,675

Prob. 10-6B, Concluded

2. (c)

BOYD IMPORTS
Balance Sheet
December 31, 19—

Assets

Current assets:		
Cash		$22,550
Accounts receivable	$37,500	
Less allowance for doubtful accounts	2,175	35,325
Merchandise inventory—at lower of cost		
(first-in, first-out method) or market		89,600
Total current assets		$147,475
Plant assets:		
Equipment	$37,500	
Less accumulated depreciation	26,800	
Total plant assets		10,700
Total assets		$158,175

Liabilities

Current liabilities:		
Accounts payable..........................	$24,500	
Notes payable	10,000	
Total liabilities................................		$ 34,500

Owner's Equity

P. L. Boyd, capital............................		123,675
Total liabilities and owner's equity...........		$158,175

Prob. 10-7B

1.   **HEIMS CO.**

	Cost	Retail
Merchandise inventory, July 1....	$259,800	$370,000
Purchases.......................	$366,840	
Less purchases discounts........	2,940	
Net purchases...................	363,900	521,000
Merchandise available for sale....	$623,700	$891,000

Ratio of cost to retail price:

$$\frac{\$623,700}{\$891,000} = 70\%$$

Sales		$600,000
Less sales returns and allowances		5,000
Net sales.........................		595,000
Merchandise inventory, July 31, at retail		$296,000
Merchandise inventory, July 31, at estimated cost ($296,000 × 70%)		$207,200

2. a.   **G.N. PALMER CO.**

Merchandise inventory, April 1..................		$317,500
Purchases......................................	$410,250	
Less purchases discounts	5,250	
Net purchases..................................		405,000
Merchandise available for sale..................		$722,500
Sales	$625,000	
Less sales returns and allowances..............	5,000	
Net sales	$620,000	
Less estimated gross profit ($620,000 × 40%) ...	248,000	
Estimated cost of merchandise sold............		372,000
Estimated merchandise inventory, May 31		$350,500

b.

Estimated merchandise inventory, May 31	$350,500
Physical inventory count, May 31	338,750
Estimated loss due to theft or damage, April 1–May 31...	$ 11,750

Mini-Case 10

1. a. First-in, first-out method:

1,000 units at $17.00	$17,000
1,000 units at $15.75	15,750
1,000 units at $15.50	15,500
3,000 units...	$48,250

b. Last-in, first-out method:

3,000 units at $13.20	$39,600

c. Average cost method:

3,000 units at $14.50	$43,500

($391,500 ÷ 27,000 = $14.50)

2.

	Fifo	Lifo	Average Cost
Sales....................................	$454,000	$454,000	$454,000
Cost of merchandise sold*	343,250	351,900	348,000
Gross profit	$110,750	$102,100	$106,000
*Cost of merchandise available for sale..	$391,500	$391,500	$391,500
Less ending inventory..................	48,250	39,600	43,500
Cost of merchandise sold...............	$343,250	$351,900	$348,000

3. a. The lifo method is often viewed as the best basis for reflecting income from operations. This is because the lifo method matches the most current cost of merchandise purchases against current sales. The matching of current costs with current sales results in a gross profit amount that many consider to best reflect the results of current operations. For Garvey Company, the gross profit of $102,100 reflects the matching of the most current costs of the product of $351,900 against the current period sales of $454,000. This matching of current costs with current sales also tends to minimize the effects of price trends on the results of operations.

    The lifo method will not match current sales and the current cost of merchandise sold if the current period quantity of sales exceeds the current period quantity of purchases. In this case, the cost of merchandise sold will include a portion of the cost of the beginning inventory, which may have a unit cost from purchases made several years prior to the current period. The results of operations may then be distorted in the sense of the current matching concept. This situation occurs rarely in most businesses because of consistently increasing quantities of year-end inventory from year to year.

Note to Instructors: The matching concept mentioned above is further discussed in Chapter 13.

    While the lifo method is often viewed as the best method for matching revenues and expenses, the fifo method is often in harmony

Mini-Case 10, Continued

with the physical movement of merchandise in an enterprise, since most businesses tend to dispose of commodities in the order of their acquisition. To the extent that this is the case, the fifo method approximates the results that will be attained by a specific identification of costs.

The average cost method is, in a sense, a compromise between lifo and fifo. The effect of price trends is averaged, both in the determination of net income and in the determination of inventory cost.

Which inventory costing method best reflects the results of operations for Garvey Company depends upon whether one emphasizes the importance of matching revenues and expenses (the lifo method) or whether one emphasizes the physical flow of merchandise (the fifo method). The average cost method might be considered best if one emphasizes the matching and physical flow of goods concepts equally.

b. The fifo method provides the best reflection of the replacement cost of the ending inventory for the balance sheet. This is because the amount reported on the balance sheet for merchandise inventory will be assigned costs from the most recent purchases. For most businesses, these costs will reflect purchases made near the end of the period. For example, Garvey Company's ending inventory on December 31, 1993, is assigned costs totaling $48,250 under the fifo method. These costs represent purchases made during the period October through December. This fifo inventory amount ($48,250) more closely approximates the replacement cost of the ending inventory than either the lifo ($39,600) or the average cost ($43,500) figures.

c. During periods of rising prices, such as shown for Garvey Company, the lifo method will result in a lesser amount of net income than the other two methods. Hence, for Garvey Company, the lifo method would be preferred for the current year, since it would result in a lesser amount of income tax.

During periods of declining prices, the fifo method will result in a lesser amount of net income and would be preferred for income tax purposes during such periods.

d. The advantages of the perpetual inventory system include the following:

1. A perpetual inventory system provides an effective means of control over inventory. A periodic comparison of the amount of inventory on hand with the balance of the subsidiary account can be used to determine the existence and seriousness of any inventory shortages.

2. A perpetual inventory system provides an accurate method for determining inventories used in the preparation of interim statements.

3. A perpetual inventory system provides an aid for maintaining inventories at optimum levels. Frequent review of the perpetual inventory records helps management in the timely reordering of merchandise, so that loss of sales and excessive accumulation of

Mini-Case 10, Concluded

inventory are avoided. An analysis of Garvey Company purchases and sales, as shown below, indicates that the company may have accumulated excess inventory from May through August because the amount of month-end inventory increased materially, while sales remained relatively constant for the period.

Month	Purchases	Sales	Increase (Decrease) in Inventory	Inventory at End of Month	Next Month's Sales
April	5,000 units	2,000 units	3,000 units	3,000 units	2,000 units
May	5,000	2,000	3,000	6,000	3,500
June	5,000	3,500	1,500	7,500	4,000
July	5,000	4,000	1,000	8,500	3,500
August	3,000	3,500	(500)	8,000	3,500
September	—	3,500	(3,500)	4,500	2,250
October	2,000	2,250	(250)	4,250	2,250
November	1,000	2,250	(1,250)	3,000	1,000

It appears that during April through July, the company ordered a predetermined amount of inventory (5,000 units) each month, without regard to the accumulation of excess inventory. A perpetual inventory system might have prevented this excess accumulation from occurring.

The primary disadvantage of the perpetual inventory system is the cost of maintaining the necessary inventory records. However, computers may be used to reduce this cost.

CHAPTER 11

DISCUSSION QUESTIONS

1. a. Tangible
   c. Capable of repeated use in the operations of the business
   f. Long-lived

2. a. Plant assets
   b. Current assets (merchandise inventory)

3. Real estate acquired as speculation should be listed in the balance sheet under the caption "Investments," below the Current Assets section.

4. $105,000

5. a. Sales tax on purchase price
   b. Transportation charges
   c. Insurance while in transit
   d. Cost of special foundation
   f. Fee paid to factory representative for installation

6. a. Transportation charges
   b. Installation costs
   d. Replacement of worn-out parts

7. (a) Land, (b) Land, (c) Land

8. Ordinarily not; if the book values closely approximate the market values of plant assets, it is coincidental.

9. a. No, it does not provide a special cash fund for the replacement of assets. Unlike most expenses, however, depreciation expense does not require an equivalent outlay of cash in the period to which the expense is allocated.
   b. Depreciation is the cost of plant assets periodically charged to revenue over their expected useful life.

10. Initial plant asset cost, the useful life of the plant asset, and residual value.

11. 4 years

12. (a) No, (b) No

13. Straight-line method

14. $20,000

15. (a) $9,000, (b) $6,000

16. (a) 25%, (b) 20%, (c) 10%, (d) 5%, (e) 4%, (f) 2½%, (g) 2%

17. $20,000 (20% × $100,000)

18. a. 10
   b. $10,000 (4/10 × $25,000)
   c. $7,500 (3/10 × $25,000)

19. a. Accelerated depreciation methods are most appropriate for situations in which the decline in productivity or earning power of the asset is proportionately greater in the early years of use than in later years, and the repairs tend to increase with the age of the asset.
   b. They reduce income tax expense in earlier periods and correspondingly increase the amount of funds available to pay for the asset or for other purposes.
   c. MACRS was enacted by the Tax Reform Act of 1986 and provides for depreciation for plant assets acquired after 1986.

20. a. $5,000
   b. $105,000 ($205,000 − $100,000)
   c. $4,000 [($105,000 − $5,000) ÷ 25]

21. a. 10% ($60,000 ÷ $600,000)
   b. 11% ($66,000 ÷ $600,000)

22. a. Capital expenditures are those properly chargeable to an asset account or to an accumulated depreciation account; revenue expenditures are chargeable to current operations.
   b. Because the items are minor in amount.

23. Capital expenditure

24. a. No, the accumulated depreciation for an asset cannot exceed the cost of the asset.
   b. The cost and accumulated depreciation should be removed from the accounts when the asset is no longer useful and is removed from service. Presumably the asset will then be sold, traded in, or discarded as junk.

25. Other Income and Other Expense sections

26. a. $70,000 ($120,000 − $50,000)
   b. $110,000 ($40,000 + $70,000) or ($120,000 − $10,000)
   c. Same as (b)

27. a. $120,000
   b. $130,000 ($70,000 + $60,000) or ($120,000 + $10,000)

28. Capital leases are defined as leases that include one or more of the following provisions: (1) the lease transfers ownership of the leased asset to the lessee at the end of the lease term, (2) the lease contains an option for a bargain purchase of the leased asset by the lessee, (3) the lease term extends over most of the economic life of the leased asset, or (4) the lease requires rental payments that approximate the fair market value of the leased asset. Leases which do not meet the preceding criteria are classified as operating leases.

29. All purchases of plant assets should be approved by an appropriate level of management. In addition, competitive bids should be solicited to ensure the company is acquiring the assets at the lowest possible price.

30. An inventory of plant assets will verify the accuracy of accounting records. It will also detect missing plant assets that should be removed from the inventory records and obsolete or idle plant assets that should be disposed of.

31. (a) Depletion, (b) Amortization

32. a. Over the years of its expected usefulness.
    b. Expense as incurred.

33. a. The balance of each major class of depreciable assets should be disclosed in the balance sheet or notes thereto, together with the related accumulated depreciation, either by major class or in total.
    b. Intangible assets are usually presented in the balance sheet in a separate section immediately following plant assets. The balance of each major class should be disclosed as an amount net of amortization taken to date.

34. a. Yes. All expenditures incurred for the purpose of making the land suitable for its intended use should be debited to the land account.
    b. No. Land is not depreciated.

35. No. Accounting Principles Board Opinion No. 20, *Accounting Changes,* is quite specific about the treatment of changes in depreciable assets' estimated service lives. Such changes should be reflected in the amounts for depreciation expense in the current and future periods. The amounts recorded for depreciation expense in the past are not affected.

36. These leases would be classified as capital leases because the lease agreements allow for an option to purchase the facilities at a bargain price. In addition, the requirement that the company insure and maintain the facilities implies a transfer of ownership rights.

ETHICS DISCUSSION CASE It is generally considered unethical for employees to use company assets for personal reasons, because such use reduces the useful life of the assets for normal business purposes. Thus, it is unethical for Alice Parker to use Wilson Co.'s microcomputers and laser printers to service her part-time accounting business, even on an after-hours basis. In addition, it is improper for Alice's clients to call her during regular working hours. Such calls may interrupt or interfere with Alice's ability to carry out her assigned duties for Wilson Co.

EXERCISES

Ex. 11-1 Initial cost of land ($10,000 + $50,000)............ $60,000

Plus: Legal fees.................................	$2,500	
Delinquent taxes...........................	4,000	
Demolition of building.....................	5,500	12,000
		$72,000
Less: Salvage of materials.......................		1,000
Cost of land......................................		$71,000

Ex. 11-2 a. No. The $725,000 represents the original cost of the equipment. Its replacement cost, which may be more or less than $725,000, is not reported in the financial statements.

b. No. The $510,000 is the accumulation of the past depreciation charges on the equipment. The recognition of depreciation expense has no relationship to the cash account or accumulation of cash funds.

Ex. 11-3 $\dfrac{\$170,000 - \$20,000}{50,000 \text{ hours}} = \$3$ depreciation per hour

360 hours at $3 = $1,080 depreciation for November

Ex. 11-4 a.

Truck No.	Rate per Mile	Miles Operated	Credit to Accumulated Depreciation
1	20.0¢	25,000	$5,000
2	15.0¢	20,000	3,000
3	16.0¢	4,500	700*
4	9.0¢	12,000	1,080
Total			$9,780

*Mileage depreciation of $720 is limited to $700, which reduces the book value of the truck to $4,000, its residual value.

b.

Depreciation Expense—Trucks...................	9,780	
Accumulated Depreciation—Trucks		9,780

Ex. 11-5

	First Year	Second Year
a.	10% of $220,000 = $22,000	10% of $220,000 = $22,000
b.	20% of $220,000 = $44,000	20% of $176,000 = $35,200
c.	10/55 of $220,000 = $40,000	9/55 of $220,000 = $36,000

Ex. 11-6 a. 12½% of ($45,200 − $2,000) = $5,400

b. 25% of ($45,200 − $11,300) = $8,475

c. 7/36 of ($45,200 − $2,000) = $8,400

Ex. 11-7 a. First year: $3/4 \times 40\%$ of $\$33,000 = \$9,900$
Second year: 40% of $(\$33,000 - \$9,900) = \$9,240$

b. First year: $3/4 \times 5/15 \times \$30,000 = \$7,500$
Second year: $(1/4 \times 5/15 \times \$30,000) + (3/4 \times 4/15 \times \$30,000)$
$= \$8,500$

Ex. 11-8 Book value, January 1, 1994 ($\$32,500 - \$12,000$) . . . . $\$20,500$
Less revised estimated residual value 2,100
Revised remaining depreciation . . . . $\$18,400$
Depreciation expense for 1994 ($\$18,400 \div 8$) . . . . $\$ \ 2,300$

Ex. 11-9 a. 15% of $\dfrac{\$297,750 + \$333,250}{2} = \$47,325$

b. 15% of $(\$297,750 + \$41,250 - \$16,500) = \$48,375$

Ex. 11-10

    a. $\$400,000 \div 25 = \$16,000$ annual depreciation
    b. Accumulated Depreciation—Building
    c. $\$800,000 - (\$400,000 - \$90,000) = \$490,000$
    d. $\$490,000 \div 35$ (25 years life remaining prior to repairs plus 10 additional years) $= \$14,000$ depreciation for current year

Ex. 11-11

    a. Cost of equipment . . . . $\$57,500$
Accumulated depreciation at December 31,
   1994 (4 years at $\$10,000$ per year) 40,000
Book value at December 31, 1994 . . . . $\$17,500$

    b. (1) Depreciation Expense—Equipment 5,000
         Accumulated Depreciation—Equipment   5,000

       (2) Cash 9,000
         Accumulated Depreciation—Equipment . . 45,000
         Loss on Disposal of Plant Assets 3,500
         Equipment   57,500

Ex. 11-12

a. 1991 depreciation expense: $5,000 [($25,000 − $5,000) ÷ 4]
   1992 depreciation expense: $5,000
   1993 depreciation expense: $5,000

b. $10,000 ($25,000 − $15,000)

c. Cash 8,500
   Accumulated Depreciation—Equipment 15,000
   Loss on Disposal of Plant Assets 1,500
      Equipment 25,000

d. Cash 11,500
   Accumulated Depreciation—Equipment 15,000
      Equipment 25,000
      Gain on Disposal of Plant Assets 1,500

Ex. 11-13

a. Depreciation Expense—Office Equipment 7,500
      Accumulated Depreciation—Office Equipment 7,500

b. Accumulated Depreciation—Office Equipment 57,500
   Office Equipment 125,000
   Loss on Disposal of Plant Assets 10,000
      Office Equipment 82,500
      Cash 30,000
      Notes Payable 80,000

Ex. 11-14

a. Depreciation Expense—Office Equipment 7,500
      Accumulated Depreciation—Office Equipment 7,500

b. Accumulated Depreciation—Office Equipment 70,000
   Office Equipment 122,500
      Office Equipment 82,500
      Cash 20,000
      Notes Payable 90,000

Ex. 11-15

a. 1. 20% of ($28,500 − $2,000) = $5,300
   2. same as (1)

b. 1. 20% of ($30,000 − $2,000) = $5,600
   2. 20% of ($31,000 − $2,000) = $5,800

Ex. 11-16

The managers at Programs Co. are not required to obtain approval before disposing of plant assets. Managers may be disposing of assets that are in good working order and that are needed at another location within the company. Alternatively, managers may be persuaded to sell used assets to employees and replace them with new assets, even though the older items are still in good working order.

Ex. 11-17

a. $3,000,000 ÷ 15,000,000 = $.20 depletion per ton
   600,000 × $.20 = $120,000 depletion expense

b. Depletion Expense.......................... 120,000
      Accumulated Depletion   120,000

Ex. 11-18

a. ($59,500 ÷ 17) + ($19,600 ÷ 14) = $4,900 total patent expense

b. Amortization Expense—Patents............ 4,900
      Patents....................................   4,900

WHAT'S WRONG WITH THIS?

1. Plant assets should be reported at cost and not replacement cost.
2. Land does not depreciate.
3. Patents and goodwill are intangible assets and should be listed in a separate section following the plant assets section.

PROBLEMS

Prob. 11-1A

1.

Item	Land	Land Improvements	Building	Other Accounts
a.	$225,000			
b.	15,000			
c.	900			
d.	18,500			
e.	11,250			
f.	1,500*			
g.	13,500			
h.			$ 105,000	
i.			9,000	
j.		$17,500		
k.		10,000		
l.	4,500			
m.				$ 3,500
n.				800
o.				3,300*
p.			85,000	
q.				1,000,000*
r.			1,250,000	
s.			750*	

*Indicates receipt

2. The periodic cost expiration for a plant asset due to the loss of the asset's ability to provide services is called depreciation. Since land used as a plant site does not lose its ability to provide services, it is not depreciated. However, land improvements do lose their ability to provide services as time passes and are therefore depreciated.

Prob. 11-2A

Depreciation Expense

Year	Straight-line method	Units-of-production method	Declining-balance method	Sum-of-the-years-digits method
1993	$28,000	$24,000	$60,000	$42,000
1994	28,000	33,600	20,000	28,000
1995	28,000	26,400	4,000	14,000
Total	$84,000	$84,000	$84,000	$84,000

Calculations:

Straight-line method:
($90,000 − $6,000) ÷ 3 = $28,000 each year

Units-of-production method:
($90,000 − $6,000) ÷ 7,000 = $12 per operating hour
1993 2,000 hours @ $12 = $24,000
1994 2,800 hours @ $12 = $33,600
1995 2,200 hours @ $12 = $26,400

Declining-balance method:
1993 $90,000 × 2/3 = $60,000
1994 ($90,000 − $60,000) × 2/3 = $20,000
1995 ($90,000 − $80,000) × 2/3 = $6,667. But maximum depreciation is $4,000 to not reduce book value below residual value of $6,000.

Sum-of-the-years-digits method:
1993 ($90,000 − $6,000) × 3/6 = $42,000
1994 ($90,000 − $6,000) × 2/6 = $28,000
1995 ($90,000 − $6,000) × 1/6 = $14,000

Prob. 11-3A

a. Straight-line method:

1993: [($72,000 − $3,000) ÷ 3] × 1/2 .... $11,500
1994: ($72,000 − $3,000) ÷ 3............................ 23,000
1995: ($72,000 − $3,000) ÷ 3............................ 23,000
1996: [($72,000 − $3,000) ÷ 3] × 1/2 11,500

b. Units-of-production method:

1993: 700 hours @ $10 .... $ 7,000
1994: 2,800 hours @ $10................................... 28,000
1995: 2,400 hours @ $10................................... 24,000
1996: 1,000 hours @ $10................................... 10,000

c. Declining-balance method:

1993: $72,000 × 2/3 × 1/2................................. $24,000
1994: ($72,000 − $24,000) × 2/3.......................... 32,000
1995: ($72,000 − $24,000 − $32,000) × 2/3 10,667
1996: $72,000 − $24,000 − $32,000 − $10,667 − $3,000* 2,333
*Book value should not be reduced below $3,000, the residual value.

d. Sum-of-the-years-digits method:

1993: [($72,000 − $3,000) × 3/6] × 1/2 .... $17,250
1994: [($72,000 − $3,000) × 3/6] × 1/2 +
      [($72,000 − $3,000) × 2/6] × 1/2 28,750
1995: [($72,000 − $3,000) × 2/6] × 1/2 +
      [($72,000 − $3,000) × 1/6] × 1/2 17,250
1996: [($72,000 − $3,000) × 1/6] × 1/2 5,750

Prob. 11-4A

1.

	Year	Depreciation Expense	Accumulated Depreciation, End of Year	Book Value, End of Year
a.	1	$18,750	$18,750	$61,250
	2	18,750	37,500	42,500
	3	18,750	56,250	23,750
	4	18,750	75,000	5,000
b.	1	$40,000	$40,000	$40,000
	2	20,000	60,000	20,000
	3	10,000	70,000	10,000
	4	5,000	75,000	5,000
c.	1	$30,000	$30,000	$50,000
	2	22,500	52,500	27,500
	3	15,000	67,500	12,500
	4	7,500	75,000	5,000

2. Book value of old equipment .... $ 10,000
Boot given (cash and notes payable) 185,000
Cost of new equipment $195,000

or

Price of new equipment $200,000
Less unrecognized gain on exchange.............. 5,000
Cost of new equipment $195,000

3. Accumulated Depreciation—Equipment 70,000
Equipment...................................... 195,000
   Equipment.. 80,000
   Cash 15,000
   Notes Payable 170,000

4. $195,000 (Same as 2.)

5. Accumulated Depreciation—Equipment 70,000
Equipment...................................... 200,000
Loss on Disposal of Plant Assets.................... 5,000
   Equipment.. 80,000
   Cash 15,000
   Notes Payable 180,000

Prob. 11-4A, Concluded

6. Book value of old equipment .... $ 10,000
    Boot given (cash and notes payable)   195,000
    Cost of new equipment $205,000

                             or

    Price of new equipment......................... $200,000
    Plus unrecognized loss on old equipment   5,000
    Cost of new equipment $205,000

Prob. 11-5A

a. (Equipment) Repair Expense...........................   750
       Factory Equipment....................................   750
b. Depreciation Expense—Office Equipment   100
       Accumulated Depreciation—Office Equipment........   100
    Accumulated Depreciation—Office Equipment..........   1,025
       Office Equipment   975
       Gain on Disposal of Plant Assets.....................   50
c. Land   4,000
       Property Tax Expense   4,000
d. Gain on Disposal of Plant Assets   3,800
       Office Equipment   3,800
e. Accumulated Depreciation—Delivery Equipment........   1,100
       Delivery Expense.....................................   1,100
f. Factory Equipment....................................   450
       Transportation In   450
g. Land   30,000
       Loss on Disposal of Plant Assets....................   30,000
h. Land   7,500
       Miscellaneous Expense...............................   7,500
i. (Building) Repair Expense   7,750
       Building   7,750

Prob. 11-6A

1993

July	3	Delivery Equipment	15,000	
		Cash		15,000
	6	Delivery Equipment	1,000	
		Cash		1,000
Dec.	7	Truck Repair Expense	215	
		Cash		215

1994

June	30	Depreciation Expense—Delivery Equipment	4,000	
		Accumulated Depreciation—Delivery Equipment (25% × $16,000)		4,000
	30	Income Summary	4,215	
		Depreciation Expense—Delivery Equipment		4,000
		Truck Repair Expense		215
Aug.	29	Truck Repair Expense	240	
		Cash		240
Oct.	31	Depreciation Expense—Delivery Equipment	1,000	
		Accumulated Depreciation—Delivery Equipment		1,000
	31	Accumulated Depreciation—Delivery Equipment	5,000	
		Delivery Equipment	27,000	
		Delivery Equipment		16,000
		Cash		16,000

1995

June	30	Depreciation Expense—Delivery Equipment	3,600	
		Accumulated Depreciation—Delivery Equipment (8/12 × 20% × $27,000)		3,600
		Income Summary	4,840	
		Depreciation Expense—Delivery Equipment		4,600
		Truck Repair Expense		240

1996

Apr.	1	Delivery Equipment	30,000	
		Cash		30,000
	2	Depreciation Expense—Delivery Equipment	3,510	
		Accumulated Depreciation—Delivery Equipment [9/12 × 20%($27,000 − $3,600)]		3,510
	2	Cash	20,500	
		Accumulated Depreciation—Delivery Equipment	7,110	
		Delivery Equipment		27,000
		Gain on Disposal of Plant Assets		610

Prob. 11-6A, Continued

				Dr.	Cr.
June 30	Depreciation Expense—Delivery Equipment			1,875	
	Accumulated Depreciation—Delivery Equipment				
	(3/12 × 25% × $30,000).....................				1,875
30	Income Summary			4,775	
	Gain on Disposal of Plant Assets.................			610	
	Depreciation Expense—Delivery Equipment.....				5,385

Delivery Equipment   122

					Balance	
Date		Item	Dr.	Cr.	Dr.	Cr.
1993						
July	3	....	15,000	......	15,000	......
	6	....	1,000	......	16,000	......
1994						
Oct.	31	....	27,000	......	43,000	......
	31	....	......	16,000	27,000	......
1996						
Apr.	1	....	30,000	......	57,000	......
	2	....	......	27,000	30,000	......

Accumulated Depreciation—Delivery Equipment   123

1994						
June	30	....	......	4,000	......	4,000
Oct.	31	....	......	1,000	......	5,000
	31	....	5,000	......	—	—
1995						
June	30	....	......	3,600	......	3,600
1996						
Apr.	2	....	......	3,510	......	7,110
	2	....	7,110	......	—	—
June	30	....	......	1,875	......	1,875

Prob. 11-6A, Concluded

Depreciaton Expense—Delivery Equipment 616

Date	Item	Dr.	Cr.	Balance Dr.	Balance Cr.
1994					
June 30	....	4,000	......	4,000	......
30	....	......	4,000	—	—
Oct. 31	....	1,000	......	1,000	......
1995					
June 30	....	3,600	......	4,600	......
30	....	......	4,600	—	—
1996					
Apr. 2	....	3,510	......	3,510	......
June 30	....	1,875	......	5,385	......
30	....	......	5,385	—	—

Truck Repair Expense 617

Date	Item	Dr.	Cr.	Balance Dr.	Balance Cr.
1993					
Dec. 7	....	215	......	215	......
1994					
June 30	....	......	215	—	—
Aug. 29	....	240	......	240	......
1995					
June 30	....	......	240	—	—

Gain on Disposal of Plant Assets 812

Date	Item	Dr.	Cr.	Balance Dr.	Balance Cr.
1996					
Apr. 2	....	......	610	......	610
June 30	....	610	......	—	—

Prob. 11-7A

1, 2, and 3.

1993			
June 30	Printing Equipment	108,000	
	Accounts Payable—Kunz Manufacturing Co ..		108,000
Dec. 31	Depreciation Expense—Printing Equipment	73,400	
	Accumulated Depreciation—Printing Equipment.................................		73,400

Prob. 11-7A, Continued

1994

			Dr.	Cr.
Sep.	30	Depreciation Expense—Printing Equipment	3,750	
		Accumulated Depreciation—Printing Equipment..................................		3,750
	30	Accumulated Depreciation—Printing Equipment.....................................	25,000	
		Printing Equipment	60,000	
		Loss on Disposal of Plant Assets	2,000	
		Printing Equipment		42,000
		Cash		20,000
		Notes Payable		25,000

GENERAL LEDGER

Printing Equipment 125

Date	Item	Dr.	Cr.	Balance Dr.	Balance Cr.
1993					
Jan. 1	Balance......................	......	......	527,650	......
June 30	....	108,000	......	635,650	....
1994					
Sep. 30	....	60,000	......	695,650	....
30	....	....	42,000	653,650	....

Accumulated Depreciation—Printing Equipment 126

Date	Item	Dr.	Cr.	Balance Dr.	Balance Cr.
1993					
Jan. 1	Balance......................	......	....	....	205,700
Dec. 31	....	......	73,400	....	279,100
1994					
Sep. 30	....	....	3,750	....	282,850
30	....	25,000	......	....	257,850

Prob. 11-7A, Concluded

PRINTING EQUIPMENT LEDGER

Linotype 125–30

Date	Explanation	Asset			Accumulated Depreciation			Book Value
		Dr.	Cr.	Bal.	Dr.	Cr.	Bal.	
12-31-93	....	......	.....	....	......	2,700	17,100	11,400

Press 125–31

Date	Explanation	Asset			Accumulated Depreciation			Book Value
		Dr.	Cr.	Bal.	Dr.	Cr.	Bal.	
12-31-93	....	......	.....	....	......	5,000	21,250	20,750
9-30-94	....	......	.....	....	......	3,750	25,000	17,000
9-30-94	....	......	42,000	—	25,000	.....	—	—

Power Binder 125–32

Date	Explanation	Asset			Accumulated Depreciation			Book Value
6-30-93	....	108,000	.....	108,000	......	......	......	108,000
12-31-93	....	......	.....	....	......	4,500	4,500	103,500

Press 125–33

Date	Explanation	Asset			Accumulated Depreciation			Book Value
9-30-94	....	60,000	.....	60,000	......	.....	......	60,000

4. a. $1/4 \times (20\% \times \$60,000) = \$3,000$ b. $20\% \times (\$60,000 - \$3,000) = \$11,400$

Prob. 11-8A

1.

MARTIN COMPANY
Income Statement
For Year Ended December 31, 19—

Sales		$996,950
Cost of merchandise sold:		
Merchandise inventory, January 1, 19—	$178,700	
Purchases	702,350	
Merchandise available for sale	$881,050	
Less merchandise inventory, December 31, 19—	171,000	
Cost of merchandise sold		710,050
Gross profit		$286,900
Operating expenses		182,000*
Income from operations		$104,900
Other expense:		
Interest expense		1,900
Net income		$103,000

*Computation of operating expenses:

Operating expenses (trial balance before adjustments)	$140,500
Uncollectible accounts expense ($6,100 − $500)	5,600
Insurance and other prepaid operating expenses	7,250
Depreciation expense—office equipment [($27,900 + $31,100) ÷ 2] × 10%	2,950
Depreciation expense—store equipment [($48,500 + $51,500) ÷ 2] × 8%	4,000
Depreciation expense—delivery equipment [($57,150 + $57,850) ÷ 2] × 20%	11,500
Depreciation expense—buildings $225,000 × 2%	4,500
Amortization expense—patents	3,000
Wages and other operating expenses	2,700
Operating expenses (after adjustments)	$182,000

Prob. 11-8A, Concluded

2.

MARTIN COMPANY
Balance Sheet
December 31, 19—

Assets

Current assets:

Cash		$ 30,100
Accounts receivable	$60,200	
Less allowance for doubtful accounts	6,100	54,100
Merchandise inventory		171,000
Prepaid expense		4,000
Total current assets		$259,200

Plant assets:

	Cost	Accumulated Depreciation	Book Value
Land	$ 50,000	—	$ 50,000
Buildings	225,000	$90,500	134,500
Office equipment	31,100	14,550	16,550
Store equipment	51,500	25,400	26,100
Delivery equipment	57,850	33,250	24,600
Total plant assets			251,750

Intangible assets:

Patents	15,000
Total assets	$525,950

Liabilities

Current liabilities:

Accounts payable	$ 40,200
Notes payable	20,000
Accrued liabilities	3,000
Total liabilities	$ 63,200

Owner's Equity

R.C. Martin, capital*		462,750
Total liabilities and owner's equity		$525,950

*Computation of owner's equity:

Balance, January 1, 19—		$429,750
Net income for year	$103,000	
Less withdrawals	70,000	33,000
Balance, December 31, 19—		$462,750

Prob. 11-9A

1. a. $50,000 ÷ 500,000 board feet = $.10 per board foot; 75,000 board feet × $.10 per board foot = $7,500

   b. $160,000 ÷ 40 years (maximum period of amortization) = $4,000

   c. $24,800 ÷ 8 years = $3,100; 1/2 of $3,100 = $1,550

2. a. Depletion Expense.................................... 7,500
         Accumulated Depletion............................   7,500

   b. Amortization Expense—Goodwill................. 4,000
         Goodwill..   4,000

   c. Amortization Expense—Patents................... 1,550
         Patents...   1,550

Prob. 11-1B

1.

Item	Land	Land Improvements	Building	Other Accounts
a.	$190,000	....	....	....
b.	8,750	....	....	....
c.	5,800	....	....	....
d.	900	....	....	....
e.	9,700	....	....	....
f.	....	....	$ 60,000	....
g.	....	....	5,500	....
h.	....	....	750,000	....
i.	....	....	....	$ 1,500
j.	....	$12,500	....	....
k.	....	15,000	....	....
l.	2,500	....	....	....
m.	....	....	....	500
n.	....	....	39,000	....
o.	....	13,500	....	....
p.	1,100*	....	....	....
q.	....	....	....	600,000*
r.	....	....	....	1,000*
s.	....	....	350*	....

*Indicates receipt

2. The periodic cost expiration for a plant asset due to the loss of the asset's ability to provide services is called depreciation. Since land used as a plant site does not lose its ability to provide services, it is not depreciated. However, land improvements do lose their ability to provide services as time passes and are therefore depreciated.

Prob. 11-2B

Depreciation Expense

Year	Straight-line method	Units-of-production method	Declining-balance method	Sum-of-the-years-digits method
1993	$30,000	$30,000	$66,000	$45,000
1994	30,000	38,000	22,000	30,000
1995	30,000	22,000	2,000	15,000
Total	$90,000	$90,000	$90,000	$90,000

Calculations:

Straight-line method:
($99,000 − $9,000) ÷ 3 = $30,000 each year

Units-of-production method:
($99,000 − $9,000) ÷ 9,000 = $10 per operating hour
1993   3,000 hours @ $10 = $30,000
1994   3,800 hours @ $10 = $38,000
1995   2,200 hours @ $10 = $22,000

Declining-balance method:
1993 $99,000 × 2/3 = $66,000
1994   ($99,000 − $66,000) × 2/3 = $22,000
1995   ($99,000 − $88,000) × 2/3 = $7,333. But maximum depreciation is $2,000 to not reduce book value below residual value of $9,000.

Sum-of-the-years-digits method:
1993   ($99,000 − $9,000) × 3/6 = $45,000
1994   ($99,000 − $9,000) × 2/6 = $30,000
1995   ($99,000 − $9,000) × 1/6 = $15,000

Prob. 11-3B

a. **Straight-line method:**

1993: [($90,000 − $6,000) ÷ 3] × 1/2	**$14,000**
1994: ($90,000 − $6,000) ÷ 3................................	**28,000**
1995: ($90,000 − $6,000) ÷ 3................................	**28,000**
1996: [($90,000 − $6,000) ÷ 3] × 1/2	**14,000**

b. **Units-of-production method:**

1993: 1,400 hours @ $6*	**$ 8,400**
1994: 5,600 hours @ $6	**33,600**
1995: 4,800 hours @ $6	**28,800**
1996: 2,200 hours @ $6	**13,200**

*($90,000 − $6,000) ÷ 14,000 = $6

c. **Declining-balance method:**

1993: $90,000 × 2/3 × 1/2	**$30,000**
1994: ($90,000 − $30,000) × 2/3.............................	**40,000**
1995: ($90,000 − $30,000 − $40,000) × 2/3	**13,333**
1996: $90,000 − $30,000 − $40,000 − $13,333 − $6,000*	**667**

*Book value should not be reduced below $6,000, the residual value.

d. **Sum-of-the-years-digits method:**

1993: [($90,000 − $6,000) × 3/6] × 1/2	**$21,000**
1994: [($90,000 − $6,000) × 3/6] × 1/2 +	
[($90,000 − $6,000) × 2/6] × 1/2	**35,000**
1995: [($90,000 − $6,000) × 2/6] × 1/2 +	
[($90,000 − $6,000) × 1/6] × 1/2	**21,000**
1996: [($90,000 − $6,000) × 1/6] × 1/2	**7,000**

Prob. 11-4B

1.

	Year	Depreciation Expense	Accumulated Depreciation, End of Year	Book Value, End of Year
a.	1	$24,000	$ 24,000	$101,000
	2	24,000	48,000	77,000
	3	24,000	72,000	53,000
	4	24,000	96,000	29,000
	5	24,000	120,000	5,000
b.	1	$50,000	$ 50,000	$ 75,000
	2	30,000	80,000	45,000
	3	18,000	98,000	27,000
	4	10,800	108,800	16,200
	5	6,480	115,280	9,720
c.	1	$40,000	$ 40,000	$ 85,000
	2	32,000	72,000	53,000
	3	24,000	96,000	29,000
	4	16,000	112,000	13,000
	5	8,000	120,000	5,000

2. Book value of old equipment.................................... $ 16,200
Boot given (cash and notes payable) 150,000
Cost of new equipment $166,200

or

Price of new equipment.. $170,000
Less unrecognized gain on exchange........................... 3,800
Cost of new equipment $166,200

3. Accumulated Depreciation—Equipment.............. 108,800
Equipment 166,200
  Equipment 125,000
  Cash... 25,000
  Notes Payable..................................... 125,000

4. $166,200 (Same as 2.)

5. Accumulated Depreciation—Equipment.............. 108,800
Equipment 170,000
Loss on Disposal of Plant Assets.................... 6,200
  Equipment 125,000
  Cash... 25,000
  Notes Payable..................................... 135,000

Prob. 11-4B, Concluded

6. Book value of old equipment........................... $ 16,200
   Boot given (cash and notes payable)   160,000
   Cost of new equipment $176,200

   or

   Price of new equipment............................... $170,000
   Plus unrecognized loss on old equipment   6,200
   Cost of new equipment $176,200

Prob. 11-5B

a. (Equipment) Repair Expense............................   900
      Equipment...   900

b. Gain on Disposal of Plant Assets 3,800
      Store Equipment...................................   3,800

c. Land... 3,000
      Property Tax Expense   3,000

d. Depreciation Expense—Office Equipment   800
      Accumulated Depreciation—Office Equipment........   800

   Accumulated Depreciation—Office Equipment..........   6,800
      Office Equipment   6,050
      Gain on Disposal of Plant Assets.................   750

e. Accumulated Depreciation—Delivery Equipment........   2,250
      Delivery Expense..................................   2,250

f. (Building) Repair Expense 12,500
      Building   12,500

g. Land 25,000
      Loss on Disposal of Plant Assets..................   25,000

h. Land   4,000
      Miscellaneous Expense   4,000

i. Store Equipment   250
      Transportation In   250

Prob. 11-6B

1993

Jan.	2	Delivery Equipment	10,800	
		Cash..		10,800
	5	Delivery Equipment	1,200	
		Cash..		1,200
Sep.	17	Truck Repair Expense.............................	225	
		Cash..		225
Dec.	31	Depreciation Expense—Delivery Equipment	6,000	
		Accumulated Depreciation—Delivery Equipment		
		(50% × $12,000).............................		6,000
	31	Income Summary	6,225	
		Depreciation Expense—Delivery Equipment.....		6,000
		Truck Repair Expense..........................		225

1994

June	30	Depreciation Expense—Delivery Equipment	1,500	
		Accumulated Depreciation—Delivery Equipment		1,500
	30	Accumulated Depreciation—Delivery Equipment ..	7,500	
		Delivery Equipment	24,500	
		Delivery Equipment............................		12,000
		Cash..		20,000
Nov.	4	Truck Repair Expense	195	
		Cash..		195
Dec.	31	Depreciation Expense—Delivery Equipment	4,900	
		Accumulated Depreciation—Delivery Equipment		
		(6/12 × 40% × $24,500).......................		4,900
	31	Income Summary	6,595	
		Depreciation Expense—Delivery Equipment.....		6,400
		Truck Repair Expense..........................		195

1995

Oct.	1	Delivery Equipment	24,400	
		Cash..		24,400
	2	Depreciation Expense—Delivery Equipment	5,880	
		Accumulated Depreciation—Delivery Equipment		
		[9/12 × 40% × ($24,500 − $4,900)]		5,880
	2	Cash..	15,000	
		Accumulated Depreciation—Delivery Equipment ..	10,780	
		Delivery Equipment............................		24,500
		Gain on Disposal of Plant Assets		1,280

Prob. 11-6B, Continued

Dec. 31	Depreciation Expense—Delivery Equipment	1,525	
	Accumulated Depreciation—Delivery Equipment (3/12 × 25% × $24,400).....................		1,525
31	Income Summary	6,125	
	Gain on Disposal of Plant Assets.................	1,280	
	Depreciation Expense—Delivery Equipment.....		7,405

Delivery Equipment   122

					Balance	
Date	Item	Dr.	Cr.	Dr.	Cr.
1993					
Jan. 2	....	10,800	......	10,800	......
5	....	1,200	......	12,000	......
1994					
June 30	....	24,500	......	36,500	......
30	....	......	12,000	24,500	......
1995					
Oct. 1	....	24,400	......	48,900	......
2	....	......	24,500	24,400	......

Accumulated Depreciation—Delivery Equipment   123

1993					
Dec. 31	....	......	6,000	......	6,000
1994					
June 30	....	......	1,500	......	7,500
30	....	7,500	......	—	—
Dec. 31	....	......	4,900	......	4,900
1995					
Oct. 2	....	......	5,880	......	10,780
2	....	10,780	......	—	—
Dec. 31	....	......	1,525	......	1,525

Prob. 11-6B, Concluded

Depreciation Expense—Delivery Equipment   616

Date	Item	Dr.	Cr.	Balance Dr.	Balance Cr.
1993					
Dec. 31	....	6,000	......	6,000	......
31	....	......	6,000	—	—
1994					
June 30	....	1,500	......	1,500	......
Dec. 31	....	4,900	......	6,400	......
31	....	......	6,400	—	—
1995					
Oct. 2	....	5,880	......	5,880	......
Dec. 31	....	1,525	......	7,405	......
31	....	......	7,405	—	—

Truck Repair Expense   617

Date	Item	Dr.	Cr.	Balance Dr.	Balance Cr.
1993					
Sep. 17	....	225	......	225	......
Dec. 31	....	......	225	—	—
1994					
Nov. 4	....	195	......	195	......
Dec. 31	....	......	195	—	—

Gain on Disposal of Plant Assets   812

Date	Item	Dr.	Cr.	Balance Dr.	Balance Cr.
1995					
Oct. 2	....	......	1,280	......	1,280
Dec. 31	....	1,280	......	—	—

Prob. 11-7B

1, 2, and 3.

1993			
Sep. 1	Printing Equipment	60,000	
	Accounts Payable—King Manufacturing Co.		60,000
Dec. 31	Depreciation Expense—Printing Equipment	77,900	
	Accumulated Depreciation—Printing Equipment .		77,900

Prob. 11-7B, Continued

1994

Mar. 31 Depreciation Expense—Printing Equipment 1,250
        Accumulated Depreciation—Printing Equipment .   1,250

    31 Accumulated Depreciation—Printing Equipment... 22,500
       Printing Equipment 47,000
           Printing Equipment   42,000
           Cash   7,500
           Notes Payable   20,000

GENERAL LEDGER

Printing Equipment   **125**

Date	Item	Dr.	Cr.	Balance Dr.	Balance Cr.
1993					
Jan. 1	Balance......................	......	......	527,650	......
Sep. 1	....	60,000	......	587,650	......
1994					
Mar. 31	....	47,000	......	634,650	......
31	....	......	42,000	592,650	......

Accumulated Depreciation—Printing Equipment   **126**

Date	Item	Dr.	Cr.	Balance Dr.	Balance Cr.
1993					
Jan. 1	Balance......................	......	......	......	205,700
Dec. 31	....	......	77,900	......	283,600
1994					
Mar. 31	....	......	1,250	......	284,850
31	....	22,500	......	......	262,350

Prob. 11-7B, Concluded

PRINTING EQUIPMENT LEDGER

Linotype   125–30

Date	Explanation	Asset			Accumulated Depreciation			Book Value
		Dr.	Cr.	Bal.	Dr.	Cr.	Bal.	
12-31-93	....	......	......	....	......	2,700	17,100	11,400

Press   125–31

Date	Explanation	Dr.	Cr.	Bal.	Dr.	Cr.	Bal.	Book Value
12-31-93	....	......	......	....	......	5,000	21,250	20,750
3-31-94	....	......	......	....	......	1,250	22,500	19,500
3-31-94	....	......	42,000	—	22,500	.....	—	—

Power Binder   125–32

Date	Explanation	Dr.	Cr.	Bal.	Dr.	Cr.	Bal.	Book Value
9-1-93	....	60,000	.....	60,000	......	.....	......	60,000
12-31-93	....	......	.....	....	......	2,000	2,000	58,000

Press   125–33

Date	Explanation	Dr.	Cr.	Bal.	Dr.	Cr.	Bal.	Book Value
3-31-94	....	47,000	.....	47,000	......	.....	......	47,000

4. a. $3/4(20\% \times \$47,000) = \$7,050$ b. $20\%(\$47,000 - \$7,050) = \$7,990$

Prob. 11-8B

1.

TREADWAY COMPANY
Income Statement
For Year Ended December 31, 19—

Sales		$999,750
Cost of merchandise sold:		
Merchandise inventory, January 1, 19—	$179,200	
Purchases.......................................	706,550	
Merchandise available for sale	$885,750	
Less merchandise inventory, December 31, 19— ..	171,000	
Cost of merchandise sold		714,750
Gross profit.....................................		$285,000
Operating expenses		186,806*
Income from operations		$ 98,194
Other expense:		
Interest expense................................		1,850
Net income		$ 96,344

*Computation of operating expenses:	
Operating expenses (trial balance before	
adjustments)...................................	$144,600
Uncollectible accounts expense ($7,200 − $500).....	6,700
Insurance and other prepaid operating expenses	6,750
Depreciation expense—office equipment	
[($37,900 + $41,100) ÷ 2] × 10%.................	3,950
Depreciation expense—store equipment	
[($49,200 + $52,200) ÷ 2] × 8%.................	4,056
Depreciation expense—delivery equipment	
[($57,150 + $57,850) ÷ 2] × 20%.................	11,500
Depreciation expense—buildings	
$225,000 × 2%	4,500
Amortization expense—patents.....................	3,000
Wages and other operating expenses...............	1,750
Operating expenses (after adjustments)	$186,806

Prob. 11-8B, Concluded

2.
TREADWAY COMPANY
Balance Sheet
December 31, 19—

Assets

Current assets:

Cash			$ 30,700
Accounts receivable		$62,600	
Less allowance for doubtful accounts		7,200	55,400
Merchandise inventory			171,000
Prepaid expense			4,000
Total current assets			$261,100

Plant assets:

	Cost	Accumulated Depreciation	Book Value	
Land	$ 55,000	—	$ 55,000	
Buildings	225,000	$94,500	130,500	
Office equipment	41,100	21,550	19,550	
Store equipment	52,200	26,156	26,044	
Delivery equipment	57,850	33,250	24,600	
Total plant assets				255,694

Intangible assets		
Patents		15,000
Total assets		$531,794

Liabilities

Current liabilities:

Accounts payable		$ 43,200
Notes payable		30,000
Accrued liabilities		2,000
Total liabilities		$ 75,200

Owner's Equity

D. D. Treadway, capital*		456,594
Total liabilities and owner's equity		$531,794

*Computation of owner's equity:

Balance, January 1, 19—		$430,250
Net income for year	$ 96,344	
Less withdrawals	70,000	26,344
Balance, December 31, 19—		$456,594

Prob. 11-9B

1. **a.** $60,000 ÷ 500,000 board feet = $.12 per board foot; 50,000 board feet × $.12 per board foot = $6,000

b. $150,000 ÷ 40 years (maximum period of amortization) = $3,750

c. $20,000 ÷ 8 years = $2,500; 1/2 of $2,500 = $1,250

2. **a.**

Depletion Expense.............................	6,000	
Accumulated Depletion........................		6,000

b.

Amortization Expense—Goodwill	3,750	
Goodwill		3,750

c.

Amortization Expense—Patents................	1,250	
Patents..		1,250

Mini-Case 11

1. **a.** Straight-line method:

1994: ($120,000 ÷ 5) × 1/2.............................	$12,000
1995: ($120,000 ÷ 5).....................................	24,000
1996: ($120,000 ÷ 5).....................................	24,000
1997: ($120,000 ÷ 5).....................................	24,000
1998: ($120,000 ÷ 5).....................................	24,000
1999: ($120,000 ÷ 5) × 1/2.............................	12,000

b. MACRS:

1994: ($120,000 × 20%)	$24,000
1995: ($120,000 × 32%)	38,400
1996: ($120,000 × 19.2%)	23,040
1997: ($120,000 × 11.5%)	13,800
1998: ($120,000 × 11.5%)	13,800
1999: ($120,000 × 5.8%).................................	6,960

Mini-Case 11, Continued

2. **a.** <u>Straight-line method</u>

			Year				
		1994	1995	1996	1997	1998	1999
Income before depreciation	...	$200,000	$200,000	$200,000	$200,000	$200,000	$200,000
Depreciation expense	...	12,000	24,000	24,000	24,000	24,000	12,000
Income before income tax	...	$188,000	$176,000	$176,000	$176,000	$176,000	$188,000
Income tax	...	56,400	52,800	52,800	52,800	52,800	56,400
Net income	...	$131,600	$123,200	$123,200	$123,200	$123,200	$131,600

b. **MACRS**

			Year				
		1994	1995	1996	1997	1998	1999
Income before depreciation	...	$200,000	$200,000	$200,000	$200,000	$200,000	$200,000
Depreciation expense	...	24,000	38,400	23,040	13,800	13,800	6,960
Income before income tax	...	$176,000	$161,600	$176,960	$186,200	$186,200	$193,040
Income tax	...	52,800	48,480	53,088	55,860	55,860	57,912
Net income	...	$123,200	$113,120	$123,872	$130,340	$130,340	$135,128

Mini-Case 11, Concluded

3. For financial reporting purposes, Wilde should select the method that provides the net income figure that best represents the results of operations. (*Note to Instructors:* The concept of matching revenues and expenses is discussed in Chapter 3 and also in Chapter 13.) However, for income tax purposes, Wilde should consider selecting the method that will minimize taxes. Based upon the analyses in (2), both methods of depreciation will yield the same total amount of taxes over the useful life of the equipment. MACRS results in less taxes paid in the early years of useful life and more in the later years. For example, in 1994 the MACRS amount is less than the straight-line amount. Wilde and Company can invest such differences in the early years and earn income.

   In some situations, it may be more beneficial for a taxpayer not to choose MACRS. These situations usually occur when a taxpayer is expected to be subject to a low tax rate in the early years of use of an asset and a higher tax rate in the later years of the asset's useful life. In this case, the taxpayer may be better off to defer the larger deductions to offset the higher tax rate.

CHAPTER 12

DISCUSSION QUESTIONS

1. Payroll

2. a. Yes
   b. Yes

3. Bonus = .06 ($250,000 − Bonus − Taxes)
   Taxes = .35 ($250,000 − Bonus)
       B = .06 [$250,000 − B − .35($250,000 − B)]
       B = .06 ($250,000 − B − $87,500 + .35B)
       B = $15,000 − .06B − $5,250 + .021B
   1.039B = $9,750
       B = $9,384.02

4. a. Gross pay is the total earnings of an employee for a payroll period.
   b. Net, or take-home, pay is the amount to be paid to an employee on payday. Gross pay (earnings) for the payroll period less the deductions yields the amount to be paid.

5. Combined federal programs for old-age and disability benefits, insurance benefits to survivors, and health insurance for the aged (Medicare).

6. a. Income or withholding taxes and FICA.
   b. Employees Income Tax Payable and FICA Tax Payable.

7. There is a ceiling on (a) FICA tax and (c) federal unemployment compensation tax.

8. $990 [(40 × $18) + (10 × $27)]

9. $720.75 ($990 − $74.25 − $195)

10. The FICA tax, the federal unemployment compensation tax, and the state unemployment compensation tax.

11. The deductions from employee earnings are for amounts owed (liabilities) to others for such items as federal taxes, state and local income taxes, and contributions to pension plans.

12. Payroll taxes levied against employers become liabilities only at the time the related remuneration is paid to the employees.

13. Yes. Unemployment compensation taxes are paid by the employer on the first $7,000 of annual earnings for each employee. Therefore, hiring two employees, each earning $12,500 per year, would require the payment of more unemployment tax than if only one employee, earning $25,000, was hired.

14. a. employees only: (2) federal income tax
    b. employers only: (3) federal unemployment compensation tax and (4) state unemployment compensation tax
    c. both employees and employers: (1) FICA tax

15. The employee's earnings record reveals the cumulative earnings for the year to date. This information is used to determine the amount of FICA tax to be withheld from the earnings of each employee and to prepare quarterly and annual payroll tax returns. The earnings record may also be used in determining the rights of employees to bonuses, pensions, and vacation leaves, and in answering questions in connection with the Federal Wage and Hour Law.

16. a. Obtaining the exact amount of money needed for the payroll provides control over the funds. Errors in inserting the currency in the envelopes are less likely to occur, and if any do occur, they are more likely to be discovered. There is also less likelihood of theft by employees.
    b. List names and net pay of employees on an analysis sheet, with a column for each denomination, beginning with the largest to be used (perhaps $20 bill) and proceeding down to 1¢. For each amount of net pay, determine and insert in the columns the number of each denomination needed. The accuracy (barring compensating errors) of the numbers can be proved by adding each column, multiplying by the respective values of the bills and coins and comparing the sum of these products with the total amount of the net pay.

17. The use of special payroll checks relieves the treasurer or other executives of the task of signing a large number of regular checks each payday. Another advantage of this system is that reconciling the regular bank statement is simplified. The paid payroll checks are returned by the bank separately from regular checks and are accompanied by a statement of the special bank account. Any balance shown on the bank's statement will correspond to the sum of the payroll checks outstanding because the amount of each deposit is exactly the same as the total amount of checks drawn.

18. a. Deposits are made at the end of each pay period, that is, weekly.
    b. The amount of the deposit is equal to the net amount to be paid, according to the payroll register.
    c. There is no need for a payroll bank account in the ledger because the total of the payroll

checks drawn on the account is equal to the amount of the deposit.

    d. The credit balance of $7,127.50 represents the total amount of payroll checks that have not been presented to the bank for payment; it is the sum of the outstanding checks.

19. a. Input data that remain relatively unchanged from period to period (and therefore do not need to be reintroduced into the system frequently) are called constants.
    b. Input data that differ from period to period are called variables.

20. Personnel Department

21. a. If employee's attendance records are kept and their preparation supervised in such a manner as to prevent errors and abuses, then one can be assured that wages paid are based upon hours actually worked. The use of "In and Out" cards, whereby employees indicate by punching a time clock their time of arrival and departure, is especially useful. Employee identification cards or badges can be very helpful in giving additional assurance.
    b. The requirement that the addition of names on the payroll be supported by written authorizations from the Personnel Department can help ensure that payroll checks are not being issued to fictitious persons. Endorsements on payroll checks can be compared with other samples of employees' signatures.

22. Employee fringe benefits are benefits in addition to salary and wages earned, such as vacations, employee pension plans, and health, life and disability insurance.

23. If the vacation payment is probable and can be reasonably estimated, the vacation pay expense should be recorded during the period in which the vacation privilege is earned.

24. A contributory pension plan requires contributions by both the employer and employee. A noncontributory plan requires contributions by only the employer.

25. Employee life expectancies, expected employee retirement dates, employee turnover, employee compensation levels, and investment income on pension contributions.

26. Prior service cost arises in a new or revised pension plan when a company grants pension benefits to employees for prior years of service.

27. Current liability or long-term liability, depending upon when the unfunded pension liability is to be paid.

28. Alternative (2) would be preferred by the bank. Under both alternatives, the interest rate is 10% and interest earned is $500 ($30,000 × 60/360 × 10%). However, alternative (1) would require lending $30,000, while alternative (2) would require lending only $29,500 ($30,000 − $500 discount).

29. a. Accounts Payable 15,000
       Notes Payable......... 15,000
    b. Notes Payable 15,000
       Interest Expense 375
       Cash 15,375

30. No. After the bank deducts the amount of the discount of $1,000 (12% × $50,000 × 60/360) from the face amount, the proceeds are $49,000.

31. To match revenues and expenses properly, the liability to cover product warranties should be recorded in the period during which the sale of the product is made.

32. a. Product Warranty
      Expense 48,614,000
      Product Warranty
      Payable 48,614,000
    b. When the defective product is repaired, the repair costs would be recorded by debiting Product Warranty Payable and crediting Cash, Supplies, or another appropriate account.

33. Since the $5,000 is payable within one year, Company A should present it as a current liability at September 30.

ETHICS DISCUSSION CASE Ellen should bring the error to the attention of her employer. To do otherwise would not be trustworthy. An essential element of the character of a professional is a high level of personal integrity. Thus, it would be unethical for Ellen to cash her payroll check without bringing the error to the attention of her employer.

EXERCISES

Ex. 12-1 a. Bonus = .05($400,000)
B = $20,000

b. Bonus = .05($400,000 − Bonus − Taxes)
Taxes = .35($400,000 − Bonus)
B = .05[$400,000 − B − .35($400,000 − B)]
B = .05($400,000 − B − $140,000 + .35B)
B = $20,000 − .05B − $7,000 + .0175B
1.0325B = $13,000
B = $12,590.80

Ex. 12-2 a. Summary: (1) $88,900; (3) $95,000; (7) $1,150; (11) $16,000
Details:

Net amount paid		$75,550
Total deductions		19,450
(3) Total earnings		$95,000
Overtime		6,100
(1) Regular		$88,900
Total deductions		$19,450
FICA tax	$ 6,500	
Income tax withheld	10,750	
Medical insurance	1,050	18,300
(7) Union dues		$ 1,150
Total earnings		$95,000
Factory wages	$71,500	
Office salaries	7,500	79,000
(11) Sales salaries		$16,000

b.

Factory Wages Expense	71,500	
Sales Salaries Expense	16,000	
Office Salaries Expense	7,500	
FICA Tax Payable		6,500
Employees Income Tax Payable		10,750
Union Dues Payable		1,150
Medical Insurance Payable		1,050
Salaries Payable		75,550

c.

Salaries Payable	75,550	
Accounts Payable		75,550

d.

Accounts Payable	75,550	
Cash		75,550

e. The amount of FICA tax withheld, $6,500, is less than 7.5% of the total earnings of $95,000. This indicates that the cumulative earnings of some employees exceed $60,000. Therefore, it is unlikely that this payroll was paid during the first few weeks of the calendar year.

Ex. 12-3 Gem City Sounds does have an internal control procedure which should detect the payroll error. Before funds are transferred from the regular bank account to the payroll account, the owner authorizes a voucher for the total amount of the week's payroll. The owner should catch the error, since the extra 360 hours will cause the weekly payroll to be substantially higher than usual.

Ex. 12-4 a. Appropriate. The use of a special payroll account assists in preventing fraud and makes it easier to reconcile the company's bank accounts.

b. Inappropriate. Access to the check-signing machine should be restricted.

c. Inappropriate. Each employee should record his or her own time out for lunch. Under the current procedures, one employee could clock in several employees who are still out to lunch. The company would be paying employees for more time than they actually worked.

d. Appropriate. All changes to the payroll system, including wage rate increases, should be authorized by someone outside the Payroll Department.

e. Inappropriate. Payroll should be informed when any employee is terminated. A supervisor or other individual could continue to clock in and out for the terminated employee and collect the extra paycheck.

Ex. 12-5 a.

FICA [(7.5% × $510,000) + (1.5% × $30,000)]		$38,700
State unemployment (4.3% × $15,000)		645
Federal unemployment (.8% × $15,000)		120
		$39,465

b.

Payroll Taxes Expense	39,465	
FICA Tax Payable		38,700
State Unemployment Tax Payable		645
Federal Unemployment Tax Payable		120

Ex. 12-6

Vacation Pay Expense	15,500	
Vacation Pay Payable		15,500
($186,000 × 1/12)		

Ex. 12-7 a.

Pension Expense	75,000	
Unfunded Pension Liability		75,000

b.

Unfunded Pension Liability	75,000	
Cash		75,000

Ex. 12-8 a.

1.	Cash	98,000	
	Interest Expense	2,000	
	Notes Payable		100,000
2.	Notes Payable	100,000	
	Cash		100,000

Ex. 12-8, Concluded

b.	1.	Notes Receivable	100,000	
		Cash		98,000
		Interest Income		2,000
	2.	Cash	100,000	
		Notes Receivable....................		100,000

Ex. 12-9

a. $6,250 ($250,000 × 90/360 × 10%)

b. 1. $243,750
   2. $250,000

c. Option 2 is more favorable to the borrower than option 1 because it gives the use of a larger amount of money for the 90-day period, without any additional interest expense. *Note to Instructors:* The effective interest rate on option (2) is approximately 10.3% [($6,250/$243,750) × 4].

Ex. 12-10

a.	Building..................................	670,000	
	Land......................................	200,000	
	Mortgage Note Payable		720,000
	Cash		150,000
b.	Mortgage Note Payable	40,000	
	Interest Expense..........................	36,000	
	Cash		76,000
c.	Mortgage Note Payable	40,000	
	Interest Expense..........................	34,000	
	Cash		74,000

Ex. 12-11

Product Warranty Expense (2% × $750,000)	15,000	
Product Warranty Payable		15,000

WHAT'S WRONG WITH THIS?

There is nothing wrong with the procedures used by K. L. Clark Co. Employers are required to compute and report all payroll taxes on the calendar-year basis, regardless of the fiscal year they may use for financial reporting purposes.

PROBLEMS

Prob. 12-1A

1. **a.** Bonus = .05($309,000)

   B = $15,450

   b. Bonus = .05($309,000 − Bonus)

   B = $15,450 − .05B

   1.05B = $15,450

   B = $14,714.29

   c. Bonus = .05($309,000 − Taxes)

   Taxes = .40($309,000 − Bonus)

   B = .05[$309,000 − .40($309,000 − B)]

   B = .05($309,000 − $123,600 + .4B)

   B = $15,450 − $6,180 + .02B

   .98B = $9,270

   B = $9,459.18

   d. Bonus = .05($309,000 − Bonus − Taxes)

   Taxes = .40($309,000 − Bonus)

   B = .05[$309,000 − B − .40($309,000 − B)]

   B = .05($309,000 − B − $123,600 + .4B)

   B = $15,450 − .05B − $6,180 + .02B

   1.03B = $9,270

   B = $9,000

2. **a.** The COO would prefer the bonus plan that computes the bonus on income before deductions for bonus and income taxes. This plan would provide the COO with the highest amount of bonus.

   b. Bonus plan (a) would always be preferred by the COO, since it will always provide the highest amount of bonus.

Prob. 12-2A

1. **a.** Dec. 30 Sales Salaries Expense 86,500

   Warehouse Salaries Expense 18,980

   Office Salaries Expense.................... 9,520

      FICA Tax Payable 8,175

      Employees Income Tax Payable.......... 18,050

      Group Insurance Payable................. 1,350

      Bond Deductions Payable 1,200

      Salaries Payable 86,225

   b. 30 Payroll Taxes Expense 8,625

      FICA Tax Payable 8,175

      State Unemployment Tax Payable 378

      Federal Unemployment Tax Payable 72

2. **a.** Dec. 31 Sales Salaries Expense 86,500

   Warehouse Salaries Expense 18,980

   Office Salaries Expense.................... 9,520

      FICA Tax Payable 8,625

      Employees Income Tax Payable.......... 18,050

      Group Insurance Payable................. 1,350

      Bond Deductions Payable 1,200

      Salaries Payable 85,775

Prob. 12-2A, Concluded

b. Jan. 5 Payroll Taxes Expense 14,375
                FICA Tax Payable 8,625
                State Unemployment Tax Payable 4,830
                Federal Unemployment Tax Payable 920

Prob. 12-3A

1. 19—

Dec. 12 Sales Salaries Expense 3,463.00
        Office Salaries Expense 1,420.00
        Delivery Salaries Expense 1,120.00
                FICA Tax Payable......................... 383.03
                Employees Income Tax Payable 937.00
                Medical Insurance Payable 157.60
                Salaries Payable......................... 4,525.37

2. Dec. 12 Salaries Payable 4,525.37
                Accounts Payable 4,525.37

        Accounts Payable 4,525.37
                Cash in Bank............................. 4,525.37

3. Dec. 12 Payroll Taxes Expense 422.81
                FICA Tax Payable......................... 383.03
                State Unemployment Tax Payable........ 31.62
                Federal Unemployment Tax Payable 8.16

4. Dec. 16 Employees Income Tax Payable 937.00
        FICA Tax Payable.......................... 766.06
                Accounts Payable 1,703.06

     16 Accounts Payable 1,703.06
                Cash in Bank............................. 1,703.06

Prob. 12-4A

1.

Employee	Gross Earnings	Federal Income Tax Withheld	FICA Tax Withheld
Alvarez	$32,200.00	$ 5,416.50	$ 2,415.00
Cruz	5,000.00	788.00	375.00
Funk	50,400.00	10,740.00	3,780.00
Little	18,700.00	3,498.00	1,402.50
Powell	64,800.00	16,488.00	4,572.00
Soong	28,800.00	5,216.00	2,160.00
Wilson	42,000.00	9,072.00	3,150.00
			$17,854.50

2. a. FICA tax paid by employer............................. $17,854.50
    b. Earnings subject to unemployment compensation tax:
       (6 × $7,000) + $5,000 = $47,000
      State unemployment compensation tax: $47,000 × 4.2%   1,974.00
    c. Federal unemployment compensation tax: $47,000 × .8%   376.00
    d. Total payroll taxes expense $20,204.50

Prob. 12-5A

1.

PAYROLL FOR WEEK ENDING December 7, 1993

NAME	TOTAL HOURS	EARNINGS REGULAR	OVERTIME	TOTAL	DEDUCTIONS FICA TAX	FEDERAL INCOME TAX	U.S. SAVINGS BONDS	TOTAL	PAID NET AMOUNT	CK. NO.	ACCOUNTS DEBITED SALES SALARIES EXPENSE	OFFICE SALARIES EXPENSE
A......	40	800.00	......	800.00	60.00	166.00	25.00	251.00	549.00	818	800.00	......
B......	42	800.00	60.00	860.00	64.50	265.00	37.50	367.00	493.00	819	860.00	......
C......	40	1,200.00	......	1,200.00	18.00	300.00	50.00	368.00	832.00	820	......	1,200.00
D......	40	440.00	......	440.00	33.00	68.00	......	101.00	339.00	821	440.00	......
E......	40	600.00	......	600.00	45.00	115.00	25.00	185.00	415.00	822	600.00	......
F......	48	510.00	153.00	663.00	49.73	125.00	......	174.73	488.27	823	663.00	......
G......	40	560.00	......	560.00	42.00	93.00	25.00	160.00	400.00	824	560.00	......
H......		350.00	......	350.00	26.25	35.00	......	61.25	288.75	825	......	350.00
I......	20	220.00	......	220.00	16.50	15.00	......	31.50	188.50	826	220.00	......
J......	40	600.00	......	600.00	45.00	81.00	......	126.00	474.00	827	600.00	......
		6,080.00	213.00	6,293.00	399.98	1,263.00	162.50	1,825.48	4,467.52		4,743.00	1,550.00

Prob. 12-5A, Concluded

2. **Sales Salaries Expense** 4,743.00
   Office Salaries Expense 1,550.00
     FICA Tax Payable. 399.98
     Employees Federal Income Tax Payable. 1,263.00
     Bond Deductions Payable. 162.50
     Salaries Payable. 4,467.52

Prob. 12-6A

2.

VOUCHER REGISTER

Date	Vou. No.	Payee	Date Paid	Ck. No.	Accts. Pay. Cr.	Other Accounts Dr.		
						Account	Post. Ref.	Amount
Dec. 2	637	Marine Nat'l Bank	12/2	620	715	Bond Ded. Pay.	218	715
3	638	Marine Nat'l Bank	12/3	621	13,500	FICA Tax Pay.	213	6,000
						Emp. Fed. Inc. Tax Payable	214	7,500
14	646	Payroll Bank Acct.	12/14	627	35,845	Salaries Pay.	212	35,845
17	647	Marine Nat'l Bank	12/17	633	14,290	FICA Tax Pay.	213	6,500
						Emp. Fed. Inc. Tax Payable	214	7,790
18	650	Wilson Ins. Co.	12/19	639	3,875	Med. Ins. Pay.	219	3,875
28	684	Payroll Bank Acct.	12/28	671	34,765	Salaries Pay.	212	34,765
30	690	Marine Nat'l Bank	12/30	680	630	Bond Ded. Pay.	218	630
30	691	Marine Nat'l Bank	12/30	681	13,260	Emp. State Inc. Tax Payable	215	13,260

CHECK REGISTER

Date	Check No.	Payee	Vou. No.	Accounts Payable Dr.	Cash in Bank Cr.
Dec. 2	620	Marine National Bank	637	715	715
3	621	Marine National Bank	638	13,500	13,500
14	627	Payroll Bank Acct.	646	35,845	35,845
17	633	Marine National Bank	647	14,290	14,290
19	639	Wilson Insurance Co.	650	3,875	3,875
28	671	Payroll Bank Acct.	684	34,765	34,765
30	680	Marine National Bank	690	630	630
30	681	Marine National Bank	691	13,260	13,260

Prob. 12-6A, Continued

2.

19—

Dec. 14	Sales Salaries Expense	611	30,600	
	Officers Salaries Expense	711	15,200	
	Office Salaries Expense	712	3,800	
	FICA Tax Payable	213		3,250
	Employees Federal Income Tax Payable.	214		7,790
	Employees State Income Tax Payable ..	215		1,920
	Bond Deductions Payable	218		315
	Medical Insurance Payable	219		480
	Salaries Payable	212		35,845
14	Payroll Taxes Expense	719	3,448	
	FICA Tax Payable	213		3,250
	State Unemployment Tax Payable	216		163
	Federal Unemployment Tax Payable....	217		35
28	Sales Salaries Expense	611	28,500	
	Officers Salaries Expense	711	15,200	
	Office Salaries Expense	712	3,800	
	FICA Tax Payable	213		3,010
	Employees Federal Income Tax Payable.	214		7,565
	Employees State Income Tax Payable ..	215		1,845
	Bond Deductions Payable	218		315
	Salaries Payable	212		34,765
28	Payroll Taxes Expense	719	3,203	
	FICA Tax Payable	213		3,010
	State Unemployment Tax Payable	216		160
	Federal Unemployment Tax Payable....	217		33

3. **Adjusting Entry**

31	Sales Salaries Expense	611	2,950	
	Officers Salaries Expense	711	1,640	
	Office Salaries Expense	712	410	
	Salaries Payable	212		5,000

4. **Closing Entry**

31	Income Summary		1,229,781	
	Sales Salaries Expense	611		693,350
	Officers Salaries Expense	711		343,840
	Office Salaries Expense	712		93,510
	Payroll Taxes Expense	719		99,081

Prob. 12-6A, Continued

1, 2, 3, and 4.

Salaries Payable   212

Date	Item	Post. Ref.	Dr.	Cr.	Balance Dr.	Balance Cr.
19—						
Dec. 14	....	J	......	35,845	......	35,845
14	....	VR	35,845	....	—	—
28	....	J	......	34,765	......	34,765
28	....	VR	34,765	....	—	—
31	....	J	......	5,000	......	5,000

FICA Tax Payable   213

Date	Item	Post. Ref.	Dr.	Cr.	Balance Dr.	Balance Cr.
19—						
Dec. 1	Balance	√	......	....	......	6,000
3	....	VR	6,000	....	—	—
14	....	J	......	3,250	......	3,250
14	....	J	......	3,250	......	6,500
17	....	VR	6,500	....	—	—
28	....	J	......	3,010	......	3,010
28	....	J	......	3,010	......	6,020

Employees Federal Income Tax Payable   214

Date	Item	Post. Ref.	Dr.	Cr.	Balance Dr.	Balance Cr.
19—						
Dec. 1	Balance	√	......	....	......	7,500
3	....	VR	7,500	....	—	—
14	....	J	......	7,790	......	7,790
17	....	VR	7,790	....	—	—
28	....	J	......	7,565	......	7,565

Employees State Income Tax Payable   215

Date	Item	Post. Ref.	Dr.	Cr.	Balance Dr.	Balance Cr.
19—						
Dec. 1	Balance	√	......	....	......	13,260
14	....	J	......	1,920	......	15,180
28	....	J	......	1,845	......	17,025
30	....	VR	13,260	....	......	3,765

State Unemployment Tax Payable   216

Date	Item	Post. Ref.	Dr.	Cr.	Balance Dr.	Balance Cr.
19—						
Dec. 1	Balance	√	......	....	......	1,710
14	....	J	......	163	......	1,873
28	....	J	......	160	......	2,033

Prob. 12-6A, Continued

Federal Unemployment Tax Payable   217

Date	Item	Post. Ref.	Dr.	Cr.	Balance Dr.	Balance Cr.
19—						
Dec. 1	Balance	√	......	....	....	360
14		J	......	35	....	395
28		J	......	33	....	428

Bond Deductions Payable   218

Date	Item	Post. Ref.	Dr.	Cr.	Balance Dr.	Balance Cr.
19—						
Dec. 1	Balance	√	......	....	....	715
2		VR	715	....	....	—
14		J	......	315	....	315
28		J	......	315	....	630
30		VR	630	....	....	—

Medical Insurance Payable   219

Date	Item	Post. Ref.	Dr.	Cr.	Balance Dr.	Balance Cr.
19—						
Dec. 1	Balance	√	......	....	....	3,875
14		J	......	480	....	4,355
18		VR	3,875	....	....	480

Sales Salaries Expense   611

Date	Item	Post. Ref.	Dr.	Cr.	Balance Dr.	Balance Cr.
19—						
Dec. 1	Balance	√	......	....	631,300	......
14		J	30,600	....	661,900	......
28		J	28,500	....	690,400	......
31		J	2,950	....	693,350	......
31		J	......	693,350	—	—

Officers Salaries Expense   711

Date	Item	Post. Ref.	Dr.	Cr.	Balance Dr.	Balance Cr.
19—						
Dec. 1	Balance	√	......	....	311,800	......
14		J	15,200	....	327,000	......
28		J	15,200	....	342,200	......
31		J	1,640	....	343,840	......
31		J	......	343,840	—	—

Prob. 12-6A, Concluded

Office Salaries Expense   712

Date	Item	Post. Ref.	Dr.	Cr.	Balance Dr.	Balance Cr.
19—						
Dec. 1	Balance	√	......	....	85,500	......
14	....	J	3,800	....	89,300	......
28	....	J	3,800	....	93,100	......
31	....	J	410	....	93,510	......
31	....	J	......	93,510	—	—

Payroll Taxes Expense   719

Date	Item	Post. Ref.	Dr.	Cr.	Balance Dr.	Balance Cr.
19—						
Dec. 1	Balance	√	......	....	92,430	......
14	....	J	3,448	....	95,878	......
28	....	J	3,203	....	99,081	—
31	....	J	......	99,081	—	—

Prob. 12-7A

1.

Jan.	15	Purchases	7,800	
		Accounts Payable—Wyatt Co.		7,800
Mar.	1	Purchases	9,600	
		Accounts Payable—Evans Co.		9,600
	6	Accounts Payable—Wyatt Co.	7,800	
		Notes Payable		7,800
	10	Accounts Payable—Evans Co.	9,600	
		Cash		9,504
		Purchases Discounts		96
Apr.	5	Notes Payable	7,800	
		Interest Expense	78	
		Cash		7,878
July	15	Cash	8,000	
		Notes Payable		8,000
	25	Cash	19,000	
		Interest Expense	1,000	
		Notes Payable		20,000
Oct.	13	Notes Payable	8,000	
		Interest Expense	260	
		Notes Payable		8,000
		Cash		260
Nov.	12	Notes Payable	8,000	
		Interest Expense	100	
		Cash		8,100
	22	Notes Payable	20,000	
		Cash		20,000
Dec.	1	Office Equipment	57,500	
		Notes Payable		50,000
		Cash		7,500
	31	Notes Payable	5,000	
		Interest Expense	50	
		Cash		5,050
	31	Pension Expense	40,000	
		Cash		27,500
		Unfunded Pension Liability		12,500
2.	a.	Vacation Pay Expense	15,000	
		Vacation Pay Payable		15,000
	b.	Product Warranty Expense	12,750	
		Product Warranty Payable		12,750

Prob. 12-7A, Concluded

3.   Interest Expense 450

        Interest Payable   450

        ($5,000 × .12 × 30/360 × 9 = $450)

4. $5,500 ($5,000 principal; $50,000 × .12 × 30/360 = $500 interest)

Prob. 12-1B

1. a.   Bonus = .04($720,000)

         B = $28,800

    b.   Bonus = .04($720,000 − Bonus)

         B = $28,800 − .04B

         1.04B = $28,800

         B = $27,692.31

    c.   Bonus = .04($720,000 − Taxes)

         Taxes = .40($720,000 − Bonus)

         B = .04[$720,000 − .40($720,000 − B)]

         B = .04($720,000 − $288,000 + .4B)

         B = $28,800 − $11,520 + .016B

         .984B = $17,280

         B = $17,560.98

    d.   Bonus = .04($720,000 − Bonus − Taxes)

         Taxes = .40($720,000 − Bonus)

         B = .04[$720,000 − B − .40($720,000 − B)]

         B = .04($720,000 − B − $288,000 + .4B)

         B = $28,800 − .04B − $11,520 + .016B

         1.024B = $17,280

         B = $16,875

2. a.   The COO would prefer the bonus plan that computes the bonus on income before deductions for bonus and income taxes. This plan would provide the COO with the highest amount of bonus.

    b.   Bonus plan (a) would always be preferred by the COO, since it will always provide the highest amount of bonus.

Prob. 12-2B

1. a. Dec. 30 Sales Salaries Expense 148,700
Warehouse Salaries Expense 21,280
Office Salaries Expense................... 12,020
FICA Tax Payable 8,460
Employees Income Tax Payable........ 33,850
Bond Deductions Payable 4,400
Group Insurance Payable.............. 2,800
Salaries Payable 132,490

b. 30 Payroll Taxes Expense 9,150
FICA Tax Payable 8,460
State Unemployment Tax Payable 570
Federal Unemployment Tax Payable ... 120

2. a. Dec. 30 Sales Salaries Expense 148,700
Warehouse Salaries Expense 21,280
Office Salaries Expense................... 12,020
FICA Tax Payable 13,650
Employees Income Tax Payable........ 33,850
Bond Deductions Payable 4,400
Group Insurance Payable.............. 2,800
Salaries Payable 127,300

b. Jan. 4 Payroll Taxes Expense 22,022
FICA Tax Payable 13,650
State Unemployment Tax Payable 6,916
Federal Unemployment Tax Payable ... 1,456

Prob. 12-3B

1. 19—

Dec. 12	Sales Salaries Expense	3,463.00	
	Office Salaries Expense	1,420.00	
	Delivery Salaries Expense	1,120.00	
	FICA Tax Payable........................		383.03
	Employees Income Tax Payable		937.00
	Medical Insurance Payable		157.60
	Salaries Payable........................		4,525.37

2. Dec. 12

Salaries Payable	4,525.37	
Accounts Payable		4,525.37
Accounts Payable	4,525.37	
Cash in Bank...........................		4,525.37

3. Dec. 12

Payroll Taxes Expense....................	429.95	
FICA Tax Payable........................		383.03
State Unemployment Tax Payable........		38.76
Federal Unemployment Tax Payable		8.16

4. Dec. 15

Employees Income Tax Payable	937.00	
FICA Tax Payable.........................	766.06	
Accounts Payable		1,703.06

15	Accounts Payable	1,703.06	
	Cash in Bank...........................		1,703.06

Prob. 12-4B

1.

Employee	Gross Earnings	Federal Income Tax Withheld	FICA Tax Withheld
Allen	$17,500.00	$ 2,919.00	$ 1,312.50
Cox	50,400.00	10,248.00	3,780.00
Gower	38,000.00	7,480.00	2,850.00
Nunn	48,000.00	9,720.00	3,600.00
Quinn	5,400.00	978.00	405.00
Ruiz	23,800.00	3,918.50	1,785.00
Wu	60,950.00	14,501.50	4,514.25
			$18,246.75

2. a. FICA tax paid by employer............................. $18,246.75
   b. Earnings subject to unemployment compensation tax:
      (6 × $7,000) + $5,400 = $47,400
      State unemployment compensation tax: $47,400 × 3.8%   1,801.20
   c. Federal unemployment compensation tax: $47,400 × .8%   379.20
   d. Total payroll taxes expense $20,427.15

Prob. 12-5B

1.

PAYROLL FOR WEEK ENDING *December 7, 1993*

| NAME | TOTAL HOURS | EARNINGS | | | DEDUCTIONS | | | | PAID | | ACCOUNTS DEBITED | |
		REGULAR	OVERTIME	TOTAL	FICA TAX	FEDERAL INCOME TAX	U.S. SAVINGS BONDS	TOTAL	NET AMOUNT	CK. NO.	SALES SALARIES EXPENSE	OFFICE SALARIES EXPENSE
A	44	800.00	120.00	920.00	69.00	280.00	37.50	386.50	533.50	981	920.00	......
B	40	800.00	......	800.00	60.00	166.00	25.00	251.00	549.00	982	800.00	......
C	40	1,120.00	......	1,120.00	16.80	270.00	50.00	336.80	783.20	983	......	1,120.00
D	40	600.00	......	600.00	45.00	81.00	......	126.00	474.00	984	600.00	......
E	40	600.00	......	600.00	45.00	115.00	25.00	185.00	415.00	985	600.00	......
F	48	510.00	153.00	663.00	49.73	125.00	......	174.73	488.27	986	663.00	......
G	40	560.00	......	560.00	42.00	93.00	25.00	160.00	400.00	987	560.00	......
H	40	400.00	......	400.00	30.00	40.00	......	70.00	330.00	988	......	400.00
I	20	220.00	......	220.00	16.50	15.00	......	31.50	188.50	989	220.00	......
J	40	440.00	......	440.00	33.00	68.00	......	101.00	339.00	990	440.00	......
		6,050.00	273.00	6,323.00	407.03	1,253.00	162.50	1,822.53	4,500.47		4,803.00	1,520.00

Prob. 12-5B, Concluded

2. Sales Salaries Expense 4,803.00
    Office Salaries Expense 1,520.00
      FICA Tax Payable........................   407.03
      Employees Federal Income Tax Payable...........   1,253.00
      Bond Deductions Payable........................   162.50
      Salaries Payable................................   4,500.47

Prob. 12-6B

2.

VOUCHER REGISTER

| | | | | | | Other Accounts Dr. | | |
Date	Vou. No.	Payee	Date Paid	Ck. No.	Accts. Pay. Cr.	Account	Post. Ref.	Amount
Dec. 2	745	First Nat'l Bank	12/2	728	800	Bond Ded. Pay.	218	800
3	746	First Nat'l Bank	12/3	729	16,620	FICA Tax Pay.	213	7,550
						Emp. Fed. Inc. Tax Payable	214	9,070
14	757	Payroll Bank Acct.	12/14	738	39,401	Salaries Pay.	212	39,401
17	758	First Nat'l Bank	12/17	744	15,719	FICA Tax Pay.	213	7,150
						Emp. Fed. Inc. Tax Payable	214	8,569
18	760	Pico Ins. Co.	12/19	750	3,200	Med. Ins. Pay.	219	3,200
28	795	Payroll Bank Acct.	12/28	782	38,213	Salaries Pay.	212	38,213
30	801	First Nat'l Bank	12/30	791	750	Bond Ded. Pay.	218	750
30	802	First Nat'l Bank	12/30	792	14,586	Emp. State Inc. Tax Payable	215	14,586

CHECK REGISTER

Date	Check No.	Payee	Vou. No.	Accounts Payable Dr.	Cash in Bank Cr.
Dec. 2	728	First National Bank	745	800	800
3	729	First National Bank	746	16,620	16,620
14	738	Payroll Bank Acct.	757	39,401	39,401
17	744	First National Bank	758	15,719	15,719
19	750	Pico Insurance Co.	760	3,200	3,200
28	782	Payroll Bank Acct.	795	38,213	38,213
30	791	First National Bank	801	750	750
30	792	First National Bank	802	14,586	14,586

Prob. 12-6B, Continued

2.

19—

Dec. 14	Sales Salaries Expense...................	611	33,660	
	Officers Salaries Expense	711	16,720	
	Office Salaries Expense	712	4,180	
	FICA Tax Payable	213		3,575
	Employees Federal Income Tax Payable.	214		8,569
	Employees State Income Tax Payable ..	215		2,112
	Bond Deductions Payable	218		375
	Medical Insurance Payable.............	219		528
	Salaries Payable	212		39,401
14	Payroll Taxes Expense..................	719	3,772	
	FICA Tax Payable	213		3,575
	State Unemployment Tax Payable	216		162
	Federal Unemployment Tax Payable....	217		35
28	Sales Salaries Expense...................	611	31,350	
	Officers Salaries Expense	711	16,720	
	Office Salaries Expense	712	4,180	
	FICA Tax Payable	213		3,311
	Employees Federal Income Tax Payable.	214		8,322
	Employees State Income Tax Payable ..	215		2,029
	Bond Deductions Payable	218		375
	Salaries Payable	212		38,213
28	Payroll Taxes Expense..................	719	3,505	
	FICA Tax Payable	213		3,311
	State Unemployment Tax Payable	216		161
	Federal Unemployment Tax Payable....	217		33

3.   Adjusting Entry

31	Sales Salaries Expense...................	611	3,245	
	Officers Salaries Expense	711	1,800	
	Office Salaries Expense	712	450	
	Salaries Payable	212		5,495

4.   Closing Entry

31	Income Summary.......................		1,352,715	
	Sales Salaries Expense	611		762,685
	Officers Salaries Expense	711		378,220
	Office Salaries Expense	712		102,860
	Payroll Taxes Expense.................	719		108,950

Prob. 12-6B, Continued

1, 2, 3, and 4.

Salaries Payable   212

Date	Item	Post. Ref.	Dr.	Cr.	Balance Dr.	Balance Cr.
19—						
Dec. 14	....	J	......	39,401	....	39,401
14	....	VR	39,401	....	—	—
28	....	J	......	38,213	....	38,213
28	....	VR	38,213	....	—	—
31	....	J	......	5,495	....	5,495

FICA Tax Payable   213

Date	Item	Post. Ref.	Dr.	Cr.	Balance Dr.	Balance Cr.
19—						
Dec. 1	Balance	√	......	....	....	7,550
3	....	VR	7,550	....	....	—
14	....	J	......	3,575	....	3,575
14	....	J	......	3,575	....	7,150
17	....	VR	7,150	....	....	—
28	....	J	......	3,311	....	3,311
28	....	J	......	3,311	....	6,622

Employees Federal Income Tax Payable   214

Date	Item	Post. Ref.	Dr.	Cr.	Balance Dr.	Balance Cr.
19—						
Dec. 1	Balance	√	......	....	....	9,070
3	....	VR	9,070	....	....	—
14	....	J	......	8,569	....	8,569
17	....	VR	8,569	....	....	—
28	....	J	......	8,322	....	8,322

Employees State Income Tax Payable   215

Date	Item	Post. Ref.	Dr.	Cr.	Balance Dr.	Balance Cr.
19—						
Dec. 1	Balance	√	......	....	....	14,586
14	....	J	......	2,112	....	16,698
28	....	J	......	2,029	....	18,727
30	....	VR	14,586	....	....	4,141

State Unemployment Tax Payable   216

Date	Item	Post. Ref.	Dr.	Cr.	Balance Dr.	Balance Cr.
19—						
Dec. 1	Balance	√	......	....	....	1,881
14	....	J	......	162	....	2,043
28	....	J	......	161	....	2,204

Prob. 12-6B, Continued

Federal Unemployment Tax Payable   217

Date	Item	Post. Ref.	Dr.	Cr.	Balance Dr.	Balance Cr.
19—						
Dec. 1	Balance	√	......	....	....	396
14		J	......	35	....	431
28		J	......	33	....	464

Bond Deductions Payable   218

Date	Item	Post. Ref.	Dr.	Cr.	Balance Dr.	Balance Cr.
19—						
Dec. 1	Balance	√	......	....	....	800
2		VR	800	....	—	—
14		J	......	375	....	375
28		J	......	375	....	750
30		VR	750	....	—	—

Medical Insurance Payable   219

Date	Item	Post. Ref.	Dr.	Cr.	Balance Dr.	Balance Cr.
19—						
Dec. 1	Balance	√	......	....	....	3,200
14		J	......	528	....	3,728
18		VR	3,200	....	....	528

Sales Salaries Expense   611

Date	Item	Post. Ref.	Dr.	Cr.	Balance Dr.	Balance Cr.
19—						
Dec. 1	Balance	√	......	....	694,430	.....
14		J	33,660	....	728,090	.....
28		J	31,350	....	759,440	.....
31		J	3,245	....	762,685	.....
31		J	......	762,685	—	—

Officers Salaries Expense   711

Date	Item	Post. Ref.	Dr.	Cr.	Balance Dr.	Balance Cr.
19—						
Dec. 1	Balance	√	......	....	342,980	.....
14		J	16,720	....	359,700	.....
28		J	16,720	....	376,420	.....
31		J	1,800	....	378,220	.....
31		J	......	378,220	—	—

Prob. 12-6B, Concluded

Office Salaries Expense   712

Date	Item	Post. Ref.	Dr.	Cr.	Balance Dr.	Balance Cr.
19—						
Dec. 1	Balance	√	......	....	94,050	.....
14	....	J	4,180	....	98,230	.....
28	....	J	4,180	....	102,410	.....
31	....	J	450	....	102,860	.....
31	....	J	......	102,860	—	—

Payroll Taxes Expense   719

Date	Item	Post. Ref.	Dr.	Cr.	Balance Dr.	Balance Cr.
19—						
Dec. 1	Balance	√	......	....	101,673	.....
14	....	J	3,772	....	105,445	.....
28	....	J	3,505	....	108,950	.....
31	....	J	......	108,950	—	—

Prob. 12-7B

1.

Mar.	2	Purchases	5,000	
		Accounts Payable—Clark Co.		5,000
	8	Purchases	10,000	
		Accounts Payable—Malone Co.		10,000
	12	Accounts Payable—Clark Co.	5,000	
		Cash		4,900
		Purchases Discounts		100
Apr.	1	Accounts Payable—Malone Co.	10,000	
		Notes Payable		10,000
May	10	Cash	42,900	
		Interest Expense	2,100	
		Notes Payable		45,000
	31	Notes Payable	10,000	
		Interest Expense	200	
		Cash		10,200
Aug.	5	Cash	7,500	
		Notes Payable		7,500
Sep.	7	Notes Payable	45,000	
		Cash		45,000
Oct.	4	Notes Payable	7,500	
		Interest Expense	175	
		Notes Payable		7,500
		Cash		175
Nov.	3	Notes Payable	7,500	
		Interest Expense	100	
		Cash		7,600
	15	Store Equipment	50,000	
		Notes Payable		42,000
		Cash		8,000
Dec.	15	Notes Payable	6,000	
		Interest Expense	60	
		Cash		6,060
	31	Pension Expense	45,000	
		Cash		32,400
		Unfunded Pension Liability		12,600
2.	a.	Vacation Pay Expense	17,900	
		Vacation Pay Payable		17,900
	b.	Product Warranty Expense	15,000	
		Product Warranty Payable		15,000

Prob. 12-7B, Concluded

3.   Interest Expense 552
         Interest Payable 552
         ($6,000 × .12 × 46/360 × 6 = $552)

4. $6,420 ($6,000 principal; $42,000 × .12 × 30/360 = $420 interest)

Mini-Case 12

1. No. The president's bonus, based on reported income after deducting the bonus but before deducting income taxes, should have been $97,500, determined as follows:

$$B = .12(\$910,000 - B)$$
$$B = \$109,200 - .12B$$
$$1.12B = \$109,200$$
$$B = \$97,500$$

The president has improperly determined the bonus of $109,200 ($910,000 × .12) by basing it on income before deducting the bonus and income taxes.

2. a. Failure to accrue payroll and payroll tax expense for the five days, December 27–31, 1993.
  b. Failure to accrue the semiannual pension cost for the last six months of 1993.
  c. Failure to accrue the product warranty liability for 1993.
  d. Failure to record insurance expired during July through December on the policy purchased on July 1.
  e. Failure to accrue the vacation pay liability for December 1993.

3. Reported 1993 income before bonus and income taxes........ $910,000
Less: Payroll expense for December 27–31,
    1993 .... $12,000
    Payroll tax expense for Dec. 27–31, 1993:
    FICA tax $900
    State unemployment tax............. 384
    Federal unemployment tax 96   1,380
    Pension cost 22,500
    Product warranty...................... 12,000
    Insurance expense..................... 5,320
    Vacation pay expense.................. 12,000   65,200
Adjusted 1993 income before bonus and income taxes........ $844,800

Note to Instructors: Since the payroll was not paid until January 9, 1994, all of the December 27–31 payroll is subject to FICA tax of 7.5% and unemployment compensation taxes.

Bonus computation: $B = .12(\$844,800 - B)$
                       $B = \$101,376 - .12B$
                  $1.12B = \$101,376$
                       $B = \$90,514.29$

Mini-Case 12, Concluded

4. $18,685.71 ($109,200 − $90,514.29)

5. The major advantage of income-sharing bonus contracts is the ability to motivate executives to higher levels of achievement. When the bonus is based on income, executives are directly rewarded and are thus motivated to achieve high levels of income.

The major disadvantage of income-sharing bonus contracts is that they may be misused by executives. For example, a bonus based on income might lead to attempts to misstate income, such as illustrated, or decisions to maximize short-run income at the expense of long-term profitability.

COMPREHENSIVE PROBLEM 4

1. **a.** Petty Cash 300
    Accounts Payable 300

Accounts Payable 300
    Cash in Bank 300

b. Office Supplies 95
Miscellaneous Selling Expense 97
Miscellaneous Administrative Expense 90
    Accounts Payable 282

c. Purchases 4,950
    Accounts Payable 4,950

d. Accounts Payable 4,950
Discounts Lost 50
    Cash in Bank 5,000

e. Cash in Bank 9,050
Cash Short and Over 10
    Sales 9,060

f. Notes Receivable 30,000
    Accounts Receivable 30,000

g. Cash in Bank 30,195
    Notes Receivable 30,000
    Interest Income 195

h. Accounts Receivable 30,500
    Cash in Bank 30,500

i. Cash in Bank 30,805
    Accounts Receivable 30,500
    Interest Income 305

j. Cash in Bank 800
Allowance for Doubtful Accounts 700
    Accounts Receivable 1,500

Comp. Prob. 4, Continued

k.	Accounts Receivable	700	
	Allowance for Doubtful Accounts		700
	Cash in Bank.....................................	700	
	Accounts Receivable		700
l.	Office Equipment	120,000	
	Accumulated Depreciation—Office Equipment	65,000	
	Office Equipment.................................		90,000
	Accounts Payable		95,000
m.	Sales Salaries Expense	9,500	
	Office Salaries Expense...........................	4,500	
	Employees Federal Income Tax Payable		2,950
	FICA Tax Payable................................		900
	Salaries Payable.................................		10,150
n.	Payroll Taxes Expense	992	
	FICA Tax Payable................................		900
	State Unemployment Tax Payable		76
	Federal Unemployment Tax Payable		16
o.	Cash in Bank.....................................	24,250	
	Interest Expense	750	
	Notes Payable....................................		25,000
p.	Notes Payable	25,000	
	Accounts Payable		25,000
q.	Pension Expense	34,000	
	Accounts Payable		25,000
	Unfunded Pension Liability		9,000

2.

KEY COMPANY
Bank Reconciliation
November 30, 19—

Balance according to bank statement		$ 89,030
Add deposit in transit, not recorded by bank..............		27,600
		$116,630
Deduct outstanding checks		56,630
Adjusted balance		$ 60,000
Balance according to depositor's records.................		$ 60,130
Deduct:		
Bank service charges...................................	$40	
Error in recording check...............................	90	130
Adjusted balance		$ 60,000

3.	Miscellaneous Administrative Expense.................	40	
	Accounts Payable	90	
	Cash in Bank......................................		130

Comp. Prob. 4, Continued

4. **a.** Uncollectible Accounts Expense.................. 6,850
       Allowance for Doubtful Accounts 6,850

b. Merchandise Inventory 220,250
     Income Summary 220,250

Item	Cost	
C10	45 at $1,940	$ 87,300
D35	(25 at $1,100) + (5 at $1,185)	33,425
L11	(75 at $550) + (5 at $575)	44,125
K72	15 at $2,600	39,000
V17	4 at $4,100...	16,400
Total	....	$220,250

c. Insurance Expense 18,400
     Prepaid Insurance 18,400

d. Office Supplies Expense....................... 5,100
     Office Supplies................................ 5,100

e. Depreciation Expense—Buildings 4,500
     Depreciation Expense—Office Equipment 18,000
     Depreciation Expense—Store Equipment 15,000
        Accumulated Depreciation—Buildings 4,500
        Accumulated Depreciation—Office Equipment ... 18,000
        Accumulated Depreciation—Store Equipment.... 15,000

   Depreciation Expense:
   Buildings ($225,000 × 2%) .... $ 4,500
   Office Equipment [1/2 × 5/15 ×
      ($120,000 − $12,000)]........................ 18,000
   Store Equipment ($60,000 × 25%) 15,000

f. Amortization Expense—Patents 3,000
     Patents 3,000

g. Depletion Expense 12,000
     Accumulated Depletion......................... 12,000

h. Vacation Pay Expense 7,000
     Vacation Pay Payable.......................... 7,000

i. Product Warranty Expense 4,500
     Product Warranty Payable...................... 4,500

Comp. Prob. 4, Continued

5.

KEY COMPANY
Balance Sheet
December 31, 19—

Assets

Current assets:

Petty cash		$ 300
Cash		59,250
Marketable equity securities	$ 40,000	
Less allowance for decline to market	4,510	35,490
Notes receivable		50,000
Accounts receivable	$152,300	
Less allowance for doubtful accounts	5,950	146,350
Merchandise inventory—at cost (last-in, first-out)		220,250
Prepaid insurance		12,950
Office supplies		2,300
Total current assets		$526,890

Plant assets:

	Cost	Accumulated Depreciation (Depletion)	Book Value	
Land	$ 50,000	—	$ 50,000	
Buildings	225,000	$ 4,500	220,500	
Office equipment	120,000	18,000	102,000	
Store equipment	60,000	15,000	45,000	
Mineral rights	50,000	12,000	38,000	
Total plant assets	$505,000	$49,500		455,500

Intangible assets:

Patents	15,000
Total assets	$997,390

Comp. Prob. 4, Concluded

Liabilities

Current liabilities:

FICA tax payable	$ 2,100	
Employees federal income tax payable	2,950	
State unemployment tax payable.........	1,520	
Federal unemployment tax payable	320	
Salaries payable	14,000	
Accounts payable.........................	88,000	
Product warranty payable.................	4,500	
Vacation pay payable	5,000	
Notes payable (current portion)	50,000	
Total current liabilities		$168,390

Long-term liabilities:

Vacation pay payable	$ 2,000	
Unfunded pension liability	2,000	
Notes payable	400,000	
Total long-term liabilities		404,000
Total liabilities...........................		$572,390

Owner's Equity

Jim Key, capital		425,000
Total liabilities and owner's equity..........		$997,390

6. The bonus would be $8,000, determined as follows:

$$B = .04(\$208,000 - B)$$
$$B = \$8,320 - .04B$$
$$1.04B = \$8,320$$
$$B = \$8,000$$

7. The merchandise inventory destroyed was $182,500, determined as follows:

Merchandise inventory, January 1.................		$220,250
Purchases, January 1–February 7		189,750
Merchandise available for sale		$410,000
Sales, January 1–February 7.....................	$350,000	
Less estimated gross profit ($350,000 × 35%)	122,500	
Estimated cost of merchandise sold...............		227,500
Estimated merchandise inventory destroyed		$182,500

CHAPTER 13

DISCUSSION QUESTIONS

1. a. Accounting principles do not have the same authoritativeness as do universal principles related to the physical sciences. Accounting principles are developed by individuals to enhance the usefulness of accounting data in an ever-changing society. They represent the best possible guides, based on reason, observation, and experimentation, to the achievement of the desired results.
    b. General acceptability of guides and standards by the accounting profession is the criterion for determining accounting principles.
    c. Accounting principles are not fixed and unchanging laws. They must be continually re-examined and reviewed to keep pace with changes in the economic environment and with the increasing complexity of business operations.

2. The Financial Accounting Foundation appoints members of the standard-setting boards (FASB and GASB) and advisory councils, raises funds for the operation of the standard-setting process, and provides general oversight of the standard-setting process.

3. a. Financial Accounting Standards Board (FASB)
    b. Governmental Accounting Standards Board (GASB)

4. As accounting problems are identified, the FASB conducts extensive research to identify issues and possible solutions, then publishes discussion memos and preliminary proposals and evaluates responses from interested parties, and finally publishes *Statements of Financial Accounting Standards*.

5. a. Financial Accounting Standards Board
    b. Financial Accounting Foundation
    c. Governmental Accounting Standards Board
    d. American Institute of Certified Public Accountants
    e. American Accounting Association
    f. Securities and Exchange Commission
    g. Internal Revenue Service

6. Business entity concept

7. It is customary to assume that a business entity has a reasonable expectation of continuing in business at a profit for an indefinite period of time. This assumption is referred to as the going concern concept.

8. No. If there is conclusive evidence that a business entity has a limited life, such as an entity in receivership, the going concern concept should not be used in preparing its financial statements. In such a case, the financial statements should clearly disclose the limited life of the enterprise and should be prepared from the liquidation point of view.

9. The most objective information available minimizes the possibility of error, intentional bias, or fraud, and therefore provides statements that can be accepted with confidence.

10. a. Yes. This is quite possible.
    b. Plant assets are not reported at their estimated market values because the enterprise is viewed as a going concern and there is no expectation of disposing of the assets.

11. The general effect of the change in price level on Pendleton Company was an increase in purchasing power, because the $1,000,000 loan was paid off in dollars representing only two-thirds of the purchasing power of the dollars borrowed.

12. a. $10,000 ($75,000 less accumulated depreciation of $65,000)
    b. $120,000

13. a. $50,000
    b. No. The amount of cash remaining would be equal to the cost of merchandise sold, and this amount is insufficient to pay for the replacement of the merchandise.

14. The conventional financial statements can be supplemented by statements that reflect changing prices based on current costs or constant dollars.

15. Current cost is the amount of cash that would have to be paid currently to acquire assets of the same age and in the same condition as existing assets.

16. $60,000 ($50,000 × 210/175)

17. To obtain a complete and accurate picture of an enterprise's success or failure, it would need to discontinue operations, convert its assets into cash, and pay off its debts.

18. At the time of sale

19. a. $320,000
    b. $120,000 (40% gross profit × $300,000, or $320,000/$800,000 × $300,000)

20. a. $3,600,000 (40% × $9,000,000)
    b. $3,110,000
    c. $490,000 ($3,600,000 − $3,110,000)

21. Generally accepted accounting principles were not followed. No revenue should have been realized because the land has not been sold. The cost of the tract of land, including development costs, should be matched with the related revenue. Since no revenue has been realized, the total cost of the tract of land, $425,000 is an unexpired cost or asset.

22. No. Properties acquired by an enterprise are generally recorded at cost. A savings, but not income, results if the enterprise constructs property at a lower cost than the outside contractor stated in the bid. The savings will be reflected in lower depreciation charges during periods in which the property is used than would have been the case had the property been constructed by the outside contractor. No income has been realized by the construction.

23. a. Depreciation is an allocation of the expiration of cost of plant assets to the period during which the expiration took place. This allocation should be made regardless of changes in the market values of the plant assets.
    b. Plant assets are generally recorded at cost, and current market values are not recorded in the accounts. If the difference is significant, market values of plant assets may be presented in supplementary financial schedules.

24. Inventory cost flow and pricing methods; depreciation methods; revenue recognition methods, such as installment sales and percentage of completion; allowance and direct write-off methods for uncollectible receivables.

25. Readers of the financial statements should be able to assume that the successive financial statements of an enterprise are based consistently on the same generally accepted accounting principles. Any changes revealed by the statements from one period to the next are assumed to be the result of changes in business conditions or managerial effectiveness. Therefore, significant changes in accounting methods must be disclosed so that the reader is alerted to the effect of those changes on the financial statements.

26. Yes. The concept of consistency does not prohibit changes in accounting methods where another method would more fairly state net income and financial position. In this case, the change in method should be made and its effect should be disclosed in the financial statements for the period in which the change was made.

27. a. Reported net income has been increased by $30,000. If the change in method had not been made, the reported net income would have been $60,000.
    b. Yes. This is a relative matter for which no absolute criteria can be formulated. A difference in net income of 1/3, however, would appear to be material.
    c. Yes. The net income reported for the current year is not directly comparable with the net income of past years. For example, if the net income reported for the preceding year had been $75,000, it would appear, in the absence of an explanation, that the net income of the current year had increased by $15,000, whereas, when placed on a comparable basis, there was a decrease of $15,000.

28. The concept of materiality

29. a. This practice is conservative for 1975 because depreciation expense is high compared with later years.
    b. This method is not conservative for 2024 because depreciation expense is low compared with that of earlier years.

30. Cost is the proper basis for presenting land in the financial statements of the developer. However, footnote or other supplementary disclosure of the land's appraised value, and the basis of the appraisal, may be useful information to the reader of the financial statements.

31. $187,007,000 ($191,507,000 + $72,300,000 − $76,800,000)
    Note to Instructors: The impact of the current costs on reported earnings must be determined by considering the effects of current costs on both the ending and beginning inventories.

32. a. A subsequent event is an event occurring or becoming known after the close of the accounting period.
    b. Examples of subsequent events include crippling losses from a fire or other catastrophe, issuance of long-term debt or capital stock, purchase of another business enterprise, and litigation.

ETHICS DISCUSSION CASE The amounts reported in the financial statements as fees earned from clients must be based upon objective evidence that the services have been rendered. It would be unethical for Janet Smoltz to include amounts in the financial statements as earned fees if no services have been rendered. However, in negotiating the sale of her practice, Janet Smoltz may include estimates of expected fees to be earned in the future in a separate schedule. As long as Janet Smoltz clearly indicates that the separate schedule includes estimated fees expected to be earned in the future, she is behaving in an ethical manner. It is up to Richard Statham to challenge the reasonableness of these estimates in negotiating the purchase of the practice.

EXERCISES

Ex. 13-1 a. $70,000 ($170,000 − $100,000)
     b. 1. $60,000 [(240/150 × $100,000) − $100,000]
        2. $10,000 ($70,000 − $60,000), or [$170,000 − (240/150 × $100,000)]

Ex. 13-2 a. $36,000 in current year; $54,000 in future period. The revenue is realized as the concerts are performed; therefore, two-fifths of the contract has been fulfilled during the current year, and three-fifths will be fulfilled during a future period.

  b. None in current year; perhaps $420,000 in future period(s). Revenue is measured by the amount charged to customers for merchandise sold. Such revenue is not realized until the buyer acquires the right of ownership to the merchandise.

  c. $1,500 in current year; $750 in future period(s). Revenue from interest on loans is realized during the period in which it is earned. It is immaterial whether the interest is received at the beginning of the loan or at its termination.

  d. $955,000 in current year; none in the following year. Revenue from the sale of merchandise is realized when title passes to the buyer.

  e. Revenue recognized in current year: 20% × $11,000,000 = $2,200,000. Revenue recognized in future period(s): $11,000,000 − $2,200,000 = $8,800,000.

  f. $20,000 in current year; $40,000 in future period. The total revenue of $60,000 to be earned should be realized over the period of the lease. In accordance with the going concern concept, it is assumed that the owner will supply the use of the land during the term of the lease.

  g. None in current year; $49,250 in future period. Revenue from the sale of merchandise is customarily realized when title passes to the buyer. The amount charged to the customer for merchandise delivered is revenue of the following year.

  h. None in current year; $10,000 in future period. The revenue is realized when title to the merchandise passes from the seller. A claim for merchandise is still outstanding, and the recognition of revenue must be postponed until the seller fulfills this obligation. A refund may be necessary for the outstanding certificates.

  i. $450 in current year; $900 in future period. Revenue from interest is realized during the period in which it is earned.

Ex. 13-3 a.

Sales...		$950,000
Less cost of merchandise sold:		
Inventory, beginning of year	$175,000	
Purchases	657,500	
Merchandise available for sale	$832,500	
Less inventory, end of year	167,500	
Cost of merchandise sold............		665,000
Gross profit		$285,000

    b. Percent of gross profit to sales:
        $285,000/$950,000 = 30%
    Gross profit:
        $350,000 × 30% = $105,000

Ex. 13-4 a. $7,500 + $4,500 = $12,000
      b. $60,000 + $7,500 − $500 + $1,750 = $68,750
      c. $50,000 + $725 + $1,500 = $52,225

Ex. 13-5 a. 1st year, net income overstated $20,000.
          2d year, net income overstated $7,500.
          3d year, net income understated $4,000.
          4th year, net income understated $23,500.
      b. 1st year, commissions payable understated $20,000 and owner's
          equity overstated $20,000.
          2d year, commissions payable understated $27,500 and owner's
          equity overstated $27,500.
          3d year, commissions payable understated $23,500 and owner's
          equity overstated $23,500.
          4th year, no understatements or overstatements.

Ex. 13-6 a. 1st year, net income understated $6,500.
          2d year, net income overstated $1,500.
          3d year, net income understated $2,500.
      b. 1st year, accounts receivable and owner's equity understated
          $6,500.
          2d year, accounts receivable and owner's equity understated
          $5,000.
          3d year, accounts receivable and owner's equity understated
          $7,500.

Ex. 13-7 Material and should be disclosed: a, b, c, e
         Immaterial and need not be disclosed: d

Ex. 13-8 a. $58,500 [$65,000 − ($86,500 − $80,000)]
      b. $68,500 [$65,000 + ($90,000 − $86,500)]
      c. Lifo
      d. Yes

Ex. 13-9 a. Agree with the accountant's decision. Such detailed information is not needed by the reader of the financial statements for adequate disclosure, and to include it on the balance sheet would impede rather than aid understanding.

  b. Disagree with the accountant's decision. Changes in market values of plant assets are not recognized in the accounts. The practice of recording acquisition cost is supported by the going concern concept, which assumes that the business entity has a reasonable expectation of continuing in business for an indefinite period of time with no immediate expectation of selling the plant assets.

  c. Agree with the accountant's decision. The principle of materiality justifies treating minor expenditures for plant assets as expenses.

  d. Agree with the accountant's decision. Title to merchandise transferred on a consignment basis and not sold remains with the consignor and should be included in the consignor's inventory. Sales are customarily recorded when title passes to a buyer to match revenue and expenses properly.

  e. Disagree with the accountant's decision. Depreciation expense is an allocation of the expiration of the cost of plant assets to the period during which the expiration took place and not a process of providing for the replacement of plant assets. Therefore, the depreciation expense should be a portion of the cost of $250,000.

  f. Disagree with the accountant's decision. The most objective evidence available should be used in making the accounting entries. In this case, the inventory should be determined by counting the inventory and applying the appropriate unit cost as evidenced by purchase invoices. An estimate of inventory cost based on observed past gross profit rates would be an acceptable alternate method.

  g. Agree with the accountant's decision. Because the firm is considered to be a going concern, the cost of the unused catalogs will serve the purpose for which they were acquired. Therefore, the unused portion is an asset and this investment will be recovered in future years.

  h. Disagree with the accountant's decision. The concept of consistency requires the use of the same accounting principles from year to year unless a change to a different principle will more fairly state net income and financial position. Thus a change merely to smooth periodic net income is not an acceptable reason for a change.

  i. Agree with the accountant's decision. Supplementary financial data indicating the effect of changing prices is not only acceptable but is encouraged.

WHAT'S WRONG WITH THIS?

Generally accepted accounting principles require that inventory be valued at cost or lower of cost or market. The method used, including the manner in which cost is determined, should be disclosed in the statements. However, adequate disclosure of an unaccepted principle does not compensate for the lack of compliance with generally accepted accounting principles.

PROBLEMS

Prob. 13-1A

1. Gross profit percentages:
    First year: $127,600 ÷ $398,750 = 32%
    Second year: $112,200 ÷ $340,000 = 33%
    Third year: $133,700 ÷ $382,000 = 35%

2.

	First Year	Second Year	Third Year
Gross profit realized on collections from sales of:			
First year: 32% × $121,250..........	$ 38,800		
32% × $157,500..........		$50,400	
32% × $120,000..........			$ 38,400
Second year: 33% × $95,000...........		31,350	
33% × $145,000..........			47,850
Third year: 35% × $99,000...........			34,650
Total gross profit realized	$ 38,800	$81,750	$120,900
Operating expenses....................	60,000	51,500	62,250
Net income (loss)	$(21,200)	$30,250	$ 58,650

Prob. 13-2A

1. **First year:**

Selling price of set	$800
Cost of set	640
Gross profit	$160

Rate of gross profit: $\dfrac{\$160}{\$800} = 20\%$

Gross profit recognized (20% × $150 collected)	$ 30

2. **Second year:**

Gross profit recognized (20% × $300 collected)	$ 60

3. **Third year:**

Installment payments canceled	$350
*Gross profit lost (20% × $350)	70
Unrecovered portion of original cost	$280
Sales price of set repossessed	250
*Loss on repossession and sale	$ 30

*Note that the $70 of gross profit is not a deduction from other revenue. It is an anticipated gross profit that is never realized. It is replaced by the $30 loss which is the excess of the unrecovered portion of its original cost over the sales price of the set.

Prob. 13-3A

	1993	1994	1995
Revenue recognized:			
Contract 1:			
40% × $5,000,000	$2,000,000		
35% × $5,000,000		$1,750,000	
25% × $5,000,000			$1,250,000
Contract 2:			
30% × $10,000,000	3,000,000		
30% × $10,000,000		3,000,000	
30% × $10,000,000			3,000,000
Contract 3:			
50% × $8,000,000	4,000,000		
50% × $8,000,000		4,000,000	
Total revenue recognized	$9,000,000	$8,750,000	$4,250,000
Costs incurred:			
Contract 1	$1,810,000	$1,575,000	$1,090,000
Contract 2	2,550,000	2,625,000	2,695,000
Contract 3	3,710,000	3,815,000	
Total costs incurred	$8,070,000	$8,015,000	$3,785,000
Income from contracts	$ 930,000	$ 735,000	$ 465,000

Prob. 13-4A

	First Year	Second Year	Third Year
Net income reported	$105,000	$142,000	$175,000
Increase (decrease) in net income attributable to change in method of determining:			
Uncollectible accounts expense	$ (1,500)	$ (700)	$ 1,700
Ending merchandise inventory	(1,750)	(10,150)	(7,350)
Depreciation expense	(20,000)	(12,040)	900
Total	$ (23,250)	$ (22,890)	$ (4,750)
Net income as recomputed	$ 81,750	$119,110	$170,250

Prob. 13-5A

a. Allowance for Doubtful Accounts   8,000
    Accounts Receivable—J. J. Jeffries Co.   8,000

b. No entry. Land is recorded at cost in the accounts and not at appraisal value.

c. No entry. Only contingent liabilities that are probable and the amounts reasonably estimated should be recorded in the accounts.

d. Insurance Expense   4,975
    Prepaid Insurance   4,975

e. Depreciation Expense—Buildings   52,100
    Accumulated Depreciation—Buildings   52,100

f. Interest Receivable.   2,000
    Interest Income   2,000

g. No entry. Merchandise inventory is recorded in the accounts at lower of cost or market. If current market price exceeds cost, it is not recognized in the accounts.

Prob. 13-6A

1. and 2.

THE GALLERY
Work Sheet
For Year Ended December 31, 19—

Account Title	Trial Balance Dr.	Trial Balance Cr.	Adjustments* Dr.	Adjustments* Cr.	Income Statement Dr.	Income Statement Cr.	Balance Sheet Dr.	Balance Sheet Cr.
Cash	7,750						7,750	
Equipment	17,250		(d) 5,000 (d) 4,000				26,250	
Chris Bosio, Capital		37,500						37,500
Sales		98,700		(f) 6,700		105,400		
Purchases	73,500		(k) 5,000	(d) 5,000 (j) 1,000	72,500			
Salary Expense	17,850		(m) 350		18,200			
Rent Expense	13,000			(l) 1,000	12,000			
Utilities Expense	5,100				5,100			
Miscellaneous Expense	1,750			(i) 850	900			
	136,200	136,200						
Notes Payable				(d) 4,000				4,000
Depreciation Expense**			(e) 1,975		1,975			
Accumulated Depreciation				(e) 1,975				1,975
Accounts Receivable			(f) 6,700				6,700	
Uncollectible Accounts Expense			(g) 475		475			
Allowance for Doubtful Accounts				(g) 475				475
Merchandise Inventory			(h) 12,750				12,750	
Income Summary				(h) 12,750		12,750		
Prepaid Insurance			(i) 350				350	
Insurance Expense			(i) 500		500			
Supplies			(j) 250				250	
Supplies Expense			(j) 750		750			
Accounts Payable				(k) 5,000				5,000
Prepaid Rent			(l) 1,000				1,000	
Salaries Payable				(m) 350				350
			39,100	39,100	112,400	118,150	55,050	49,300
Net Income					5,750			5,750
					118,150	118,150	55,050	55,050

*Letters correspond to information stated in problem.
**Computation of depreciation expense: January acquisition ($17,250 ÷ 10)...... $1,725
July acquisition ($5,000 ÷ 10) × 6/12 ... 250
$1,975

Prob. 13-6A, Continued

3.

THE GALLERY
Income Statement
For Year Ended December 31, 19—

Sales		$105,400
Cost of merchandise sold:		
Purchases	$72,500	
Less merchandise inventory, December 31, 19—.......	12,750	
Cost of merchandise sold............................		59,750
Gross profit		$ 45,650
Operating expenses:		
Salary expense	$18,200	
Rent expense.................................	12,000	
Utilities expense.............................	5,100	
Depreciation expense	1,975	
Supplies expense	750	
Insurance expense	500	
Uncollectible accounts expense.................	475	
Miscellaneous expense........................	900	
Total operating expenses........................		39,900
Net income		$ 5,750

THE GALLERY
Statement of Owner's Equity
For Year Ended December 31, 19—

Chris Bosio, capital, January 3, 19—.....................		$30,000
Additional investment, June 10	$7,500	
Net income for the year.................................	5,750	
Increase in owner's equity		13,250
Chris Bosio, capital, December 31, 19—.................		$43,250

Prob. 13-6A, Concluded

THE GALLERY
Balance Sheet
December 31, 19—

Assets

Current assets:

Cash		$ 7,750
Accounts receivable	$6,700	
Less allowance for doubtful accounts	475	6,225
Merchandise inventory		12,750
Prepaid rent		1,000
Prepaid insurance		350
Supplies		250
Total current assets		$28,325
Plant assets:		
Equipment	$26,250	
Less accumulated depreciation	1,975	24,275
Total assets		$52,600

Liabilities

Current liabilities:

Notes payable		$ 4,000
Accounts payable		5,000
Salaries payable		350
Total liabilities		$ 9,350

Owner's Equity

Chris Bosio, capital	43,250
Total liabilities and owner's equity	$52,600

Prob. 13-1B

1. Gross profit percentages:
    First year: $105,000 \div \$300,000 = 35\%$
    Second year: $115,600 \div \$340,000 = 34\%$
    Third year: $158,400 \div \$440,000 = 36\%$

Prob. 13-1B, Concluded

2.

	First Year	Second Year	Third Year
Gross profit realized on collections from sales of:			
First year: 35% × $75,000	$ 26,250		
35% × $125,000		$43,750	
35% × $100,000			$ 35,000
Second year: 34% × $110,000		37,400	
34% × $180,000			61,200
Third year: 36% × $115,000			41,400
Total gross profit realized	$ 26,250	$81,150	$137,600
Operating expenses....................	62,500	68,500	98,400
Net income (loss)	$(36,250)	$12,650	$ 39,200

Prob. 13-2B

1. First year:

Selling price of set	$900
Cost of set	720
Gross profit	$180

Rate of gross profit: $\dfrac{\$180}{\$900} = 20\%$

Gross profit recognized (20% × $150 collected)	$ 30

2. Second year:

Gross profit recognized (20% × $360 collected)................	$ 72

3. Third year:

Installment payments canceled	$390
*Gross profit lost (20% × $390)..............................	78
Unrecovered portion of original cost	$312
Sales price of set repossessed	350
*Gain on repossession and sale...............................	$ 38

*Note that the $78 of gross profit is not a deduction from other revenue. It is an anticipated gross profit that is never realized. It is replaced by the $38 gain, which is the excess of the sales price of the set over the unrecovered portion of its original cost.

Prob. 13-3B

	1993	1994	1995
Revenue recognized:			
Contract 1:			
40% × $6,000,000	$2,400,000		
60% × $6,000,000		$3,600,000	
Contract 2:			
20% × $4,000,000	800,000		
40% × $4,000,000		1,600,000	
40% × $4,000,000			$1,600,000
Contract 3:			
15% × $3,500,000	525,000		
30% × $3,500,000		1,050,000	
50% × $3,500,000			1,750,000
Total revenue recognized	$3,725,000	$6,250,000	$3,350,000
Costs incurred:			
Contract 1	$2,175,000	$3,250,000	
Contract 2	600,000	1,375,000	$1,500,000
Contract 3	455,000	985,000	1,575,000
Total costs incurred	$3,230,000	$5,610,000	$3,075,000
Income from contracts	$ 495,000	$ 640,000	$ 275,000

Prob. 13-4B

	First Year	Second Year	Third Year
Net income reported	$ 40,200	$ 60,750	$69,900
Increase (decrease) in net income attributable to change in method of determining:			
Uncollectible accounts expense	$ (575)	$ (550)	$ 250
Ending merchandise inventory	3,250	(4,350)	2,600
Depreciation expense	(19,000)	(12,100)	(6,620)
Total	$(16,325)	$(17,000)	$ (3,770)
Net income as recomputed	$ 23,875	$ 43,750	$66,130

Prob. 13-5B

a. Depreciation Expense—Equipment...................... 29,600
    Accumulated Depreciation—Equipment 29,600

b. No entry. Land is recorded at cost in the accounts and not at appraisal value.

c. Interest Expense....................................... 500
    Interest Payable..................................... 500

d. Office Supplies Expense............................... 6,000
    Office Supplies 6,000

e. No entry. Merchandise inventory is recorded in the accounts at lower of cost or market. If current market price exceeds cost, it is not recognized in the accounts.

f. Allowance for Doubtful Accounts...................... 11,700
    Accounts Receivable—Baker and Wilson Co........... 11,700

g. No entry. Only contingent liabilities that are probable and the amounts reasonably estimated should be recorded in the accounts.

h. Accounts Receivable—Cowens Co...................... 41,215
    Cash in Bank....................................... 41,215

Prob. 13-6B

1. and 2.

THE ART MART
Work Sheet
For Year Ended December 31, 19—

Account Title	Trial Balance Dr.	Trial Balance Cr.	Adjustments* Dr.	Adjustments* Cr.	Income Statement Dr.	Income Statement Cr.	Balance Sheet Dr.	Balance Sheet Cr.
Cash	8,000						8,000	
Equipment	12,000		(j) 6,000 / (j) 7,000				25,000	
Alice Marx, Capital		25,500						25,500
Sales		146,750		(f) 10,250		157,000		
Purchases	90,500		(l) 17,500	(j) 6,000 / (o) 2,400	99,600			
Salary Expense	38,410		(i) 925		39,335			
Rent Expense	16,800			(h) 1,400	15,400			
Utilities Expense	4,225				4,225			
Miscellaneous Expense	2,315			(n) 1,250	1,065			
	172,250	172,250						
Accounts Receivable			(f) 10,250				10,250	
Merchandise Inventory			(g) 23,425				23,425	
Income Summary				(g) 23,425		23,425		
Prepaid Rent			(h) 1,400				1,400	
Salaries Payable				(i) 925				925
Notes Payable				(j) 7,000				7,000
Uncollectible Accounts Expense			(k) 950		950			
Allowance for Doubtful Accounts				(k) 950				950
Accounts Payable				(l) 17,500				17,500
Depreciation Expense**			(m) 1,550		1,550			
Accumulated Depreciation				(m) 1,550				1,550
Prepaid Insurance			(n) 400				400	
Insurance Expense			(n) 850		850			
Supplies			(o) 800				800	
Supplies Expense			(o) 1,600		1,600			
			72,650	72,650	164,575	180,425	69,275	53,425
Net Income					15,850			15,850
					180,425	180,425	69,275	69,275

*Letters correspond to information stated in problem.

**Computation of depreciation expense: February acquisition:

($12,000 ÷ 10) × 11/12 ... $1,100

April acquisition: ($6,000 ÷ 10) × 9/12 ... 450

$1,550

Prob. 13-6B, Continued

3.

THE ART MART
Income Statement
For Year Ended December 31, 19—

Sales		$157,000
Cost of merchandise sold:		
Purchases	$99,600	
Less merchandise inventory, December 31, 19—	23,425	
Cost of merchandise sold...........................		76,175
Gross profit		$ 80,825
Operating expenses:		
Salary expense	$39,335	
Rent expense...................................	15,400	
Utilities expense................................	4,225	
Supplies expense	1,600	
Depreciation expense	1,550	
Uncollectible accounts expense...................	950	
Insurance expense	850	
Miscellaneous expense...........................	1,065	
Total operating expenses......................		64,975
Net income		$ 15,850

THE ART MART
Statement of Owner's Equity
For Year Ended December 31, 19—

Alice Marx, capital, January 26, 19—		$17,500
Additional investment, June 1	$ 8,000	
Net income for the year................................	15,850	
Increase in owner's equity		23,850
Alice Marx, capital, December 31, 19—		$41,350

Prob. 13-6B, Concluded

THE ART MART
Balance Sheet
December 31, 19—

Assets

Current assets:		
Cash		$ 8,000
Accounts receivable	$10,250	
Less allowance for doubtful accounts	950	9,300
Merchandise inventory.........................		23,425
Prepaid rent		1,400
Supplies		800
Prepaid insurance..............................		400
Total current assets........................		$43,325
Plant assets:		
Equipment	$25,000	
Less accumulated depreciation	1,550	23,450
Total assets		$66,775

Liabilities

Current liabilities:		
Notes payable		$ 7,000
Accounts payable..............................		17,500
Salaries payable		925
Total liabilities................................		$25,425

Owner's Equity

Alice Marx, capital.............................	41,350
Total liabilities and owner's equity..............	$66,775

Mini-Case 13

1. a. Revenue should be recognized on credit sales at the time that title to the merchandise passes to the buyer. For J. B. Parts Co., this occurs at the time that merchandise is delivered to the customer.

   b. In the retail field, it is common to make sales on the installment plan. Installment sales should ordinarily be treated in the same manner as any other credit sale, in which case the revenue should be recognized at the time that merchandise is delivered to the customer. In exceptional cases where the circumstances are such that the collection of receivables is not reasonably assured, an alternate method of determining revenue may be used. Under the alternate method, known as the installment method, each cash payment is treated as being composed of cost of goods sold and gross profit amounts. J. B. Parts Co. should choose the revenue recognition method that best reflects the results of operations.

Mini-Case 13, Concluded

2. a. Only in rare instances is a business organized with the expectation of remaining in existence for a specified period of time. In most cases, it is not possible to determine in advance the length of life of an enterprise, and so an assumption must be made. The nature of the assumption will affect the manner of recording some of the business transactions, which in turn will affect the data reported in the financial statements.

    It is customary to assume that a business entity has a reasonable expectation of continuing in business at a profit for an indefinite period of time. This going concern concept provides much of the justification for recording assets at acquisition cost and reporting them without reference to their current realizable values. It is pointless to report assets on the balance sheet at their estimated realizable value if there is no immediate expectation of selling them. For example, it is irrelevant whether the current market value of plant assets is less than the book value or greater than the book value if there is no expectation that the plant assets will be sold in the immediate future. Similarly, the going concern assumption supports the treatment of prepaid expenses as assets, even though they may be virtually unsalable. When there is conclusive evidence that a specific business entity has a limited life, the accounting procedures should then be modified to the expected terminal date of the entity.

    b. The use of a monetary unit that is assumed to be stable ensures objectivity. In spite of inflationary trends in the United States, historical-dollar financial statements are considered to be superior to statements based on movements of changing prices.

    c. A number of accepted alternative accounting principles affecting the determination of the income statement and the balance sheet amounts may be used in preparing financial statements. The concept of consistency requires than an entity use the same accounting principles from year to year. Changes are not acceptable just to improve "net income." However, changes in the accounting methods would be permissible when it is believed that adoption of a different principle will more fairly state net income and financial position. In addition, the principle of adequate disclosure requires that when there are several acceptable alternative accounting methods available, the particular method adopted should be disclosed.

    d. Many years ago, accountants tended to be conservative. In selecting among alternatives, they favored the method or procedure that yielded the lesser amount of net income or asset value. Such an attitude or pessimism was due, in part, to the need for an offset to the optimism of business management. It could also be argued that potential future losses to an enterprise from poor management decisions would be lessened if net income and assets were understated. Current accounting thought has shifted somewhat from this philosophy of conservatism. The element of conservatism is considered only when other factors affecting a choice of alternatives are neutral.

CHAPTER 14

DISCUSSION QUESTIONS

1. Unlimited liability. Each partner in a general partnership is individually liable to creditors for debts incurred by the partnership.

2. In a limited partnership, the liability of the "limited" partners may be limited to the amount of their capital investment. General partners—and there must be at least one—have unlimited liability.

3. Yes. A partnership may incur losses in excess of the total investment of all partners. The division of losses among the partners would be made in accordance with their agreement. In addition, because of the unlimited liability of each partner for partnership debts, a particular partner may actually lose a greater amount than his or her capital balances.

4. (a) Yes. (b) No. A partnership is a nontaxable entity, but it must file an informational tax return with the Internal Revenue Service.

5. 3:2. In the absence of an agreement to the contrary, net losses are shared in the same ratio as is net income.

6. Equally

7. No. He would have to bear his share of losses. In the absence of any agreement as to division of net income or net loss, his share would be one-third. In addition, because of the unlimited liability of each partner, DiPano may lose more than one-third of the losses if one partner is unable to absorb his share of the losses.

8. The disadvantages of a partnership are its life is limited, each partner has unlimited liability, one partner can bind the partnership to contracts, and raising large amounts of capital is more difficult for a partnership than a corporation.

9. The delivery equipment should be recorded at $15,000, the valuation agreed upon by the partners.

10. The accounts receivable should be recorded by a debit of $200,000 to Accounts Receivable and a credit of $20,000 to Allowance for Doubtful Accounts.

11. No. In the absence of any agreement as to division of net income or net loss, all partners share equally.

12. Yes. Partnership net income is divided in accordance with the income-sharing ratio regardless of the amount of the withdrawals by the partners. Therefore, it is very likely that the partners' monthly withdrawals from a partnership will not exactly equal their shares of net income.

13. a. Debit the partner's drawing account and credit Cash.
    b. Debit the income summary account for the amount of the net income and credit the partners' capital accounts for their respective shares of the net income.
    c. No. Payments to partners and the division of net income are separate. The amount of one does not affect the amount of the other.

14. The division of income can be reported in a separate section added to the income statement or in a separate statement of owner's equity.

15. a. Under common law, the partnership is dissolved if a partner assigns his or her interest to an outside party. Under the Uniform Partnership Act, a partner can dispose of his or her interest without the consent of the remaining partners. The person who buys the interest acquires the seller's rights in income and assets.
    b. No. The consent of all partners is required to admit a new partner.

16. a. By purchase of an interest, the capital interest of the new partner is obtained from the old partner, and neither the total assets nor the total equity of the partnership are affected.
    b. By investment, both the total assets and the total equity of the partnership are increased.

17. (a) and (b)

Kirk, Capital	30,000	
Taylor, Capital		30,000

18. It is important to state all partnership assets in terms of current prices at the time of the admission of a new partner because failure to do so might result in participation by the new partner in gains or losses attributable to the period prior to admission to the partnership. To illustrate, assume that A and B share net income and net loss equally and operate a partnership that owns land recorded at and costing $20,000. C is admitted to the partnership and the three partners share in income equally. The day after C is admitted to the partnership, the land is sold for $35,000 and, since the land was not revalued, C receives a one-third distribution of the $15,000 gain. In this case, C participates in the gain attributable to the period prior to admission to the partnership.

19. A bonus paid to the original partners should be allocated to the capital accounts of the original partners in accordance with their income-sharing agreement.

20. A new partner who is expected to improve the fortunes (income) of the partnership might be given equity in excess of the amount invested to join the partnership.

21. a. Dissolution refers to any change in the personnel of the partnership that has the effect of dissolving the partnership. Liquidation, as used in its broad sense, refers to the entire winding-up process of a firm that is going out of business.
   b. The sale of the assets is referred to as realization.

22. a. Losses and gains on realization are divided among partners in the income-sharing ratio.
   b. Cash is distributed to the partners in accordance with their ownership claims, as indicated by the credit balances in their capital accounts, after taking into consideration the potential deficiencies that may result from the inability to collect from a deficient partner.

23. a. $5,000 loss
   b. $2,500 to each
   c. $2,500 to Logan; $17,500 to Mayes

24. a. deficiency
   b. $60,000
   c. Reed must pay the amount of the deficiency ($17,500) to the partnership.

25. Short's debit balance of $15,000 must be divided between Tull and Wade in the income-sharing ratio of 2:1 (2/3 and 1/3): $10,000 to Tull and $5,000 to Wade.

26. $2,000,000,000 ÷ 350 partners = $5,714,286, or approximately $5,700,000 per partner.

ETHICS DISCUSSION CASE Donald Newton behaved in an ethical manner in signing the contract without notifying Eileen Logan. Any partner has the legal authority to commit the partnership to contractual obligations. Although Newton behaved ethically, it is usually preferable to notify all partners in a partnership of pending transactions which might significantly affect the operations of the partnership. To do otherwise may create ill will and dissension among the partners.

EXERCISES

Ex. 14-1

Cash..	4,500	
Accounts Receivable	92,500	
Merchandise Inventory	81,500	
Equipment	75,000	
Allowance for Doubtful Accounts		7,500
Albert Sommers, Capital......................		246,000

Ex. 14-2

	Kahn	Lell
a.	$30,000	$30,000
b.	40,000	20,000
c.	28,800	31,200
d.	27,500	32,500
e.	30,500	29,500

Details

	Kahn	Lell	Total
a. Net income (1:1)	$30,000	$30,000	$60,000
b. Net income (2:1)	$40,000	$20,000	$60,000
c. Interest allowance	$12,000	$ 6,000	$18,000
Remaining income (2:3).........	16,800	25,200	42,000
Net income....................	$28,800	$31,200	$60,000
d. Salary allowance.................	$20,000	$25,000	$45,000
Remaining income (1:1).........	7,500	7,500	15,000
Net income	$27,500	$32,500	$60,000
e. Interest allowance	$12,000	$ 6,000	$18,000
Salary allowance.................	20,000	25,000	45,000
Excess of allowances over income (1:1)	(1,500)	(1,500)	(3,000)
Net income	$30,500	$29,500	$60,000

Ex. 14-3

	Kahn	Lell
a.	$45,000	$45,000
b.	60,000	30,000
c.	40,800	49,200
d.	42,500	47,500
e.	45,500	44,500

Ex. 14-3, Concluded

	Details		
	Kahn	**Lell**	**Total**
a. Net income (1:1)	$45,000	$45,000	$90,000
b. Net income (2:1)	$60,000	$30,000	$90,000
c. Interest allowance	$12,000	$ 6,000	$18,000
Remaining income (2:3)...........	28,800	43,200	72,000
Net income.....................	$40,800	$49,200	$90,000
d. Salary allowance..................	$20,000	$25,000	$45,000
Remaining income (1:1)...........	22,500	22,500	45,000
Net income	$42,500	$47,500	$90,000
e. Interest allowance	$12,000	$ 6,000	$18,000
Salary allowance..................	20,000	25,000	45,000
Remaining income (1:1)...........	13,500	13,500	27,000
Net income.....................	$45,500	$44,500	$90,000

Ex. 14-4

	Ruth Neff	**Don Raub**	**Total**
	---	---	---
Salary allowances	20,000	$ 30,000	$ 50,000
Remainder ($60,000) (net loss, $10,000 plus $50,000 salary allowances), divided equally ...	(30,000)	(30,000)	(60,000)
Net loss.....................	$(10,000)	$ 0	$(10,000)

Ex. 14-5 a.

(1)
Income Summary	80,000	
J.C. Reed, Capital		40,000
Victor Scott, Capital		40,000

(2)
J.C. Reed, Capital........................	36,000	
Victor Scott, Capital	42,000	
J.C. Reed, Drawing.....................		36,000
Victor Scott, Drawing		42,000

Ex. 14-5, Concluded

b.

REED AND SCOTT
Statement and Owner's Equity
For Year Ended December 31, 19–

	J.C. Reed	Victor Scott	Total
Capital, January 1, 19–......................	$ 80,000	$ 95,000	$175,000
Additional investment during the year......	10,000	....	10,000
	$ 90,000	$ 95,000	$185,000
Net income for the year...................	40,000	40,000	80,000
	$130,000	$135,000	$265,000
Withdrawals during the year..............	36,000	42,000	78,000
Capital, December 31, 19–................	$ 94,000	$ 93,000	$187,000

Ex. 14-6 a. $2,068,000 ($4,947,800,000 ÷ 2,393)
     b. $210,000 ($500,000,000 ÷ 2,393)
     c. A new partner might contribute more than $210,000 because of goodwill attributable to the firm's reputation, future income potential, a strong client base, etc.

Ex. 14-7 a. (1) Alan Evans, Capital 20,000
          Mary Farr, Capital......................... 14,000
             Don Reese, Capital 34,000

        (2) Cash 30,000
            Gloria Swain, Capital.................. 30,000

     b. Alan Evans................................. $60,000
        Mary Farr 56,000
        Don Reese 34,000
        Gloria Swain 30,000

Ex. 14-8 a. Cash 40,000
        Mike Cash, Capital........................... 5,000
        Ed Doerr, Capital 5,000
          Paula Goles, Capital....................... 50,000

     b. Mike Cash................................... $51,000
        Ed Doerr 49,000
        Paula Goles 50,000

Ex. 14-9 a. Merchandise Inventory..................... 7,500

Allowance for Doubtful Accounts.........	1,550
Paul Blasi, Capital........................	2,550
Sandra Young, Capital	1,700
Ralph Zimmer, Capital	1,700

b. Paul Blasi, Capital 202,550

Cash.......................................	52,550
Notes Payable	150,000

Ex. 14-10

	Bond	Fico
Capital balances before realization	$51,000	$36,000
Division of loss on sale of noncash assets ($87,000 − $67,000).........................	10,000	10,000
Capital balances after realization and distribution of cash.........................	$41,000	$26,000

Ex. 14-11

a. Cash should be distributed as indicated in the following tabulation:

	Gray	Hall	Ide	Total
Capital invested	$175	$125	$—	$300
Net income................	+ 75	+ 75	+ 75	+ 225
Capital balances and cash distribution	$250	$200	$75	$525

b. Ide has a capital deficiency of $50, as indicated in the following tabulation:

	Gray	Hall	Ide	Total
Capital invested	$175	$125	$—	$300
Net loss..................	− 50	− 50	− 50	− 150
Capital balances	$125	$ 75	$50 Dr.	$150

Ex. 14-12

Gertz, Hart, and Imes
Statement of Partnership Liquidation
For Period July 1–29, 19–

	Cash	+	Noncash Assets	=	Liabilities	+	Capital Gertz (3/6)	+	Hart (2/6)	+	Imes (1/6)
Balances before realization	$11,000		$85,000		$30,000		$24,000		$28,000		$14,000
Sale of assets and division of loss	+ 49,000		− 85,000		—		− 18,000		− 12,000		− 6,000
Balances after realization	$60,000		0		$30,000		$ 6,000		$16,000		$ 8,000
Payment of liabilities	− 30,000		—		− 30,000		—		—		—
Balances after payment of liabilities	$30,000		0		0		$ 6,000		$16,000		$ 8,000
Distribution of cash to partners	− 30,000		—		—		− 6,000		− 16,000		− 8,000
Final balances	0		0		0		0		0		0

WHAT'S WRONG WITH THIS?

The partners can divide net income in any ratio that they wish. However, in the absence of an agreement, net income is divided equally between the partners. Therefore, Jim's conclusion was correct but for the wrong reasons.

PROBLEMS

Prob. 14-1A

1.
May 1	Cash		10,500	
	Merchandise Inventory		39,500	
	Anna Austin, Capital			50,000
1	Cash		5,300	
	Accounts Receivable		19,500	
	Equipment		45,000	
	Allowance for Doubtful Accounts			800
	Accounts Payable			14,000
	Notes Payable			15,000
	Dave Walls, Capital			40,000

2.

AUSTIN AND WALLS
Balance Sheet
May 1, 19—

Assets

Current assets:			
Cash		$15,800	
Accounts receivable	$19,500		
Less allowance for doubtful accounts	800	18,700	
Merchandise inventory		39,500	
Total current assets			$ 74,000
Plant assets:			
Equipment			45,000
Total assets			$119,000

Liabilities

Current liabilities:			
Accounts payable		$14,000	
Notes payable		15,000	
Total liabilities			$ 29,000

Owner's Equity

Anna Austin, capital		$50,000	
Dave Walls, capital		40,000	
Total owner's equity			90,000
Total liabilities and owner's equity			$119,000

Prob. 14-1A, Concluded

3. April 30 Income Summary........................... 68,000

               Anna Austin, Capital......................   33,000*

               Dave Walls, Capital.......................   35,000*

      30 Anna Austin, Capital....................... 20,000

           Dave Walls, Capital 26,000

               Anna Austin, Drawing   20,000

               Dave Walls, Drawing   26,000

*Computations:

	Austin	Walls	Total
Interest allowance	$ 5,000	$ 4,000	$ 9,000
Salary allowance..........................	18,000	21,000	39,000
Remaining income (1:1)....................	10,000	10,000	20,000
Net income................................	$33,000	$35,000	$68,000

Prob. 14-2A

	(1) $45,000		(2) $120,000	
Plan	Bode	Dyke	Bode	Dyke
a.	$22,500	$22,500	$60,000	$60,000
b.	30,000	15,000	80,000	40,000
c.	15,000	30,000	40,000	80,000
d.	25,500	19,500	63,000	57,000
e.	18,000	27,000	55,500	64,500
f.	18,000	27,000	48,000	72,000

Prob. 14-2A, Concluded

		Details			
		$45,000		**$120,000**	
		Bode	**Dyke**	**Bode**	**Dyke**
a.	Net income (1:1)	$22,500	$22,500	$60,000	$60,000
b.	Net income (2:1)	$30,000	$15,000	$80,000	$40,000
c.	Net income (1:2)	$15,000	$30,000	$40,000	$80,000
d.	Interest allowance	$12,000	$ 6,000	$12,000	$ 6,000
	Remaining income (1:1)	13,500	13,500	51,000	51,000
	Net income	$25,500	$19,500	$63,000	$57,000
e.	Interest allowance	$12,000	$ 6,000	$12,000	$ 6,000
	Salary allowance	15,000	30,000	15,000	30,000
	Excess of allowances over income (1:1)	(9,000)	(9,000)		
	Remaining income (1:1)			28,500	28,500
	Net income	$18,000	$27,000	$55,500	$64,500
f.	Interest allowance	$12,000	$ 6,000	$12,000	$ 6,000
	Salary allowance	15,000	30,000	15,000	30,000
	Bonus allowance				15,000
	Excess of allowances over income (1:1)	(9,000)	(9,000)		
	Remaining income (1:1)			21,000	21,000
	Net income	$18,000	$27,000	$48,000	$72,000

Prob. 14-3A

1.

ACOSTA AND MORRIS
Income Statement
For Year Ended December 31, 19—

Professional fees			$265,650
Operating expenses:			
Salary expense		$75,500	
Depreciation expense—building		10,500	
Property tax expense		8,000	
Heating and lighting expense...............		7,900	
Supplies expense		2,850	
Depreciation expense—office equipment....		2,800	
Miscellaneous expense.......................		6,100	
Total operating expenses.................			113,650
Net income			$152,000

	Juan Acosta	Marsha Morris	Total
Division of net income:			
Salary allowance.............................	$30,000	$40,000	$ 70,000
Interest allowance	9,000	6,000	15,000
Remaining income	33,500	33,500	67,000
Net income	$72,500	$79,500	$152,000

2.

ACOSTA AND MORRIS
Statement of Owner's Equity
For Year Ended December 31, 19—

	Juan Acosta	Marsha Morris	Total
Capital, January 1, 19—....................	$ 75,000	$ 50,000	$125,000
Additional investment during the year	—	5,000	5,000
	$ 75,000	$ 55,000	$130,000
Net income for the year....................	72,500	79,500	152,000
	$147,500	$134,500	$282,000
Withdrawals during the year	60,000	75,000	135,000
Capital, December 31, 19—.................	$ 87,500	$ 59,500	$147,000

Prob. 14-3A, Concluded

3.

ACOSTA AND MORRIS
Balance Sheet
December 31, 19—

Assets

Current assets:

Cash	$17,000	
Accounts receivable	28,900	
Supplies	1,900	
Total current assets		$ 47,800

Plant assets:

Land		$25,000	
Building	$130,000		
Less accumulated depreciation	69,200	60,800	
Office equipment	$ 39,000		
Less accumulated depreciation	21,500	17,500	
Total plant assets			103,300
Total assets			$151,100

Liabilities

Current liabilities:

Accounts payable	$ 2,100	
Salaries payable	2,000	
Total liabilities		$ 4,100

Owner's Equity

Juan Acosta, capital	$87,500	
Marsha Morris, capital	59,500	
Total owner's equity		147,000
Total liabilities and owner's equity		$151,100

Prob. 14-4A

1.

April 30	Asset Revaluations		2,950	
		Accounts Receivable		2,500
		Allowance for Doubtful Accounts		450
30	Merchandise Inventory		2,300	
		Asset Revaluations		2,300
30	Accumulated Depreciation—Equipment		65,000	
		Equipment		50,000
		Asset Revaluations		15,000
30	Asset Revaluations		14,350	
		Dave Eagan, Capital		7,175
		Agnes Mobley, Capital		7,175

Prob. 14-4A, Concluded

2. May 1 Agnes Mobley, Capital 20,000
              Ann Wild, Capital   20,000
    1 Cash.. 20,000
              Ann Wild, Capital   20,000

3.   EAGAN, MOBLEY, AND WILD
                              Balance Sheet
                               May 1, 19—

Assets

Current assets:

Cash		$27,900
Accounts receivable	$20,000	
Less allowance for doubtful accounts.......	1,000	19,000
Merchandise inventory......................		52,900
Prepaid insurance..........................		1,650
Total current assets		$101,450
Plant assets:		
Equipment		95,000
Total assets		$196,450

Liabilities

Current liabilities:

Accounts payable...........................		$12,100
Notes payable		10,000
Total liabilities.............................		$ 22,100

Owner's Equity

Dave Eagan, capital.........................		$87,175
Agnes Mobley, capital		47,175
Ann Wild, capital		40,000
Total owner's equity		174,350
Total liabilities and owner's equity...........		$196,450

Prob. 14-5A

1.
ARK, BIRK, AND CASE
Statement of Partnership Liquidation
For Period May 3–29, 19—

					Capital	
	Cash	+ Noncash Assets	= Liabili- ties	+ Ark (50%)	+ Birk (25%)	+ Case (25%)
Balances before realization......	$ 1,900	$62,000	$30,000	$20,000	$ 3,900	$10,000
Sale of assets and division of loss..........	+22,000	−62,000	—	−20,000	−10,000	−10,000
Balances after realization	$23,900	0	$30,000	0	$ 6,100(Dr.)	0
Receipt of deficiency......	+ 6,100	—	—	—	+ 6,100	—
Balances..........	$30,000	0	$30,000	0	0	0
Payment of liabilities.......	−30,000	—	−30,000	—	—	—
Final balances....	0	0	0	0	0	0

2. The $6,100 deficiency of Birk would be divided between the other partners, Ark and Case, in their income-sharing ratio (50:25 respectively). Therefore, Ark would absorb 50/75 of the $6,100 deficiency, or $4,066.67, and Case would absorb 25/75 of the $6,100 deficiency, or $2,033.33.

Prob. 14-6A

1.

GRAY, HALE, AND IVES
Statement of Partnership Liquidation
For Period December 1–20, 19—

	Cash	+ Noncash Assets	= Liabilities	+ Gray (50%)	+ Hale (30%)	+ Ives (20%)
				Capital		
Balances before realization	$15,400	$87,100	$50,000	$30,400	$ 8,000	$14,100
Sale of assets and division of loss	+37,100	−87,100	—	−25,000	−15,000	−10,000
Balances after realization	$52,500	0	$50,000	$ 5,400	$ 7,000(Dr.)	$ 4,100
Payment of liabilities.......	−50,000	—	−50,000	—	—	—
Balances after payment of liabilities.......	$ 2,500	0	0	$ 5,400	$ 7,000(Dr.)	$ 4,100
Receipt of deficiency	+ 7,000	—	—	—	+ 7,000	—
Balances.........	$ 9,500	0	0	$ 5,400	0	$ 4,100
Distribution of cash to partners	− 9,500	—	—	− 5,400	—	− 4,100
Final balances....	0	0	0	0	0	0

2. **a.** Cash 37,100
Loss and Gain on Realization 50,000
   Assets 87,100

b. Tom Gray, Capital 25,000
Clyde Hale, Capital 15,000
Curtis Ives, Capital 10,000
   Loss and Gain on Realization 50,000

c. Liabilities 50,000
   Cash 50,000

d. Cash 7,000
   Clyde Hale, Capital 7,000

e. Tom Gray, Capital 5,400
Curtis Ives, Capital 4,100
   Cash 9,500

Prob. 14-7A

1.

JUST, KANE, AND LOWE
Statement of Partnership Liquidation
For Period October 1–30, 19—

		Noncash	Liabili-	Just	Kane	Lowe
					Capital	
	Cash	+ Assets =	ties +	(2/5) +	(2/5) +	(1/5)
Balances before realization......	$ 20,000	$250,000	$50,000	$100,000	$ 90,000	$30,000
Sale of assets and division of gain	+300,000	−250,000	—	+ 20,000	+ 20,000	+10,000
Balances after realization	$320,000	0	$50,000	$120,000	$110,000	$40,000
Payment of liabilities	− 50,000	—	−50,000	—	—	—
Balances after payment of liabilities	$270,000	0	0	$120,000	$110,000	$40,000
Distribution of cash to partners........	−270,000	—	—	−120,000	−110,000	−40,000
Final balances....	0	0	0	0	0	0

2.

JUST, KANE, AND LOWE
Statement of Partnership Liquidation
For Period October 1–30, 19—

		Noncash	Liabili-	Just	Kane	Lowe
					Capital	
	Cash	+ Assets =	ties +	(2/5) +	(2/5) +	(1/5)
Balances before realization......	$ 20,000	$250,000	$50,000	$100,000	$ 90,000	$30,000
Sale of assets and division of loss..........	+150,000	−250,000	—	− 40,000	− 40,000	−20,000
Balances after realization	$170,000	0	$50,000	$ 60,000	$ 50,000	$10,000
Payment of liabilities	− 50,000	—	−50,000	—	—	—
Balances after payment of liabilities	$120,000	0	0	$ 60,000	$ 50,000	$10,000
Distribution of cash to partners........	−120,000	—	—	− 60,000	− 50,000	−10,000
Final balances....	0	0	0	0	0	0

Prob. 14-7A, Concluded

3.

JUST, KANE, AND LOWE
Statement of Partnership Liquidation
For Period October 1–30, 19—

	Cash	+	Noncash Assets	=	Liabili-ties	+	Just (2/5)	+	Kane (2/5)	+	Lowe (1/5)
							Capital				
Balances before realization	$ 20,000		$250,000		$50,000		$100,000		$90,000		$30,000
Sale of assets and division of loss	+ 80,000		−250,000		—		− 68,000		−68,000		−34,000
Balances after realization	$100,000		0		$50,000		$ 32,000		$22,000		$ 4,000(Dr.)
Payment of liabilities.	− 50,000		—		−50,000		—		—		—
Balances after payment of liabilities.	$ 50,000		0		0		$ 32,000		$22,000		$ 4,000(Dr.)
Receipt of deficiency	+ 4,000		—		—		—		—		+ 4,000
Balances	$ 54,000		0		0		$ 32,000		$22,000		0
Distribution of cash to partners	− 54,000		—		—		− 32,000		−22,000		—
Final balances. . .	0		0		0		0		0		0

Prob. 14-1B

1. Nov. 1

Cash	10,000	
Merchandise Inventory	55,000	
Dan Neja, Capital		65,000

1

Cash	6,550	
Accounts Receivable	30,500	
Merchandise Inventory	40,900	
Equipment	27,750	
Allowance for Doubtful Accounts		1,000
Accounts Payable		9,700
Notes Payable		10,000
Paul Ott, Capital		85,000

Prob. 14-1B, Concluded

2.

NEJA AND OTT
Balance Sheet
November 1, 19—

Assets

Current assets:

Cash..		$16,550	
Accounts receivable	$30,500		
Less allowance for doubtful accounts.......	1,000	29,500	
Merchandise inventory......................		95,900	
Total current assets.......................			$141,950

Plant assets:

Equipment		27,750
Total assets		$169,700

Liabilities

Current liabilities:

Accounts payable..........................	$ 9,700	
Notes payable	10,000	
Total liabilities.............................		$ 19,700

Owner's Equity

Dan Neja, capital	$65,000	
Paul Ott, capital	85,000	
Total owner's equity		150,000
Total liabilities and owner's equity...........		$169,700

3.

Oct. 31	Income Summary	65,000		
	Dan Neja, Capital..........................		34,500*	
	Paul Ott, Capital		30,500*	
31	Dan Neja, Capital..........................	26,000		
	Paul Ott, Capital	17,500		
	Dan Neja, Drawing		26,000	
	Paul Ott, Drawing		17,500	

*Computations:

	Neja	Ott	Total
Interest allowance	$ 6,500	$ 8,500	$15,000
Salary allowance............................	24,000	18,000	42,000
Remaining income (1:1)....................	4,000	4,000	8,000
Net income.................................	$34,500	$30,500	$65,000

Prob. 14-2B

Plan		(1) $75,000		(2) $45,000	
		Logan	Mair	Logan	Mair
a.	....	$37,500	$37,500	$22,500	$22,500
b.	....	30,000	45,000	18,000	27,000
c.	....	50,000	25,000	30,000	15,000
d.	....	42,000	33,000	24,000	21,000
e.	....	43,500	31,500	28,500	16,500
f.	....	46,500	28,500	28,500	16,500

Details

		$75,000		$45,000	
		Logan	Mair	Logan	Mair
a.	Net income (1:1)	$37,500	$37,500	$22,500	$22,500
b.	Net income (60:90)............	$30,000	$45,000	$18,000	$27,000
c.	Net income (2:1)	$50,000	$25,000	$30,000	$15,000
d.	Interest allowance	$ 6,000	$ 9,000	$ 6,000	$ 9,000
	Remaining allowance (3:2)	36,000	24,000	18,000	12,000
	Net income	$42,000	$33,000	$24,000	$21,000
e.	Interest allowance	$ 6,000	$ 9,000	$ 6,000	$ 9,000
	Salary allowance	30,000	15,000	30,000	15,000
	Excess of allowances over income (1:1)			(7,500)	(7,500)
	Remaining income (1:1)	7,500	7,500		
	Net income	$43,500	$31,500	$28,500	$16,500
f.	Interest allowance	$ 6,000	$ 9,000	$ 6,000	$ 9,000
	Salary allowance	30,000	15,000	30,000	15,000
	Bonus allowance	6,000			
	Excess of allowances over income (1:1)			(7,500)	(7,500)
	Remaining income (1:1)	4,500	4,500		
	Net income	$46,500	$28,500	$28,500	$16,500

Prob. 14-3B

1.

MUZI AND NALL
Income Statement
For Year Ended December 31, 19—

Professional fees...............................		$296,750
Operating expenses:		
Salary expense.................................	$79,500	
Depreciation expense—building.............	10,500	
Property tax expense	10,000	
Heating and lighting expense...............	9,900	
Supplies expense	5,750	
Depreciation expense—office equipment	5,000	
Miscellaneous expense......................	6,100	
Total operating expenses..................		126,750
Net income		$170,000

	Ed Muzi	Ellen Nall	Total
Division of net income:			
Salary allowance............................	$25,000	$35,000	$ 60,000
Interest allowance..........................	9,000	6,000	15,000
Remaining income	47,500	47,500	95,000
Net income	$81,500	$88,500	$170,000

2.

MUZI AND NALL
Statement of Owner's Equity
For Year Ended December 31, 19—

	Ed Muzi	Ellen Nall	Total
Capital, January 1, 19—....................	$ 75,000	$ 50,000	$125,000
Additional investment during the year	—	5,000	5,000
	$ 75,000	$ 55,000	$130,000
Net income for the year...................	81,500	88,500	170,000
	$156,500	$143,500	$300,000
Withdrawals during the year	50,000	60,000	110,000
Capital, December 31, 19—................	$106,500	$ 83,500	$190,000

Prob. 14-3B, Concluded

3.

MUZI AND NALL
Balance Sheet
December 31, 19—

Assets

Current assets:			
Cash		$ 19,500	
Accounts receivable		30,500	
Supplies		2,400	
Total current assets			$ 52,400
Plant assets:			
Land		$ 50,000	
Building	$150,000		
Less accumulated depreciation	77,500	72,500	
Office equipment	$ 40,000		
Less accumulated depreciation	22,400	17,600	
Total plant assets			140,100
Total assets			$192,500

Liabilities

Current liabilities:		
Accounts payable	$ 1,000	
Salaries payable	1,500	
Total liabilities		$ 2,500

Owner's Equity

Ed Muzi, capital	$106,500	
Ellen Nall, capital	83,500	
Total owner's equity		190,000
Total liabilities and owner's equity		$192,500

Prob. 14-4B

1.	May 31	Asset Revaluations	5,000	
		Accounts Receivable		4,250
		Allowance for Doubtful Accounts		750
	31	Merchandise Inventory	1,100	
		Asset Revaluations		1,100
	31	Accumulated Depreciation—Equipment	72,500	
		Equipment		52,000
		Asset Revaluations		20,500
	31	Asset Revaluations	16,600	
		Alan Lair, Capital		8,300
		Don Mara, Capital		8,300

Prob. 14-4B, Concluded

2. June 1   Alan Lair, Capital   25,000
                  Fran Voss, Capital   25,000

     1   Cash..   25,000
                  Fran Voss, Capital   25,000

3.

LAIR, MARA, AND VOSS
Balance Sheet
June 1, 19—

Assets

Current assets:		
Cash		$ 34,500
Accounts receivable	$25,000	
Less allowance for doubtful accounts......	1,250	23,750
Merchandise inventory....................		61,200
Prepaid insurance........................		2,000
Total current assets....................		$121,450
Plant assets:		
Equipment		110,000
Total assets		$231,450

Liabilities

Current liabilities:		
Accounts payable........................		$ 9,850
Notes payable		20,000
Total liabilities..............................		$ 29,850

Owner's Equity

Alan Lair, capital	$103,300	
Don Mara, capital.........................	48,300	
Fran Voss, capital.........................	50,000	
Total owner's equity		201,600
Total liabilities and owner's equity...........		$231,450

Prob. 14-5B

1.

FOX, GOVE, AND HOWE
Statement of Partnership Liquidation
For Period May 10–30, 19—

	Cash	+	Noncash Assets	=	Liabili- ties	+	Fox (50%)	+	Gove (25%)	+	Howe (25%)
							Capital				
Balances before realization......	$ 6,500		$89,100		$45,600		$27,800		$ 8,300		$13,900
Sale of assets and division of loss..........	+33,500		−89,100		—		−27,800		−13,900		−13,900
Balances after realization	$40,000		0		$45,600		0		$ 5,600(Dr.)		0
Receipt of deficiency......	+ 5,600		—		—		—		+ 5,600		—
Balance...........	$45,600		0		$45,600		0		0		0
Payment of liabilities	−45,600		—		−45,600		—		—		—
Final balances....	0		0		0		0		0		0

2. The $5,600 deficiency of Gove would be divided between the other partners, Fox and Howe, in their income-sharing ratio (50:25, respectively). Therefore, Fox would absorb 50/75 of the $5,600 deficiency, or $3,733.33, and Howe would absorb 25/75 of the $5,600 deficiency, or $1,866.67.

Prob. 14-6B

1.

GRAY, HALE, AND IVES
Statement of Partnership Liquidation
For Period December 1–20, 19—

					Capital	
	Cash	+ Noncash Assets =	Liabili- ties	+ Gray (50%) +	Hale (30%) +	Ives (20%)
Balances before realization	$15,400	$87,100	$50,000	$30,400	$ 8,000	$14,100
Sale of assets and division of loss	+37,100	−87,100	—	−25,000	−15,000	−10,000
Balances after realization	$52,500	0	$50,000	$ 5,400	$ 7,000(Dr.)	$ 4,100
Payment of liabilities.......	−50,000	—	−50,000	—	—	—
Balances after payment of liabilities.......	$ 2,500	0	0	$ 5,400	$ 7,000(Dr.)	$ 4,100
Division of deficiency	—	—	—	− 5,000	+ 7,000	− 2,000
Balances.........	$ 2,500	0	0	$ 400	0	$ 2,100
Distribution of cash to partners	− 2,500	—	—	− 400	—	− 2,100
Final balances....	0	0	0	0	0	0

2. **a.** Cash 37,100
    Loss and Gain on Realization....................... 50,000
      Assets 87,100

    b. Tom Gray, Capital 25,000
        Clyde Hale, Capital 15,000
        Curtis Ives, Capital 10,000
          Loss and Gain on Realization 50,000

    c. Liabilities 50,000
          Cash 50,000

    d. Tom Gray, Capital 5,000
        Curtis Ives, Capital 2,000
          Clyde Hale, Capital 7,000

    e. Tom Gray, Capital 400
        Curtis Ives, Capital 2,100
          Cash 2,500

Prob. 14-7B

1.

ANKU, BASS, AND COX
Statement of Partnership Liquidation
For Period May 3–29, 19—

	Cash	+ Noncash Assets =	Liabili- ties	+ Anku (1/5) +	Bass (2/5) +	Cox (2/5)
					Capital	
Balances before realization......	$ 10,000	$285,000	$55,000	$30,000	$ 90,000	$120,000
Sale of assets and division of gain	+335,000	−285,000	—	+10,000	+ 20,000	+ 20,000
Balances after realization	$345,000	0	$55,000	$40,000	$110,000	$140,000
Payment of liabilities	− 55,000	—	−55,000	—	—	—
Balances after payment of liabilities	$290,000	0	0	$40,000	$110,000	$140,000
Distribution of cash to partners........	−290,000	—	—	−40,000	−110,000	−140,000
Final balances....	0	0	0	0	0	0

2.

ANKU, BASS, AND COX
Statement of Partnership Liquidation
For Period May 3–29, 19—

	Cash	+ Noncash Assets =	Liabili- ties	+ Anku (1/5) +	Bass (2/5) +	Cox (2/5)
					Capital	
Balances before realization........	$ 10,000	$285,000	$55,000	$30,000	$90,000	$120,000
Sale of assets and division of loss............	+185,000	−285,000	—	−20,000	−40,000	−40,000
Balances after realization	$195,000	0	$55,000	$10,000	$50,000	$ 80,000
Payment of liabilities	− 55,000	—	−55,000	—	—	—
Balances after payment of liabilities	$140,000	0	0	$10,000	$50,000	$ 80,000
Distribution of cash to partners..........	−140,000	—	—	−10,000	−50,000	− 80,000
Final balances......	0	0	0	0	0	0

Prob. 14-7B, Concluded

3.

ANKU, BASS, AND COX
Statement of Partnership Liquidation
For Period May 3–29, 19—

	Cash	+	Noncash Assets	=	Liabili- ties	+	Anku (1/5)	+	Bass (2/5)	+	Cox (2/5)
							Capital				
Balances before realization	$ 10,000		$285,000		$55,000		$30,000		$90,000		$120,000
Sale of assets and division of loss	+ 115,000		−285,000		—		−34,000		−68,000		− 68,000
Balances after realization	$125,000		0		$55,000		$ 4,000(Dr.)		$22,000		$ 52,000
Payment of liabilities......	− 55,000		—		−55,000		—		—		—
Balances after payment of liabilities......	$ 70,000		0		0		$ 4,000(Dr.)		$22,000		$ 52,000
Receipt of deficiency	+ 4,000		—		—		+ 4,000		—		—
Balances	$ 74,000		0		0		0		$22,000		$ 52,000
Distribution of cash to partners	− 74,000		—		—		—		−22,000		− 52,000
Final balances...	0		0		0		0		0		0

Mini-Case 14

1.

Net Income, $100,000

Proposal I	Lewis	Meyer	Total
Salary allowance	$ 30,000	$ 45,000	$ 75,000
Interest allowance*	16,000	29,000	45,000
Remaining income (excess of allowances over income)	(10,000)	(10,000)	(20,000)
Net income	$ 36,000	$ 64,000	$100,000

Proposal II	Lewis	Meyer	Total
Salary allowance	$ 20,000	$ 30,000	$ 50,000
Bonus to Meyer	—	10,000	10,000
Remaining income	20,000	20,000	40,000
Net income	$ 40,000	$ 60,000	$100,000

Net Income, $140,000

Proposal I	Lewis	Meyer	Total
Salary allowance	$30,000	$45,000	$ 75,000
Interest allowance*	16,000	29,000	45,000
Remaining income (excess of allowances over income)	10,000	10,000	20,000
Net income	$56,000	$84,000	$140,000

Proposal II	Lewis	Meyer	Total
Salary allowance	$20,000	$30,000	$ 50,000
Bonus to Meyer	—	18,000	18,000
Remaining income	36,000	36,000	72,000
Net income	$56,000	$84,000	$140,000

Net Income, $200,000

Proposal I	Lewis	Meyer	Total
Salary allowance	$30,000	$ 45,000	$ 75,000
Interest allowance*	16,000	29,000	45,000
Remaining income (excess of allowances over income)	40,000	40,000	80,000
Net income	$86,000	$114,000	$200,000

Proposal II	Lewis	Meyer	Total
Salary allowance	$20,000	$ 30,000	$ 50,000
Bonus to Meyer	—	30,000	30,000
Remaining income	60,000	60,000	120,000
Net income	$80,000	$120,000	$200,000

*Lewis: $200,000 × 8% = $16,000
Meyer: $362,500 × 8% = $29,000

2.

The proposal that would maximize Meyer's share of the profits depends upon the future levels of income of the partnership. If Meyer believes that the partnership income will exceed $140,000, she should choose Proposal I. If Meyer believes that income will be less than $140,000, she should choose Proposal II.

3.

$46,875 ($250,000 – $203,125). Brill is paying $250,000 for a one-fourth interest of $203,125 ($200,000 capital of Lewis plus $362,500 capital of Meyer plus $250,000 contribution by Brill divided by four).